One Hundred Years of the

MOTOR CAR

1886 to 1986

One Hundred Years of the
MOTOR CAR
1886 to 1986

Marco Ruiz

Griffith Borgeson · Maurizio Caldera · Michele Fenu · Ray Hutton
Giulio Mangano · Gianni Rogliatti · Edouard Seidler

WILLOW BOOKS
Collins
8 Grafton Street, London
1985

The Publisher would like to thank the public relations departments of automobile companies throughout the world for kindly supplying textual and photographic material. Special thanks are also extended to Mr. Peter Brockes of The National Motor Museum, Beaulieu, Hampshire, England.

Translated from the Italian by Maria Piotrowska

© 1984 Arnoldo Mondadori Editore S.p.A., Milan
© 1985 English translation by Arnoldo Mondadori Editore S.p.A., Milan
Produced by ERVIN s.r.l., Rome
under the supervision of ADRIANO ZANNINO
editorial assistant SERENELLA GENOESE ZERBI

First published in Britain in 1985 by
Willow Books
William Collins Sons & Co Ltd
London · Glasgow · Sydney
Auckland · Toronto · Johannesburg

Contributors:

Griffith Borgeson
European correspondent for *Automobile Quarterly*   Indianapolis

Maurizio Caldera
Journalist   American Motors – Austin Rover – Chrysler – Ford – General Motors/Opel – Honda – Jaguar – Lamborghini – Lotus – Maserati – Mitsubishi – Peugeot-Talbot – Renault – Saab – Toyota – Volvo – Other companies

Michele Fenu
Motoring editor for *La Stampa*   The Manufacturers' Championship

Ray Hutton
Freelance motoring journalist and editor   Sport Between the Two Wars

Giulio Mangano
Sports editor of *Il Giornale di Sicilia*   Citroën – Lancia – Mazda – Nissan – Rolls-Royce

Gianni Rogliatti
Editor of *Motor Italia*   The Formula One Years – The World Land Speed Record – The Great Inventions – Ferrari – Fiat

Marco Ruiz
Journalist   The History of the Motor Car – An Industry Without Frontiers – The Automobile Today: A World-wide Phenomenon – The Evolution of Design: The Coachbuilders – Rallies – Alfa Romeo – Aston Martin – Audi – BMW – Mercedes – Porsche – Volkswagen

Edouard Seidler
Editor of *L'Equipe*   The Heroic Age

Illustrations by:

BMW 68-69-81
Amedeo Gigli 12-17-20-21-23-27-35-55-59-60-64-65-66-67-71-83-87-137-138-141-151-153-155-157-159-161-178-181-183-185-193-197-199-205-211-217-223-227-230-236-240-241-247-249-255-262-265-268
Egidio Imperi 80-83-84-86-88-89-91-94-110-113-129-130-131-132-257
Kromos 10-11-12-15-16-18-19-22-24-25-26-28-29-32-33-34-36-37-47-48-49-50-51-52-53-54-56-57-58-68-69-77-78-79-85-86-92-107-109-110-111-112-113-122-123-128-145-165-167-173-175-187-195-203-215-225-235-239-243-249-251
Mazda 216
Mercedes-Benz 13-14-69
Pierluigi Pinto 26-70-71-79-80-81-82-84-85-86-89-91-93-94-109-111-112-113-233-261
Porsche 84
Quattroruote 105-106-119-120-121-123-134-147-154-162-166-169-177-189-200-206-209-219-244-252-266
Fabio Luigi Rapi 51-59-61-62-63-64-66-70-173
Renault 104
Maurizio e Paolo Riccioni 19-30-31-38-39-40-41-42-43-44-45-72-73-74-75-76-77-80-86-89-90-95-96-97-98-99-100-101-102-103-104-105-106-107-114-115-116-117-118-119-121-123-124-125-126-127-128

Ruiz, Marco
    One hundred years of the motor car; 1886-1986.
    1. Automobiles—History
    I. Title
    629.2'222'0904   TL15

ISBN 0-00-218194-0

Filmset by Rowland Phototypesetting (London) Ltd, 30 Oval Road, London NW1, England
Printed in Italy by Arnoldo Mondadori Editore, Officine Grafiche, Verona

CONTENTS

The hundred years since the birth of the motor car have seen a complex interplay of technical, industrial and human effort, supporting one of the most radical new developments ever to have captured the interest of mankind. It is with good reason that the automobile is one of the great symbols of twentieth-century civilization, having proved fundamental to its well-being and progress.

The aim of this book is to commemorate the centenary of the automobile, leaving aside claims as to where, when and by whom it was first invented, in a celebratory tribute that brings together great names from all nations. Although the intricate process of the invention of the new means of transport took place in Western Europe, and although the United States of America takes the credit for having developed its industrial potential, which has been increased dramatically by Japan's recent rise in production and technological development, the scenario for the future evolution of the automobile transcends all national and international boundaries. In this book we have aimed to trace the evolution of the automobile from the very first pioneer experiments, which developed from the achievements of Benz and Daimler into a continual striving for technical perfection, to the world-wide scale of the motor industry since the Second World War. To this end, we have considered particular aspects of the industry in the various countries involved, in the light of their own specific technical and industrial developments, without forgetting that the relationship which binds Man to the motor car has always contained an element of emotional irrationality, reflecting an intimate response to the need for self-assertion and freedom. The feats of the great drivers of the past and their sophisticated machines therefore served the fascinating dual purpose of being the ultimate expression of a passion for speed, and providing an infinitely valuable testing ground for each new technical development.

A century of motoring has seen the breaking of exhilarating new ground in terms of both quality and quantity. Today's runabouts offer a degree of comfort and performance which until a few years ago were reserved for luxurious saloons and exclusive GTs. At the same time, the 350 million cars on the road throughout the world (in 1886 there were no more than two) and the opening up of countries such as China to the motor car, are proof of the fact that civil and economic growth cannot go on without it.

In recognition of the contribution made by the existing automobile companies to this evolution, we have devoted the second part of the book to their most important achievements and to their most significant products. Our grateful thanks are therefore extended to the presidents of all companies who kindly agreed to make a personal statement on the historic contribution of the marques they represent.

Celebrating a success often means regretting the end of the enthusiasm which made it possible. In the case of the motor car, however, these hundred years end on a note of such technological fervour that the expectations for the future leave no room for nostalgia.

Fuel economy, environmental protection, safety and cost are the challenges to meet for the next hundred years.

ONE HUNDRED YEARS OF PROGRESS

THE HISTORY OF THE MOTOR CAR

If we define the word "automobile" as a vehicle capable of generating its own power, then we should attribute the concept of the motor car to the inventor of a particular desire – the desire to travel quickly and independently, to explore new horizons, and experience the exhilaration and exciting possibilities afforded by the luxury of speed.

To search for the embryo of what may be considered – for better or worse – the symbol of modern civilization would be to search in vain, for the idea of the automobile has existed through the ages in the dreams and imagination of all men and may be recognized among the sketches of Leonardo da Vinci, in his *Codice Atlantico*, and even in the works of Hero of Alexandria who foresaw the possibility of using steam to replace horses and create movement as early as 150 B.C.

The search can be narrowed down by restricting the problem to a consideration of the modern concept of a vehicle driven by its own power. However, since the process of conceiving and developing the motor car followed a great number of courses, some converging and some running parallel, recognizing one exclusive patent holder was to prove extremely difficult, if not impossible.

The road to success reached a decisive stage in the last twenty years of the nineteenth century, when great pioneers worked together with simple mechanics whose ideas, perhaps less important, probably remained buried in the shadows of their workshops.

To give some form of cohesion to this search, one can say that the modern automobile is the result of a single process, in so far as the definition of the vehicle and its general lines are concerned, and a threefold process with regard to the development of the power system. Until the early twentieth century, in fact, the steam engine, the internal combustion engine and the electric motor – a less fortunate outsider which has still not been completely abandoned – all competed for a place in the newly born automobile.

Steam

The first convincing experiments into steam as a source of pro-pulsion date back to the second half of the seventeenth century. After the discovery of the power of atmospheric pressure in 1643 by Evangelista Torricelli, the Dutchman Christian Huygens in 1680 designed the first power unit to be based on the principle (which had already been used a couple of years previously by the French Abbé Hautefeuille for his water suction machine) of the vacuum produced in a cylinder by exploding gunpowder. This was effectually the first internal combustion engine. The explosive method was soon replaced with a less violent fuel – steam – by the French physicist Denis Papin. In 1690 he built the first condensing engine known as the autoclave: this consisted of a piston pushed up inside a cylinder by boiling water and then pushed back down again as a result of subsequent cooling to produce motive power. The entire process was achieved by placing a furnace underneath the cylinder, which also served as a boiler; once the piston had risen, the furnace was removed to facilitate cooling.

Later, two Englishmen, Newcomen and Cawley, one a blacksmith and the other a glazier, perfected the system by separating the boiler from the cylinder and adding a cold water tank. This was operated by cocks, one for the steam and the other for the water, which were alternately opened and shut off. Beighton then converted the cock operation into a true timing system.

Newcomen's machine soon became widely popular and, after undergoing improvements such as the double action system introduced by James Watt in 1765, the steam engine, which saw its most important developments in England, was then sufficiently evolved for use on vehicles, even though, because of its size, it was really more suitable for use on stationary machines. Watt also applied his developments to industry and built engines for the textile trade.

The steam engine was first used on a means of locomotion by the French engineer and amateur military strategist, Nicolas Joseph Cugnot, who built a vehicle in 1763 or 1765 which could carry four passengers at an average speed of 3.5 km/h (2.17 mph) with

The Newton Reaction Carriage – 1680 (GB) This carriage was more a fanciful visual expression of the principle of reaction than a true vehicle design. Although it was probably extremely difficult to handle, it represented one of the first studies into the possibility of using steam as a source of power.

The Verbiest Steam Carriage – 1672 (B) In this very basic vehicle conceived by the Belgian missionary Ferdinand Verbiest, the steam from the boiler was directed through a nozzle on to the blades of a turbine, which in turn transmitted the drive through gears to the wheels. It was extremely limited in range.

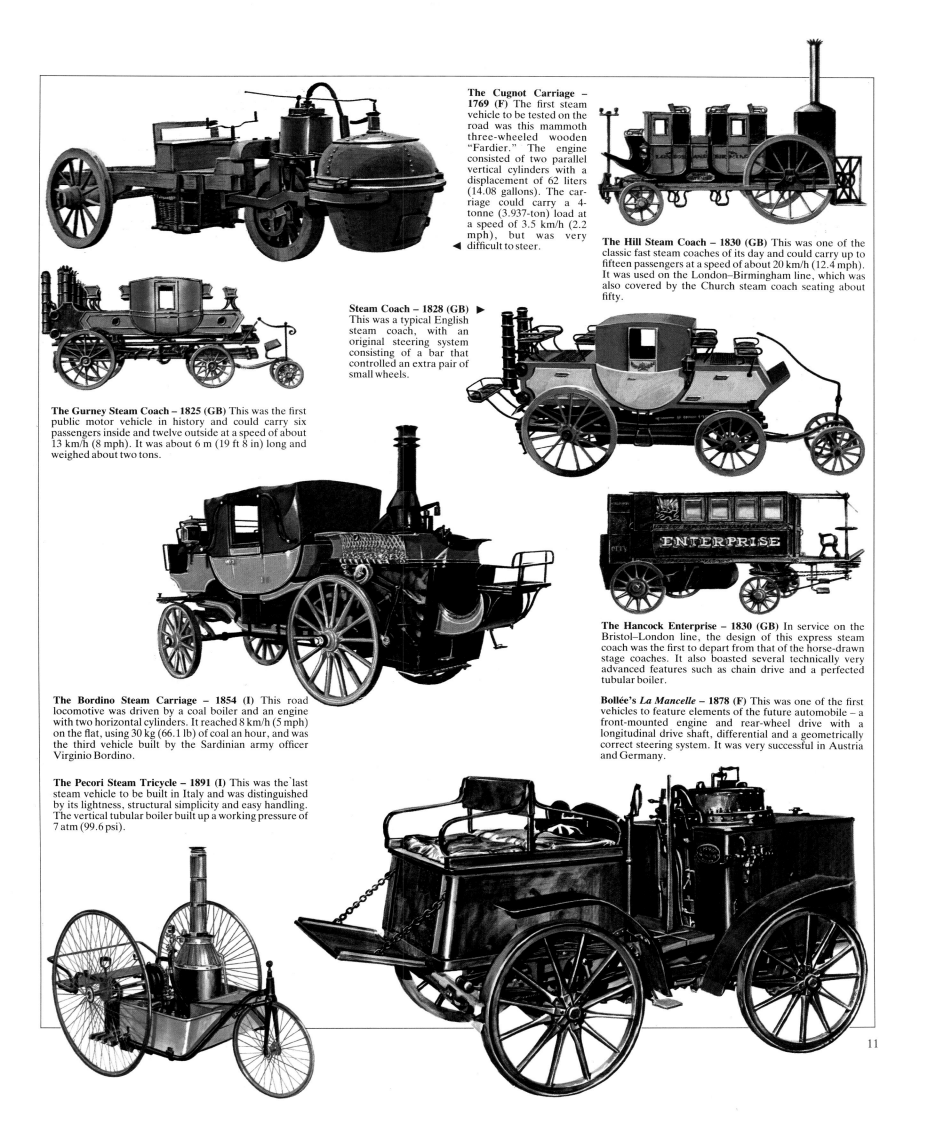

The Cugnot Carriage – 1769 (F) The first steam vehicle to be tested on the road was this mammoth three-wheeled wooden "Fardier." The engine consisted of two parallel vertical cylinders with a displacement of 62 liters (14.08 gallons). The carriage could carry a 4-tonne (3.937-ton) load at a speed of 3.5 km/h (2.2 mph), but was very difficult to steer. ◀

The Hill Steam Coach – 1830 (GB) This was one of the classic fast steam coaches of its day and could carry up to fifteen passengers at a speed of about 20 km/h (12.4 mph). It was used on the London–Birmingham line, which was also covered by the Church steam coach seating about fifty.

Steam Coach – 1828 (GB) ▶ This was a typical English steam coach, with an original steering system consisting of a bar that controlled an extra pair of small wheels.

The Gurney Steam Coach – 1825 (GB) This was the first public motor vehicle in history and could carry six passengers inside and twelve outside at a speed of about 13 km/h (8 mph). It was about 6 m (19 ft 8 in) long and weighed about two tons.

The Hancock Enterprise – 1830 (GB) In service on the Bristol–London line, the design of this express steam coach was the first to depart from that of the horse-drawn stage coaches. It also boasted several technically very advanced features such as chain drive and a perfected tubular boiler.

Bollée's *La Mancelle* **– 1878 (F)** This was one of the first vehicles to feature elements of the future automobile – a front-mounted engine and rear-wheel drive with a longitudinal drive shaft, differential and a geometrically correct steering system. It was very successful in Austria and Germany.

The Bordino Steam Carriage – 1854 (I) This road locomotive was driven by a coal boiler and an engine with two horizontal cylinders. It reached 8 km/h (5 mph) on the flat, using 30 kg (66.1 lb) of coal an hour, and was the third vehicle built by the Sardinian army officer Virginio Bordino.

The Pecori Steam Tricycle – 1891 (I) This was the`last steam vehicle to be built in Italy and was distinguished by its lightness, structural simplicity and easy handling. The vertical tubular boiler built up a working pressure of 7 atm (99.6 psi).

11

The Lenoir Vehicle – 1863 (F) Despite advanced technical features such as final chain drive, steering wheels and elliptical leaf-spring suspension, this vehicle failed to produce the results hoped for because of its limited engine power. The three-phase operating cycle was completed in two strokes of the piston: on the first stroke, the gas–air mixture was aspirated and subsequently exploded, without compression, by the spark from a sparking-plug, then exhaust took place towards the top of the second stroke.

The Markus Automobile – 1873–5 (A) Between 1873 and 1875, the Austrian Siegfried Markus experimented with a vehicle which was fitted with interesting technical innovations. It had a four-stroke, single-cylinder petrol engine with a spray carburettor, magneto ignition and a rudimentary water-cooling system. However, Markus had problems with the police when he tested it on the road, because the vehicle was so noisy and smoky.

Delamarre-Deboutteville – 1884 (F) After building a rudimentary motor tricycle in 1881, Delamarre-Deboutteville patented this four-wheeled vehicle on 12 February 1884. The rear-mounted engine had two separate horizontal cylinders. The drive shaft was fitted with a large central flywheel and was connected by a chain to a transverse transmission shaft which transferred the drive to the rear wheels by means of two side chains.

a top speed of 9.5 km/h (5.9 mph). After his first attempt, Cugnot developed a carriage for transporting canons which was tested several times by the military authorities before they abandoned it because of its very short running time – about fifteen minutes.

Meanwhile, in England, the perfection of the steam engine was progressing at a very steady pace. After the unsuccessful experiments of Francis Moore, William Murdock and William Symington, based on Watt's engine, Richard Trevithick arrived on the scene. He was responsible for building the first locomotive to run on tracks for a Welsh coal mine and the first steam-powered threshing machine, as well as a series of small goods transporters; in 1802, he presented a safe and efficient passenger vehicle capable of reaching a speed of 15 km/h (9.3 mph) on the flat and 6 km/h (3.72 mph) uphill. Steam carriages were also becoming more widely used in the United States: Nathan Read astounded the citizens of Philadelphia in 1790 with his steam carriage, though not nearly as much as his fellow citizen Oliver Evans, who, fourteen years later, developed the first amphibian vehicle.

After the Napoleonic wars, during which experiments were interrupted, research immediately began again on the steam engine, which by 1821 was well developed and fairly reliable. From then on, all progress made with steam-powered vehicles contributed significantly to the evolution of the automobile. In 1825, Sir Goldsworthy Gurney set up the first regular steam service on the 171 km (106.25 miles) from London to Bath using a steam coach he had patented himself. This was the beginning of the age of the fast steam coach which was later discontinued in England, although it became very popular in France and Italy. These vehicles reached their peak with Amédée Bollée's 4500-kg (9921-lb) steam coach *L' Obéissante* (1873) and particularly with the more compact 2500-kg (5511-lb) *La Mancelle*, capable of reaching speeds of over 35 km/h (21.75 mph): both were forerunners of the techniques and designs that were later to characterize the first

The Benz Patent Motor Car – 1886 (D)
This was the first automobile to introduce a revolutionary new idea in vehicles, in that the engine and chassis' formed a single unit. It was officially launched on 3 July 1886 in Mannheim, when the car reached 15 km/h (9.3 mph) with a single-cylinder 984-cc engine developing 0.9 hp at 400 rpm.

The Daimler Motor Car – 1886 (D)
Having already been fitted on a motor cycle and on a river launch, Daimler and Maybach's engine was now fitted on a small carriage – further proof of its versatility. It was a single-cylinder 469-cc engine developing 1.5 hp at 700 rpm and capable of reaching 16 km/h (10 mph).

real automobiles. In fact it was Bollée who patented the first geometrically correct steering system, grouping the instruments and controls together in anticipation of what we now know as the dashboard. In spite of the great progress made with the combustion engine, steam still gave greater guarantees of regular, silent running and continued to have many strong supporters.

As well as Bollée, who built other light vehicles, among them *La Rapide* in 1881, timed at 60 km/h (37.3 mph), and *La Nouvelle* in 1873, which had an axle with independent front wheels, Léon Serpollet also produced a number of vehicles between 1887 and 1907 which reached very high levels of efficiency thanks to the light and compact instant action steam generator patented in 1889.

De Dion-Bouton, founded in 1883 in Paris, also spent their first ten years building steam vehicles whose finest hour was winning first place in the Paris–Rouen Reliability Trial of 1894. However, Panhard-Levassor's successes with petrol led to De Dion's changing over to the internal combustion engine; inheriting their father's company, the Bollée brothers did likewise. Later, with the disappearance of the Serpollet, steam-driven vehicles began to fall into decline, although they remained in use in the United States until 1930.

The combustion engine and the birth of the automobile

The principle of the combustion engine was based on the pistol constructed by Alessandro Volta in 1777. This worked on the principle of the explosion of a mixture of marsh gas and air fired by an electric spark instead of gunpowder. On the basis of this discovery, Isaac de Rivaz of Switzerland took out a patent in 1807 to use the gas–air mixture as a source of mechanical energy. His engine was fitted into a carriage and consisted of a cylinder in which the explosion pushed up a piston which operated a rocker arm or pulleys as it returned back down. The use of gas was not without risks, and the war – de Rivaz was one of Napoleon's officers – interrupted the develop-

ment of what was the first important forerunner of the automobile.

Other experiments were carried out with inflammable gases at the beginning of the century by the Englishman Robert Street, the Frenchman Philippe Lebon and the American Peter Cooper; and in 1825 Michael Faraday succeeded in extracting benzene from fossil coal, producing the first liquid fuel suitable for use in internal combustion engines.

A succession of vehicles was produced up to 1830 which were not as yet true combustion engines but engines in which the gas–air mixture was used in place of steam. This proved of no great advantage and was not without risk to the running cycle. Patents were obtained for these engines by, among others, the two Englishmen Brown (1823) and Wright (1833).

It was not until 1841 that the basis for a light, compact engine was laid with the igneo-pneumatic machine built by the Italian Luigi De Cristoforis. This consisted of a pump which used naphtha, a

combustible liquid, as fuel for the first time. Eugenio Barsanti and Felice Matteucci developed this idea further and, after obtaining the British patent in 1854, brought out the first true internal combustion engine two years later. It worked on a three-stroke cycle (omitting the compression stroke) and was water-cooled. The fuel source was a mixture of air and coal gas, although other combustible liquids had also been considered, and it developed 5 hp. A second two-cylinder engine with opposed pistons was built in 1858 and a small number were produced from 1860 onwards by the Eschel-Wyss company in Zürich. The premature death of Barsanti in 1864 and the delicate health of Matteucci prevented the two from reaping the rewards of their work, both materially and spiritually. At the same time, the Frenchman Etienne Lenoir was bringing to completion a project which his compatriot Hugon had started in 1858 and later abandoned; and in 1860 Lenoir patented an internal combustion engine which was later to enjoy great

commercial success. This engine also ran on coal gas with a three-stroke cycle. An attempt was made in 1863 to fit it into a carriage, but its 1.5 hp at 100 rpm was not enough to move it. At the Paris Exposition of 1867, the Gasmotorenfabrik Deutz (Deutz Gas Motor Works), a company formed by the engineer Nikolaus Otto and the industrialist Eugen Langen, successfully introduced an engine inspired by the Barsanti-Matteucci which was lighter and suffered less from vibration, and which therefore soon took over from the Lenoir. In 1872, Gottlieb Daimler joined the Deutz company as chief engineer, and Wilhelm Maybach as chief designer: their contributions over the next ten years were reflected in the 2,000 Otto engines sold in Europe in 1875. It was in that same year, and using an Otto engine, that the Austrian Siegfried Markus built the first, albeit rudimentary, automobile, though no official record of it exists.

The real breakthrough in the development of the combustion engine was the introduction of the four-stroke cycle patented by the Frenchman Alphonse Beau de Rochas in 1862, which was firmly established with the 8-hp engine introduced by Otto in 1876.

Development of the internal

Benz Velo – 1894 (D) Originally fitted with a 1050-cc 1.5-hp engine, this vehicle was later equipped with an engine giving 2.75 hp at 500 rpm and capable of reaching up to 20 km/h (12.4 mph). In 1895, a third gear was added as a result of the addition of a supplementary planetary gear; in 1898, a 1140-cc engine was fitted, developing 3 hp at 4000 rpm.

combustion engine was also under way in the United States, most notably in the work of George Brayton, an engineer from Boston who brought out his engine, tested on a vehicle, in 1876. At the Philadelphia Centennial Exhibition in the same year, Brayton and Otto met and exchanged ideas. Another American, George Baldwin Selden, obtained a patent in 1877 for a vehicle driven by a Brayton engine which saw the start of locomotion in America.

In Italy, Guiseppe Murnigotti patented the application of an original four-stroke engine (achieved by the piston moving only twice) to a three-wheel velocipede, and Edouard Delamare-Deboutteville, assisted by his faithful and skilled mechanic Léon Malandin, built a four-wheel car in France with a high compression engine fed on a light essence of petroleum. Features such as overhead valves and a power rating of about 2.5 hp show the degree of sophistication attained. However, in spite of the fact that by many this was at the time considered the first automobile, Delamare-Deboutteville failed to exploit his work on an industrial scale and his name disappeared from the history of the motor car.

In 1882, Daimler and Maybach left Deutz to start up on their own in Cannstatt near Stuttgart. In 1883, they brought out their first high-speed lightweight engine which weighed about 80 kg (176.4 lb), in comparison with the 300 kg (661.4 lb) of the other more sophisticated combustion engines of the time. The engine speed was between 450 and 900 rpm, assisted by the new hot tube ignition system, consisting of a platinum tube heated by an outer burner. However, its limited power of 0.5 hp meant that it could be used realistically only on a lighter vehicle such as a motor bicycle.

Meanwhile, another German, Karl Benz, the owner of Benz & Company in Mannheim, developed his own engine with electric ignition and brought out a three-wheel vehicle in 1886 which, because of the perfect integration of its engine and chassis, can be considered the first true automobile. In the same year, Daimler fitted his improved and upgraded engine into a body which did not undergo subsequent modifications, thus consolidating a trend which was already firmly rooted. The appearance of Benz and Daimler's cars marked the completion of the invention stage of the automobile.

While Benz perfected his tricycle (no great need for a four-wheel vehicle was felt yet) in his attempt to design the best possible engine-chassis assembly, Daimler was concerned with the commercialization of his engines, which were very popular even outside Germany. In about 1890, something like 1,900 manufacturing licenses were granted for Daimler engines, which were also produced in New York by William Steinway, founder of the Steinway & Sons piano company. In 1889, a two-cylinder 20-degree V engine was brought out with a capacity of 565 cc, developing 1.75 hp at 920 rpm; it was water-cooled with a centrifugal pump and finned radiator. Thanks also to its light tubular chassis, the *Stahlradwagen* (metal-wheeled car) in which it was fitted was capable of reaching speeds of up to 17 km/h (10.5 mph). This vehicle competed with the latest Benz model for the attention of visitors to the Paris Exhibition of 1889, at which Daimler also concluded talks begun four years previously on the concession of a manufacturing license for his engines to Panhard-Levassor.

This French company, founded in 1864 for the construction of wood-working machines, thus went on to the production of internal combustion engines. Its first customer was Armand Peu-geot who, after a few prototypes, brought out a four-wheel vehicle in 1891 with a two-cylinder V engine producing 2 hp at 1000 rpm. With the engine speed limited to 550 rpm, it was capable of reaching 18 km/h (11.2 mph) and was cooled by water circulating through its tubular chassis. That same year, Panhard-Levassor brought out their own automobile – a front-engined model with a gear transmission which Levassor himself described as "brutal."

Automobile production could still not be said to be fully under way, since in 1891 only seven Benzs, six Panhard-Levassors and four Peugeots were in fact produced. Nevertheless, in the improvements made by the major manufacturers lay the basis for early popularization of the automobile on a larger scale, and the motor car became even more firmly established from 1895 onwards, particularly in France, where the road network was much better developed than in the rest of Europe.

The four-wheel Benz Viktoria came out in 1893, with a single-cylinder, 2.9-liter engine developing 3 hp, which was later increased to 5 hp after improvements had been made to the cooling system. The lighter Velo of the following

Benz Viktoria – 1893 (D) The first four-wheel Benz had a single-cylinder 2900-cc engine, available in a 3- or 5-hp version. It had a constant level carburettor; a regulator tap for the gas–air mixture and a butterfly valve and spark advance regulator ensured flexibility of operation.

The Bernardi Tricycle – 1896 (I) This vehicle weighed a total of 300 kg (661.4 lb) and had a single-cylinder 624-cc engine which developed 4 hp at 800 rpm. The gearbox had three speeds plus reverse and chain drive. The tricycle could reach speeds of 35 km/h (21.7 mph).

year was the German company's first series-produced car. The 1894 Panhard-Levassor automobile was the best attempt to date at moving away from the typical lines of the horse-drawn carriage. In the following year, the French company abandoned the Daimler engine in favour of a two-cylinder in-line Phoenix engine and held a prime position on the technological forefront until the beginning of the century.

As far as activity in Italy was concerned, the first vehicle to be driven by an internal combustion engine was built in 1890 by Count Enrico Bernardi, who had already made great innovatory contributions in this field with his removable cylinder head, rod and rocker valve operation, and constant-level carburettor. Bernardi cars did not enjoy great commercial success, mainly because the Italian economy was not yet ready to develop the industry, but they did represent achievements of significant technical value. The first four-wheel Italian vehicle was manufactured by the Turin industrialist Michele Lanza in the Martini brothers' workshop, but again, attempts to begin large-scale production proved unsuccessful.

By 1895, 350 automobiles were already on the road in France and 75 in Germany. Although production was still limited, an industry on a somewhat grander scale seemed finally to have been launched: 135 Benzs had been produced, and the Panhard-Levassor and the Peugeot companies had each built 72 vehicles.

The electric motor

The advantages for the automobile offered by electric power through rechargeable accumulators – no vibration or exhaust emissions and nearly 90 per cent efficiency as opposed to about 25 per cent with the combustion engine – were enjoyed from the first half of the nineteenth century onwards.

Early attempts were aimed at finding an alternative source of energy for the smoky, noisy train engines, but very soon experiments were applied to automobiles and the first example of a

light electric vehicle was the small car produced by the Englishman J. K. Starley in 1888. The first satisfactory result, however, was obtained in 1893 by Jeantaud and Rafford, who produced an automobile in which the batteries – two 200 Ah elements situated in the rear – weighed a total of 420 kg (925 lb). The output was about 2.5 kW (3.5 hp) at 1300 rpm. The most difficult problem with electric cars, however, remained their limited range, and this was the real reason why experiments stopped in about 1910, at a time when the lightness and improved performance of the combustion engine made the search for other forms of power less pressing.

As far as speed was concerned, however, electric vehicles achieved remarkable results; in 1897, the British Gladiator Pinganet electric tandem covered the flying kilometer in 1 min 46 secs and five miles in 8 mins 56 secs. Five electric cars were entered for the Paris–Rouen race of 1894, but the greatest moment for this type of vehicle was undoubtedly when *La Jamais Contente*, driven by Camille Jenatzy, reached 100 km/h (62 mph), exceeding 105.882 km/h (65.792 mph) at Achères in 1899, in a furious duel with another electric car, Comte Gaston de Chasseloup-Laubat's Jeantaud. Jenatzy's car was also the first to have a studied aerodynamic design – rudimentary though this was – suitable for high speeds, al-

though its designer had almost certainly overlooked the shape of the driver, who stuck out from the waist upwards. Nevertheless, this record was one of the final moments of glory for the electric car, whose theoretical advantages were later outweighed by problems of cost and range, practically the same as those still put forward today against the creation of an accumulator engine which would be a sufficiently viable alternative.

The most important manufacturers of electric cars included the French firm Kriéger, who had enjoyed great success from 1895 to 1909 both at home and abroad, working through associated companies such as British Electromobile, Namag in Germany and STAE in Italy.

The range of the first Kriéger model in 1897, capable of speeds up to 24 km/h (15 mph) with a weight of 1100 kg (2425 lb), 350 kg (771.6 lb) of which were the batteries, was about 60 km (37.3 miles), but two years later, a more powerful vehicle with two 6-hp engines could run 90 km (56 miles) without having to recharge its batteries. Electric cars enjoyed greater success in the United States, where Fred M. Kimball built the first vehicle of this type in 1888. The first series production was begun by the Electric Carriage and Wagon Company of Philadelphia, which supplied the New York City Council with a

number of electric taxis in 1897. The first electric Studebakers appeared in 1902, and by 1912 there were 20,000 passenger carriers with accumulator engines on the road. However, interest in direct-current traction gradually waned in favour of the combustion engine, which was the only form to guarantee long journeys.

Hand-built cars

By 1895, output by the major manufacturers – Daimler and Benz in Germany, and Panhard-Levassor, De Dion-Bouton and Serpollet in France – had placed the automobile on the road to a secure future, although production was still far from being on an industrial scale. Each vehicle was virtually custom-built according to the customer's particular wishes; with regard to bodywork and fittings, particularly in the case of the most prestigious models, these finishing touches were added by specialist firms, still accustomed to the rich, graceful lines of the horse-drawn carriage. The automobile was in fact much less comfortable than the latter, which represented perfection itself in terms of elegance, refinement and serviceability.

The bodywork was in perfectly seasoned wood, often with elaborate and painstaking attention to detail. Integration of the mechanical parts with the bodywork was still rudimentary – the tank was usually under the front or back seat, so filling it up without spilling a good deal of fuel on the ground was quite a feat. The electrical system had exposed wires which were open to dirt and vibrations. The steering column was vertical at first, and the driver, particularly in early vehicles where the seats faced each other, had to position himself carefully to obtain even minimum visibility. The first angled steering column was used on the Panhard-Levassor winner of the 1894 Paris–Rouen race.

Since the brakes only worked in forward motion, a stone was always carried and placed immediately behind a wheel if the car stopped on a hill: however, some cars, such as the Panhard-Levassor, had a special prong – then known as a "sprag" or "*béquille*" – which was dropped when needed.

Baker – 1902 (USA) Baker began producing electric cars in 1897, but stopped after merging with Rauch & Lang in 1914. By 1902, they were already using advanced features such as the characteristic drive shaft on the voiturette (illustrated above), which measured about 2.4 m (7 ft 9 in) in length. This model was, however, rather limited in range, and the batteries had to be recharged every six to eight hours. A competition version with a bullet-shaped body, the Torpedo Kid, was developed from this model and won several national races.

Peugeot-Daimler – 1894 (F) This first
Peugeot was fitted with a 565-cc twin-
cylinder Daimler engine and was brought
out in 1891. It was in production until 1894,
by which time sixty-four had been built in
various versions. In the same year, the
1645-cc 4-hp model was introduced, with a
four-speed gearbox with reverse. It was
capable of speeds up to 30 km/h (18.6
mph). The model illustrated was an
intermediate version with a 1206-cc 2.5-hp
engine.

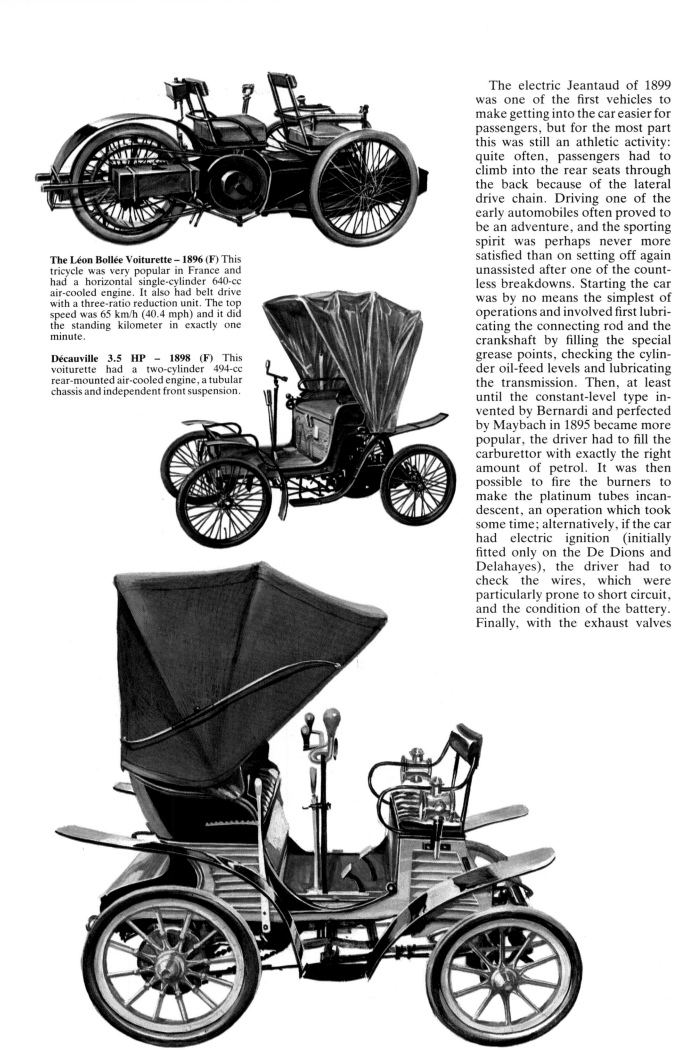

The Léon Bollée Voiturette – 1896 (F) This tricycle was very popular in France and had a horizontal single-cylinder 640-cc air-cooled engine. It also had belt drive with a three-ratio reduction unit. The top speed was 65 km/h (40.4 mph) and it did the standing kilometer in exactly one minute.

Décauville 3.5 HP – 1898 (F) This voiturette had a two-cylinder 494-cc rear-mounted air-cooled engine, a tubular chassis and independent front suspension.

The electric Jeantaud of 1899 was one of the first vehicles to make getting into the car easier for passengers, but for the most part this was still an athletic activity: quite often, passengers had to climb into the rear seats through the back because of the lateral drive chain. Driving one of the early automobiles often proved to be an adventure, and the sporting spirit was perhaps never more satisfied than on setting off again unassisted after one of the countless breakdowns. Starting the car was by no means the simplest of operations and involved first lubricating the connecting rod and the crankshaft by filling the special grease points, checking the cylinder oil-feed levels and lubricating the transmission. Then, at least until the constant-level type invented by Bernardi and perfected by Maybach in 1895 became more popular, the driver had to fill the carburettor with exactly the right amount of petrol. It was then possible to fire the burners to make the platinum tubes incandescent, an operation which took some time; alternatively, if the car had electric ignition (initially fitted only on the De Dions and Delahayes), the driver had to check the wires, which were particularly prone to short circuit, and the condition of the battery. Finally, with the exhaust valves open to avoid undue high compression and with the clutch engaged, the driver could crank the starting handle which acted on the flywheel. As soon as the engine started to turn, the driver closed the exhaust valves, cleaned his hands and took his position at the wheel.

Actually buying an automobile was not particulary easy, as growing demand towards the end of the nineteenth century had created a waiting list of two months for delivery of a Darracq, six for a Peugeot, eight for a Mors and up to twenty months for a Panhard.

New companies are born

The close of the nineteenth and early years of the twentieth century saw the arrival of many new names on the automobile scene, although some did not become established on an industrial scale until after the First World War. Of the nations, France contributed most to the rise of car fever: her traditional open mind to new experiences, a sufficiently modern road network and a host of rich and enthusiastic potential clients, offered new and exciting possibilities. By the end of 1900, there were twenty-five specialist magazines and the

Fiat 3.5 HP – 1899 (I) The first Fiat in history was designed by Aristide Faccioli and had a two-cylinder 679-cc engine with a power rating of 4 hp at 400 rpm. The constant mesh gearbox had three speeds and no reverse. Its top speed was about 35 km/h (21.7 mph) and fuel consumption was 8.5 liters/100 km (33.2 mpg). The car was 2.30 m (7 ft 6 in) long, 1.38 m (4 ft 6 in) wide and weighed 280 kg (617.3 lb).

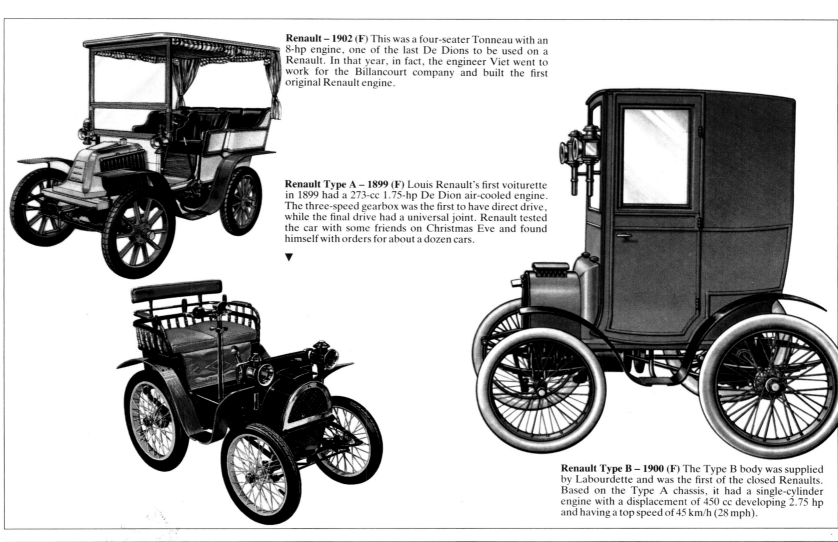

Renault – 1902 (F) This was a four-seater Tonneau with an 8-hp engine, one of the last De Dions to be used on a Renault. In that year, in fact, the engineer Viet went to work for the Billancourt company and built the first original Renault engine.

Renault Type A – 1899 (F) Louis Renault's first voiturette in 1899 had a 273-cc 1.75-hp De Dion air-cooled engine. The three-speed gearbox was the first to have direct drive, while the final drive had a universal joint. Renault tested the car with some friends on Christmas Eve and found himself with orders for about a dozen cars.

Renault Type B – 1900 (F) The Type B body was supplied by Labourdette and was the first of the closed Renaults. Based on the Type A chassis, it had a single-cylinder engine with a displacement of 450 cc developing 2.75 hp and having a top speed of 45 km/h (28 mph).

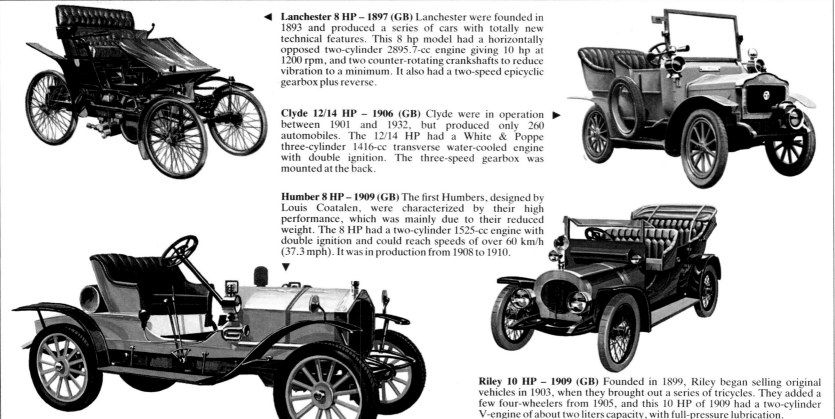

Lanchester 8 HP – 1897 (GB) Lanchester were founded in 1893 and produced a series of cars with totally new technical features. This 8 hp model had a horizontally opposed two-cylinder 2895.7-cc engine giving 10 hp at 1200 rpm, and two counter-rotating crankshafts to reduce vibration to a minimum. It also had a two-speed epicyclic gearbox plus reverse.

Clyde 12/14 HP – 1906 (GB) Clyde were in operation between 1901 and 1932, but produced only 260 automobiles. The 12/14 HP had a White & Poppe three-cylinder 1416-cc transverse water-cooled engine with double ignition. The three-speed gearbox was mounted at the back.

Humber 8 HP – 1909 (GB) The first Humbers, designed by Louis Coatalen, were characterized by their high performance, which was mainly due to their reduced weight. The 8 HP had a two-cylinder 1525-cc engine with double ignition and could reach speeds of over 60 km/h (37.3 mph). It was in production from 1908 to 1910.

Riley 10 HP – 1909 (GB) Founded in 1899, Riley began selling original vehicles in 1903, when they brought out a series of tricycles. They added a few four-wheelers from 1905, and this 10 HP of 1909 had a two-cylinder V-engine of about two liters capacity, with full-pressure lubrication.

De Dion-Bouton Populaire – 1903 (F) The establishment of De Dion-Bouton et Trépardoux dates back to 1883, when Count Albert De Dion went into partnership with George Bouton and his brother-in-law to design a steam boiler which was also used by the French Navy. Meanwhile, the first experimental steam vehicles were giving good results, for example the 1-hp 50-kg (110.2-lb) tricycle which was the only entrant, and hence the winner, of the first recorded speed trial in 1887, organized by the newspaper *Le Vélocipède*. It reached a speed of 60 km/h (37.3 mph). De Dion was also studying a combustion engine at the time, and although he won the Paris–Rouen race of 1893 with one of his steam cars, in 1895 he began to use petrol engines only. By 1893, the year in which the revolutionary rear axle was patented, Trépardoux had left the company and it became officially known as De Dion-Bouton & Company. The first petrol vehicle, brought out in 1895, was a tricycle which had relatively little success despite the fact that it won a number of races, an achievement considered by Count De Dion as fundamentally important to the promotion of sales. His first success on the market was the tubular chassis vis-à-vis which came out in 1899. Production on an industrial scale began with the Populaire, which was in production until 1907 in various versions with one, two and four cylinders. The De Dion innovative spirit was later stifled when production concentrated on eight-cylinder luxury vehicles. This signalled the beginning of the company's decline, since it could no longer offer the economical, widely popular car which might have been the answer to its financial problems. After completing a few military orders during the war, the company finally ceased production in 1933.

Automobile Club de France, one of the first to be founded (on the initiative of Comte Albert De Dion), encouraged and stimulated the development of civil and competition motoring. As well as De Dion, Peugeot and Renault (who, founded in 1899, almost definitively established the small-engine car), a large number of different makes appeared. Delahaye were among the first to rationalize production, manufacturing up to 600 vehicles between 1895 and 1899. The first cars produced by this company were virtual copies of the Daimler and Benz of the time, but during nearly fifty years of technical direction by Charles Weiffenbach, from 1902 onwards a more individual range was established.

Darracq, on the other hand, operated on a more international scale and by 1900, 1,200 cars had been produced. After a few experiments with an electric car and a rotary-engined tricycle, Alexandre Darracq, who until then had been involved in the construction of bicycles, obtained a franchise for the production of a small Léon Bollée car which was to prove quite popular, although it was later outclassed by Renault's small but true automobiles. The company was also very active in competitions, but is remembered mainly for its international role: Opel developed their business by building Darracq models under license in 1902, and a factory was set up in Italy where the small, two-cylinder 8/10 hp and the four-cylinder 14/16 hp were assembled. However, these cars received a lukewarm reception on the market and were taken over by ALFA (Anonima Lombarda Fabbrica Automobili), known from the beginning by the acronym Alfa. Darracq first operated in

Great Britain through the G & J Weir Company; the Englishman Owen Clegg then took control of the French company and, after purchasing Clément-Talbot and Sunbeam at the end of the war, formed the STD group (Sunbeam-Talbot-Darracq).

The first Mors came out in 1896 and the company enjoyed varying degrees of success in the field of racing. The 6 hp was a vis-à-vis which had a four-cylinder engine with a mixed cooling system (water-cooled heads and air-cooled cylinder barrels) and an original ignition system. Production, ranging from small two-cylinder to luxurious six-cylinder 8500-cc engines, continued until the post-war crisis compromised the profitability of small and medium-sized companies such as Mors, who were progressively absorbed by Citroën from 1919 onwards.

Décauville were in operation between 1897 and 1911, and their first voiturette was a vis-à-vis with two 1.75-hp engines. Their cars were produced under license in Germany by Dixi and in Italy by Marchand, and it was a Décauville which gave Royce the inspiration

for his first car, completed in 1903.

A prominent character on the French automobile scene was Alphonse Clément, who was originally involved in bicycle production. He first obtained the agency for the new Dunlop tyres and then in 1895 went on to produce tricycles with De Dion engines. After creating the Anglo-French group Clément-Gladiator-Humber (from which first Clément-Talbot and then Talbot were formed), he produced a series of cars in his own right under the name Clément-Bayard. They enjoyed considerable success both commercially and in competitions and were taken over by Citroën in 1919.

During this period, three companies were formed which excelled in their respective fields and were later to become legends: Hispano-Suiza, who were founded in 1904 in Spain, but became French after the First World War; Bugatti; and Delage, who were rather overshadowed by the prestige and racing successes of the first two, despite the quality of their own products.

In England, development of the automobile industry was still in its

embryonic stage, hampered by the hostile attitude of the authorities and large sections of the public towards the new means of transport. The Red Flag Act, a law introduced in 1861 after pressure on Parliament by influential groups of railway workers and employees of transport companies which still used horse-drawn carriages, had practically brought the evolution of the motor car to a halt, claiming that it was dangerous. Motor vehicles had to respect a speed limit as low as 6 km/h (4 mph) on the open road and 3 km/h (2 mph) in towns, and also had to be preceded on urban stretches by a man on foot waving a red flag to announce their arrival. The law was repealed in 1896, but the birth of new car companies was still hampered by bitter disputes with the metal industry unions and by the monopolistic attitude of Henry J. Lawson, who founded the British Motor Syndicate and in 1893 took over Daimler (set up in 1893 to exploit the expertise of the German builder Daimler in the United Kingdom). Lawson blocked the granting of fundamental patents and franchises, and did not hesitate to prevent the

introduction of new companies into the market, but his plans to control the industry were thwarted by a court decision in 1901.

Many engineering companies, mainly those which had specialized in the manufacture of bicycles, changed over to the motor car, and many new names appeared in this growing industry. A concentration of companies grew up in the West Midlands around Coventry which was later to become the capital of the British motor industry. Wolseley were founded in 1895 and brought out their first four-wheel vehicle four years later; then came Riley with De Dion type cars from 1899 onwards; and Napier, whose first cars in the early twentieth century were modified Panhard-Levassors. The first year of the new century saw the birth of Sunbeam, making their début with the small Mabley, which had an original rhomboid wheel arrangement; and Humber who had broken away from the Lawson group. Other makes were also introduced within a few years: Rover (1904), Singer (1905), Austin and Royce (1906), and Hillman (1907). Some of them

Peugeot Double Phaeton – 1903 (F) This car was structurally built for a four-cylinder bi-bloc front-mounted 3635-cc engine with the gearbox-differential unit in the center, in front of the rear axle. The pressed steel chassis had side- and cross-members, and the steering was highly accurate, with a worm and nut system.

were destined to become of major importance. By 1913, the British motor industry had a good eleven companies capable of producing over 1,000 cars a year.

In Germany, Daimler and Benz continued their outstanding technical achievements, and in 1900 Daimler began a new era for the automobile with the 35-hp Mercedes. For the first time, very high performance was obtained with a vehicle of limited weight – the power-to-weight ratio of 6.8 kg/cv (15.2 lb/hp) was to remain unsurpassed for a long time to come – and it included innovations such as the light alloy engine block and vertical valves operated by an outer timing shaft. The honeycomb radiator was completely new, and the petrol and ignition systems were also very advanced for their time. Finally, the chassis was lower, and a comfortable new selective gear change was introduced. Yet, in spite of this and other technically advanced motor cars, the industry had difficulties in achieving high-level production, a result in particular of limited home demand. Suffice it to say that, for a number of years, more Benzs were exported to France than were sold on home territory. Despite the fact that there were about fifty companies in operation in 1907, production was equal to about one-fifth of that in France and about half of that in Britain. It is symptomatic that, of the new companies which came out in that period, small to medium firms such as Opel and Adler achieved better results commercially than industrial giants such as AEG and Siemens, who failed in their attempts to break into the market.

Opel of Rüsselsheim presented their first car in 1898, while the Adler bicycle factory changed over to motor cars in the following year, using De Dion engines and introducing universal transmission almost at the same time as Renault. One example of a company operating on an international scale was De Dietrich. The motor company in Alsace, having established itself firmly in the railway industry, found itself to be German instead of French after the Treaty of Frankfurt in 1870, when Alsace was annexed to Germany. A second factory was built later at Luneville in France,

Opel – 1898 (D) Friedrich Lutzmann, who had built a car inspired by the Benz Viktoria, took out patents in 1897 which were to form the basis for the first Opel, brought out in 1898. Its main features were the rear-mounted single-cylinder engine and the gearbox under the driver's seat. Only a few were built while it was in production, up to 1900.

Benz 20/35 – 1910 (D) This car was part of the Phaeton series, with four-cylinder 35–60-hp engines, produced by Benz between 1908 and 1912. The 20/35 was a 4851-cc version, also available as an open top.

Adler 7/15 HP – 1912 (D) The British Morgan coachworks imported Adler chassis from 1912. The 7/15 HP was one of the results of this association. Driven by a four-cylinder L-head bi-bloc engine, it had double ignition and a three-speed gearbox.

and in 1897 an agreement was made with Amédée Bollée jr. for the construction and sale of his cars in both countries.

At the beginning of the century, production at the two associated companies was divided: De Dietrich in France obtained a license for the exclusive production of Turcat-Méry cars (another French company, founded in 1899 and renowned for the high quality and excellent performance of its products), whereas the German section persuaded Ettore Bugatti to work for them, attracting him to Alsace from Italy with a financial offer which he apparently could not refuse. Between 1902 and 1904, this famous designer produced two models, the 5300 cc 24/26 hp and the 7430 cc 30/33 hp. Production stopped in Germany as soon as Bugatti left, whereas in France it continued until 1935 with the marque Lorraine-Dietrich.

The year 1899 also saw the début of Horch, who were to rival Mercedes in the quality of their construction and technical details.

If the manufacture of motor cars was having difficulties getting into its stride in the rest of Europe, in Italy it was still little more than a cottage industry. To take advantage of the economic situation of the time, numerous attempts to enter the market were made but most of them were short-lived.

By 1896, Miari Giusti & Company in Padua were producing Professor Bernardi's tricycle in very limited numbers, while Prinetti & Stucchi built a vehicle between 1898 and 1906, virtually on a design by Ettore Bugatti, which had a two-cylinder 4.5-hp engine. In 1901, Bugatti had left the company and founded another with Count Gulinelli, to produce a three-liter, four-cylinder car capable of reaching speeds up to 65 km/h (40.4 mph).

Michele Lanza also tried to find a production outlet for his own cars, but the factory he founded in 1898 ceased operation five years later. For Lanza, each single car had to be an individual piece, built with all the refinements available at the time, and the moulds used for each body were immediately destroyed. In 1905, Max Turkheimer, who had previously been in the bicycle business, founded OTAV in Milan. He enjoyed a certain amount of commercial

Rolls-Royce Silver Ghost – 1909 (GB) This car was in production from 1907 to 1925, and for its first two years had a fixed L-head straight-six 7036-cc engine. The engine was extremely quiet, being fixed to the chassis by a patented elastic mounting. The four-speed gearbox had direct third and overdrive on fourth.

success with his first 5.5-hp single-cylinder and 18/24-hp cars, which encouraged him to set up a company with Giovanni Ceirano jr. to sell their cars in England. However, the economic crisis of 1907 put an irreversible end to the company's activities.

By 1906, there were fifty or so companies involved in the construction of motor cars, and interest was growing all the time. Gradually, Turin became the linchpin of the new industry, which owed much to the industrial zeal of three brothers, Giovanni Battista, Matteo and Giovanni Ceirano. The first two built bicycles from 1886 under the name Welleyes, and the same name was used in 1889 for their 3.5-hp vehicles, designed by Aristide Facciolo. This model was very much to the liking of the newly formed FIAT (Fabbrica Italiana di Automobili Torino) which for L30,000, took over the entire company, including such persona-

lities as Vincenzo Lancia, the accountant, and Felice Nazzaro, the mechanic. Very soon, the two Ceirano brothers set up on their own to produce certain models with De Dion and Aster engines. In 1903, their paths divided: Giovanni Battista founded STAR (Società Torinese Automobili Rapid), with a production level of about 600 vehicles until their disappearance in 1912. In 1904 Matteo became a general partner of SA Itala, who, thanks partly to their competition successes, including victory in the 1907 Peking–Paris race, were very successful until after the First World War. In 1905 Matteo left Itala and set up a company with Michele Ansaldi which remained in operation until 1918. In 1922, this company was taken over by the Perrone brothers, owners of Ansaldo.

The third brother, Giovanni, entered the motor industry in 1904, with the founding of Junior,

two years later capable of producing 130 vehicles. In 1906, Ceirano left Junior, later merged with OTAV, to join SCAT (Società Ceirano Automobili Torino). This company was taken over by Hispano-Suiza in 1917 after enjoying considerable success.

The most important company during this pioneering period in Italy was, of course, FIAT, from the end of 1906 known by the acronym Fiat, whose more solid financial base (it was founded in 1899 with L800,000) enabled it to survive the 1907 crisis, which wreaked havoc with many other manufacturers. In the first decade of the new century, however, companies such as Isotta Fraschini (1904), Lancia (1906) and Alfa (1909) were formed which were to become great names in the history of the motor car. The first four-wheel vehicle to be produced was brought out in 1899 by Edoardo Bianchi, who was to be Fiat's strongest rival between the

two wars. Diatto, founded in 1905 for the construction of Clément-Bayard models under license, played a less important role from the industrial standpoint – though their technical contribution was considerable – and subsequently moved on to the manufacture of original models for the sports market.

A number of Belgian, Austrian and Dutch concerns, some of which achieved the highest levels of craftsmanship, complete the panorama of European production at the time. Of these, the most commercially successful were FN (Fabrique Nationale d'Armes de Guerre). Their first car, of which over a hundred were produced in 1900, was designed by the Italian De Cosmo, previously employed by Delahaye and Singer. FN remained in operation until 1934, gradually expanding its range to include prestige models. The Compagnie Belge de Construction d'Automobiles built a series

Spyker – 1905 (NL) The Dutch company Spyker was in operation at the beginning of the century and produced this interesting four-cylinder 2536-cc car with a three-speed gearbox and semi-elliptic leaf-springs.

Albion A6 – 1906 (GB) The A6 had chain drive and a 4140-cc engine which developed 24 hp at 1200 rpm and could reach 65 km/h (40.4 mph). A very successful luxury car, it was in production from 1906 to 1914.

Gaggenau Type 10/18 – 1907 (D) The output from the 2600-cc engine in this car, which was in production until 1910, was 20 hp at 1600 rpm. Its top speed was 80 km/h (50 mph), and it had double ignition and a four-speed gearbox.

Brasier VL – 1908 (F) Richard Brasier were formed in 1903 by Georges Richard and Henri Brasier, and won several important races. Richard left the partnership to form Unic in 1905. The VL had a two-cylinder 1520-cc engine, with a three-speed gearbox.

Germain 18/22 HP – 1908 (B) A development of the 14/22 of 1905, this car had a T-head 3595-cc engine with a three-speed gearbox, giving a top speed of 68 km/h (42.2 mph). Founded in 1897 to assemble Daimler cars, Germain remained in operation until 1914.

Lanchester – 1908 (GB) Built with great attention to detail, the 20 HP had a three-speed preselector gearbox with a self-adjusting multiple disc clutch in an oil bath. The engine capacity was 2485 cc and the top speed 80 km/h (50 mph).

Martini 12/16 CV – 1909 (CH) This was considered one of the most modern cars of the period and had a four-cylinder 2212-cc OHV engine with cardan shaft transmission. Martini remained in operation from 1902 to 1934.

Métallurgique 12 CV – 1910 (B) This Belgian company's small, four-cylinder car was characterized by its pointed radiator. The 2614-cc engine had three valves per cylinder and gave a top speed of 84 km/h (52.2 mph).

Scania Vabis 18/29 HP – 1911 (S) This car was only in production for one year. The 2270-cc engine had a top speed of 65 km/h (40.4 mph). It had a four-speed gearbox and semi-elliptic leaf springs.

Clément-Bayard 4M – 1911 (F) This small, 1300-cc car was an excellent combination of size and economy. It had a three-speed gearbox, semi-elliptic leaf-spring suspension and a top speed of 84 km/h (52.2 mph).

Wolseley 16/20 – 1911 (GB) In production from 1911 to 1915, this was the best seller in England in its class. It had a 3080-cc 20-hp engine capable of up to 60 km/h (37.3 mph), a four-speed gearbox and leaf-spring suspension.

Turcat-Méry 18 CV – 1911 (F) This De Dietrich-built car was characterized by its cardan shaft transmission and four-speed gearbox. It had a capacity of 3307 cc.

Singer 10 HP – 1912 (GB) Designed by Alderson, the 10 HP had a four-cylinder 1096-cc engine with a thermosiphon cooling system and an optional electric light system. It was periodically modernized and remained in production until just before the Second World War.

Stoewer B2 – 1912 (D) Stoewer were in operation in Stettin from 1897 to 1937 and began producing automobiles with De Dion engines in 1899. This 22-hp 2-liter car, built between 1910 and 1913, had an L-head, side-valve engine and a four-speed gearbox. The footbrake acted on the transmission and the handbrake on the rear drums.

Rover 12 HP – 1912 (GB) Designed by Owen Clegg, the Rover 12 had a four-cylinder L-head 2297-cc engine with a three-speed gearbox and cardan shaft transmission. It was one of the very first cars to be supplied with a dipstick. A total of 1,600 were produced in 1913.

Apollo 4/12 PS – 1913 (D) Apollo Werke AG began building automobiles in 1904 as Ruppe & Sohn, changing the name to Apollo in 1910. The 4/12 PS had a very light chassis and an engine of about 1000 cc which developed 12 hp at 1800 rpm. Its top speed was 70 km/h (43.5 mph).

Standard Rhyl – 1913 (GB) Standard were founded by R.W. Maudsley in 1903 and introduced their economical four-cylinder 1088-cc car in 1913. Two years later, they were producing fifty a week. After the war, the Rhyl was given a 1328-cc engine and renamed the SLS. A 1.6-liter model, the SLO, was subsequently also brought out.

Calthorpe Minor – 1913 (GB) The Calthorpe company, founded by G.W. Hands, came on to the automobile scene in 1905. The Minor was brought out in 1913 with a four-cylinder 1087-cc engine that could reach 80 km/h (50 mph). It was renamed the Sporting Four after the war and given a larger, 1261-cc engine. Calthorpe ceased production in 1927.

Delaunay Belleville HB – 1911 (F) In 1904, after many years' experience of heavy engineering, Delaunay Belleville went into the production of luxury automobiles with very advanced features, for example full-pressure lubrication, patented in 1897. The 4426-cc HB was part of a six-cylinder series built after 1908.

Le Zèbre A – 1911 (F) These voiturettes, designed by Jules Solomon (later of Citroën) and produced between 1909 and 1919, achieved a wide distribution. The A-type was a small single-seater with a single-cylinder 616-cc engine giving 5 hp and a top speed of 50 km/h (31 mph). In 1913, the four-seater Model B came out with a four-cylinder 785-cc engine. The last version was the D, brought out in 1919.

Grègoire 13/18 – 1911 (F) This car, with its 2212-cc engine and three-speed gearbox, won itself an excellent reputation for handling and reliability. It led to the production of the 14/24 CV, with a 3217-cc engine and a four-speed gearbox – one of the most successful cars produced by this French company, which was active from 1903 to 1924.

Bianchi 20/30 HP – 1910 (I) This car had a four-cylinder 4939-cc L-head bi-bloc engine with high tension magneto ignition, a four-speed gearbox and cardan shaft transmission. A 5700-cc monobloc engine was later fitted which gave a top speed of 80 km/h (50 mph).

Lancia Theta – 1913 (I) The Theta was the first car in Europe to have a pedal-controlled electric starter. It had a four-cylinder in-line engine of 4940 cc, developing 70 hp at 2200 rpm, with a top speed of 120 km/h (74.5 mph). Between 1913 and 1919, 1,696 were built.

of models under the name Pipe; they were in operation between 1898 and the beginning of the 1920s, and enjoyed varying degrees of success in European competitions. In 1905, they adopted overhead valves and shock-absorbers – indicators of the high class of their production.

Various small manufacturers also in operation in Belgium included Métallurgique, who became quite important. Their best products were the work of Ernst Lehmann, a capable designer who

had benefited from years of experience with the German company Daimler. Métallurgique were taken over in 1928 by Minerva, another Belgian company, founded in 1900 by the Dutchman Sylvain de Jong. Minerva produced a vast range of models with engines from one to six cylinders until the beginning of the Second World War.

Like the Imperia (1908–35), inspired by Hispano-Suiza, the Excelsior, in production from 1901, had by 1932 become synony-

mous with luxury as a result of its high level of performance.

In Austria, too, production was dominated by a number of companies specializing in high-class vehicles. Before the First World War, there were perhaps ten firms in operation, producing up to 6,000 automobiles a year.

The Viennese coachbuilder Lohner began to build electric cars in 1898 and called upon the young Ferdinand Porsche to attempt to resolve the perennial problems of weight and range. The result was

an interesting mixed system in which a petrol power unit supplied the necessary energy to two electric motors applied to the front wheels. The patent was taken out by Daimler. In 1905, Porsche moved to Austro-Daimler, who began to break away from the German mother-company. Emil Jellinek, who had brought about the association with the Canstatt company, used his commercial drive to start production of a 4500-cc 24/28-hp vehicle, the Maja, named after his second

Fiat Zero 12/15 HP – 1912 (I) Only a roadster version of this car was produced between 1912 and 1915. The Zero had a four-cylinder 1844-cc 19-hp monobloc engine with a top speed of 70 km/h (43.5 mph). Although it was not particularly cheap, it was one of the first examples of standardized production in Italy.

Renault 9 CV ("Marne Taxi") – 1906 (F) The 9 CV was one of the first vehicles designed for public transport and 1,500 were commissioned by the Compagnie des Fiacres in Paris. They boasted a device for calculating the cost of a journey based on the speed and the distance covered. The two-cylinder 1205-cc 9-hp engine gave a top speed of 65 km/h (40.4 mph).
    During the First World War, these taxis played an important role in the defense of Paris against the advancing German troops. They were requisitioned by General Gallieni on 7 September 1914 to transport a group of reservists to the Paris–Meaux road, in order to strike the flank of von Kluck's German forces, which had already reached the Marne. The enemy troops were driven into retreat.

child, the sister of Mercedes; however, the car did not enjoy the success it deserved, as a result, among other things, of the delay with which the project got off the ground. Porsche's contribution to Austro-Daimler lasted until 1923, and resulted in sophisticated automobiles and a great number of competition successes. In 1934, the company became part of the Steyr-Daimler-Puch-AG group

and its name eventually disappeared.
    Steyr was an old arms factory in Graz which since 1894 had constructed bicycles and during the war built aeronautical engines; in 1917 it turned to automobile production. Puch, which was also in Graz, was founded in 1899 by Johann Puch to produce bicycles, engines and motor cycles. Their first car was made in 1906 and the

range was already well diversified in all areas of the market by the outbreak of the war.
    Holland was not excluded from the list of nations with a developed automobile industry either, thanks to Spyker, whose first original car was produced in 1900. Although at first the company copied the much-abused lines of De Dion-Bouton, it then distinguished itself with highly

adventurous, expensive innovations, such as an engine block integrated with the chassis, airtight anti-dust bonnets and specially designed full-length undershields. The first car with four-wheel drive – the 32/40 hp with a six-cylinder bi-bloc engine – came out in 1903. Quality of construction was the characteristic of all Spyker vehicles, the last of which was produced in 1925.

Züst 25/35 HP – 1913 (I) Züst began
producing automobiles in 1905, building
large-capacity, high-class cars while the
affiliated company Brixia Züst built less
prestigious vehicles between 1906 and
1912. The two companies then merged
under the single name "Züst," remaining
in production until 1917, when they were
taken over by the Officine Meccaniche
(Miani, Silvestri & Company) and formed
OM. The 25/35 had a four-cylinder 4714-cc
engine and a four-speed gearbox.

Panhard-Levassor X 17 SS – 1912 (F)
Under the direction of their engineer,
Krebs, Panhard-Levassor experimented
with Charles Knight sleeve-valve engines
on their cars from 1908 onwards, after they
had been adopted by British Daimler and
Minerva. One of the first valveless
Panhard-Levassors was the X 17 SS, which
had a four-cylinder 2614-cc engine. The
company came on to the automobile
market after its agreement with Daimler
Motoren Gesellschaft was terminated.

Fischer 10/33 HP – 1913 (CH) Founded in
Zurich in 1909, Fischer produced technically highly advanced cars until 1914.
The 10/33 HP had a four-cylinder 2723-cc
water-cooled sleeve-valve engine which
developed 33 hp. It had cardan shaft
transmission and a patented four-speed
gearbox having pinion gears with internal
toothing.

Thomas Flyer 35 and 6-60 – 1907 (USA) This American car, with its four-cylinder 9369-cc 70-hp engine, won the 1907 New York–Paris speed and endurance trial over 20,000 km (12,427 miles) including the sea stretch between the USA and Japan. The six-cylinder 12,936-cc 72-hp 6-60 repeated its success the following year.

With the exception of basketball and handball, the British invented nearly all major sports while the French organized most of the great competitions. In the case of motor sports, however, the French have been entirely responsible for both creating and organizing them. The reasons for this are twofold: if we except the work of Benz and Daimler in Germany, both the automobile and the automobile industry were born in France. Laws in force in England not only banned the organization of car races, but even prohibited normal use of the motor car. Until 1896, speed limits were imposed in Britain of 6 km/h (4 mph) on the open road and 3 km/h (2 mph) in built-up areas, and every car had to be preceded by a man on foot, walking at least sixty paces ahead of the car, carrying a red flag. It was not until the Light Automotive Act in 1896 that the speed limit was increased to 32 km/h (20 mph). That same year the London-to-Brighton run was organized – not a race as such, for though there were perhaps thirty cars at the starting line and fourteen finishers, there was no declared winner.

Motor racing in earnest had started a good deal earlier in France under the patronage of a group of aristocrats, wealthy gentlemen and car manufacturers, all of them motor car enthusiasts. Although the first recognized race was the Paris–Rouen, which took place on 22 July 1894, sportsmen of the time had already been enjoying the headiness of speed for several years, both alone and in competitions. A steam tricycle race had been organized on the banks of the Seine in the Bois de Boulogne on 28 April 1887, but with only one entrant: Bouton at the wheel of a De Dion-Bouton-Trepardoux. Four years later a similar race was organized, this time with three competitors at the starting line.

The 1894 Paris–Rouen marked the beginning of an era of city-to-city races, though it was not in fact a true speed race. The twenty-one starters – fourteen petrol and seven steam vehicles – to survive the qualifying rounds were not judged entirely on performance: first prize was awarded to the car also considered best in terms of manage-

ability, economy and safety. So although Bouton was the fastest finisher at the wheel of his De Dion-Bouton, a joint first prize was awarded to Peugeot and Panhard-Levassor (the latter built Daimler engines under license which were fitted both on their own cars and on the Peugeots).

The first recognized race was the Paris–Bordeaux–Paris, which covered 1200 km (732 miles) and took place on 11-15 June 1895; it was won by Levassor in a Panhard ahead of three Peugeots and a Benz. This was the first of many city-to-city races organized either by Paris newspapers or by the Automobile Club de France. This club was founded by the Marquis de Dion on 5 November 1895 and organized thirty-four inter-city races during the first eight years of its existence. Among them were the first international race, Paris–Amsterdam–Paris, in 1898, won by Charron in a Panhard; the first race to include a woman driver, the 1901 Paris–Berlin, with Madame Camille du Gast, also driving a Panhard; and – the climax and also the last race of all – the Paris–Madrid of May 1903.

There were 179 vehicles at the start, including some enormous cars by Mercedes, Panhard and Mors with *minimum* weights of 1000 kg (.984 tons), engines up to 18 or 20 liters and top speeds of over 120 km/h (75 mph). However, this last race was not completed: so many were the deaths and injuries during the course of the event that the French government insisted that the race be stopped at the first leg in Bordeaux. Five of the drivers and mechanics died, including Marcel Renault, Louis's brother, and there were countless accidents involving some of the estimated three million spectators along the route.

Fernand Gabriel, who set off five and a half hours after the first car left Paris, overtook 163 competitors to arrive first in Bordeaux at the wheel of his 70-mph Mors. He was the first and last winner of this interrupted race, which marked the end of the great road marathons: it was not until the 1927 Mille Miglia and the Transamerican that this kind of free trial on open roads was to be repeated.

Races *did* continue, supported by the

Itala 35/45 – 1907 (I) Borghese, Barzini and Guizzardi were the first to cross the finishing line of the Peking–Paris race of 1907 in this car, with a lead of more than twenty days over the second to classify. The Itala had a four-cylinder 7433-cc engine, a four-speed gearbox and semi-elliptic leaf-spring suspension. A strictly standard series version (except for small details on the coachwork and extra tanks) covered the 16,000 km (10,000 miles) in forty-four days.

Mors – 1901 (F) Mors won the Paris–Berlin race in 1901 and the Paris–Bordeaux in 1903 with this model. The 10,087-cc V4 engine developed 60 hp at 950 rpm. The following year's model was the very first car to have shock-absorbers.

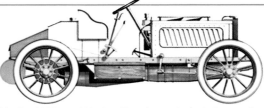

Napier 30 HP – 1902 (GB) Despite a relatively low engine capacity (6435 cc) which gave it just 44.5 hp, this car won the Gordon Bennett Cup because it was so light and easy to handle. It had a four-cylinder engine and a live axle.

Wolseley 96 – 1904 (GB) Nicknamed "The Beetle," this car developed 96 hp at 1300 rpm (the number in its title was its power output) from a four-cylinder 11,896-cc transverse engine. Designed by Herbert Austin, it qualified in twelfth place, with Jarrott driving, in the Gordon Bennett Cup.

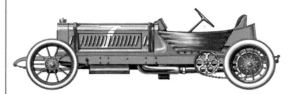

Richard-Brasier – 1904 (F) The 1904 Gordon Bennett was won by Léon Théry in a four-cylinder 9896-cc Richard-Brasier which developed 80 hp at 1300 rpm. Jenatzy came second in a Mercedes and H. Rougier was third in a Turcat-Méry.

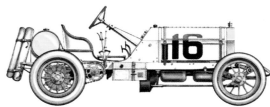

Locomobile – 1906 (USA) The Vanderbilt Cup held on Long Island in 1908 was won by Robertson driving a Locomobile Type 1906. His average speed was 103.500 km/h (64.32 mph). (Four cylinders, 17,657 cc, 90 hp at 1050 rpm.)

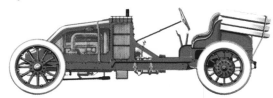

Renault GP – 1906 (F) This car won the first French Grand Prix with a four-cylinder in-line 12,986-cc engine developing 90 hp at 1200 rpm. The secret of its success lay in the detachable rear rims, which made it possible for two men to change the wheels in just four minutes.

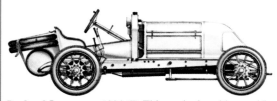

Panhard-Levassor – 1904 (F) This car had problems with overheating in the 1904 Gordon Bennett because of its new streamlining, designed to "cut through the wind," which did not include a honeycomb radiator. (Four cylinders, 15,435 cc, 90 hp.)

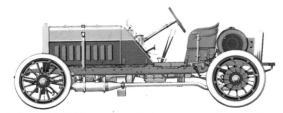

Itala – 1907 (I) There was no limit on the cylinder capacity of the cars for the 1907 Grand Prix Formula, so Itala built this 15-liter version, which developed 120 hp at 1200 rpm. It won the Brescia Speed Cup ahead of a Darracq and two De Dietrichs, and was also successful in other races.

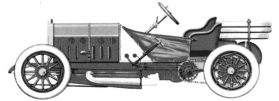

Fiat 130 HP – 1907 (I) This car was built in compliance with the 1907 Grand Prix rules, which limited fuel consumption to 30 liters/100 km (9.5 mpg). It had a four-cylinder bi-bloc supersquare engine of 16,286 cc, developing 130 hp at 1600 rpm and weighed 1000 kg (.984 tons).

enthusiasm of drivers and the public, as well as by the promotional interests of the car manufacturers; but the old city-to-city races were gradually replaced by long-distance rallies, speed trials and circuit races.

The first great rally was the 1907 Peking to Paris via Siberia, which took the winner two months to complete. There were five entrants in all, and the first to finish was the 40-hp Itala belonging to Prince Scipione Borghese, who was accompanied by his driver, Ettore Guizzardi and the reporter Luigi Barzini, covering the rally for the *Corriere della Sera* and *The Daily Telegraph*. Speed trials began in late 1898, introduced by *La France Automobile*, the first of the specialist magazines to appear. On 18 December, in Achères, north of Paris, Comte Gaston de Chasseloup-Laubat set the first official road-speed record at the wheel of an electric Jeantaud when he covered the flying kilometer at an average speed of 63.158 km/h (39.25 mph). This speed trial was followed by a long series of challenges between Chasseloup-Laubat and the Belgian Camille Jenatzy, who was to have the last word with *La Jamais Contente* in April 1899 when he covered the distance in thirty-four seconds at an average speed of 105.9 km/h (65.8 mph).

After a number of successful attempts, including one by Henry Ford in a Ford Arrow he had built himself (reaching 147.01 km/h (91.35 mph) on the frozen surface of Lake St Clair near Detroit on 12 January 1904), it was not until 8 November 1909 that the 200-km/h (124.27-mph) barrier was broken by Héméry driving a Benz at 202.65 km/h (125.92 mph) on the new Brooklands permanent circuit in Surrey, England. Even before this, the first permanent circuit, was opened in July 1907, the number of road trials on routes closed to traffic had multiplied, largely due to the Trophy created in Paris in 1900 by James Gordon Bennett, owner of the *New York Herald Tribune*. This event was an international competition in which teams of three cars from each competing country took part. The first Gordon Bennett Cups did not arouse great interest as they were held at the time of the prestigious city-to-city races and were cast in the shade by the Paris–Lyon of 1900, the 1901 Paris–Berlin and the 1902 Paris–Vienna. The fourth Cup was to have been held in England, but the British government refused to close the roads, so it finally took place in Curragh, Ireland, where it was won by the "Red Devil," Camille Jenatzy, in a Mercedes.

After 1904, the Gordon Bennett became one of the pinnacles of the racing calendar. In this year it was held on the German Taunus circuit and was won by Francois Théry in a Richard-Brasier. In 1905 it took place at Clermont-Ferrand, where Théry won again in the same car ahead of Nazzaro and Cagno's Fiats. However, the Cup finally became the victim of conflicting interest: the French wanted to introduce entry quotas, limiting the number of entrants in proportion to the respective importance of each nation's motor industry. As a result, there was no Gordon Bennett Cup in 1906, when it was replaced by the *Grand Prix de France*, held at Le Mans.

The previous year, the Tourist Trophy had been launched on the Isle of Man and in 1906 the Targa Florio was also inaugurated on the difficult Sicilian Madonie circuit. In Belgium, the Ardennes circuit was raced from 1902, while in the USA, after the accidents which had marred earlier Vanderbilt Cups on Long Island and at Santa Monica, William K. Vanderbilt in 1908 built the Long Island Motor Parkway. In 1909, the famous Speedway was built in Indianapolis, where the first Indianapolis 500 mile race was organized in 1911. Everywhere safety on closed and

Mercedes GP – 1908 (D) This Mercedes won the 1908 French Grand Prix at an average speed of 101 km/h (62.8 mph), beating at least forty-eight competitors as it covered the 800 km (497 miles) of the Dieppe circuit. The four-cylinder 12,781-cc engine developed 135 hp and gave a speed of 160 km/h (99.5 mph).

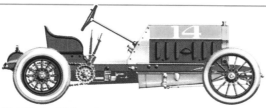

Fiat SB 4 – 1908 (I) On 8 July 1908, this car won a famous duel with the six-cylinder 200-hp Napier on the Brooklands circuit. The SB 4 had a four-cylinder 18,146-cc engine, giving 175 hp at 1200 rpm, and reached 190 km/h (118 mph).

Lancia Alpha – 1908 (I) This was the first competition car built by Vincenzo Lancia. It had a four-cylinder 2453-cc engine, giving 53 hp at 1800 rpm. It was brought out in 1907 and 108 had been sold by the end of the summer of 1909.

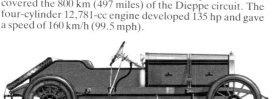

Austin – 1908 (GB) The Austin took part in the 1908 French Grand Prix, won by Lautenschlager in a 12.8-liter Mercedes. Driven by Moore and Brabazon, it came eighteenth. (Six cylinders, 9635 cc, developing 95 hp at 1350 rpm.)

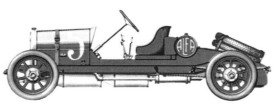

ALFA 24 HP – 1910 (I) In the 1911 Targa Florio, this car was in the lead until it was forced to retire, not because of any failure in its monobloc engine, but because spraying mud blinded the driver. (Four cylinders, 4084 cc.)

Buick Bug – 1910 (USA) This was one of the first American attempts at a competition car. Although it was not particularly successful, it was interesting for its aerodynamic lines and its original wrap-around radiator. (Four cylinders, 5750 cc, 130 hp at 2400 rpm.)

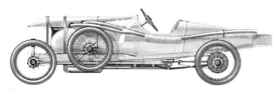

Sizaire et Naudin – 1912 (F) Three of these were built for the 1912 French Grand Prix and were entered in the under 3-liter class. Two of them were driven by the men who had built them and after whom they were named. (Four cylinders, 2982 cc, 95 hp at 2100 rpm.)

Sunbeam 3 liters – 1912 (GB) This car proved highly competitive, winning the first three places in the *Coupe de l'Auto* for voiturettes and overall third, fourth and fifth in the placings of the French Grand Prix. It had a four-cylinder 2986-cc engine, giving 75 hp at 2800 rpm.

Mercedes 1914 (D) With Louis Wagner at the wheel, this car came second in the ACF Grand Prix in 1914. The other Mercedes, driven by Christian Lautenschlager, came first. (Four cylinders, 4483 cc, 115 hp at 3200 rpm.)

supervised road circuits prevailed over the madness of the earlier races on the open road.

At the same time, very heavy, giant-engined cars were being gradually excluded from the events. Huge engines were no longer seen as necessarily the recipe for success. Besides, Marcel Renault, driving a small, 3.7-liter light car in the Paris–Vienna race of 1902, had already managed to beat the 18-liter engines which reigned supreme at the time. In 1905, the French daily *L'Auto*, the forerunner of *L'Equipe*, created the *Coupe des voiturettes* (Voiturette Cup) to encourage the construction of light cars, and certain manufacturers subsequently made their fortunes by producing cyclecars. Regulations were brought into force around 1910 to eliminate oversized engines from races and at about the same time Ettore Bugatti designed a competition engine of just 1400 cc at Molsheim in Alsace.

Although the first Monte Carlo Rally attracted twenty-three entries in 1911 and the 1912 rally had eighty-seven starters, the events of the Grand Prix – in particular the race organized by the Automobile Club de France – reigned supreme until 1924, the year when rallying took off again. Thirty-seven cars (limited to 4500 cc with a maximum weight of 1100 kg/1.08 tons) representing six countries lined up at the start of the 1914 Grand Prix on a rolling, winding 37.5-km (23.3-mile) circuit near Lyon for a race of twenty laps.

Mercedes turned out in force, determined to assert German supremacy, but the Frenchman Boillot dominated the race in his Peugeot until he lost a cylinder. Three hundred thousand spectators saw Lautenschlager win in his Mercedes, though he was not the only one to overtake Boillot: the Peugeot finished fourth, second and third places also going to Mercedes. Fifth position had been held by Fagnano, but the Fiat he was in developed mechanical trouble, so that he finished eleventh and last. There was no immediate return race, for this one marked the end of the heroic age of motor sports. Three weeks later, the war gave Europe a totally different kind of sport to think about.

Peugeot GP – 1912 (F) The twin overhead camshafts and four valves per cylinder on the Peugeot GP anticipated technical features still considered sophisticated today. It won the French Grand Prix in 1912 and 1913, Boillot driving.

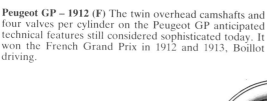

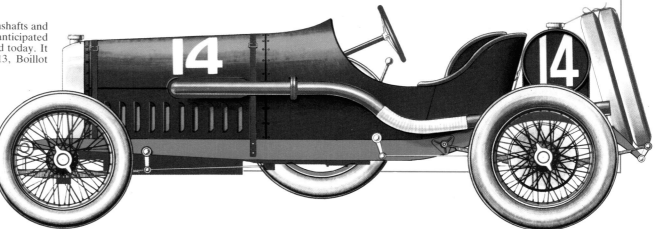

The industrialization of the automobile

If Europe was responsible for the birth of the automobile, it was the United States that saw its production on an industrial scale. In Europe, the new means of transport was considered a sophisticated toy, exciting sportsmen in particular. The emphasis on craftsmanship was also the result of a cultural approach to the automobile diametrically opposed to the demands of mass production, a concept which was clearly accepted on the other side of the Atlantic. The fact that practically every model built included countless innovations was certainly more important to technical advancement than satisfying the requirements of standardization. In addition, although at the time the automobile was still geared to a limited group of users, rationalization of production was certainly needed to bring about the changeover to popularity on a larger scale.

By 1902, the Olds Motor Vehicle Company of Detroit was building 2,500 Oldsmobile Curved Dashes, tiny runabouts with single-cylinder 7-hp engines that sold for $650. Production increased to 4,000 in 1903, then 6,500 in 1905, when thirty-five were being produced a day. By that year, there were already over 77,000 vehicles on the road in the United States, and in 1910 a total of 181,000 were produced.

The birth of the American motor car dates back to 1894 with the motor carriage built by two brothers, Charles and Frank Duryea. Their second model, which had a horizontal two-cylinder engine, three-speed gears and belt drive, was the first to cross the finishing line, in front of a Benz, in the first organized American race, held on Thanksgiving Day in 1895 over the 80 km (50 miles) from Chicago to Evanston. Production of the Duryea continued until 1917 and was characterized by outstanding technical innovations such as the Middleby air-cooled four-cylinder engine of 1906, or the two-stroke, two-cylinder horizontally opposed engine of the Buggyaut.

The pattern of development of the new means of transport was, however, set by a Clarkson

Selden – 1877 (USA) An enormous loophole in the patent system made it possible for George Selden to claim patent rights on the automobile until Henry Ford, in a long court battle which lasted until 1911, proved that the claim was unfounded. In 1879, Selden had applied for the registration of a vaguely defined "horseless" carriage, the prototype of which, ostensibly dated 1877, appears in fact to have been built later.

Oldsmobile Curved Dash – 1901 (USA) This was the first car to be built in a large series and was in production from 1901 to 1907. Four thousand were built in 1903, accounting for over a third of total US production that year. It had a single-cylinder 7-hp engine, giving a top speed of 30 km/h (18.6 mph). The two-speed gearbox also had reverse, and the transmission was gear-driven.

lawyer, George Baldwin Selden. He took advantage of the fact that the automobile was subject, not to a single patent for the whole vehicle, but to several patents for the main individual components, and in 1877 requested a single patent in his own name, to be subject to any modifications he might make as and when he collected new ideas on his frequent trips to Europe. This definitive patent came into effect in 1895, and on the strength of it, in 1903, Selden won a court action against the Winston Motor Carriage Company, who were forced to pay him damages and costs. The decision of the court prompted the majority of car manufacturers at the time to join together to form the ALAM (Association of Licensed Automobile Manufacturers), which granted a royalty to Selden of 1.25 per cent on every car – national or foreign – sold in the United States, and also ensured protection against new companies that were not associates.

Ford was among those unwilling to pay the percentage and, after an eight-year legal action and with the backing of Panhard-Levassor, Henry Ford managed to disprove and break Selden's patent. The only ALAM agreement to remain in force after this covered technical co-operation and was periodically renewed until 1955.

The economic position of the United States undoubtedly supported the development of the automobile industry and the basic innovations made by Ford, who recognized the profitability of popularizing a simple, functional, cheap but sturdy vehicle, were particularly important. With his very first Model A in 1903, the concept of building to order was abandoned, but the true industrial revolution began later, in 1908, with the Model T. Designed with a view to cutting production costs drastically, this four-cylinder 2880-cc 20-hp car was characterized by a number of unusual technical features such as epicyclic gears with pedal control. Increasing production went ahead hand in hand with a fall in sales prices of quite dizzying speed: in 1909, 12,292 cars were sold at $950 each; in 1911, 40,402 at $690; in 1913, 182,809 at $550. An even greater boost in output, however, was the introduction in 1914 of the first

Ford A – 1903 (USA) This was the first model produced by Ford and had a horizontal two-cylinder 8-hp engine positioned under the seat. It had a two-speed epicyclic gearbox and chain drive. Two hundred were sold in 1903.

Cadillac A – 1903 (USA) The first Cadillac was introduced at the New York Motor Show in January 1903 and had a single-cylinder 1610-cc 7-hp engine. Various versions of the car were built up to 1908 and it could travel up to 320 km (199 miles) on a full tank.

Peerless 24 HP – 1904 (USA) This was the first car of this marque to have a four-cylinder in-line engine. It could reach over 80 km/h (50 mph), had a four-speed gearbox and semi-elliptic leaf-spring suspension both front and rear.

Duryea – 1893 (USA) The motorized carriage (right) built by Charles and Frank Duryea represents the birth of the American automobile. The two-stroke engine was a rear-mounted single-cylinder version with electric ignition and a spray carburettor. The 1910 model (below) had a two-cylinder 12/15-hp engine and kept to the old carriage structure.

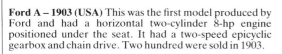

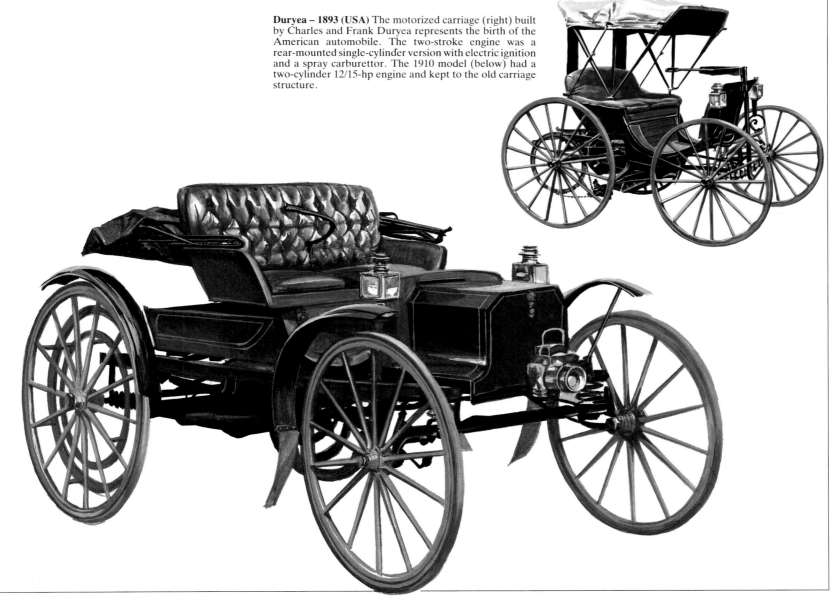

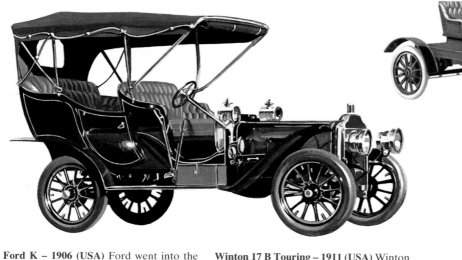

Brush – 1910 (USA) Although they were in existence for only a short time (1907–10), Brush made their mark by introducing coil-sprung suspension into the USA, as used on this runabout with a vertical single-cylinder 10-hp engine and a wooden chassis.

Ford K – 1906 (USA) Ford went into the large-engine sector of the market due to pressure from some of the shareholders, despite the fact that Ford himself was against the idea. The result was the Model K, a six-cylinder 7000-cc car which sold for $2,500. It was not a great success because of faults such as its inadequate two-speed gearbox.

Winton 17 B Touring – 1911 (USA) Winton came on to the motor car market in 1897 after introducing one of the very first electric starters. They specialized in prestige cars, which they produced up to 1924. The 17 B had a six-cylinder 9500-cc 48-hp tri-bloc engine.
▼

Rambler Cross Country 38 HP – 1912 (USA) Thomas B. Jeffery sold his cars under the name "Rambler" from 1901, when he founded his company, to 1913, after which he operated under his own name until taken over by Nash in 1917. The 38 HP had a perfectly square four-cylinder 6.7-liter engine.

KRIT 25/30 HP – 1912 (USA) Founded by Kenneth Krittenden and in operation 1909–16, KRIT produced the 25/30 HP, a four-cylinder 2998-cc vehicle with a three-speed gearbox, in 1912.

Stanley 10 HP – 1911 (USA) The Stanley company remained faithful to steam power and was the last to succumb to the petrol engine. It continued in operation until 1929. Francis and Freelan, the twins the company was named after, tested their first vehicle in 1887. The 10 HP was driven by a two-cylinder 10-hp engine.

White 0 – 1909 (USA) From 1900 to 1911, White produced a long series of steam cars ◄ before changing over to petrol engines. Immediately after the war, it stopped automobile production altogether. The Model 0 had a compound two-cylinder double-effect 20-hp engine.

Ford T – 1908 (USA) With more than 15,000,000 produced in nineteen years, the Model T was the car that put the USA on wheels. It was very sturdy, easy to drive and economical, and its price made it really popular, dropping to an all-time low of $260 in 1925. Designed by J. Galamb and G. H. Wills under Ford's supervision, it had a four-cylinder 2892-cc side-valve engine developing 20 hp at 1500 rpm, a detachable head, and magneto and fly-wheel low tension ignition. The top speed was over 60 km/h (37.3 mph).

complete production line, which allowed a Model T to be fitted out in just ninety minutes as opposed to the twelve hours needed with the most advanced of the existing systems.

The following year, more than 355,000 cars were produced by Ford and, because the new production methods were more economical than the old, the price dropped to $440. In 1923, on the threshold of two million cars a year, the price of a "Lizzie," as the Ford utility car was familiarly known, dropped to only $290 and its share of the market went up from 38 per cent in 1913 to 55 per cent in 1921. There is no doubt that the highly improved production methods, which by 1909 were bringing out cars identical even in

colour, were partly responsible for this great success story. The market at the time was still in its early stages of motorization and readily accepted such standardized products; by the early 1920s, however, production based on one single model no longer satisfied buyers' demands. It was at this point that the average American was almost obliged to choose his replacement for the monotype Model T from the wide range of cars offered by General Motors, which until then had remained in second place.

After competing at the top with Ford, between 1926 and 1930 General Motors took over as the leading manufacturer, gaining a position they were never to lose. The appearance of Chrysler in

1924 added the third to the trio of great names that were to form the basis of the American automobile industry.

Nevertheless, thanks to the wealth and size of the market, craftsman-based production along the lines of the European industry was still commercially viable and continued to exist in the USA alongside mass production. In 1909, there were at least sixty-nine companies manufacturing cars. As well as the makes that were later to join General Motors, for example Oldsmobile, Cadillac, Buick and Chevrolet, names such as Packard, Pierce-Arrow, Auburn, Marmon, Stutz and Mercer also appeared in the early years of the century, all of them specializing in products of the highest

quality. There were even a few companies remaining faithful to steam, and Stanley, who entered in the field in 1897, achieved excellent results in competitions with this form of power. Steam vehicles had reached the height of perfection in terms of comfort and therefore continued to sell until the end of the 1920s, despite great competition from the combustion engine.

White also began production of steam automobiles in 1900, but in 1910 changed over to the Otto cycle, in 1915 building an interesting coupé called the GMT, with a four-cylinder, sixteen-valve 5300-cc engine. However, the best results with steam were achieved by Doble, who only entered the market in 1912, by which time the

Hudson 37 – 1913 (USA) The Hudson company was formed in 1908 and had its biggest success with the Super Six in 1916, but even before then produced quality cars such as the 37, a four-cylinder 435-cc model with a three-speed gearbox. Hudson joined American Motors in 1954.

Wood Mobilette – 1914 (USA) The Wood company was founded in Chicago in 1899 and remained in operation until 1919, specializing in the construction of electric cars or mixed power plants. The Mobilette was a small, four-cylinder 1132-cc car which did up to 56 km/h (34.8 mph).

Pierce Arrow 48 – 1915 (USA) After it had brought out the Motorette with a De Dion engine in 1900 and the 15 HP with a Panhard-Levassor engine in 1903, Pierce introduced the Great Arrow 24/28 HP in 1904 and had a lot of success, both on the market and in competitions. In 1909, the company was renamed Pierce Arrow and began to produce prestige American cars. The Model 48 was part of the series of large-capacity six-cylinder cars designed by David Fergusson, the man behind all the company's cars until 1921. It had an 8577-cc engine giving 70 hp at 2500 rpm. Technical stagnation, however, caused the company to go into a slow decline. After a short-lived association with Studebaker (1928–33), Pierce Arrow finally went out of production in 1938.

Stearns 45–90 HP – 1908 (USA) Founded in 1896, Stearns began operation with a series of light voiturettes, but later concentrated on large-engine prestige cars of which the 45–90 HP was a typical example. With a six-cylinder bi-bloc side-valve engine of 13,088 cc, with a top speed of 140 km/h (87 mph), it was built to order and cost $6,250. After 1912, the company used Knight sleeve-valve engines until the 1929 crash put it out of production.

Stutz Bearcat – 1911 (USA) Harry Stutz, who had worked for Marmon, set up on his own in 1911, building cars with a markedly sporty line. Among the most famous was the Bearcat, which had a four-cylinder 6396-cc 60-hp engine. Some versions had four valves per cylinder. Production was brought up to date in 1926 with the eight-cylinder 4.7-liter AA series. The 5-liter DV 23 was the last car to come out before the company went out of production in 1934.

Maxwell 50–6 – 1914 (USA) The 50–6 was this small Indiana company's luxury model. It had a six-cylinder 6246-cc 41-hp engine, a three-speed gearbox, wooden wheels, double ignition and an electric starter, but was too heavy by comparison with its competitors.

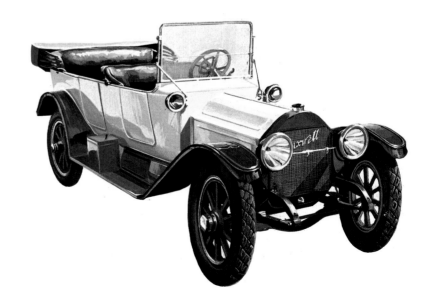

Eleven hundred and over

While the American motor industry was producing cars in large series, with the result that the number of cars on the road in the USA went up from 0.105 cars per 1,000 population in 1900 to 4.98 in 1910, 76.92 in 1920 and 150.2 in 1925, it also offered cars of exceptional quality, engine capacity and price. Although popular products such as the Model T Ford still resembled the "European model" to a certain extent, the élite models gave a foretaste of the dinosaur breeds to come in the 1930s, which were also to influence the size of later cheap models. Production was still half hand-built in style and so was particularly vulnerable to the risks of a changeable market, while the financial situation of the various companies was sorely tried by the 1909 slump and the 1929 crash, resulting in the disappearance of many names, including even the famous. None of these companies was in operation after the Second World War, but the very shortness of their existence on the market enveloped their extraordinary cars in a halo of legend.

Chadwick Six Model 19 – 1910 (USA) Lee Chadwick's cars, built between 1904 and 1913, were distinguished by their advanced technical features. The best-known model was the Great Six of 1906, with a tri-bloc side-valve engine on which, from 1907, a supercharger could be fitted – something completely new for tourers. The 11,578-cc Model 19 of 1910 developed 120 hp and gave a top speed of 160 km/h (100 mph). Chadwicks cost between $5,500 and $8,000 in 1908.

◄ **Lozier 50 HP – 1913 (USA)** Lozier started out by manufacturing bicycles and brought out their first car in 1904. The company had its greatest successes with the six-cylinder series, which began in 1907. On the racing side, a strictly series Lozier came second at Indianapolis in 1911. The 911-cc 50 HP was a typical example of the sports/tourer combination of these cars. The company went out of production in 1917.

Simplex 50 HP – 1912 (USA) This was the first car produced by Herman Broesel and it made great use of expensive materials. The four-cylinder 9777.5-cc T-head engine had an aluminium sump and two side camshafts. Transmission was chain-driven. After the 75 HP and the 36 HP, the last Simplex was the 46 HP, rated at 100 hp in 1914. Production continued until the early 1920s with the Crane Simplex marque.
▼

petrol engine was already well established.

Dobles were large automobiles which were extremely silent, comfortable and fast, capable of speeds up to 140 km/h (87 mph) with no vibration at all. Since the mechanical differences were not at all visible, the elegant coachwork was indistinguishable from the most prestigious petrol models of the time. Production ceased in 1930, as a result of the crisis of the previous year rather than as a reflection of the quality of the cars, but Abner Doble, the driving force behind the company, continued to perfect his own engines up to the end of the 1950s.

Ray Hutton SPORT BETWEEN THE TWO WARS

The ground rules for the early 1920s had been established in the immediate pre-war years. The monsters of the first period of motor racing had been slain; smaller, lighter cars with more sophisticated engines and transmissions developed from the turning-point of the 1912 Grand Prix at Dieppe. A Grand Prix formula based on engine size (maximum 4.5 liters) was introduced in 1914 and replaced by a 3-liter limit in 1920. Thus Grand Prix cars followed voiturettes, which raced to a 3-liter formula before the First World War.

During the war, racing had continued in America, where the rivalry persisted between Mercedes and Peugeot that had been so marked in the 1914 Grand Prix of France at Lyons. That race had been won by Christian Lautenschlager's Mercedes, but on the American speedways Dario Resta in a Peugeot was the most consistent winner.

No races of international importance took place in 1918, but the following year's Indianapolis 500 was again won by Peugeot – the last win in this premier American event for a European marque for twenty years – and Count Florio was determined to run the Targa Florio in 1919. He did so, in November, after a rare Sicilian snowstorm, and that too was a

victory for Peugeot. The driver was André Boillot, brother of Georges Boillot, hero of the 1914 Grand Prix at Lyons, who was killed in an aerial dog-fight during the war. Apart from the honour of winning Europe's first post-war race, Boillot the Younger's drive in the Targa Florio is remembered as one of the most sensational in racing history. He went off the road six times during the race and crossed the finishing line backwards, after crashing into the grandstand. Having sorted himself out and re-crossed the line forwards to avoid disqualification, he collapsed with, it is said, a cry of *"C'est pour la France!"*

Ballot – 1921 (F) Developed from the car which had handled so well in 1920 at Indianapolis, this car won second and third places in the French Grand Prix and won the Italian GP with Goux at the wheel. (Eight cylinders, 2960 cc, 107 hp at 3800 rpm.)

Duesenberg – 1921 (USA) This was the first racing car to have all-round hydraulic brakes and it won the French Grand Prix, with Murphy driving, at an average speed of over 127 km/h (79 mph). (Eight cylinders, 2964 cc, 115 hp at 4225 rpm.)

Fiat 801 – 1921 (I) The first Italian Grand Prix, held on the Brescia circuit, saw a line-up of just three Ballots and three Fiats. Bordino's Italian car did the fastest lap. (Eight cylinders, 2973 cc, 120 hp at 4400 rpm.)

Austro-Daimler – 1921 (A) This car was boycotted on several occasions for political reasons and so never managed to prove its qualities in the early post-war years. It had a six-cylinder 2992-cc engine developing 109 hp at 4500 rpm.

Fiat 804 – 1922 (I) The 1922 French Grand Prix was won by Fiat when Nazzaro's car averaged over 126 km/h (78.3 mph) in the 803-km (499-mile) race. (Six cylinders, 1991 cc, 112 hp at 5000 rpm.)

Bugatti T 30 – 1922 (F) The Bugatti marque made its début in the Grand Prix world in the 1922 French GP with an original, aerodynamically shaped car. The T 30 came in third, driven by Pierre Marco. (Six cylinders, 1991 cc, 86 hp at 6000 rpm.)

Voisin – 1923 (F) This car had a monocoque structure and an original aerodynamic shape, and took part in the 1923 French Grand Prix. Duray's six-cylinder 1978-cc engine developed over 60 hp and he was timed at 168 km/h (104.4 mph).

Rolland Pilain – 1923 (F) This car did very well in the 1923 French Grand Prix, driven by Guyot. Various engines were fitted on this chassis, including a desmodromic valve version which was later abandoned. (Eight cylinders, 1968 cc, 135 hp at 5300 rpm.)

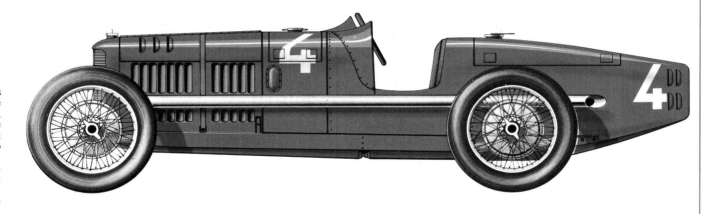

Fiat 805 – 1923 (I) This was the first Grand Prix car to be fitted with a supercharger, first the Whitting and then the Roots, increasing its output to 150 hp and giving a top speed of 219 km/h (136 mph). The 805 won the 1923 Italian Grand Prix with Salamano at the wheel. (Eight cylinders, supercharged, 1979 cc, 130 hp at 5500 rpm.)

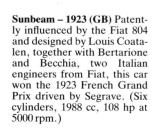

Sunbeam – 1923 (GB) Patently influenced by the Fiat 804 and designed by Louis Coatalen, together with Bertarione and Becchia, two Italian engineers from Fiat, this car won the 1923 French Grand Prix driven by Segrave. (Six cylinders, 1988 cc, 108 hp at 5000 rpm.)

Actually, by then, racing was less a matter of country competing against country, as it had been in the early days, and more one of competition between car manufacturers keen to gain a reputation for the performance and reliability of their touring cars. Racing's most famous marque has a connection with the 1919 Targa Florio, for this event was the first big race for Enzo Ferrari, driving a CMN.

Racing returned to Great Britain in 1920 with the re-opening of the Brooklands track, while in France a *Grand Prix des Voiturettes* was run on roads around a wartime American camp near Le Mans. It saw a win for the 1.4-liter Type 13 built in 1914 by Ettore Bugatti. Though the circuit was very rough and dusty, the event was a success, and the Automobile Club de France decided to revive their Grand Prix at the same venue in 1921. A rather thin entry was enhanced by the arrival of four Duesenbergs from America. Though the French Ballots were the favourites, they were roundly beaten by Jimmy Murphy's Duesenberg, a car which had benefited from the continuity of racing in the USA and brought hydraulic brakes, coil ignition and a three-valves-per-cylinder straight-eight engine to Grand Prix racing for the first time.

Le Mans was soon to become famous for a different kind of racing. The first 24-hour *Grand Prix d'Endurance* took place there in 1923, following an idea that originated in, of all places, Corsica, in 1921. The island wanted to hold an event to commemorate its most famous son, Napoléon Bonaparte. They offered free transport for competitors, a handsome cash prize (at a time when it was usual to pay a big entry fee and win just a trophy) and a new racing category. The Corsican Grand Prix was to be for four-seater touring cars of up to three liters. Thus was born sports car racing, the alternative formula to Grand Prix racing that exists to this day.

A French Bignan Sport won in Corsica, but Chenard et Walcker lasted the first Le Mans 24 Hours best. A year later, in 1924, a British Bentley scored the first of five wins for these cars in the endurance classic.

Grand Prix racing saw the end of the Peugeot period – or rather the Ernest Henry period, for it was he who designed the twin overhead camshaft, inclined valve, central plug engine configuration that was so readily copied by others. A 2-liter formula meant smaller cars and saw the dominance of Fiat in the European *Grand Epreuves* held in 1921.

Racing was adopting a pattern more familiar to today's enthusiasts. Road surfaces improved as artificial road circuits were opened – notably the 10-km (6.2-mile) track in the Royal Park at Monza in 1922. The same year, the *Grand Prix de France* at Strasburg was the first in Europe to have a massed start. Within three years the riding mechanic would be banned – the trigger was an accident in the 1924 Spanish Grand Prix – though cars continued to have two-seater bodies for some time.

A key season was 1923, which saw the first Grand Prix win by a supercharged car (Fiat, of Italy), rear-engined racers with independent rear suspension (Benz) and experiments with aerodynamic bodies (Bugatti and Voisin). The British driver Henry Segrave scored an unexpected win in the French Grand Prix driving a Fiat-inspired Sunbeam.

The following year belonged to Vittorio Jano's Alfa Romeo P2. Jano had been part of the 1923 Fiat team, but was persuaded by Enzo Ferrari to join Alfa, the team for which Ferrari drove and was later to run on behalf of the Milan factory. The P2 was, like the Fiat, a supercharged straight-eight.

The year was notable also for the introduction of the Type 35 Bugatti, a jewel of a car which was to achieve an amazing number of successes in various forms in the years to follow and which was unique at the time in being a Grand Prix car available for sale to private entrants.

Just as in the 1980s, when turbocharged engines raised the stakes in Grand Prix racing, Bugatti and Delage were against the admission of supercharged engines. Clearly, unless a new formula provided different capacity limits for supercharged and normally aspirated engines, they would have no choice but to join the forced induction club. In fact, Bugatti had the distinction of scoring the last Grand Prix victory of the period with a non-supercharged car by winning the 1925 Targa Florio.

Louis Delage was to achieve great things after he adopted supercharging for his cars, built to the new 1.5-liter formula of 1926–7. These low-slung, offset single-seaters were hot in more than one sense, for in the early races the proximity of the exhaust pipe and engine manifolds to the small cockpit gave the drivers a roasting. The problem was only solved for 1927 after an extensive re-design.

Robert Benoist was to win five major races for Delage in 1927. This beautifully engineered, supercharged straight-eight developed 170 hp – over 100 hp per liter for the first time – and ran to over 7000 rpm, much faster than its contemporaries. But compared with the Golden Years of 1922–4, the 1.5-liter formula was a disappointment. Economic conditions were poor, and it became clear that there were not enough takers to sustain a tightly controlled Grand Prix formula, with the expense and technical development that that involved. What followed was a period of *Formule Libre* – any kind of car, though mostly two-seaters which could, with more equipment, be used in sports car races and indeed on the road. The records show that, during this free-for-all period, honours were taken first by Bugatti, then Alfa Romeo and, increasingly, by Maserati.

Sports car racing became the dominant influence. At Le Mans, Alfa Romeo succeeded Bentley with four wins in a row, from 1931 to 1934. The Mille Miglia on Italian roads, recalling the great city-to-city races of the early days of the automobile, was inaugurated in 1927 and soon attracted big entries and huge crowds. In Great Britain – where racing on public roads was and is banned on the mainland – the famous Tourist Trophy was revived as a sports car race in Northern Ireland in 1928, while, a year later, a

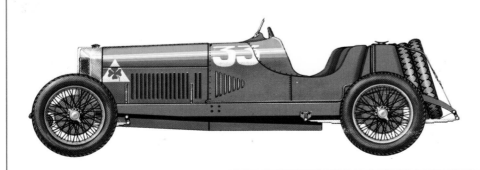

Alfa Romeo RL Targa Florio – 1923 (I) Alfa Romeo won its first Targa Florio in 1913 with Sivocci at the wheel. The car had a six-cylinder 3154-cc engine developing 95 hp at 3800 rpm. The power was increased to 125 hp and the capacity to 3620 cc for the following year's race in Sicily.

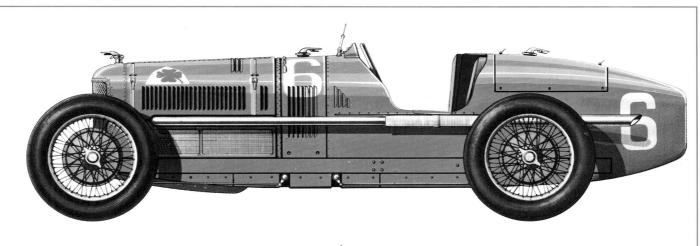

Alfa Romeo P2 – 1924 (I) This was the first Alfa Romeo designed by Vittorio Jano and was the top of its Grand Prix class for almost a decade. After 1925, it was uprated to 170 hp. Only six were built. (Eight cylinders, 1987 cc, 140 hp at 5500 rpm.)

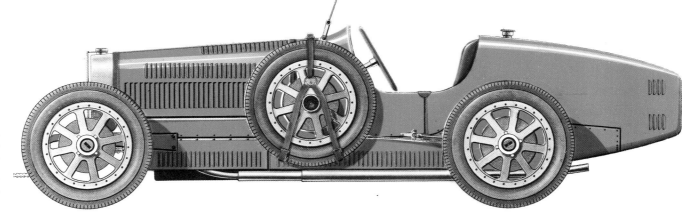

Bugatti 35 – 1930 (F) The 35 came out in 1924 and became one of the most famous models of the marque. It won countless races up to 1930. (Eight cylinders, unsupercharged, 1900 cc, 135 hp at 5300 rpm.)

Delage 1500 – 1926 (F) This Delage was built for the 1500-cc formula, which came into force in 1926. With Robert Benoist at the wheel, it won all the major European Grand Prix races of 1927. It had a straight-eight 1488-cc twin overhead camshaft engine with four valves per cylinder, developing 170 hp, and a five-speed gearbox.

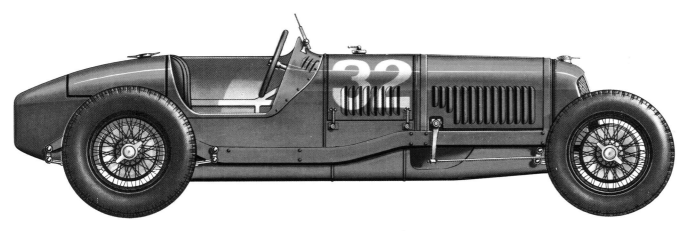

Maserati 8 CM – 1930 (I) Varzi won the Italian Grand Prix with this eight-cylinder 2991-cc car developing 165 hp at 6000 rpm. In the same year, the Maserati V4 "Sedici Cilindri" was also raced, with two engines coupled together to give a total 3958 cc and 350 hp at 5200 rpm.

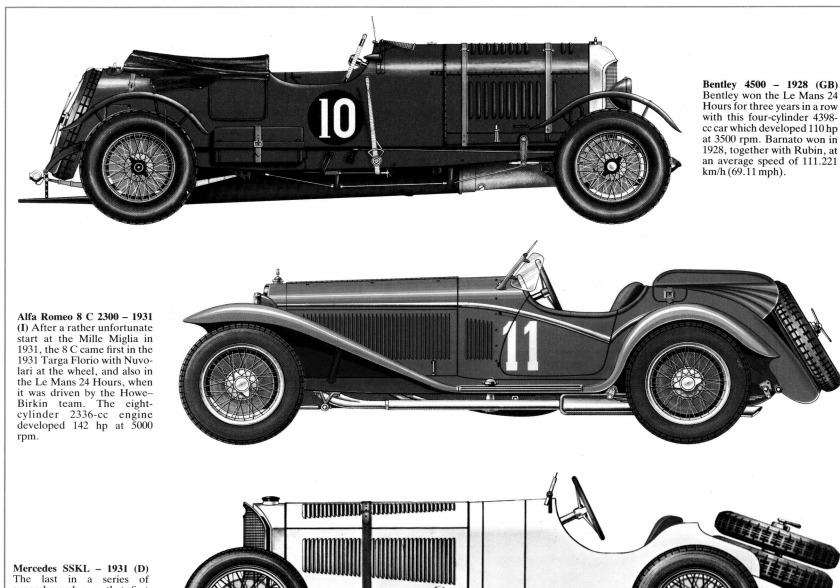

Bentley 4500 – 1928 (GB)
Bentley won the Le Mans 24 Hours for three years in a row with this four-cylinder 4398-cc car which developed 110 hp at 3500 rpm. Barnato won in 1928, together with Rubin, at an average speed of 111.221 km/h (69.11 mph).

Alfa Romeo 8 C 2300 – 1931 (I) After a rather unfortunate start at the Mille Miglia in 1931, the 8 C came first in the 1931 Targa Florio with Nuvolari at the wheel, and also in the Le Mans 24 Hours, when it was driven by the Howe–Birkin team. The eight-cylinder 2336-cc engine developed 142 hp at 5000 rpm.

Mercedes SSKL – 1931 (D) The last in a series of supercharged cars that first came out in 1926, this SSKL was driven by a six-cylinder 7068-cc engine which could develop up to 225 hp. Caracciola won the Tourist Trophy, the Spa 24 Hours and the Mille Miglia (with Sebastian), and came second at Le Mans with this car.

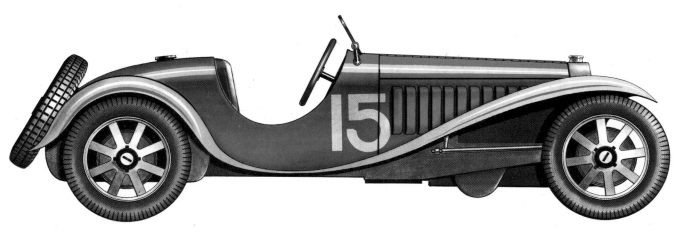

Bugatti 55 – 1932 (F) This car had an eight-cylinder 2270-cc engine developed from the one used on the GP 51 with a reduced rating of 135 hp at 5000 rpm. It competed hotly against the Alfa Romeo 8 C in various races, but proved to be less reliable. It had a top speed of 180 km/h (111.85 mph) and did 0–100 km/h (0–62.14 mph) in thirteen seconds.

five hundred mile race at Brooklands, held on the banked Outer Circuit, became the fastest long-distance race in the world, the winning Bentley averaging 173 km/h (107.5 mph).

Gradually, as the world situation improved and other countries appreciated that, if little Monaco could hold a successful race around its roads, so could they, Grand Prix racing regained some stature. The car makers returned; big-engined, central position mono-posto cars were developed. Great drivers were making their names – Caracciola, Chiron, and the great Italian rivals Nuvolari and Varzi. It was time to re-organize.

The formula proposed was simple. There would be no restriction on engine size, but the maximum weight of the cars would be 750 kg (1653 lb).

At first the pundits were doubtful about the new rules. Who would enter? By March 1933 it was clear that Mercedes-Benz would – and in a big way. Gradually it dawned that a new force had come on to the racing scene, a national force that had little to do with cars; the Third Reich had adopted the 1934 Grand Prix formula as a way of demonstrating Germany's new strength and technical ability. Funds were available not only to Mercedes but for a second Grand Prix car of more radical design by Dr Ferdinand Porsche – the P-*wagen* or Auto Union.

Though they lacked experienced Grand Prix drivers, the German teams' resources were such that they were able to produce cars the potential of which had not even been

Bugatti 59 – 1933 (F) This was one of the classics of the 1930s, first seen in the 1933 Spanish Grand Prix. The rear suspension consisted of inverted semi-elliptic leaf-springs, and the wheel rims had external spokes and aluminium inner discs. (Eight cylinders, supercharged, 3257 cc, 240 hp at 5400 rpm.)

Mercedes W 25 – 1934 (D) This car was a winner right from the beginning, when at the Nürburgring in May 1934 it competed against cars such as the Alfa Romeo P3 and the Auto Union. It had a top speed of 300 km/h (186.4 mph). (Eight cylinders, supercharged, 3360 cc, 354 hp at 5800 rpm.)

Alfa Romeo Bimotore – 1935 (I) Built at the Scuderia Ferrari in Modena, this car had a forward and a rear engine, a three-speed gearbox and two side tanks, each engine being of eight cylinders, 3165 cc, developing 540 hp at 5400 rpm.

dreamed of by the rule makers, who had sought to arrest the increase in power outputs and speeds with the weight formula. New materials and knowledge of metallurgy meant that the Mercedes and Auto Unions could keep under the weight limit while intensive engine research saw outputs rise from 430 hp for the Mercedes W 25's original 4-liter engine, to the 520-bhp V16 of the 1936 C-type Auto Union and 646 hp from the 5.66-liter eight-cylinder of the 1937 Mercedes W 125. It is worth noting that, not until the advent of turbocharged Indianapolis, CanAm, and eventually Grand Prix cars of the 1970s and 1980s, did racing cars match the output of the fabulous W 125.

By the standards of what had gone before, these were remarkably sophisticated racing machines. Independent suspension for all four wheels – and later De Dion rear ends – signalled the beginnings of understanding the science of roadholding, though the Auto Union, with its long engine and transmission at the rear, and its far forward driving position, was notably difficult to handle; in layout, though, it has the same configuration as the Formula 1 cars of today.

Despite the extravagance of their approach, the German teams were not without problems at the beginning. Yet by 1935 the challenge of Alfa Romeo and Bugatti had been over-whelmed. Tazio Nuvolari scored a notable victory in an Alfa Romeo in the 1935 German Grand Prix at the Nürburgring; otherwise only a surprise win for René Dreyfus's Delahaye at

Auto Union C-Type – 1936 (D) This mid engine, rear-wheel drive car was designed by Ferdinand Porsche and had the driver's seat very far forward. It won both the German and the Italian Grand Prix in 1936, then the Belgian GP in 1937. (Sixteen cylinders, 6006 cc, 520 hp at 5000 rpm.)

Mercedes W 154 – 1938 (D) One of the most advanced cars of its day, both from the technical point of view (independent front suspension, De Dion rear axle, with the gearbox in a block with the differential) and because of the sophisticated methyl alcohol-based mixtures which were used as fuel.

 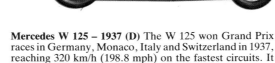 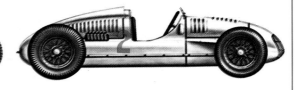

Mercedes W 125 – 1937 (D) This single-seater was a development of the previous W 25B and had a supercharged eight-cylinder 5660-cc engine developing 646 hp at 5800 rpm. In 1937, the W 125 won four Grand Prix races with Caracciola at the wheel, one with Lang and one with von Brauchitsch.

Mercedes W 125 – 1937 (D) The W 125 won Grand Prix races in Germany, Monaco, Italy and Switzerland in 1937, reaching 320 km/h (198.8 mph) on the fastest circuits. It ran on a mixture based on methyl alcohol and acetone as fuel. (Eight cylinders, 5660 cc, 646 hp at 5800 rpm.)

Auto Union D-Type – 1938 (D) One of the features of this car was the three-cam design with a single central inlet-valve camshaft and two for the exhaust valves. (Twelve cylinders, supercharged, 2990 cc, 420 hp at 7000 rpm.) In 1939, it was uprated to 485 hp.

Delahaye – 1938 (GB) This Delahaye had a De Dion rear axle and distinguished itself among the unsupercharged cars racing at the end of the 1930s, but its engine power proved to be insufficient. (Twelve cylinders, 4490 cc, 245 hp at 5000 rpm.)

ERA – 1939 (GB) Between 1934 and 1939, the most famous champions raced ERAs to success. In 1939, the 1.5-liter models took the first three places in the Nuffield Trophy, driven by Bira, Mays and Whitehead respectively. (Six cylinders, 1487 cc, 270 hp at 7500 rpm.)

Mercedes-Benz W 163 – 1939 (D) A development of the 1938 W 154, the W 163 won a good five Grand Prix races in 1939. A characteristic feature of the W 154–163 was the transaxle transmission. (Twelve cylinders, supercharged, 2962 cc, 425 hp at 8000 rpm.)

Pau in 1938 stopped a clean sweep for the silver cars.

For 1938, the formula was changed to a 3-liter engine limit with a *minimum* weight of 850 kg (1874 lb). Power outputs and speeds dropped, but by 1939, thanks mainly to two-stage supercharging, the cars were faster than the less wieldy monsters of 1937.

From 1934 to 1939, Rudolf Caracciola was the most successful driver, with seventeen wins to the ten of Auto Union's brilliant discovery, Bernd Rosemeyer, and Nuvolari's eight. The Italian champion had joined Auto Union in 1938. Had a European Champion been proclaimed in 1939, it would have been Hermann Lang, Mercedes's fastest driver of that year.

The French had retreated to sports car racing; Bugatti won the Le Mans 24 Hours in 1937 and 1939, Delahaye in 1938. The British and the Italians concentrated on voiturettes, then limited to 1.5 liters supercharged. The Italians led that class, but even here the German effort stole their thunder, for, when the showcase Tripoli Grand Prix was run for the smaller cars, Mercedes turned up with a team of scaled-down Grand Prix cars, the W 165s, and won. The Alfa Romeo 158 and the Maserati 4CL proved durable designs, however, and formed the basis for a new Grand Prix formula when the world returned to normality after the disruption and devastation caused by six years of war.

Alfa Romeo 6C 2300 B Mille Miglia – 1937 (I) This Alfa Romeo came first in the over-1500 cc Tourer class in the 1937 Mille Miglia. It had a Superlight Touring body and a higher output – 105 hp – than the basic model. It weighed 1150 kg (1.13 tons). It also won the 1937 Benghazi– Tripoli race over a distance of 1200 km (745.6 miles).

Alfa Romeo 8C 2900 – 1936 (I) Its career began with a victory in the 1936 Mille Miglia (Varzi-Bignami) and ended with first place in the same race in 1947 (Biondetti). The 2900 had an eight-cylinder 2905-cc engine giving 180 hp at 5200 rpm. It also won the Spa 24 Hours in 1936.

Alfa Romeo 308 – 1938 (I) This car had two twin-vaned vertical superchargers and was derived from no less than a standard series car, the 8C 2900 B. It had a four-speed gearbox and transverse leaf-spring rear suspension. (Eight cylinders, 2991 cc, 295 hp at 6000 rpm.)

Salmson – 1921 (F) This car won hundreds of victories in voiturette races between 1921 and 1928. It was designed by the engineer E. Petit and won the 1921 *Critérium du Mans*, driven by Lombard. (Four cylinders, 1097 cc, 38 hp at 3400 rpm.)

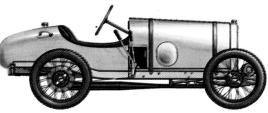

Bugatti 22 Brescia – 1921 (F) The 22 Brescia won the voiturette Grand Prix on the extremely fast circuit at Brescia with a four-cylinder 1453-cc engine which developed 30 hp at 3350 rpm.

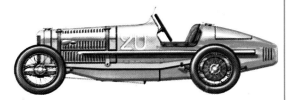

Talbot – 1924 (GB) The "invincible" Talbot-Darracqs of 1921–2 had four-cylinder engines with the same bore and stroke sizes as the eight-cylinder Grand Prix category (53 hp at 4000 rpm). In 1923, they adopted a supercharged engine which developed 100 hp at 5000 rpm.

BNC – 1927 (F) Another product of the winning "French school" of voiturettes, BNC had a four-cylinder 1098-cc engine developing 61 hp at 4900 rpm.

MG Magnette – 1934 (GB) The MG Magnette stood out among the small-capacity British cars produced in the 1930s. It was successful in both the small Grand Prix events and as a Sports version. (Six cylinders, 1087 cc, 120 hp at 6500 rpm.)

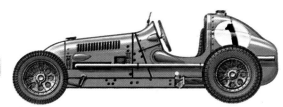

Austin 750 – 1936 (GB) This was the most sophisticated small-engine racer of the 1930s. Its twin overhead camshaft 744-cc engine developed 100 hp at 7800 rpm with the aid of a supercharger, but its potential was never fully used.

Amilcar – 1926 (F) This car had a six-cylinder 1096-cc supercharged engine and dominated the 1926 season. It had a power output of 70 hp at 5500 rpm. The French cars Amilcar, Salmson and Bugatti often competed hotly against each other in the 1100 class introduced in 1926.

ERA D-Type – 1935 (GB) With a six-cylinder 1488-cc engine developing 150 hp at 6500 rpm, the ERA was among the front-runners of the minor world competitions and won, among others, the 1936 International Trophy at Brooklands, when Bira made a final sprint across the finishing line.

▼

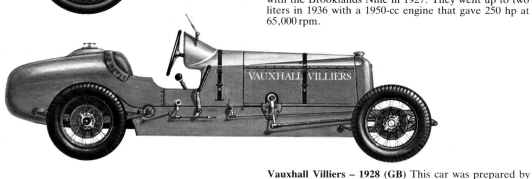

Riley – 1936 (GB) Competition Rileys featured strongly in British races and began to make a name for themselves with the Brooklands Nine in 1927. They went up to two liters in 1936 with a 1950-cc engine that gave 250 hp at 65,000 rpm.

Vauxhall Villiers – 1928 (GB) This car was prepared by Peter Berthon and was raced by Raymond Mays. A 3-liter TT model was fitted out in 1922, with an Amhurst-Villiers supercharger.

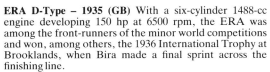

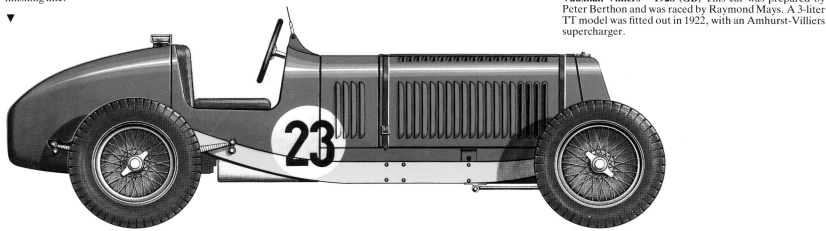

AN INDUSTRY WITHOUT FRONTIERS

As a result of military orders first from Europe and then, once the USA had entered the conflict, from the American government, the First World War boosted the rapid development of the American car industry with regard to both production and technological advancement. After the war, its improved body of technical knowledge and increased production capacity were devoted entirely to the production of automobiles. The American factories also had the advantage of not having suffered destruction, reconstruction and requisition, and so were able to continue exporting, particularly to neutral countries, even during the crucial years of the war. Once the war was over, they were immediately in a position to satisfy the great demand which had built up, and American production increased from two million vehicles in 1920 to four and a half million in 1929.

The supplies needed during the war also represented a great influx of orders and capital for European manufacturers. The automobile industry was called upon to produce aeroplane engines and munitions as well as transporters, and though in some cases heavy damage was suffered, the industry as a whole came out of the war strengthened both materially and politically, because of its proven importance in the balance of power between warring countries. Once hostilities had ceased, the technical advances that had been made were applied to the civil automobile, which benefited from many important innovations.

Metal alloys began to replace cast iron, and new but well-tried developments such as the overhead camshaft valve system were adopted from aeroplane engines. The braking system began to be applied to front wheels too, and the chain drive was finally abandoned. The extraordinary amount of interest shown in the 1919 Paris Motor Show confirmed that Europe, too, was now ready for motorization on a grand scale.

The early years after the war, however, were not easy ones for the major companies, up against an extremely complex and unstable economic situation that favoured rather the growth of an incredible number of small individual and specialist builders.

With a modest amount of capital, a workshop and a couple of mechanics, these builders were able to satisfy a passionately interested but uncertain clientele by assembling the most varied types of engine and chassis. Many of these firms disappeared within a few years, while most of them were absorbed by a process which became markedly stronger towards the middle of the 1920s, involving the concentration of production in the hands of a small number of large companies.

After the war, France confirmed its position as the leading nation in the field, and although at first production was mainly geared towards a rich élite who wanted expensive vehicles, attempts were very soon being made to broaden the range of users – following Ford's example – by standardizing production and reducing prices.

Newly born Citroën seem to have led the way, by bringing out their Model A, a 1327-cc tourer developing 18 hp at 2100 rpm, which was produced at the rate of a hundred a day, rising to five hundred in 1926, the last year of production. This was the first European example of large-scale mass production, and it was to have a significant influence, not only in France, but on the whole automobile industry. Renault updated their range with a 10-hp model inspired by the Model T which was to be offered alongside a large number of modified pre-war versions. Peugeot, too, were producing a vast range of vehicles, from the 760-cc Quadrilette cyclecar to the six-cylinder 25-hp version, but it was Citroën who made the greatest innovations with the B12, brought out in 1925, with its all-steel body and four-wheel braking.

In the 1920s, the French industry was divided between three main companies – Citroën, Peugeot and Renault – who between them produced 50 per cent of the national output. Numerous small companies were producing a range of luxury cars, for example Hispano-Suiza and Voisin. Panhard continued in an intermediate position and was able to supply complete vehicles from 1924, having acquired the Ateliers de Carrosserie of Orléans. Post-war production was resumed in 1919 and ranged from the 10- and 16-hp

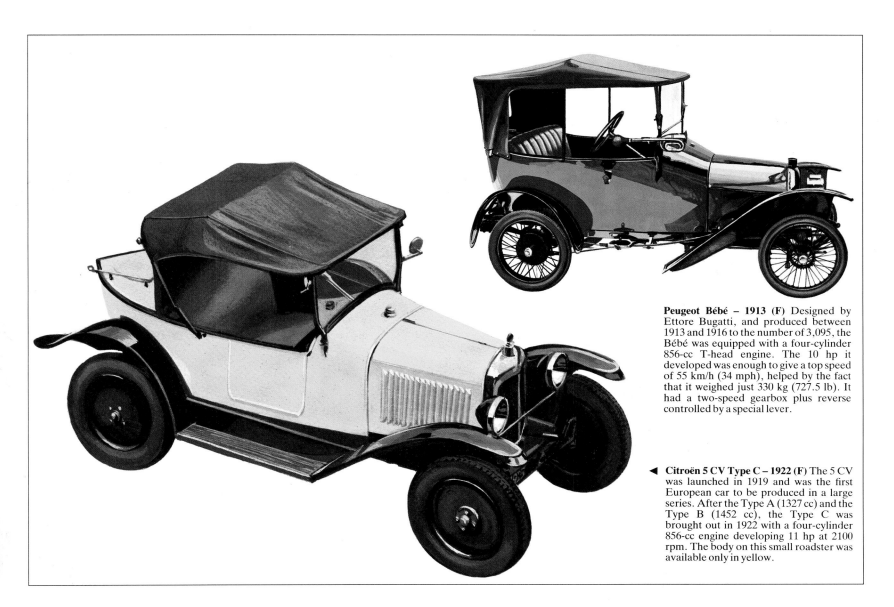

Peugeot Bébé – 1913 (F) Designed by Ettore Bugatti, and produced between 1913 and 1916 to the number of 3,095, the Bébé was equipped with a four-cylinder 856-cc T-head engine. The 10 hp it developed was enough to give a top speed of 55 km/h (34 mph), helped by the fact that it weighed just 330 kg (727.5 lb). It had a two-speed gearbox plus reverse controlled by a special lever.

◄ **Citroën 5 CV Type C – 1922 (F)** The 5 CV was launched in 1919 and was the first European car to be produced in a large series. After the Type A (1327 cc) and the Type B (1452 cc), the Type C was brought out in 1922 with a four-cylinder 856-cc engine developing 11 hp at 2100 rpm. The body on this small roadster was available only in yellow.

Austin Seven – 1924 (GB) The Austin Seven was launched in 1922 with a 696-cc engine and 300,000 were built in eighteen years. Nicknamed the "Chummy," it was modified in 1924 and had a four-cylinder 747.5-cc engine fitted, with a three-speed gearbox and brakes on all four wheels.

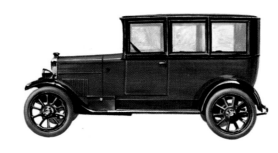

Buick Six – 1918 (USA) The Buick Six had a six-cylinder 3957-cc engine and was in production until 1923. The car had a three-speed gearbox and the last versions brought out had detachable heads and all-round brakes.

Fiat 501 – 1919 (I) Over 45,000 of these were built between 1919 and 1926, and it was the first Fiat to be built in a large series. It had a four-cylinder 1460-cc side-valve engine developing 23 hp at 2600 rpm, a four-speed gearbox and rear-wheel brakes. Its top speed was 70 km/h (43.5 mph).

Tamplin – 1920 (GB) This was a typical cyclecar with mechanics derived from the motor cycle. It had a 900-cc V2 engine with a three-speed gearbox and was pedal-started from the driving seat. It also had independent front suspension with coil springs.

Ansaldo 4C – 1923 (I) Derived from the 1800-cc 4A of 1920, this car had a 2-liter, four-cylinder engine with a removable head, a pumped water-cooling system and magneto ignition. The 4 series was the brainchild of Guido Soria.

De Dion-Bouton 25 HP – 1920 (F) This was one of the last De Dions to have a V8 engine and the car went back to the layout used on pre-war cars, with the same kind of engine. It had a 3600-cc capacity and a four-speed gearbox.

Darracq A-Type 25 HP – 1920 (F) Inspired by the American cars of the time, the A-Type had a 4594-cc V8 engine with coil ignition, a four-speed gearbox and cantilever-sprung rear suspension. It weighed 1800 kg (1.75 tons). Five hundred of them were built.

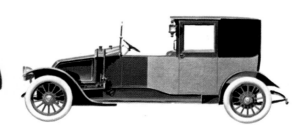

Berliet 16 HP – 1921 (F) Berliet specialized in building automobiles from 1895 until the Second World War, after which they produced only commercial vehicles. The 16 HP had a four-cylinder 3308-cc side-valve engine and a three-speed gearbox.

Renault 12 CV – 1921 (F) This car, shown here in the coupé version, had a four-cylinder 2812-cc engine and could do up to 80 km/h (50 mph). It had a four-speed gearbox, the brake pedal acted on the transmission and the handbrake on the rear wheels.

Oldsmobile 43 A – 1921 (USA) In production from 1920 to 1923, this was the last of the four-cylinder Oldsmobiles. It had an engine capacity of 3675 cc developing 22 hp, a pumped cooling system and splash lubrication. About 14,000 were built.

Wills-Sainte Claire T6 – 1925 (USA) After he had worked with Ford for sixteen years, in 1919 Harold Wills began to build his own cars, using an excellent 4.5-liter V8 engine with overhead camshafts. In 1925 the T6 was brought out with a new six-cylinder 4350-cc engine with a removable head.

Nash Four – 1921 (USA) After his success with six-cylinder cars, Nash put out a four-cylinder 2924-cc version with a three-speed gearbox. Its original price of $1,395 dropped to $985 in 1922.

Napier 40/50 – 1921 (GB) Napier, in operation between 1900 and 1924, were the first to popularize the six-cylinder engine (1904). The last car they brought out, the 40/50 (6177 cc, 82 hp), had a six-cylinder, light alloy monobloc overhead camshaft engine.

AC Six – 1922 (GB) Launched at the 1919 London Motor Show, the Six had a six-cylinder 1991-cc engine with a light alloy block, single overhead camshaft and developed 40 hp. The engine remained in production, with only minor modifications, until 1963, when the final versions developed over 100 hp.

Hotchkiss AL – 1922 (F) Hotchkiss went into the automobile business in 1904, sold its majority holdings to Peugeot in 1950 and stopped production of cars four years later. The AL four-cylinder 3962-cc model had an all-round braking system and overhead valves.

OM 469 – 1922 (I) This car was in production between 1922 and 1929, and had a four-cylinder 1496-cc engine with a removable head, a water-cooling system with a wooden fan, a four-speed gearbox and brakes on all four wheels.

Lancia Lambda – 1922 (I) The first automobile to have a unitary body and independent front suspension, this revolutionary car made its début at the 1922 Paris Salon. The V4 engine was initially 2120 cc (49 hp), but was later increased to 2570 cc (69 hp). Its top speed was 125 km/h (77.7 mph).

Audi K 14/50 PS – 1923 (D) This Audi reached a top speed of 90 km/h (56 mph) with its four-cylinder 3563-cc light alloy engine. It had a mixed braking system with a lever that acted on the transmission and a pedal operating the rear brakes.

Talbot 10/23 HP – 1923 (F) Built by Clément Talbot within the STD group, formed in 1919, the 10/23 HP had a four-cylinder 1074-cc overhead valve engine developing 23 hp. It also had a three-speed gearbox and semi-elliptic leaf-spring suspension.

Oakland 6–54 – 1924 (USA) Formed in 1907 by Edward M. Murphy and then incorporated into the General Motors group in 1909, Oakland changed its name to Pontiac in 1932 after it had brought out a successful model of that name in 1925. The 6–54 was a six-cylinder 2899-cc with four-wheel brakes.

Chiribiri Milano – 1925 (I) This was the last car brought out before the company went out of operation in 1928 (Chiribiri had been founded in 1910). The Milano was a four-cylinder 1485-cc model with a four-speed gearbox. Vittorio Valletta, the future president of Fiat, worked in an administrative capacity for the company.

Renault 6 CV NN – 1925 (F) The 6 CV was brought out in 1922 with a four-cylinder 951-cc engine. The NN roadster was brought out two years later and had four-wheel brakes, weighed 1080 kg (1.91 tons), had a top speed of 75 km/h (46.6 mph), a three-speed gearbox and transverse leaf-spring rear suspension.

Locomobile Junior Eight – 1925 (USA) Set up in 1899 to produce Stanley steam cars under license Locomobile converted to petrol engines in 1904. This car was an eight cylinder 3254 cc, with full-pressure lubrication and separate heads. Locomobile went out of production in 1929.

Willys-Overland Whippet – 1926 (USA) Founded in 1902, Overland was taken over by Willys in 1907. Willys-Overland was in turn taken over by Kaiser in 1953. The Whippet had a four-cylinder 2199-cc side-valve engine and four-wheel brakes. In 1929, 190,000 were built.

Bean 14 HP – 1924 (GB) Bean was in operation between 1919 and 1931, and introduced the 14 HP in 1924. This car had a four-cylinder 2385-cc engine with a removable head and a four-speed gearbox. Its top speed was 85 km/h (52.8 mph).

Triumph Super Seven – 1927 (GB) This rival to the Austin Seven had a four-cylinder 832-cc engine with a three-speed gearbox and hydraulic brakes. It was in production until 1934 and 15,000 were built, firmly establishing Triumph in the economical car market.

Morris Cowley 1920 (GB) A limited series of 1500 Cowleys was first built before the First World War with American parts, and it was then brought out again in 1920. It had a four-cylinder 1548-cc engine developing 26 hp at 2800 rpm. The selling price was particularly low – the open two-seater cost only £162 in 1925.

Trojan PB – 1923 (GB) Over 15,000 of these small cars were produced by Leyland prior to 1928. The wonderfully elastic four-cylinder horizontally opposed 1529-cc engine produced 11 hp at between 450 and 1200 rpm. It had a two-speed epicyclic gearbox and very economical solid tyres.

four-cylinder versions to the eight-cylinder 6355-cc version which came out in 1922. A total of 41,000 cars was produced in France in 1921, 121,000 in 1925 and 211,000 in 1929.

In Great Britain, Ford had gained a position of importance before the war through its small factory in Manchester, which assembled the American company's models from 1911 onwards. In 1914, 10,000 Model Ts were produced in comparison with the 3,000 vehicles made by the two major British companies, Wolsely and Humber. After the war, the national industry was unable to concentrate production, which remained fragmented in numerous small and medium-sized firms. This was largely due to the difficulties involved in raising the enormous capital necessary, and to union disputes which, because of the irreconcilable problems caused by the clash between modern machinery and a surfeit of manual labour, led to strikes which paralysed the automobile industry for long periods. Nevertheless, Ford still managed to produce 250,000 vehicles in 1925.

One of the important new developments on the British automobile scene at the time was the appearance of Bentley in 1919 with their 3-liter sports model (four cylinders and sixteen valves). In 1922, a model was brought out which was to play a major role in the British industry: the Austin Seven. The demand for cheap cars was growing steadily, but until then the British industry had only been able to reply to it with the cyclecar, a vehicle with a motor cycle engine and transmission, which was still chain- or

Chevrolet Superior – 1923 (USA) The four-cylinder 2.8-liter 22-hp Model M was called the Chevrolet Superior with a clear allusion to the Model T Ford. Thanks to this car, production reached 480,737 in 1923 and the first step was taken towards overtaking Ford.

Studebaker Erskine – 1927 (USA) Studebaker entered the compact economy car market with this model. It had a six-cylinder 2395-cc engine developing 17 hp, with a pumped cooling system and a three-speed gearbox. It was named after the president of the company at the time – Albert Erskine.

Kissel 8–75 – 1927 (USA) Kissel was founded in 1905 and remained in operation until 1931, producing a few four-cylinder cars followed by a successful series of fast six-cylinder models such as the 4.7-liter 60-hp 6–45. The 8–75 had an eight-cylinder Lycoming engine, which developed 71 hp at 3000 rpm, and a three-speed gearbox.

Lagonda 14/60 HP – 1925 (GB) This car was presented at the London Motor Show in 1925 and had a four-cylinder 1954-cc 60-hp engine with hemispherical combustion chambers and twin overhead camshafts, giving a top speed of 105 km/h (65.24 mph). It had a four-speed gearbox and mechanical brakes on all four wheels. The wheelbase was over 3 meters (9.8 ft).

Diatto 20 A – 1926 (I) This was a development of the 1922 20 and was the first built by the company to use overhead valves and shaft. It had a four-cylinder 1996-cc engine giving 45 hp at 3000 rpm. The 20 S was also part of the series, with an uprated 75-hp engine used in racing.

Reo Flying Cloud – 1927 (USA) In 1904, Ransom Eli Olds, the founder of Oldsmobile, set up a new company (using his initials for the name) which remained in operation until 1936. The Flying Cloud was a six-cylinder 4-liter 25-hp car with all-round hydraulic brakes and a four-speed gearbox.

belt-driven. The Austin Seven, however, was a true, small four-seater automobile with a four-cylinder 696-cc engine which was also a silent runner. Its success was enormous, and in 1923 two hundred vehicles a week were being produced. In addition to this, as a result of a rationalization of production inspired by Ford, its price dropped from £225 to £165, which was only marginally more expensive than a cyclecar. Production of this first British utility vehicle continued until 1939. A national rival to the Austin Seven was the Morris Minor.

British production increased from 60,000 a year in 1920 to 132,000 in 1925 and 182,000 in 1929. A further significant development was the purchase of Vauxhall by General Motors in 1925.

Recovery of the motor industry in Germany after the war was slower and more difficult than among the victorious nations. The lack of basic materials – fuel and rubber in particular – together with rampant inflation seriously

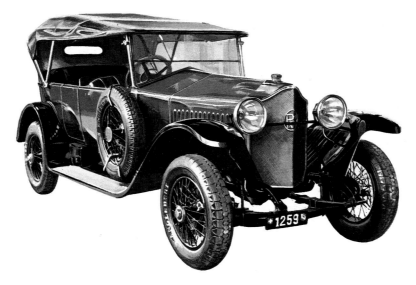

Pic Pic R2 – 1919 (CH) After having produced cars for SAG between 1904 and 1910, Paul Picard and Jules Pictet brought out their first Pic Pic – a 14/18 HP with four cylinders. The R2 had a 2950-cc sleeve-valve engine developing 50 hp at 1800 rpm. It was a particularly sophisticated vehicle, with comprehensive instrumentation, even including an oil gauge. The semi-elliptic leaf-spring suspension was integrated with hydraulic shock-absorbers. The Pic Pic marque was also active in competitions, but finally disappeared in 1924.

hampered attempts to reawaken demand and prevented Germany from making significant headway.

Opel were the first to introduce the production line in Germany, in 1924, for the manufacture of the Laubfrosch, a small, four-cylinder car which technically mirrored the successful Citroën 5 CV. Built at a rate of a hundred a day and sold initially for RM 4,000, the Laubfrosch dropped to a price of RM 2,700 in 1927. However, excessive differentiation in the range prevented Opel from taking full advantage of the possibilities of concentrating production on one single highly successful model. This was not to come about in Germany until after the Second World War, with Volkswagen.

Yet, in spite of this difficult period, a multitude of small firms flourished which were more or less of the specialist type. By the mid-1920s, there were eighty-six companies in operation, producing almost a hundred and fifty different models at a total production figure of just over 30,000 cars a year. Such was the level of

Fiat 520 Superfiat – 1921 (I) Only three of these were built before Fiat gave up their programme to build a high prestige car. It had a V12 6805-cc engine developing over 80 hp. The Superfiat could do up to 120 km/h (74.5 mph). It had a three-speed gearbox and suspension integrated with mechanical shock-absorbers.

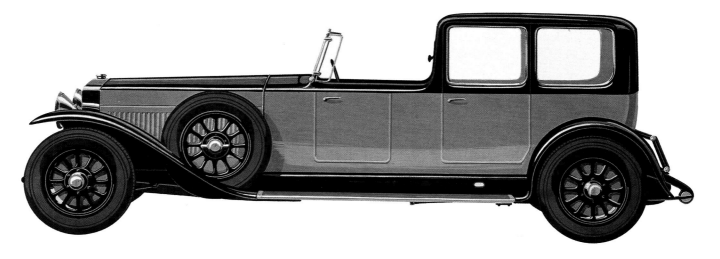

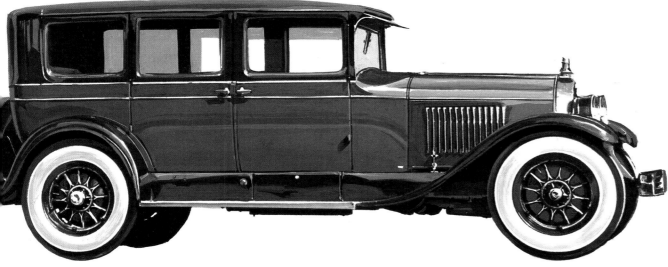

Cadillac 314–7 – 1925 (USA) This car continued the V8 series begun in 1915 on a Charles Kettering design and had a removable cylinder head and a power rating of 85.5 hp at 3000 rpm. It was one of the very first Cadillacs to have its body supplied by the Fisher company, which Lawrence P. Fisher, president of the company after 1925, owned with his five brothers.

competition that many firms collapsed or were forced to merge with large groups. A typical union at the time was that between Daimler and Benz, who joined the two makes in 1926.

Two years later, BMW and DKW came on to the German automobile scene. BMW, who specialized in the construction of motor cycles, made their début with a modified version of the Austin Seven, selling 25,000 in their first year on the market. DKW's production, on the other hand, included the P 15, a small car with a twin-cylinder two-stroke 584-cc engine.

In the second half of the 1920s, the German industry underwent a remarkable recovery, passing the 100,000 car mark for the first time in 1928.

In Italy there was a good deal of growth in the automobile industry after the First World War. Fiat controlled more than 80 per cent of the national market from the early 1920s onwards and brought out a vast range of new models. Although on the one hand this demonstrated the technical vitality of the industry, on the other it prevented sufficient rationalization of production to make for substantial reduction in costs. It was not until 1925, with the launch of the 509, and thanks also to the introduction of hire purchase sales, that Fiat were able to offer a relatively cheap product which could be sold in large numbers. The four-cylinder 990-cc 509 was put on the market at between L18,500 and L25,000, depending on the model. Fiat's closest rival in the utility car sector was Bianchi, who in 1925 brought out the S4, a four-cylinder car with a capacity of 1278 cc that was an interesting alternative to the 509 and cost only slightly more. One of the features of the S4, which remained in production until 1927, was its rods and rocker valve system; it was also equipped with a gearbox separate from the engine, but integral with the drive shaft.

Important technical advances were made by Lancia, the third largest Italian company at the time, with a production quota of about 3,000 vehicles a year. In 1922, the Lambda was the first car to have unit construction and an extremely advanced independent front suspension. Other com-

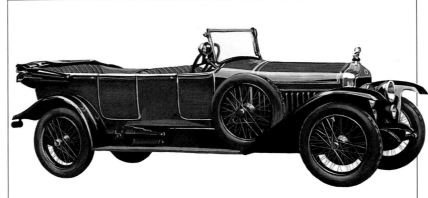

Minerva 30 HP – 1921 (B) This car had a six-cylinder 5344-cc engine. After 1922, it was fitted with a multiple disc clutch and all-round brakes. It had a four-speed gearbox and a top speed of 120 km/h (74.5 mph). The company was founded by De Jong, who died in 1928, but Minerva continued building excellent prestige vehicles (such as the eight-cylinder 6.6-liter 130-hp AL 40 HP of 1929) until 1938, though they had been taken over by Imperia three years before.

Austro-Daimler AD 617 – 1921 (A) After the First World War plunged Austria into a great economic crisis, Austro-Daimler were taken over, together with Puch and Austro-Fiat, by an Italian-Czech holding company which made it the prestige marque of the group. Subsequently Austro-Daimler brought out their first six-cylinder vehicle, designed by Porsche. The ultra-modern monobloc aluminium engine had steel cylinder linings screwed into the block and an overhead camshaft valve system. The 4420-cc engine developed 60 hp at 2300 rpm. The new version in 1923, the AD 17/60 HP, which was in production until 1926, had an integral braking system.

panies operated at much smaller production levels, but they had excellent reputations for the quality of their products and for their sporting prestige. A typical example was Alfa, whose cars were an unrivalled compromise between the saloon and the racing car. Isotta Fraschini, on the other hand, produced a limited series of prestige cars which were exported successfully even to the United States.

Italian production reached 46,000 in 1925, 37,000 of which were Fiats, increasing to 54,000 (42,000 Fiats) in 1928. Europe was, however, on the whole lagging way behind production levels in America and by the end of the 1920s equalled only 12 per cent of American output.

Great little sports cars

It was not until the 1920s that Europe began to manufacture cars on an industrial scale, although many small manufacturers were still enjoying great success in the motor world. Their products were mainly sports cars built to satisfy drivers' thirst for speed, both on the road and on the race track. France and Great Britain were the main centers of development for these special cars, which avoided all forms of ostentatious, elaborate coachwork; their appeal lay in the exhilarating performance obtained from their small capacity engines and in their excellent handling. Their bodies were basic and almost invariably open-topped. One of the best-known

manufacturers was Amilcar in France, who produced models with interesting technical features from 1921 to 1937, when they were taken over by Hotchkiss. The CGS of 1924 was an extremely light, easy-to-handle 1094-cc car, characteristic feature of which was its lack of differential. The G6 of 1926 was more sophisticated. About thirty-five of these were built, fitted with a six-cylinder 1100-cc engine which, thanks to its twin overhead camshaft, could develop up to 83 hp, giving an incredible top speed of 200 km/h (124.3 mph). A straight-eight was also brought out in 1928. Another French company, Salmson, one of Amilcar's main rivals, was set up in the 1920s to produce British GN cyclecars under license, and adopted even more elaborate technical features, examples of which are seen on the eight-cylinder 1100 cc: this model, brought out in 1928, had twin overhead camshafts, desmodromic valve control and two Cozette superchargers, and was capable of 140 hp at over 7000 rpm. The company's greatest successes included winning in its class in the 1923 Le Mans 24 Hours and the 1926 Targa Florio, as well as four consecutive category wins at the Brooklands 200 Miles from 1922 to 1925. Just before the Second World War, Salmson produced a series of more prestigious cars, the best of which was the S4E 2320-cc, which remained in production even after the war under the name "Randonée." The company's plants were taken over by Renault in 1957.

In England, Archibald Frazer-Nash started out with a partner, H.R. Godfrey, and built original cyclecars under the GN marque for several years before founding Frazer-Nash in 1924. His company produced cars which were distinguished by their original multiple-chain final drive units and very light weight, features which gave for extremely high performance, and also made them highly competitive on the race track. Superchargers were often fitted. The most important models included the 1936 Shesley (1500 cc, OHC, twin superchargers). Frazer-Nash used Anzani side-valve engines until 1929, then changed over to Meadows OHV engines. A six-cylinder BMW engine with rods and rockers was also used.

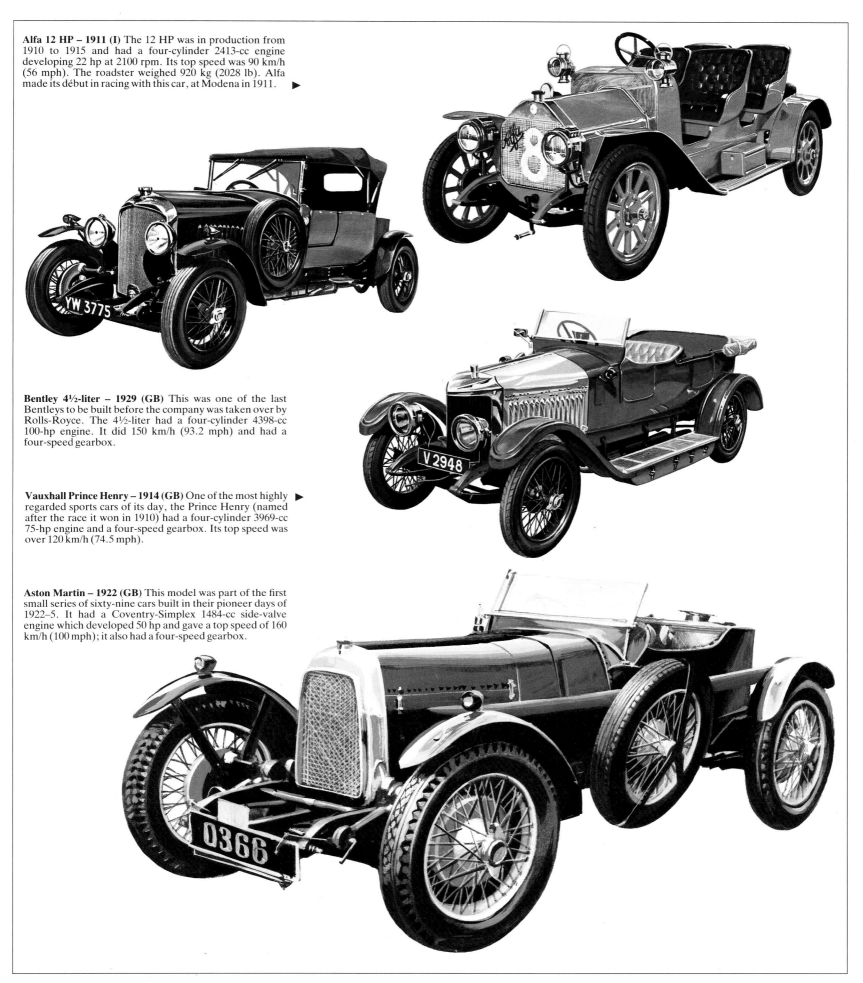

Alfa 12 HP – 1911 (I) The 12 HP was in production from 1910 to 1915 and had a four-cylinder 2413-cc engine developing 22 hp at 2100 rpm. Its top speed was 90 km/h (56 mph). The roadster weighed 920 kg (2028 lb). Alfa made its début in racing with this car, at Modena in 1911. ▶

Bentley 4½-liter – 1929 (GB) This was one of the last Bentleys to be built before the company was taken over by Rolls-Royce. The 4½-liter had a four-cylinder 4398-cc 100-hp engine. It did 150 km/h (93.2 mph) and had a four-speed gearbox.

Vauxhall Prince Henry – 1914 (GB) One of the most highly ▶ regarded sports cars of its day, the Prince Henry (named after the race it won in 1910) had a four-cylinder 3969-cc 75-hp engine and a four-speed gearbox. Its top speed was over 120 km/h (74.5 mph).

Aston Martin – 1922 (GB) This model was part of the first small series of sixty-nine cars built in their pioneer days of 1922–5. It had a Coventry-Simplex 1484-cc side-valve engine which developed 50 hp and gave a top speed of 160 km/h (100 mph); it also had a four-speed gearbox.

GN Vitesse – 1922 (GB) Trading under their initials, Godfrey and Archie Frazer-Nash began building cyclecars in 1910. They continued in business successfully until 1922, when their association was brought to an end. The Vitesse was the sports version of the voiturette that appeared in 1921, and had a 1087-cc air-cooled V2 engine giving 24 hp at 3000 rpm.

Ceirano CS – 1921 (I) Ceirano Giovanni SA was in operation between 1919 and 1923, bringing out the CS in 1921. This had a four-cylinder 2166-cc side-valve engine developing 22 hp at 2200 rpm, and a four-speed gearbox. Two sports versions were brought out, the CS 2 (2950 cc) and the CS 4 (2483 cc).

Du Pont Touring – 1921 (USA) Only 537 Du Ponts were built during the time the company was in operation, from 1919 to 1932. The Touring was a four-cylinder 4-liter model, developing 25 hp, with pump cooling and a four-speed gearbox. The most prestigious model was the eight-cylinder 5.3-liter G of 1928, which took part in the 1929 Le Mans 24 Hours.

Alvis 12/50 S – 1923 (GB) This was one of the most respected sports voiturettes of the 1920s. The 12/50 S could do up to 130 km/h (80.8 mph) and was very successful in racing. The four-cylinder engine had a displacement of 1496 cc. The series, which included a 1645-cc tourer, was nicknamed the "Duck's Back" and was in production until 1932.

Lorraine-Dietrich 15 HP B/3/6 – 1925 (F) After his experience with Delauney-Belleville, Clément and Benz, Marius Barbadoux designed all the Lorraine-Dietrich cars of 1919. The B/3/6 had a six-cylinder 3446-cc 70-hp engine, weighed 1080 kg (1.06 tons) and was one of the best-known sports cars of the period. It won at Le Mans in 1925 and 1926.

Lea-Francis Ulster – 1928 (GB) "Leaf" was in operation between 1904 and 1960, with various ups and downs in its fortunes, and built excellent sports cars in the 1920s and 1930s. The Ulster was a version of the more famous Hyper, renamed in honour of the victory in the 1928 Tourist Trophy. The four-cylinder 1496-cc engine had a Cozette supercharger and developed 61 hp at 4100 rpm in the road version.

Sunbeam 20 HP – 1925 (GB) This car appeared in 1925 with a six-cylinder 2916-cc engine developing 55 hp at 3600 rpm. The interesting but far too highly priced sports versions had twin overhead camshafts, twin carburettors and dry sump lubrication, and an output of 90 hp which could be boosted to 138 hp with the addition of a supercharger.

MG Midget M – 1929 (GB) The M was the first in a long line of Midgets which characterized the history of the company. It was based on Morris parts and had a four-cylinder 847-cc OHC engine and a four-speed gearbox, and cost £185 in 1929.

Invicta 4500 S – 1931 (GB) This was a development of the standard 1928 model with a six-cylinder 4467-cc Meadows engine developing 115 hp. Its top speed was 155 km/h (96.3 mph), and it won the Monte Carlo Rally in 1931. Invicta was founded in 1925 and went bankrupt in 1950.

Delahaye 135 – 1936 (F) The six-cylinder 135 was brought out in 1934 with a cylinder capacity of 3237 cc and an output of 130 hp at 3850 rpm. Its top speed was over 160 km/h (100 mph). The four-speed gearbox had an electromagnetic selector or, as an option, full synchromesh. The "competition" version which won the 1937 Monte Carlo Rally had a 3557-cc 160-hp engine.

The great American crisis

The extremely grave economic difficulties which followed the crash of 1929 prompted radical changes in the automobile industry in the West. In the first place, production levels were drastically rescaled, some more than others, while a large number of minor companies finally ceased operation altogether because of the impossible financial situation in which they found themselves.

Not surprisingly, the phenomenon took on macroscopic proportions in the United States, the number of cars produced dropping from 4.5 million in 1929 to 2.8 million the following year, and hitting rock bottom in 1932 with 1.1 million. It was not until the years immediately preceding the Second World War that American production levels returned to figures comparable with those before the depression. There was also another factor contributing to this spectacular reduction in the USA: the home market was already reaching its first saturation point, with an index of 187 cars for every thousand inhabitants in 1930. The slump also cut the rate of replacement of cars on the road to a minimum.

Yet it is particularly interesting to note how, in such an unfavourable climate and with 55 per cent of production concentrated in the hands of General Motors and Ford, the young Chrysler company not only managed to ride out the crisis, but also won a position of steadily growing importance in the automobile market of the United States.

Chrysler were responsible for several very important technical innovations at the beginning of the 1930s, including the "floating power" system, in which the engine was fitted on rubber mountings for the first time. In 1934, their Airflow model represented the first serious attempt to give the automobile an aerodynamic line: the engine was positioned above the front axle and the body shell extended to give a larger boot, a finer tail and better distribution of weight. The Airflow was perhaps too innovative a car, and for this reason it did not win the success it deserved. It was, however, among few others to influence the evolution of automobile design.

Meantime, as far as technical specifications and dimensions were concerned, the American motor car was taking on its own distinctive shape. Cars such as the Ford Model T, though its engine was larger, did not differ greatly from the corresponding utility cars in Europe. It was the Chevrolet AA of 1927 which had the more characteristic lines when compared with what was being produced in Europe. The enormous size of American cars was a response to the demands of the prestige car market, bringing in good returns thanks to the fortunes of certain sectors of the public, particularly the movie industry, which had been only lightly affected by the crisis. There was an unending stream of new developments in this area, which saw the production of opulent coachwork and refined technical innovations. The Cadillac V16 was a classic example of attempts at the time to develop large capacity engines that would give more silent running and reduced vibration. Cadillac, followed by Pierce-Arrow and Packard, adopted a hydraulic tappet system that guaranteed very smooth engine running. For the richer and more demanding sporting enthusiasts, Duesenberg in 1932 brought out the SJ series, which developed 320 hp at 4200 rpm, thanks to the supercharger designed by Harry Miller, who built the engines used for an entire decade in the Indianapolis races.

In 1931, there were also countercurrent attempts to launch a "miniature" vehicle (miniature in comparison with other American vehicles, that is). Emile Mathis, a Frenchman from Strasburg, made a short-lived agreement with William Durant, who was by then president of General Motors and also owner of Durant Motor Incorporated, to produce 100,000 of his small but roomy cars per year in Michigan. The PY, renamed the "Wonder Car" because it amazed the public on the other side of the Atlantic, was very popular in France. It had a four-cylinder 1230-cc 32-hp engine with a top speed of 100 km/h (62.1 mph) and was the first utility car to use hydraulic brakes. In 1935, Mathis was negotiating an agreement with Ford to produce the American company's eight-cylinder vehicle, which was to be built under the name "Matford."

Chrysler Airflow – 1934 (USA) This was one of the most innovative cars of its day, the result of intensive research in aerodynamics and advanced production technology. The eight-cylinder 4893-cc engine developed 130 hp at 3400 rpm and had a removable head, with the camshaft in the block. It had a semi-monocoque body and a wheelbase of 3.12 m (10 ft 3 in) on the saloon and 2.92 m (9 ft 7 in) on the coupé. After 1935, the gearbox had an optional automatic overdrive. It was in production until 1937 and a six-cylinder (3954-cc 100-hp) version was also available under the De Soto marque.

DELAGE

Delage D8 – 1929 (F)

In 1905, Louis Delage, who gained his experience in a long period working for Peugeot, produced his first car – a single-cylinder with a De Dion engine – with the assistance of Augustin Legros. It was built in the small works in Levallois which was destined very soon to begin production on a more industrial scale, reaching 150 units a month in 1913. In 1908, Delage won his first race, in the Dieppe Grand Prix for voiturettes. Thereafter, for as long as his company was officially involved in racing, it won some remarkable victories, including first place in the 1914 Indianapolis. It almost totally dominated the racing scene in its final season, in 1927. After the First World War, series-production was based on small, four- and six-cylinder cars, including the DI, DIS and DISS two-liter series in the four-cylinder group, in production almost until the end of the 1920s, while the second group included the DR and DM series which firmly established the Delage image. The D8 came out in 1929 with an eight-cylinder engine; depending on whether the version had one (D8), two (D8S and D8SS) or four carburettors (D8SS 100), it could develop from 80 to over 100 hp. Delage got into financial difficulties after bringing out the D6 in 1933, and were taken over by Delahaye. Production continued, but without the necessary technical development, and both companies went out of operation in 1953.

GRÄF & STIFT

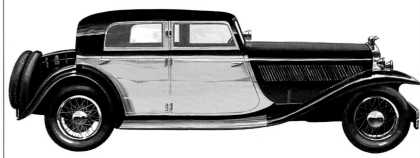

Gräf & Stift SP8 – 1932 (A)

This company was founded in Vienna in 1902 by the brothers Carl, Heinrich and Franz Gräf, who had already brought out a small, front-wheel drive voiturette with a single-cylinder De Dion engine in 1897, and Josef Hans Stift. They produced two- and four-cylinder cars until 1907 under the name of the Daimler agent Spitz, with whom they had made an agreement. Gräf & Stift cars were distinguished by their quality and prestigious image, which probably made them the most representative of the Austrian marques. It was in one of these that Archduke Franz Ferdinand was assassinated in Sarajevo. Production was originally based on large four-cylinder 50/70-hp cars with De Dion axles, but went on to six-cylinder models such as the S3, brought out in 1923. The SP8 came out in 1929 with an eight-cylinder 5923-cc 125-hp engine having a silumin block and a chain-driven overhead camshaft. The synchromesh gearbox had three speeds plus an overdrive engaged by pressing a control similar to that used for operating the hydraulic brakes. The top speed was 140 km/h (87 mph). The SP8 was in production until 1938, when the company went out of operation. Gräf & Stift had also been producing the six-cylinder Citroën MF6 under license, as well as a V8 with Ford parts from 1932.

ISOTTA FRASCHINI

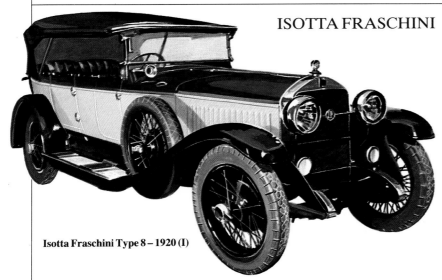

Isotta Fraschini Type 8 – 1920 (I)

The most prestigious company in Italy of the 1920s and 1930s was founded in Milan in 1900 by Cesare Isotta and the brothers Oreste, Vincenzo and Antonio Fraschini. They began operation by importing Renault-De Dion cars, but in 1902 began to build their own chassis with De Dion and Aster single- and two-cylinder engines. Between 1903 and 1905, Giuseppe Stefanini designed three four-cylinder large-capacity cars, the 12 HP, 16 HP and the 24 HP, and a 100 HP of over 17 liters which developed 120 hp and launched Isotta Fraschini on the racing circuits. Stefanini also designed the FE Grand Prix, which won the four-cylinder class in the 1908 Dieppe GP. In 1905, Isotta began an association with Giustino Cattaneo, who came from Züst, and he designed all their four-cylinder cars, leading up to the last and most famous car they ever produced, the eight-cylinder. After the crisis of 1907, Isotta drew up an agreement with Lorraine, who bought half the shares and kept them until 1910, when financial control went back to Italy. Some excellent sports cars and tourers were produced before the eight-cylinder was brought out – a car with remarkable technical features. The engine was originally 5898 cc and 90 hp, but the capacity was increased to 7370 cc in 1924, while the output gradually went up to reach 140 hp on the 8B in 1931. Isotta Fraschini went out of production in 1932.

MAYBACH

Maybach W5 – 1927 (D)

Following the death of Gottlieb Daimler, and five years after leaving the company in 1907, Wilhelm Maybach opened a factory of his own producing airship engines. His first automobile engine, of six cylinders and 5.2 liters, developing 70 hp, was built after the First World War and bought by Spyker. Later came the first full chassis, designed by Maybach's son Karl for the W3 of 1921, which had a 5.8-liter side-valve engine developing 72 hp, and though its epicyclic gearbox was just two speed, this was quite enough because the engine was so elastic. Gear selection was pedal-controlled, and it was the first German car to have mechanical brakes on all four wheels. The W5 came out in 1927, with a 6995-cc 120-hp engine and similar technical features. Overdrive was introduced in the following year on the W5 SG version; it was fitted between the gearbox and the drive shaft, and was controlled by a lever next to the seat, giving 135 km/h (83.9 mph) at just 2400 rpm. In 1929, the V12 DS 7 came out (6922 cc/155 hp), followed a year later by the DS 8 (7977 cc/200 hp), which was in production until 1939 and had a top speed of 180 km/h (111.8 mph). In 1935 it was fitted with a semi-automatic gearbox and five-speed synchromesh gears. The SW 35, SW 38 and SW 42 six-cylinder versions came out between 1936 and 1939. After the war, Maybach concentrated entirely on the production of diesel engines until Daimler-Benz took over in 1966.

MARMON

Marmon V16 – 1931 (USA)

Rolls-Royce 20/25 HP – 1929 (GB) Rolls-Royce built 3,827 of these cars using the six-cylinder 3669-cc engine which was also used on the first Bentley from 1931 onwards after the company had been bought out by Rolls-Royce. In 1932, the 20/25 HP was the first fully British car to use a four-speed synchromesh gearbox. In 1936 the engine was increased to 4257 cc.

Walter and Howard Marmon began operating in Indianapolis in 1902. The first cars they produced were V4, air-cooled models with overhead valves, their chassis giving a foretaste of the independent front suspension system that was to come. Six cylinder models came out in 1905, and in 1907 a 60-hp V8. In 1911 a six-cylinder Marmon Wasp won the first Indianapolis 500. After producing a new series, which included a six-cylinder version with a displacement of more than nine liters, the company turned its attention to more popular, affordable cars and brought out the 34, in production from 1923–7. The V16, the flagship of the range, came out in 1930, with an 8000-cc engine developing 200 hp at 3400 rpm. It was judged best car of the year by the Society of Automobile Engineers because of its excellent technical features, and the flexibility and quietness of the engine, achieved by a highly efficient timing system having the camshaft in the block. The car was only in production for two years, the Marmon marque disappearing from the American automobile scene in 1933.

Extraordinary motor cars

The period between the two wars was a time of serious world economic problems, when one would least expect to find what have since proved to be some of the most beautiful and highly refined cars that were ever made. Both in Europe and in the USA, new companies were introducing highly advanced techniques, opening up new horizons in automobile technology. These manufacturers were often intent on seeking perfection, irrespective of cost, rather than concern themselves with economy. One such manufacturer was Ettore Bugatti, an Italian living in France, who was a keen designer of his own clothes and furniture. Having already proved his caliber in turning out exceptionally prestigious models, Bugatti changed his designs in favour of less élitist cars. The same was true of Errett Lobban Cord, who was able to sell his incredible Duesenbergs for $25,000 to such stars as Gary Cooper or Clark Gable, but who also managed to inspire less famous mortals to buy his Auburns or Cords. In all cases, the

chassis were technically highly developed, with the best-researched bodies provided by specialist coachbuilders, of which the following represent but a few.

The most famous in the USA was Walter M. Murphy, who owned a company of the same name in Pasadena. He went into production in 1920, building a large number of one-offs on American and European chassis; he also acted as consultant for companies such as Packard, Stutz and the Cord group, for whom he designed over half the Auburns sold after 1925 and built at least a hundred and twenty-five bodies for Duesenberg Js and SJs.

In France in the 1920s, an innovation that proved very popular was the "sprung" body patented by Charles Torres Weymann. This prevented road shocks from the chassis from being transmitted to the body. So successful was the invention that two companies were founded in England and the USA. The Weymann system was used on Bugatti, Stutz, Delage and Hispano-Suiza cars, but its application was limited because of its high cost, and it was eventually *(cont. on p.67)*

Mercedes 770 – 1930 (D) The *Grosser Mercedes*, one of the most prestigious cars of the period, had an eight-cylinder 7655-cc engine developing 150 hp at 2800 rpm, boostable to 200 hp by a supercharger. It also had aluminium pistons and full-pressure lubrication. The four-speed gearbox had direct third and overdrive on fourth.

Tracta – 1930 (F) Tracta were among the first to use front-wheel drive and between 1925 and 1934 produced a limited series of cars which had a certain amount of success in races, particularly at Le Mans. The 1930 four-cylinder 1749-cc version had independent front suspension with hydraulic shock-absorbers. It was 4.04 m (13 ft 3 in) long and weighed 941 kg (2074.5 lb).

DUESENBERG – AUBURN – CORD

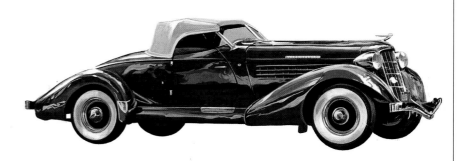

The extremely able Missouri entrepreneur Errett Lobban Cord owned a motor manufacturing group which was responsible for producing the most prestigious American cars of the 1930s, his models representing the last word in line, performance and comfort in their day. The Cord Corporation included the Auburn, Cord and Duesenberg marques.

Auburn was founded in 1900 by the Eckhart brothers, who produced a series of four- and six-cylinder cars with varying degrees of success.

Cord took over in 1924 because the company was experiencing serious financial difficulties, and changed its fortunes for the better, first by inspired restyling of unsold stock and second by introducing new models. The first of these was the 8–63 (the first figure corresponds to the number of cylinders and the second to the power output), which had an eight-cylinder engine supplied by Lycoming Motors, another of the Cord companies. Cord had great success with the 8–88, particularly with the "speedmaster" version. In 1929, 22,000 Auburns were sold, and in that same year the first car to have the Cord name, the L29, was brought out, using components built by the various factories in the group.

Duesenberg, meanwhile, had secured themselves a position of great prestige in the sports car market. The founders, Fred and Augie Duesenberg, began production in 1904, going on to win a number of victories, including the French Grand Prix in 1921 and the Indianapolis 500 in 1924, 1925 and 1926. The successful image created by their track wins was carried over to their series-produced cars, characterized by the Model A (eight cylinders, 4260 cc, 90 hp). As Cord was keen to combine a particularly well-known name with the two he already owned, he took over Duesenberg in 1928. The 740 cars in the J and SJ series, built between 1929 and 1935, although commercially negligible conferred such a degree of prestige on the group that they had a decisive influence on the sales of the less outrageously luxurious Auburns and Cords.

The J had an eight-cylinder, 6882-cc, 260-hp engine, 320-hp on the supercharged SJ version. A highly rigid chassis, excellent brakes and an exceptional standard of comfort made up the remaining features of these extraordinary cars, which were bought by many great movie stars. The price of a Duesenberg chassis was more than $10,000, as opposed to $1,500 for an Auburn and $3,500 for a Cord. A complete SJ could cost as much as $25,000. The bodywork for the group's vehicles was mostly made by Limousine Body in Kalamazoo, which was also owned by Cord.

One of the most interesting cars was the Cord 810, brought out in 1935, which had a Lycoming V8, 4730-cc engine developing 125 hp at 3200 rpm and a four-speed gearbox controlled by an electro-pneumatic Bendix selector. Like all the Cords, it was front-wheel drive and the 812 170-hp supercharged version could do 0–100 km/h (0–62 mph) in under fourteen seconds.

Auburn, for their part, had managed to bring out a twelve-cylinder car which was selling in 1932 for just $975. At that time, however, production suffered a decline, despite attempts to remedy the situation with the production of six-cylinder models. Because Cord himself was so far away and also because it was threatened in Europe with the possibility of a take-over, the group finally went into voluntary liquidation in 1937.

Cord L29 – 1929 (USA) Originally, this had an eight-cylinder 4934-cc 115-hp Lycoming engine, but in 1932 it was fitted with a 5270-cc engine developing 125 hp. It had front-wheel drive, and the Rzeppa double couplings ensured good torque transmission even to the steered drive wheels, in spite of a lack of perfectly homokinetic bearings.

Auburn 851 – 1935 (USA) Designed by Gordon Buehrig, the man who also was responsible for the lines of the Cord 810, this Auburn had an eight-cylinder, 4587-cc Lycoming engine which developed 115 hp on the aspirated version and 150 hp (at 4000 rpm) on the supercharged model.

Duesenberg A – 1922 (USA) About five hundred Model As were built between 1922 and 1926 with an eight-cylinder 4260-cc engine developing 88–90 hp at 3600 rpm. Top speed was 160 km/h (100 mph). It had a three-speed gearbox and was the first car in the USA to have all-round hydraulic brakes. An X version was brought out in 1927 with a longer wheelbase and an engine uprated to 100 hp. Only twelve were built.

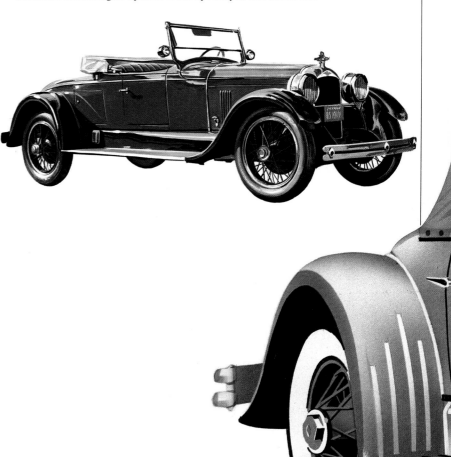

Duesenberg SJ – 1932 (USA) Although it weighed about 2.8 tonnes (2.75 tons), the 1929 J, which had some very sophisticated features, including four valves per cylinder, did 0–160 km/h (0–100 mph) in twenty-one seconds, while the supercharged SJ version introduced in 1932 took just seventeen. The three-speed gearbox was integral with the engine, and the semi-elliptical leaf-spring suspension was integrated with hydraulic shock-absorbers. The car was available in two wheelbase lengths, 3.6 or 3.9 m (11 ft 10 in or 12 ft 10 in), with an overall length of more than 5 m (16 ft 5 in).

HORCH

Horch 853 – 1936 (D)

After three years' experience with Benz, August Horch founded his own automobile factory in 1899. The first car brought out was a two-cylinder model of 5–10 hp, inspired by the Velo. The company's early period was characterized by another two-cylinder and two four-cylinder models, including the very successful 2613-cc 16/20 PS of 1904, which became even more popular after its success in racing. Very soon, however, Horch found himself at loggerheads with the board of directors and left the company to found Audi. After the war, Paul Daimler left his father's company and took over the running of Horch until 1929. The first products under the new direction were the 2.6-liter 55-hp 10/50 PS, with a modern, monobloc light alloy overhead camshaft engine, followed by the eight-cylinder 300 series in 1926, which had an initial displacement of 3230 cc. The 400 and 405 were later developments of this, and then in 1930 another completely new eight-cylinder engine was brought out and fitted on the 450 (4517 cc), the 850 (4946 cc) and also the 951 (120 hp), but only after major modifications to the latter, such as the addition of a drive shaft with ten bearings. Horch joined the Auto Union group in 1932 and brought out a perfected version of the prestigious V12, which had been launched the year before as the 600 and 670, depending on the wheelbase. The 3517-cc V8 830 B came out in 1933, but the company went back to building in-line engines with the 4944-cc 853, in production from 1936 to 1939, with an overhead camshaft and full-pressure lubrication. The five-speed gearbox had direct fourth and overdrive on fifth, and the brakes were hydraulic. When the war ended, the Zwickau headquarters of Horch found itself in East Germany, where the company was nationalized under the name "Sachsenring."

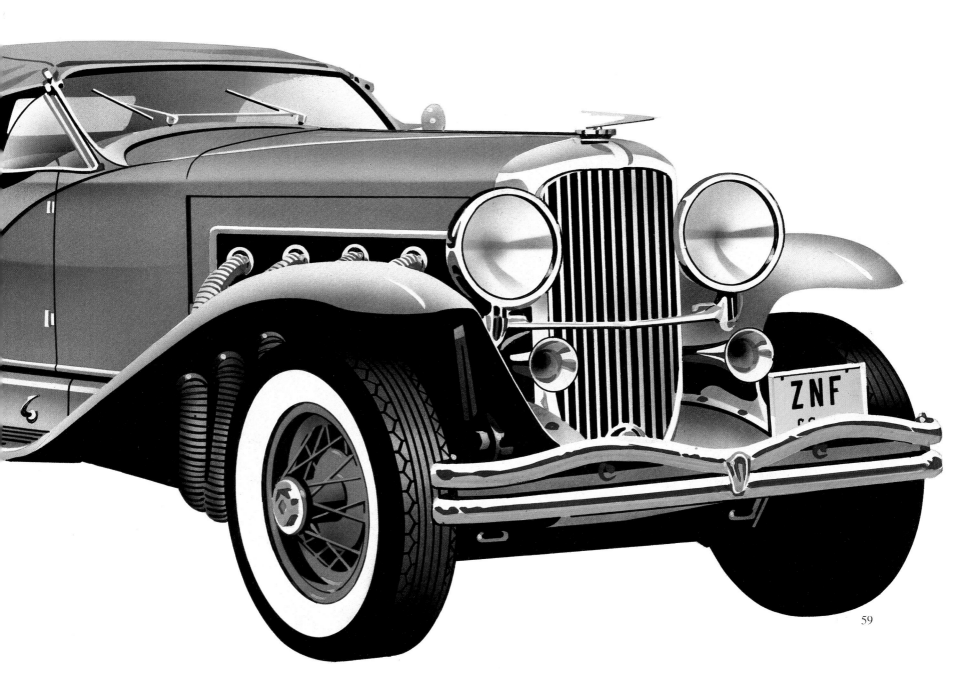

59

BUGATTI

Ettore Bugatti was born in Milan in 1881 and at eighteen he gained his first experience with automobiles with Prinetti & Stucchi. In 1901, he received financial backing from Count Gulinelli to build a four-cylinder overhead valve car, attracting the attention of De Dietrich, who decided as a result that he wanted the young designer to work with him. Bugatti stayed in Alsace until 1904, then, after a short period working with Mathis, went on to Deutz, where he was chief engineer from 1906 to 1909. During this time, he personally financed and built the *Pur Sang*, an ultra-modern prototype inspired by the Isotta Fraschini FE. In the same year that he left the company, Bugatti founded a factory in Mosheim, near Strasburg. He went into production in 1910 with the Type 13, which had a four-cylinder overhead-camshaft 1327-cc engine, but was also built in a racing version with eight cylinders and twice the engine capacity. The first car to have three valves per cylinder, a feature that was adopted on all the company's cars for over a decade, was the Black Bess 5027-cc racing model, though only very few were built, one of them for the air ace Roland Garros. The car which was to rank Bugatti among the great racing-car builders of the time (it is calculated that he had won over 3,000 races by 1940) was the Brescia, a development of the Type 13 with a 1496-cc engine and four valves per cylinder, which came out in 1921.

In the following year, the Type 30 inaugurated the series of legendary eight-cylinder engines used on all subsequent models, with the exception of the sixteen-cylinder car of 1929. The different touring saloons, sports and racing models produced (the last fitted with superchargers) were all built with unparalleled attention to detail and line. As well as the Type 35 competition version, which won all the major races of the time between 1924 and 1930, the most important model brought out by Bugatti, and the supreme expression of his automobile art, was the Type 41, known as the Royale. The 24-valve 12,763-cc light alloy engine, with nine main bearings and double ignition, could develop 300 hp at 1700 rpm and had a top engine speed of 2000 rpm. The three-speed gearbox was integral with the rear axle, and had direct second and third designed as an overdrive. Mechanical brakes were applied on all four wheels; the top speed was about 200 km/h (124.3 mph). The wheelbase was 4.57 m (15 ft) and it was about 6 m (19 ft 8 in) long, depending on the body, with a weight of 2250–3000 kg (2.2 – 3 tons). Between 1929 and 1933, only six Royales were manufactured, plus a prototype, the first to have a 14,726-cc engine and a 4.32-m (14 ft 2-in) wheelbase, which was destroyed in an accident. Only three were sold from new at a price of about 500,000 f. (about $20,000) with a lifetime guarantee. The others stayed in the Bugatti family.

In 1934, the 3.2-liter Type 57 was introduced and was the last important sedan to be produced before Ettore Bugatti died in 1947. All the company's efforts to regain its prestige and sporting glory after the war proved fruitless, as its success had been too closely tied to the personality and inventive genius of its founder.

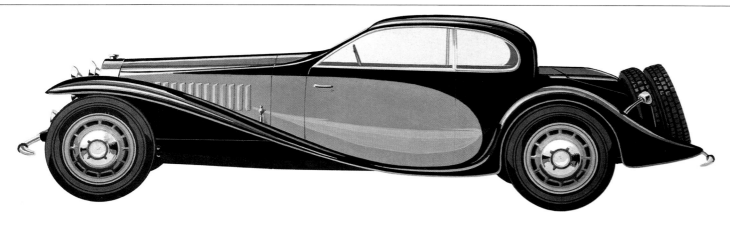

Bugatti 50 – 1933 (F) Bugatti began to use eight-cylinder engines with just two valves per cylinder on the 4972-cc 50 series introduced in 1930. The engine developed 200 hp at 4000 rpm and gave a top speed of 180 km/h (111.8 mph).

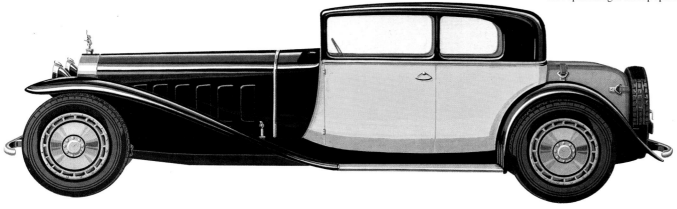

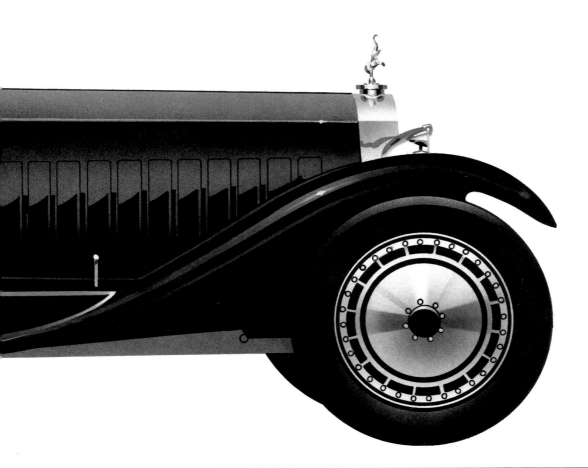

Bugatti 41 Royale – 1927–33 (F) The most luxurious and expensive car ever produced had dry sump lubrication with a 22.5-liter (5-gallon) tank capacity. The pumped cooling system was also in proportion with the enormous size of the car – the radiator held 68 liters (15 gallons) of water. The chassis side members were 25 cm (9.8 in) high in the central section. The wheels were made of light alloy and incorporated the brake drums.

Some of the seven chassis built were later fitted with different bodies (the prototype had four). The two examples shown here are the yellow and black coupé built by Weymann and the Kellner "coach" shown at the 1932 Paris Salon.

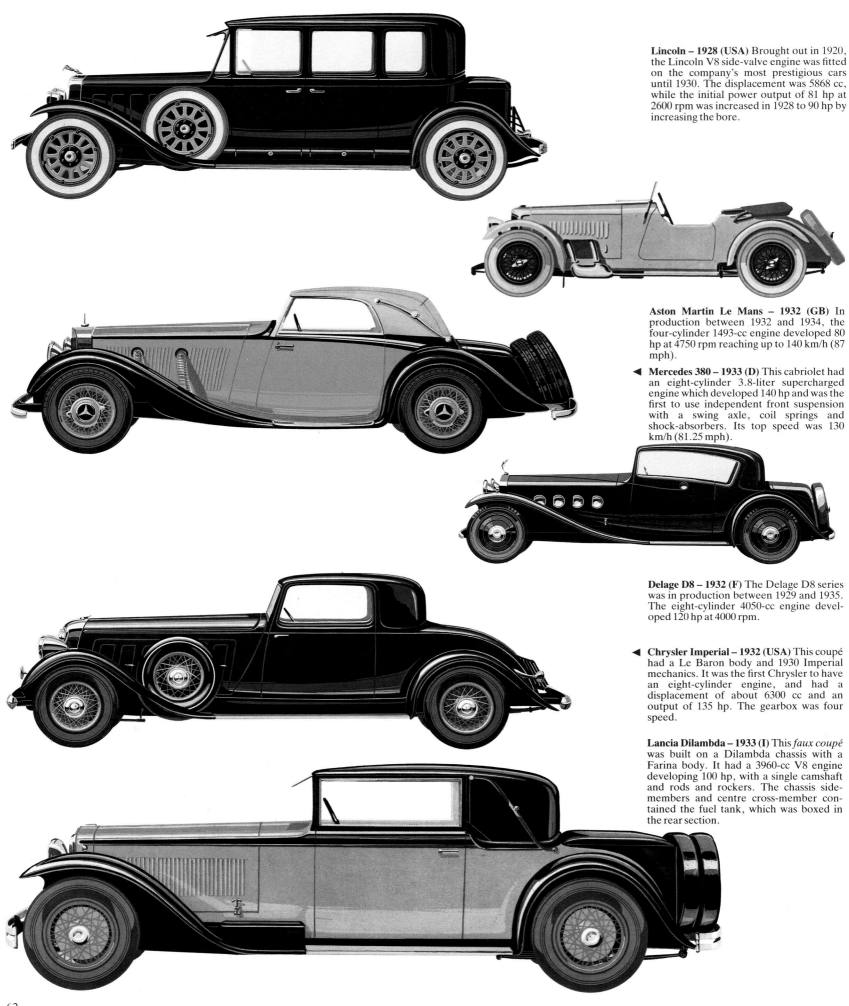

Lincoln – 1928 (USA) Brought out in 1920, the Lincoln V8 side-valve engine was fitted on the company's most prestigious cars until 1930. The displacement was 5868 cc, while the initial power output of 81 hp at 2600 rpm was increased in 1928 to 90 hp by increasing the bore.

Aston Martin Le Mans – 1932 (GB) In production between 1932 and 1934, the four-cylinder 1493-cc engine developed 80 hp at 4750 rpm reaching up to 140 km/h (87 mph).

◄ **Mercedes 380 – 1933 (D)** This cabriolet had an eight-cylinder 3.8-liter supercharged engine which developed 140 hp and was the first to use independent front suspension with a swing axle, coil springs and shock-absorbers. Its top speed was 130 km/h (81.25 mph).

Delage D8 – 1932 (F) The Delage D8 series was in production between 1929 and 1935. The eight-cylinder 4050-cc engine developed 120 hp at 4000 rpm.

◄ **Chrysler Imperial – 1932 (USA)** This coupé had a Le Baron body and 1930 Imperial mechanics. It was the first Chrysler to have an eight-cylinder engine, and had a displacement of about 6300 cc and an output of 135 hp. The gearbox was four speed.

Lancia Dilambda – 1933 (I) This *faux coupé* was built on a Dilambda chassis with a Farina body. It had a 3960-cc V8 engine developing 100 hp, with a single camshaft and rods and rockers. The chassis side-members and centre cross-member contained the fuel tank, which was boxed in the rear section.

MINERVA

Minerva built a series of very prestigious automobiles after the First World War, adopting, among other things, an integral braking system and a multiplate clutch after 1922. The model illustrated (1927) had a six-cylinder two-liter engine.

STUTZ

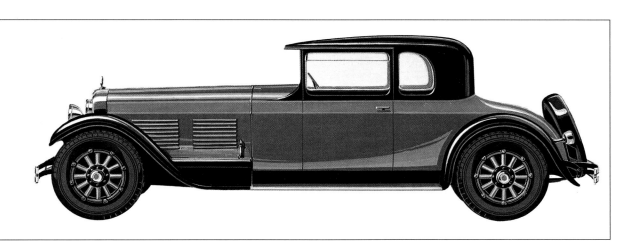

Stutz brought out its own series of eight-cylinder cars in 1926 with the 4.7-liter Model AA, which had a power output of over 90 hp, later increased to 113 hp. The Black Hawk or BB was brought out in 1928 with an increased displacement of 4.9 liters and 125 hp. The DV 32 five-liter version was the last car to be produced before the company ceased production in 1934.

BUCCIALI

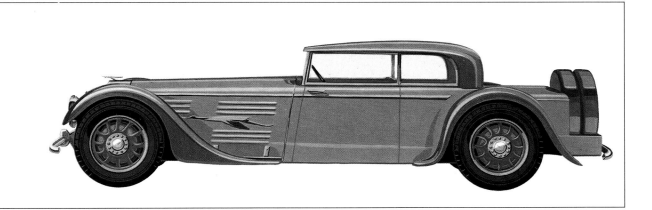

Having produced a series of cars under the BUC marque between 1922 and 1926, Angelo and Paul Albert Bucciali built a limited number of original front-wheel drive cars with very low chassis and powerful eight-cylinder Continental and twelve-cylinder Voisin engines. The *Double Huit* of 1931 did not get beyond the prototype stage, but had a sixteen-cylinder engine of eight liters, obtained by coupling two Continental units together on an original base to give a power output of 120 hp.

PANHARD

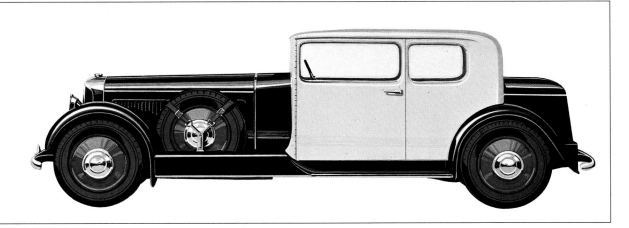

The body of this 1933 coupé was supplied by Million-Guiet and was fitted with an eight-cylinder engine of about five liters. The sleeve-valve system was used, typical of Panhards at the time.

VOISIN

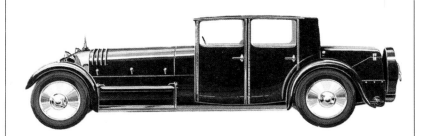

Voisin – 1930 (F)

The engineer Gabriel Voisin, who had had a lot of success with aircraft construction (many of the French planes used in the First World War were built by the Société Anonyme des Aéroplanes G. Voisin) began to produce automobiles in 1919. The first cars produced had four-cylinder 4-liter sleeve-valve engines, a system which Voisin used on all his later cars. The first 18/23 HP C1 developed 80 hp at 2500 rpm and could do up to 150 km/h (93.2 mph). It was followed by the C3 and then the C5, which had magnesium pistons and a higher compression ratio, increasing its output to 100 hp. The C4 of 1924 and the subsequent C7 of 1926 were smaller cars with 1250-cc and 1550-cc engines respectively.

The first six-cylinder was brought out in 1927 in the shape of the 2.4-liter C11. The C14 16/50 HP of 1932 had a displacement of 2327 cc, thermosiphon cooling and full-pressure lubrication. A three-speed gearbox was fitted, though a six-speed version was available on request. The limited weight of the car, 1310 kg (1.3 tons) allowed a top speed of 120 km/h (74.5 mph). The top of the range at the time was the 3-liter C23, from which the 3300-cc C28 Aérosport was developed in 1936.

A twelve-cylinder prototype, the V 12/L (6000 cc, 200 hp), was not put into production. As a result of its increasingly precarious financial position, Voisin sold out to a Belgian group in 1937 and finally ceased operation in 1939. The last car designed by Voisin was a small, single-cylinder 125-cc model known as the "Biscooter," which was produced after the war by the Spanish company Autonacional.

PACKARD

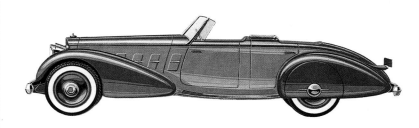

Packard Twelve Phaeton – 1936 (USA)

The major luxury car manufacturer in the world was founded in 1899 by James Ward Packard, who sold the majority shareholdings two years later to Henry B. Joy. After various versions of a single-cylinder car had been tried, the first four-cylinder, the Model K, was brought out in 1903 and set various speed records, reaching an average 125 km/h (77.7 mph) in Daytona. In 1910, Alvan Macauley took over running the company, and together with Joy and Hesse Vincent worked out the programme for the twelve-cylinder version, which was introduced in 1915 as the first series-produced car to use this format. About 9,000 were sold in 1916 and production continued until 1922. The 6950-cc side-valve V engine was also used on the single seater, which set a record of over 240 km/h (149.13 mph) for the standing-start mile in Daytona in 1919. In 1921, the Single Six made its début, followed in 1923 by the Single Eight and the 84-hp Super Eight. The new six- and eight-cylinder in-line engines (4.3 liters increased to 4.9 in the first case, 5.8 liters increased to 6.2 in the second) were characterized by an aluminium block and side valves operated by rods and rockers. The Single Eight was the first American car to have front-wheel brakes. At the top of the range there was a new V12 model with a 7292-cc engine developing 160 hp at 3200 rpm. In 1932, the company made its entry into the economy car market with the Light Eight, followed by the 120 (the wheelbase in inches), which cost only $990 for the original eight-cylinder version, and then the highly successful six-cylinder version in 1937. In that same year Packard hit their production record of 109,518 cars.

Production of the six- and eight-cylinder models began again after the Second World War, but in 1954 the company merged with Studebaker.

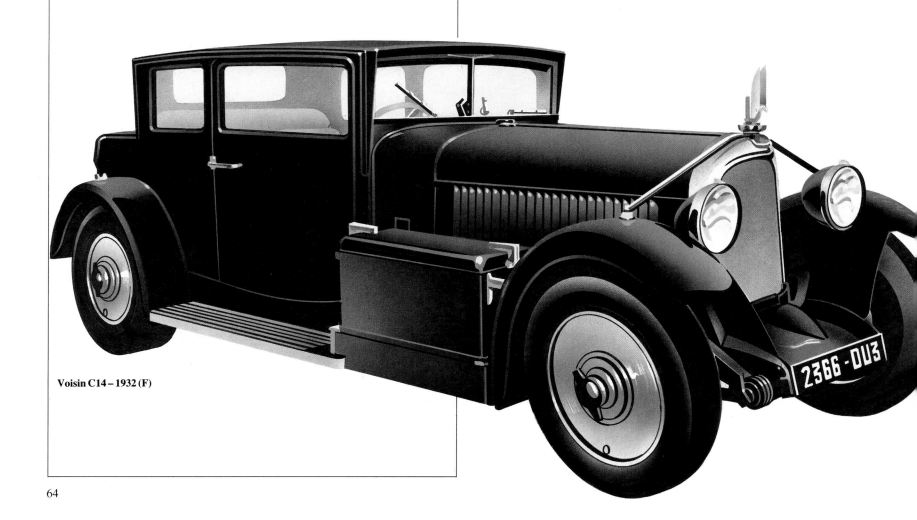

Voisin C14 – 1932 (F)

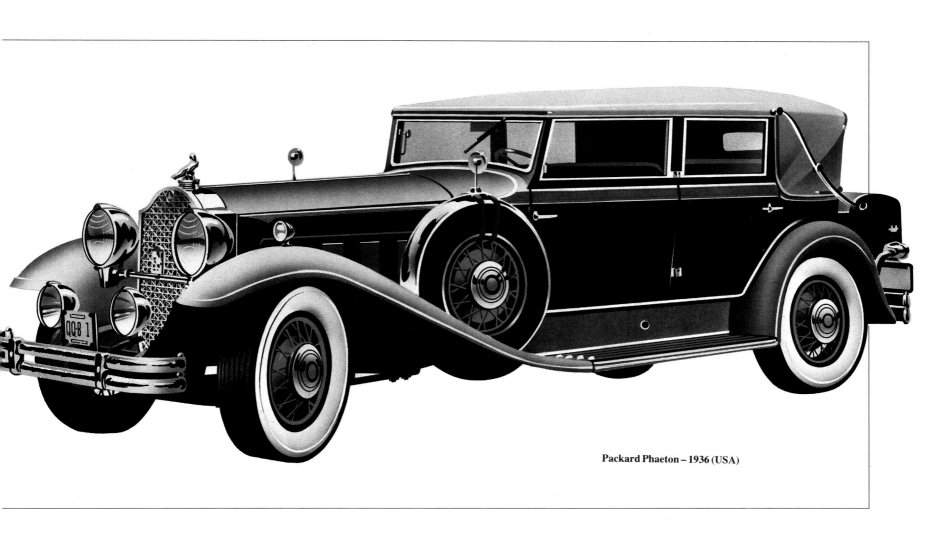

Packard Phaeton – 1936 (USA)

Rolls-Royce Phantom II – 1935 (GB) A total of 1,767 Phantom IIs were built between 1929 and 1935 as successors to the Phantom I. The chassis was completely new and had rigid axle suspension with semi-elliptic leaf-springs. The four-speed gearbox was integral with the straight-six 7.7-liter engine.

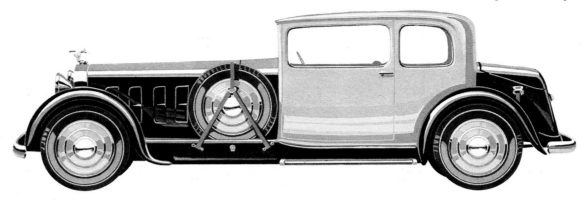

Hispano-Suiza were founded in Barcelona in 1904, when Damian Mateu took over the small Castro automobile factory where the chief engineer was the Swiss Marc Birkigt, who later designed all the cars produced by the famous Franco-Spanish company. The first model of any importance was the Alfonso of 1911, a development of the 2.6-liter car which had won *the Coupe de l'Auto* the previous year. The four-cylinder 3620-cc engine developed 60 hp with a top speed of over 100 km/h (62 mph) and its road performance ranked Hispano-Suiza among the great companies of the time.

In 1911, the French branch was opened, and soon overtook the mother company in terms of importance. During the war, Birkigt designed a series of ultra-modern V8 and V12 aircraft engines for use on French fighters, gaining experience which he then used after the war on the H 6B, the car which was to replace the Alfonso at the top of the the range. It was in production from 1919 onwards and had a six-cylinder 6597-cc engine

developing 135 hp at 3000 rpm. Its main features were its overhead camshaft, double ignition and a light alloy cylinder block. In 1924, the cylinder capacity was increased with the H 6C to 8 liters, while a 3.7-liter version was built in Spain.

The year 1931 saw the launch of what is considered by many to be Birkigt's masterpiece, the model 68 which had a V12 9424-cc engine that could develop 220 hp at 3000 rpm. The displacement was increased to 11,310 cc and the power output to 250 hp with the 68 B version of 1934, giving a top speed of 200 km/h (124.3 mph). It remained in production until 1938.

After the war, Hispano-Suiza in Spain, where minimum production had continued up to 1944, were taken over by ENASA, while the French factory, based in Bois Colombes, was unable to follow the V8 front-wheel drive prototype introduced at the 1946 Geneva Motor Show.

Delahaye 135 – 1938 (F)

Hispano-Suiza H 6B – 1930 (F/E)

DELAHAYE

Delahaye's first car came out in 1895, but it was not until Charles Weiffenbach took over as chief engineer that any real development in industrial terms took place. Weiffenbach stayed with Delahaye for nearly fifty years, introducing rational and economical production systems which allowed for the organization of one of the first true examples of series production in Europe. The first car with cardan shaft transmission was produced in 1907, and a very interesting V6 engine was brought out in 1912. Post-war production hinged on four- and six-cylinder cars, winning the company a stable position on the French market. In 1935, the company took over Delage, though their two product lines remained completely different. The 135 came out in the same year and gained important wins in several races, including the 1938 Le Mans, and the 1937 and 1939 Monte Carlo Rallies. The six-cylinder engine initially had a displacement of 3.2 liters, but this was later increased to 3557 cc with an output of 130 hp at 3850 rpm on the road version and 160 hp at 4200 rpm on the competition model. The four-speed gearbox had synchromesh, though an electromagnetic pre-selector gearchange was available. The body of the model illustrated was supplied by Figoni and Falaschi.

In 1938, the V12 4.5-liter 145 was brought out, followed after the war by the 235. Delahaye made their last official appearance at the Paris Motor Show in 1953, and were taken over by Hotchkiss in 1954, after which they concentrated on the production of lorries.

(cont. from p.57)

outmoded as a result of refinements to chassis and suspension in general. Still of French origin, Labourdette bodies were very highly regarded.

In England, Park Ward built a seven-seater limousine on a Bugatti Royale chassis. The British company was taken over by Rolls-Royce in 1939. One of the most prestigious German coachbuilders was Alexis Kellner, used particularly by Gräf & Stift, and Maybach. In 1927, the "Ballon Karrosserie" was patented, which was mounted on the chassis with just three fixing points and covered in leather.

The most refined bodies in Italy were built by Giovanni Farina and Ercole Castagna. Farina produced such famous chassis as the Lancia, Rolls-Royce, Hispano-Suiza and Isotta Fraschini with great elegance, while Castagna was also very successful in the USA, particularly with his Isotta Fraschinis. Jacques Saoutchik's bodies were also highly prized, and the Mercedes Ks, presented at the 1928 Paris Salon, were considered to be his masterpieces. Henry Binder was another famous name, remembered above all for his Bugatti Royale and for nearly two hundred Hispano-Suizas which he built between 1924 and 1937.

Europe in the 1930s

In Europe, the effects of the crisis were felt slightly later.

France saw its level of production drop by 35 per cent between 1929 and 1931, and the manufacturers to feel the greatest financial repercussions were Citroën, who, in spite of having secured a position at the top of the market with their modern production systems, had to pay for the massive investments of the 1920s. Their great commitment to technological development produced an automobile destined to break every record for durability, the Traction Avant. Production of this car involved the total refitting of the Quai de Javel plant, but the onus of the change-over was not borne by Citroën, as its majority holdings were bought out in 1934 by Michelin after the company had been declared bankrupt. In that same year, the revolutionary new car was launched on to the market in a 1298-cc 7-cv and a 1911-cc 11-cv version. Its distinguishing features included front-wheel drive, rubber engine mountings and a unit-body assembly as its main features. It remained in production until 1957.

Renault and Peugeot managed to ride out the crisis with few difficulties, because they had been less heavily committed to investment, though, despite their financial policies, still producing interesting new developments. Renault brought out various versions of the four-, six- and eight-cylinder series models until in 1937 they produced the Juvaquatre, the first car to have a monocoque body. At the Paris Motor Show in 1935, Peugeot, inspired by the Chrysler Airflow, presented the ultra-modern 402 with its low chassis, synchromesh gears, and dash-mounted handbrake and gear lever.

In 1936, France began to show clear signs of recovery, producing 180,000 vehicles and surpassing 200,000 in 1938. On the eve of the outbreak of war, the number of manufacturers dropped (from the ninety who had been in operation before the recession) to fewer than ten, two of whom were owned by foreign interests – Simca, founded in 1936 for the production of Fiat cars under license, and Matford.

In Great Britain, the 1929 crash did not have particularly serious consequences. Production suffered only minimal reduction – 13 per cent between 1929 and 1931 – and the number of automobiles built in 1930 was greater than in France. Great Britain had the

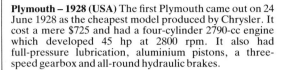

Plymouth – 1928 (USA) The first Plymouth came out on 24 June 1928 as the cheapest model produced by Chrysler. It cost a mere $725 and had a four-cylinder 2790-cc engine which developed 45 hp at 2800 rpm. It also had full-pressure lubrication, aluminium pistons, a three-speed gearbox and all-round hydraulic brakes.

Ford 18 V8 – 1932 (USA) This car was in production between 1932 and 1941 with a V8 3622-cc side-valve engine developing about 65 hp at 3400 rpm. The three-speed gearbox had synchromesh on the top two. Built in Europe, it also proved successful there in rallies such as the Monte Carlo Rally, which it won in 1936.

DKW F1 – 1931 (D) Brought out with a two-cylinder 494-cc 15-hp engine, this small front-wheel drive car was given a 584-cc, 18-hp engine when it went into series production. The basic model had a double-beam chassis and weighed just 450 kg (992 lb). It had independent suspension front and rear.

advantage of being able to export cars to Commonwealth countries, and in 1931 only about 18 per cent of its production was sold on the home market; the brief duration of the Depression in England meant that this percentage rose rapidly until it exceeded 30 per cent in 1932 and 50 per cent in 1935.

Ford and Vauxhall were the most active companies at the time. Ford opened their new and ultra modern Dagenham works in Essex in 1932, where they produced the Model Y, known as the Popular – so successful that it caused a decline in the popularity of the Austin Seven. It had a

993-cc engine, the first to have been designed independently by British Ford, which was followed by the 1147-cc engine of the Ten (the 1938 Prefect) in 1935. The Popular was renamed the Anglia in 1939.

Vauxhall's production was influenced to a certain extent by American trends. Their most successful model was the 14-hp Light Six, brought out in 1933 – a six-cylinder car that was quite cheap in spite of such refinements as a leather interior and standard sliding roof. In the second half of the 1930s, this British associate of General Motors sold a total of 26,000 cars on the home market in

1935 and 35,000 in 1938. Among the national companies, Austin's rate of production increased steadily throughout the 1930s, thanks largely to the Seven, about 300,000 of which were produced between 1922 and 1939, and the less successful Ten. Morris, leaders of the Nuffield group, which also included MG and from 1926 Wolseley, followed their luke-warm success with the Minor by launching the Eight in 1935. This had an all-metal body which, though inspired by the Ford Y, boasted a number of distinctly superior features: by July 1938, half a million had been produced. Standard were also fairly success-

ful with their wide range of cars, as was the Rootes Group, which in 1932 took on its definitive form as the holding company for Humber and Hillman, to which Karrier and Sunbeam were later added. Riley and Alvis, as well as the BSA group consisting of BSA, Daimler and Lanchester, also counted on consistent production. Riley had good results with their small but fast Four in 1935, together with luxurious V8 versions, but their financial situation deteriorated until they were finally forced to merge with the Nuffield group. Alvis came on to the automobile scene in 1919 and, after their great racing successes in the 1920s,

BMW 315/1 – 1936 (D) Designed by Fritz Fiedler, the 315 was the first BMW to have a six-cylinder engine. It had a displacement of 1490 cc, developing 34 hp on the saloon and 40 hp on the Touring Sport 315/1 model, which had a top speed of 125 km/h (77.7 mph). It was in production from 1934 to 1937.

Opel P4 – 1935 (D) The P4, a particularly cheap four-cylinder runabout which cost RM 1450, was in production for only two years. The engine had a pumped cooling system and a power output of 23 hp at 3600 rpm.

Mercedes 540 K – 1936 (D) The last in the series of great supercharged sports cars, the 540 K was in production from 1934 to 1939. Its eight-cylinder 5401-cc engine had valve gear with rods and rockers, and developed 115 hp, boosted to 180 hp by the supercharger. It had hydraulic brakes with Bosch vacuum power assistance, independent all-round suspension and a top speed of 170 km/h (105.6 mph).

Mercedes 170 – 1931 (D) The 170 had a six-cylinder 1.7-liter 32-hp engine and was the first Mercedes to have independent rear wheels with swinging half-axles and double coil springs. The 2-liter 40-hp 200 was developed from it in 1932.

BMW 326 – 1936 (D) The 326 cost RM 550 and had a six-cylinder 1971-cc 50-hp engine, Solex twin carburettors, a top speed of 115 km/h (71.5 mph) and hydraulic brakes. It was in production until 1940.

69

Citroën Traction Avant 7 CV – 1934 (F)
Brought out in April 1934 with a four-cylinder 32-hp engine, the 7A had a unitary body and front-wheel drive but it was replaced just two months later by the 7B with a 1529-cc 35-hp engine. The top speed on both versions was 100 km/h (62 mph). The 11 AL was also brought out in 1934 (1911 cc, 46 hp) and remained in production until 1957. In 1935, the 7C was launched (1628 cc, 36 hp) and continued to be produced until the outbreak of the war. The diesel version (11 UD, 1767 cc, 40 hp) followed, but remained in production for only three years. In 1938, the 15 Six G was introduced, with a six-cylinder 2867-cc 77-hp engine and a top speed of 130 km/h (80.8 mph). Altogether about 750,000 Tractions were built in twenty-three years.

presented their first British front-wheel drive vehicle, a small 1500-cc sports model, in 1928. This was followed in 1934 by the Firebird, which had a pre-selector gearbox available as an extra, and independent suspension. Rover and, in the top bracket, Rolls-Royce, who took over Bentley in 1931 when it was in financial difficulties, continued to hold a very secure position with their high quality cars.

The less serious effects of the crisis in Great Britain meant that, on the one hand, the industry was able to develop more smoothly than in other Western countries; on the other, that it did not have to restructure in the same way. In the long term, this had two negative consequences: it to a certain extent slowed down technical development, a fact which became more evident after the war, and there was less financial backing from the British government for the concentration of production. This paved the way for the American companies Ford and Vauxhall to establish themselves firmly on British soil. As a result, Britain was the leading European nation in terms of automobile production for the whole decade, reaching its highest total ever in 1937, with 379,000 cars.

The consequences of the crisis were worst felt in Germany, where production dropped from 108,000 cars in 1928 to 62,000 in 1931 and 43,000 in 1932. The automobile industry reacted mainly with a policy of mergers, a typical example being the formation of Auto Union, a combination of Audi, Horch, Wanderer and DKW in 1932. The

number of major companies dropped to around fifteen, and there was still no model available which could lead to the spread and popularization of the automobile throughout the whole country.

When Hitler rose to power in 1933, the automobile industry was in the middle of a vast development programme centered primarily on public orders and then later on the revival of private demand. Development in the private sector took off with the Volkswagen programme, which had begun in 1934 but could not be completed until after the war.

Production in Germany quickly reached its former levels, however, and by 1935 the country already occupied second place in Europe, ahead even of France. One of the most important developments in the German industry of the 1930s was the Opel Olympia, a 1.3-liter, 26-hp vehicle which was the first car in Germany to have a monocoque body. Eighty thousand were produced in

the two years from 1936 to 1937. It was also in 1937 that the Kadett 1100-cc was launched. Mercedes, too, were making important innovations. Alongside the development of the exceptional six- and eight-cylinder supercharged versions, a series of small rear-engine cars was proposed and the 260D, the first diesel car in the world, came out in 1935.

In Italy, production was drastically cut by the crisis. In 1931, only 26,000 cars were built, and the small manufacturers had no alternative but to abandon the market. Larger companies either fell under the control of Fiat or of the Italian government. The former was the case with OM, the latter with Alfa Romeo and Isotta Fraschini.

Fiat continued to dominate the home market, thanks to extremely rigid import controls, but still underwent a programme of great change. In 1932, the 995-cc 508 Balilla was launched, but the first people's car was the 500 Topolino

of 1936. The same year, work began on the Mirafiori plant, which was opened in 1939.

Thanks largely to the quality of their automobiles, Lancia managed – remarkably – to maintain a solid and independent position. The Augusta 1200 of 1932 was an attempt to reach a wider market by the introduction of a more popular vehicle, but because of its high price could not challenge Fiat. Lancia relied, rather, on their very high standards to win them a wealthy clientele which would remain faithful to the company.

On the eve of the outbreak of war, production in Italy was still very limited in comparison with other European countries, though manufacturers had managed to create for the Italian car a markedly individual image. A total of 61,000 cars were built in 1937.

For the automobile, the 1930s marked the end of a process of development in which the car industry was consolidated into a number of leading names and associations which were to remain practically unchanged even throughout the post-war recovery. Having survived the Depression, which was effectively over by about 1936, the industry was able to concentrate on popularizing private motoring, which, though interrupted by the Second World War, was after the conflict injected with even greater enthusiasm.

Until then, the automobile had been a phenomenon limited to the five countries responsible for its first fifty years of technical and industrial development. However, other nations were now

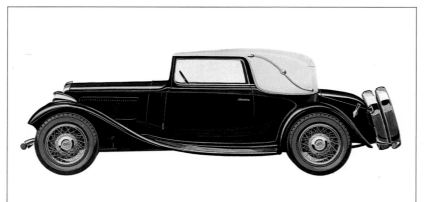

Fiat 518 L Ardita – 1933 (I) The Ardita was produced from 1933 to 1938 with four-cylinder side-valve engine of either 1758 or 1944 cc, developing 40 and 45 hp respectively. This cabriolet was built by the Castagna coachworks.

Lancia Ardea – 1939 (I) This was the first Lancia with an engine displacement of under a liter. The Ardea was influenced both technically and from a design point of view by the more famous Aprilia. The V4 903-cc engine could develop 29 hp at 4600 rpm and had a top speed of 108 km/h (67 mph).

beginning to make their début: in Sweden, Volvo and Saab were still limiting their activity to the rich and untapped home market; in Japan, the 1,800 vehicles produced in 1938 clearly indicated how far they still had to come. Even Eastern Europe was cautiously attempting to break into this new field: Skoda was achieving excellent results in Czechoslovakia, while the Soviet Union had begun producing cars in limited numbers under license from America. One fact was certain, however: the automobile had become a permanent feature of the economic fiber and life of the civilized world.

Fiat 500 Topolino – 1936 (I) Launched in 1936 at a price of less than L 10,000, the first version of the Topolino remained in production until 1948 with a four-cylinder 569-cc side-valve engine developing 13 hp at 4000 rpm and a top speed of 85 km/h (52.8 mph). The four-speed gearbox had synchromesh on the top two.

Fiat 508 Balilla – 1932 (I) The first version of the Balilla came out in 1932 and remained in production until 1934, by which time over 41,000 had been built. The four-cylinder 995-cc engine developed 20 hp at 3400 rpm and gave a top speed of 85 km/h (52.8 mph). A more powerful version was also available which developed 26 hp at 3800 rpm. It had a three-speed gearbox, measured 3.44 m (11 ft 3 in) in length and weighed 685 kg (1510 lb).

Griffith Borgeson: INDIANAPOLIS

The Indianapolis 500 has been held at the end of May every year since 1911, interrupted only by war. Thus it is the oldest continuously held automotive speed contest in the world. The hallowed track claims to be "The Greatest Race Course in the World" – a matter of opinion. What *is* an indisputable fact is that it is the world's fastest. Also indisputable are the staggering size of the purse, the colossal scale of the Roman-holiday spectacle which the race presents, and the enormous number of spectators who pay handsomely for the privilege of witnessing it. Current crowds vary between about 320,000 and 350,000 of the faithful.

All this has worked out very much according to a plan which was evolved about seventy years ago by a financial genius named Carl G. Fisher. Creator of the billion-dollar real-estate development known as Miami Beach, Florida, Fisher was born in a small village in the state of Indiana in 1874. He had little schooling and began earning his living at the age of twelve.

He saved enough to buy a bicycle, which he raced professionally. He continued to make money and in 1895, at the age of twenty-six, became the first man in Indianapolis to own a motor vehicle – a De Dion-Bouton tricycle. In 1900, Fisher became an automobile dealer in the same city and promoted his products by racing them. In 1905, he went to France to take part in that year's Gordon Bennett Cup Race. His car exceeded the weight limit, and so he witnessed Europe's biggest race as a spectator.

Two things impressed Fisher above all: one was the power of international competition between outstanding machines and drivers to attract great masses of people; the other was the inherent difficulty, on public roads, of controlling those crowds and, secondly, exploiting them. He returned to Indianapolis with the idea of building a factory – and it is still called the "plant" – for the production of motor-racing spectacles on a grand scale. It would consist of a sort of magnified velodrome, 4023 meters (2.5 miles) in

circumference, with banked curves at the two ends of the oval. The plant would be properly fenced in, but accessible to a paying public, which from the grandstands would have a panoramic view of the whole action. And to make sure that the finest performers in the country, and eventually in the world, would act upon this stage, he adopted a policy of always offering the world's richest purse.

This formula was not perfected overnight. It took time to find financial backers and to build the Speedway. Its asphalt surface was completed in time for the first race, for motor cycles, on 14 August 1909. Even with these light machines, the blacktop broke up rapidly, and the slow process of laying over three million paving bricks began. Short races were held periodically in 1910 with declining attendance, forcing the conclusion that one big event per year might be more profitable than a succession of small ones. Fisher considered twenty-four hours, but settled for the 500 miles (804.5 km).

Mercer 35 – 1911 (USA) Although they finished in twelfth and fifteenth place, the Mercer 35s were among the stars of the first Indianapolis 500. (Four cylinders, 4940 cc, 60 hp.)

National – 1912 (USA) When De Palma's Mercedes had to withdraw, Joe Dawson had a free run to first place at the wheel of his National. (Four cylinders, over 8000 cc.)

Peugeot GP – 1913 (F) The first European to win at Indianapolis was Goux in a four-cylinder sixteen-valve twin overhead camshaft Peugeot of 7600 cc, developing 130 hp at 2200 rpm.

Delage – 1914 (F) Built in 1913, the Delage GP (four cylinders, 7032 cc, with 110 hp at 2200 rpm) won in 1914. It weighed 1036 kg (1.02 tons) and reached speeds of 170 km/h (105.6 mph).

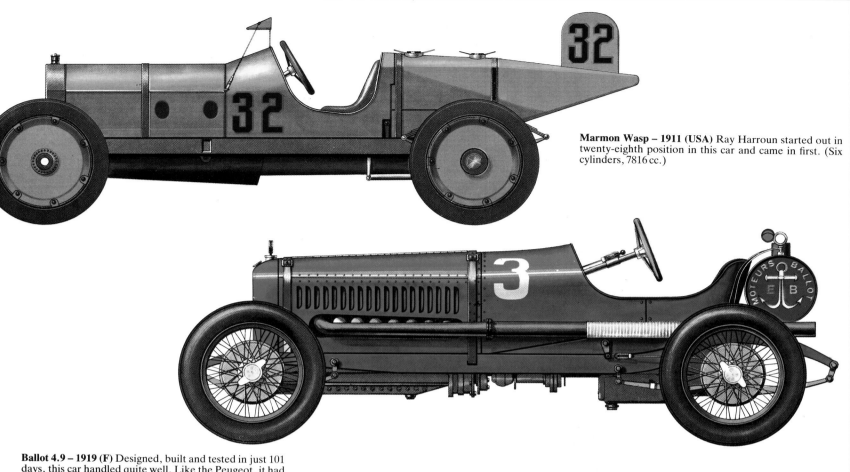

Marmon Wasp – 1911 (USA) Ray Harroun started out in twenty-eighth position in this car and came in first. (Six cylinders, 7816 cc.)

Ballot 4.9 – 1919 (F) Designed, built and tested in just 101 days, this car handled quite well. Like the Peugeot, it had a Bugatti eight-cylinder Avio-based engine. (4820 cc, 140 hp at 3000 rpm.)

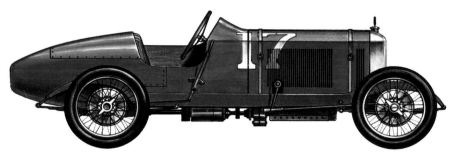

Peugeot GP – 1919 (F) Four Peugeots built by the American company Premier lined up at Indianapolis, three of 4.5 liters, one of 3. Wilcox won the race in a 4.5-liter.

Stutz – 1915 (USA) De Palma's Stutz had a four-cylinder 4839-cc engine developing 120 hp at 2700 rpm. It broke a connecting rod three laps before the end, but still managed to push Resta's Peugeot into second place.

Frontenac – 1920 (USA) Gaston Chevrolet won the 1920 race with a Monroe built by his brother Louis, who in 1921 also built the Frontenac that took Milton to victory. (Four cylinders, 2980 cc, 120 hp at 4200 rpm.)

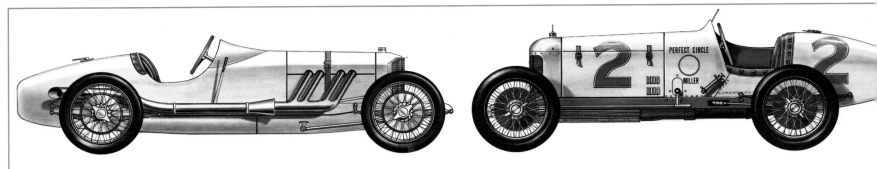

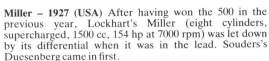

Mercedes – 1923 (D) Mercedes took part in the Indianapolis 500 between 1921 and 1925, with four-, six- and eight-cylinder cars. They entered this four-cylinder model in the 1923 race, which was for 2000-cc cars. Sailer and Werner came in eighth and eleventh respectively.

Miller – 1927 (USA) After having won the 500 in the previous year, Lockhart's Miller (eight cylinders, supercharged, 1500 cc, 154 hp at 7000 rpm) was let down by its differential when it was in the lead. Souders's Duesenberg came in first.

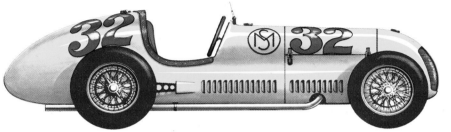

Sampson – 1940 (USA) This car had an original V16 engine made by coupling together two eight-cylinder Millers. It came in thirty-first in 1939 and sixth in 1940, with Swanson at the wheel. It developed 385 hp at 7500 rpm, with a displacement of 2956 cc and two centrifugal superchargers.

Maserati (Boyle Special) – 1938 (I) This won in 1939 and 1940, driven by Shaw. The straight-eight turbocharged 3000-cc engine was made up by coupling together two 1500-cc versions used on cars from the Modena company that year. It had a Roots two-stage supercharger and a twin carburettor. (365 hp at 6400 rpm.)

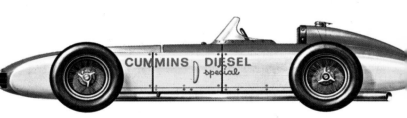

Novi Special – 1951 (USA) This car's 3-liter V8 engine delivered 600 hp at 8000 rpm, but its performance was limited by high fuel consumption (70–92 liters/100 km; 4– 1.3 mpg), which meant that it needed a good 523-liter (115-gallon) tank. It was driven by Tony Bettenhausen.

Cummins Diesel Special – 1951 (USA) This was a highly original car with a straight-six 6751-cc diesel engine turbocharged with the exhaust gases. It developed 350 hp at 4000 rpm. Agabashian was the driver, but he had to retire from the race.

The first Indianapolis 500 brought forty cars, their drivers and riding mechanics to the starting line. A crowd of around 80,000 paid well to watch the young engineer, Ray Harroun, win the almost seven-hour trial and the biggest share of a spectacularly unprecedented purse with a car which he had helped to design. Over the decades, speeds and prize money have grown considerably.

The winning average speed in 1981 is explained by the fact that much of the race was run under the caution flag. The usual upward trend was resumed immediately, and in 1984 qualifying speed reached 337.93 km/h (210 mph). Rick Mears won at an average speed of 263.25 km/h (163.58 mph), and the purse reached a record $2,795,899.

Carl Fisher's belief that racing on public roads was doomed proved to be correct, for the USA and the Speedway set a pattern that all have tried to emulate but none has equalled. This almost total concentration upon oval-track racing led to the development of a strictly American breed of competition machine. At Indianapolis, races were run in a counter-clockwise direction, and other tracks

Year	Driver	Chassis	Engine	Average Speed km/h (mph)	Highest Qualif. Speed km/h (mph)	Total Purse $
1911	Harroun	Marmon	Marmon	120.01 (74.57)	—	27,500
1921	Milton	Frontenac	Frontenac	144.191 (89.56)	162.01 (100.67)	86,650
1931	Schneider	Stevens	Miller	155.46 (96.60)	183.35 (113.93)	81,800
1941	Davis/Rose	Wetteroth	Offy	185.21 (115.08)	207.06 (128.66)	90,925
1951	Wallard	Kurtis	Offy	203.12 (126.21)	220.22 (136.84)	207,650
1961	Foyt	Watson	Offy	223.86 (139.10)	234.75 (145.87)	400,000
1971	A. Unser	P.J. Colt	Ford	253.79 (157.70)	280.80 (174.48)	1,001,604
1981	B. Unser	Penske	Ford	223.74 (139.02)	322.91 (200.65)	1,609,375

Miller – 1929 (USA) The American builder produced about fifty eight-cylinder 1500-cc supercharged cars, ten or so of them having front-wheel drive. This one, driven by Duray in 1929, came twenty-second.

Miller Ford V8 – 1935 (USA) In 1935, nine of the thirty-three starters were front-wheel drive vehicles like the Miller illustrated here, which was driven by Horn and Bailey. The 3605-cc Ford V8 engine developed 220 hp.

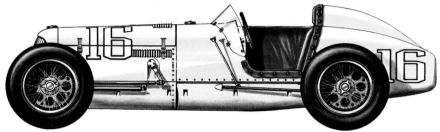

Blue Crown Spark Plug Special – 1948 (USA) This car won in 1947, 1948 (Rose) and 1949 (Holland), and came second in 1950 (Holland). The 1947 and 1948 versions had front-wheel drive, while the later models were rear-wheel drive. (Four cylinders, 4500 cc, 270 hp.)

Thorne Engineering Special – 1946 (USA) Built in 1937 by the specialist Art Sparks on behalf of Thorne, this car won in 1946 with Robson at the wheel. It had a straight-six 2946-cc engine, and the winner's average speed was about 185 km/h (115 mph).

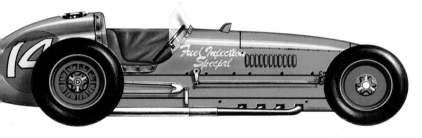

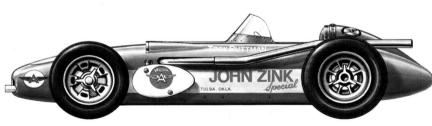

Fuel Injection Special – 1953 (USA) This 4428-cc car with a four-cylinder Offenhauser engine was driven to win in 1953 and 1954 by Bill Vucovich. It had a Kurtis Kraft 500A chassis with torsion bar suspension.

John Zink Special – 1955 (USA) In 1955–6, this car won the 500 with Sweikert and Flaherty respectively. It was fitted with the increasingly popular Offenhauser engine.

Dean Van Lines – 1957 (USA) This single-seater with an Offenhauser engine on a Kuzma chassis came third in the 1957 500 with Bryan at the wheel. Drivers such as A. Foyt and Mario Andretti raced with this marque, which had a V8 Ford engine fitted after 1965.

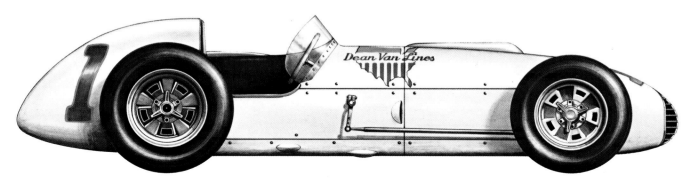

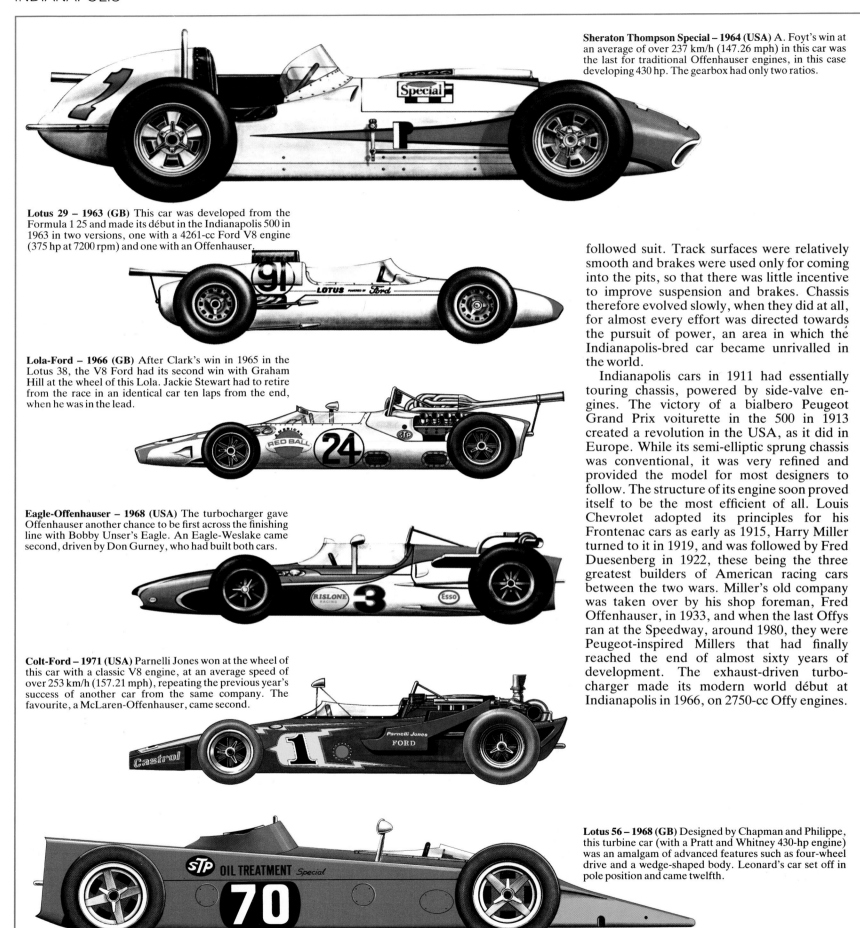

Sheraton Thompson Special – 1964 (USA) A. Foyt's win at an average of over 237 km/h (147.26 mph) in this car was the last for traditional Offenhauser engines, in this case developing 430 hp. The gearbox had only two ratios.

Lotus 29 – 1963 (GB) This car was developed from the Formula 1 25 and made its début in the Indianapolis 500 in 1963 in two versions, one with a 4261-cc Ford V8 engine (375 hp at 7200 rpm) and one with an Offenhauser.

Lola-Ford – 1966 (GB) After Clark's win in 1965 in the Lotus 38, the V8 Ford had its second win with Graham Hill at the wheel of this Lola. Jackie Stewart had to retire from the race in an identical car ten laps from the end, when he was in the lead.

Eagle-Offenhauser – 1968 (USA) The turbocharger gave Offenhauser another chance to be first across the finishing line with Bobby Unser's Eagle. An Eagle-Weslake came second, driven by Don Gurney, who had built both cars.

Colt-Ford – 1971 (USA) Parnelli Jones won at the wheel of this car with a classic V8 engine, at an average speed of over 253 km/h (157.21 mph), repeating the previous year's success of another car from the same company. The favourite, a McLaren-Offenhauser, came second.

followed suit. Track surfaces were relatively smooth and brakes were used only for coming into the pits, so that there was little incentive to improve suspension and brakes. Chassis therefore evolved slowly, when they did at all, for almost every effort was directed towards the pursuit of power, an area in which the Indianapolis-bred car became unrivalled in the world.

Indianapolis cars in 1911 had essentially touring chassis, powered by side-valve engines. The victory of a bialbero Peugeot Grand Prix voiturette in the 500 in 1913 created a revolution in the USA, as it did in Europe. While its semi-elliptic sprung chassis was conventional, it was very refined and provided the model for most designers to follow. The structure of its engine soon proved itself to be the most efficient of all. Louis Chevrolet adopted its principles for his Frontenac cars as early as 1915, Harry Miller turned to it in 1919, and was followed by Fred Duesenberg in 1922, these being the three greatest builders of American racing cars between the two wars. Miller's old company was taken over by his shop foreman, Fred Offenhauser, in 1933, and when the last Offys ran at the Speedway, around 1980, they were Peugeot-inspired Millers that had finally reached the end of almost sixty years of development. The exhaust-driven turbocharger made its modern world début at Indianapolis in 1966, on 2750-cc Offy engines.

Lotus 56 – 1968 (GB) Designed by Chapman and Philippe, this turbine car (with a Pratt and Whitney 430-hp engine) was an amalgam of advanced features such as four-wheel drive and a wedge-shaped body. Leonard's car set off in pole position and came twelfth.

Eagle-Offenhauser – 1975 (USA) Bobby Unser won the 1975 500 with a four-cylinder turbocharged 2611-cc Offenhauser which developed 625 hp at 8500 rpm. Its average speed was 240.083 km/h (149.180 mph).

Lola-Cosworth – 1978 (USA) The first win with a Cosworth supercharged 2650-cc V8 at Indianapolis came in 1978 with Al Unser's Lola, at an average speed of 259.689 km/h (161.363 mph). Eleven Cosworths took part, including one driven by Penske and Tom Sneva, which came second.

At the end, these engines, reduced to 2.6 liters, were giving in the neighbourhood of 900 hp, but they still could not hold their own against the racing Ford V8. The 500 has always been run according to a periodically revised displacement formula. Only occasionally has it coincided with the formulas established by the AIACR and FIA. Such fuels as pump and aviation gasoline, methanol, and nitro-methane blends have been authorized at different periods.

An historic innovation in chassis design took place at Indianapolis in 1925 with the introduction of Miller front-wheel drive, which launched the entire modern forward trend. Otherwise, chassis remained fairly traditional, with solid axles, until Jack Brabham's Cooper-Climax touched off the rear-engine revolution at Indianapolis in 1961. Many Italians and Italo-Americans have contributed to the Indianapolis legend, including Mario Andretti, Alberto Ascari, Pietro Bordino, Baconin Borzacchini, Ralph de Palma, Peter de Paolo, Tony Gulotta, Kelly Petillo, Giovanni Porporato, Joe and Paul Russo, Vincenzo Trucco, Luigi Villoresi and Paolo Zuccarelli.

Penske-Cosworth PC12 – 1984 (USA) This car won the 1984 Indianapolis 500 for Rick Mears at an average speed of 263.25 km/h (163.575 mph). Like most of the CART formula cars, this one had a Cosworth DFX V8 2650-cc engine, which developed about 700 hp at 11,000 rpm turbocharged. The body was aluminium reinforced with carbon fiber. Geoff Ferris designed the PC12.

THE AUTOMOBILE TODAY: A WORLD-WIDE PHENOMENON

While Europe had been badly hit by the war and was deeply involved in major reconstruction work, the American automobile industry was in a position to satisfy a demand which had been unfulfilled for a long time during the war. By 5 April 1945, the War Production Department had officially announced possibilities for financing the development of new models, and by 20 August of the same year they were once again on the market. General Motors allocated twenty million dollars for a new test center to be created and reconverted the Buick plant to produce half a million cars a year. The first models to come on to the market were mainly updated versions of pre-war cars, a typical example of this being the Ford V8 Super De Luxe which differed from the 1942 model only in a slight restyling and a few horsepower more. There were also, however, some completely new developments, with the appearance of the new Kaiser company, founded by J. Kaiser and Joe Frazer, who had formerly been a director of Willys. After the very brief appearance of a front-wheel drive version, the new company brought out a very conventional saloon, the Special, in 1946. That year, about 2,150,000 automobiles were produced in the USA and this number grew steadily until it exceeded 6,600,000 in 1950, when the number of cars on the road reached 226 per thousand inhabitants as opposed to 43 in the most advanced European country, Great Britain.

With continual but fluctuating progress in this sphere, American production settled at between five and six million cars a year in the ten years between 1950 and 1960 as a result of certain concomitant factors, namely the two periods of economic recession (1951/52 and 1957/58), the constantly increasing prices over the decade and the particular situation of the motor industry in the USA. General Motors, Ford and Chrysler had for some time enjoyed complete control of the market and followed a production policy led by General Motors designed to prevent competition and so keep investment costs down. The models offered by the "Big Three" together covered the whole range of the market from the "standard" to "medium" and "luxury" cars, which basically differed from each other only in their fittings and the fact that the most luxurious versions had V8 engines: they were all on a line as regards price and technical features. While this kind of standardization made it possible to supply mass-produced cars at relatively cheap prices at a time when demand was great, it also resulted in a complete lack of really economical cars on the one hand and of highly advanced cars on the other. The latter were of increasing appeal to young buyers, attracted by more modern and sophisticated, albeit smaller, cars, who were thus forced to turn their attention to vehicles produced on the other side of the Atlantic. In 1958, European cars accounted for 7.9 per cent of the market, even though they were unable to set up an efficient service network to rely on in America.

The early post-war years also saw the introduction of automatic gear change, an innovation which was to become highly developed in the USA. Although different types of semi-automatic transmission had been used before, such as General Motors Hydramatic (1940), which had a hydraulic joint and a four-speed epicyclic unit, the Dynaflow fitted on the 1948 eight-cylinder Buick had a torque converter and required no manual operation except on the reduced gear for use on rough ground, and on reverse. The technical credit for this kind of unit belongs to the 1946 Invicta, and it was General Motors who made it popular on a national scale. Borg-Warner immediately built an automatic gearbox on the same principle, which was used by Ford and Studebaker.

The V8 overhead valve engine designed for Cadillac in 1949 by Charles Kettering started another race for greater engine power, which was to bring about a whole series of similar engines in the 1950s, while even the more modest six-cylinder engines were being updated. At the same time, a number of "futuristic" prototypes were brought out that gave a foretaste of the later series vehicle design, with long, low lines, wrap-around windscreens and rear fins, one of the few features of American styling to

Lancia Aprilia – 1937 (I) This was the last car designed by Vincenzo Lancia. It was launched in 1937 with a V4 1351.6-cc engine, which was increased to 1486 cc two years later. The output in both series was 48 hp and the top speed 127 km/h (79 mph). The Aprilia had an original rear axle with independent wheels and central brake drums. It was in production up to 1949.

Citroën DS19 – 1955 (F) This was one of the most innovative cars of the post-war period, with features such as a highly aerodynamic line (the drag coefficient was 0.31), front-wheel drive and self-levelling air suspension using a central hydraulic unit that also fed the power-assisted steering, the clutch and four-speed gearbox and the brakes (front discs). The original engine had four cylinders with a capacity of 1911 cc, developing 75 hp at 4500 rpm.

influence European cars. Models began to be modernized at a frenetic pace: in 1949 the major companies had proposed to update nearly all their pre-war models, but by 1955 some companies had completely updated their whole range three times. The investment required to keep up with the competition cut out almost all of the "independent" builders: only American Motors, established in 1954 by a merger between Nash and Hudson, managed to win themselves a relatively strong position on the market.

The conditions behind the recovery of the automobile in Europe after the war were very different from those in America. Most of the factories had been destroyed, and raw materials were scarce, but Europe soon began to make a comeback in the automobile industry and grew increasingly stronger after a brief period of reconstruction. Firstly, as a result of strict import controls, development took place within national boundaries; and secondly, a much more varied selection of cars aimed at a much wider social framework was available, both in terms of size and engine capacity. This resulted in the preservation of national technical traditions and marques, and some companies were able to specialize in specific areas of the market, where they established outstanding reputations.

This competitive fever, accentuated by the presence of companies with American backing, prevented the major manufacturers from organizing a crystallized situation, as in the USA, and forced them to compete fiercely on the grounds of price and variety of product. This brought about a situation in Europe whereby production became concentrated into a very limited number of companies in comparison with the fragmentation that had existed before.

In France, heavy damage had been inflicted on Peugeot, Ford and Renault – Renault was subsequently nationalized – whereas Citroën and Simca were relatively unscathed by the war. Production figures increased from 30,400 cars in 1946 to 257,000 in 1950, thanks mainly to successful new runabouts such as the Renault 4 CV, the prototype of which was inspired by the Volkswagen, but which was presented at the 1946 Paris Motor Show in a more original form, and the Citroën 2 CV. Simca brought out updated versions of the 6 and the 8 based on the Fiat Topolino and the 1100 respectively.

The new Peugeot 203, on the other hand, was a medium-sized 1300-cc car which remained in production until 1960, by which time 685,000 had been built. In 1954, Simca took over the Ford plant at Poissy, where the eight-cylinder Vedette was in production for some time. The most innovative European car was the front-wheel drive Citroën DS of 1955, which had self-levelling air suspension, front disc brakes and an automatic gear change.

In 1958, the four major French companies accounted for 92 per cent of home production. Despite its highly interesting Dyna, Panhard barely managed 4 per cent. In 1959, total production exceeded a million for the first time.

The British car industry, spared crippling destruction, had managed to produce 219,000 vehicles by 1946. However, this represented the total of a large number of manufacturers, the most important being the Nuffield group of companies (Morris, MG, Riley and Wolseley), Ford, Austin, Vauxhall, Standard-Triumph and the Rootes Group (Hillman, Sunbeam, Humber and, after 1956,

Dodge Polara Lancer – 1960 (USA) The unitary-bodied Polara Lancer was a false cabriolet brought out in 1960 with a V8 5916-cc engine. It had a three-speed automatic gearbox.

Renault Colorale Prairie – 1950 (F) The Colorale series came out in 1950 and included Taxi and Savane versions. The 1950 Prairie had a four-cylinder 2383-cc engine developing 46 hp.

Datsun DS – 1949 (J) Nissan resumed production of cars after the war in 1947, but it was only in the 1950s that the Japanese government decided on a development policy for the motor industry, which was saved by strict protectionist measures combined with easy finance to support national production of small cars. The industry acquired the necessary expertise by building European runabouts under license. Nissan in particular made an agreement with Austin to build the Seven.

PANHARD

The post-war period began with Panhard at the technical forefront. In fact, in 1947, the engineer Jean-Albert Gregoire built the prototype later to be used as the basis for the first Dyna. It had a horizontal, air-cooled, two-cylinder engine, front-wheel drive and an aluminium body. The original 610-cc displacement was increased in 1949 to 745 cc, giving 35 hp. The aerodynamic Dyna 54 came out in 1953, again with an aluminium body, designed by the St Cyr Aeronautical Institute. The 850-cc engine developed 40 hp at 4000 rpm. The body frame had two sub-frames supporting the front and rear suspension. Panhard also produced some sports models, which did very well in the Le Man 24 Hours (DB Panhard), and built 35,000 vehicles in 1958, but then had to stop using aluminium because of the cost. The PL 17 came out in 1959 and was available in a Tigre version which gave 60 hp. Citroën acquired shares in Panhard in 1955 and gradually extended their influence; in fact, the new 24 C two-door saloon and the 24 CT coupé were built at their design centre in 1963. Two years later, their shareholding became a full take-over. The Panhard marque disappeared in 1967.

Panhard 24C – 1963 (F)

Renault Dauphine – 1956 (F) Over two million were produced between 1956 and 1962. The Dauphine had a four-cylinder 845-cc rear-mounted engine which developed 26.5 hp at 4250 rpm. Its top speed was 115 km/h (71.46 mph). A coupé and a cabriolet (Floride) version were also built, with the output increased to 40 hp, giving a top speed of 125 km/h (77.7 mph).

Peugeot 404 – 1960 (F) ▶ Altogether 2,450,000 404s were built, with traditional lines, the result of a long association with Pininfarina, and in a range that included two petrol versions (1486 and 1618 cc) and a diesel. This came out in 1963 and had a displacement of 1816 cc, later increased to 1948 cc. McPherson front suspension and an angled engine were two of the features that made the car so innovative for its day.

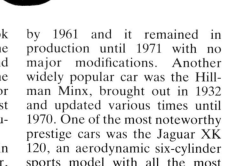

Singer). Other companies, for example, Rover, Jaguar and Rolls-Royce, concentrated on producing prestige vehicles. More than thirty different marques were in operation, but of these only Ford were strong enough to guarantee financial stability. Consequently, and also as a result of certain crises in the battle for sales with French and German cars on the foreign markets, a great number of mergers took place. The most important was the merger between Nuffield and Austin in 1952, resulting in the formation of BMC (British Motor Company), subsequently the most productive of all British manufacturers.

The most successful model in the 1950s was the Morris Minor, designed by Alec Issigonis in 1947. Over a million had been produced by 1961 and it remained in production until 1971 with no major modifications. Another widely popular car was the Hillman Minx, brought out in 1932 and updated various times until 1970. One of the most noteworthy prestige cars was the Jaguar XK 120, an aerodynamic six-cylinder sports model with all the most modern features, which remained in production for over twenty-five years. British production figures surpassed a million in 1958.

In Germany, reconstruction of the industry, which had been totally destroyed, was accelerated by massive support from the Allies and by enormous investment on the part of General Motors and Ford to help their respective subsidiaries back on their feet. In 1950, a total of 219,000 cars were built. The German motor industry

Fiat 1100 R – 1966 (I) The roots of this car went back to the 508 C of 1937, which had a four-cylinder 1098-cc 32-hp engine. The completely redesigned 1100/103 (36 hp) was brought out in 1953 and remained in production until 1962. In 1957 it was used as the base for the 55-hp 1200, with a 1221-cc engine that was later reduced in power to 50 hp and fitted in the 1100 D in 1962. The R version, which had the original displacement, but developed 48 hp was in production from 1966 to 1969. The plants were later given over to Premier.

Morris Minor – 1957 (GB) Brought out in 1949, the Minor had a four-cylinder 920-cc side-valve engine which developed 37 hp at 4600 rpm. A second series was brought out in 1957 with a large area of glass and a one-piece windscreen. Its engine capacity was increased to 948 cc, giving a speed of 117 km/h (72.7 mph).

found itself in very special circumstances, for although there was a great number of companies in operation, the largest of them held almost a monopoly in the particular areas of the market they controlled.

Such was also the case with Volkswagen at the lower end of the market. The Wolfsburg company had begun producing the Beetle again in 1945, when they built 10,000. This figure increased to 19,220 in 1948, 40,000 in 1949 and 82,000 in 1950. Heinz Nordhoff was the driving force behind this success, assisted by a completely innovative policy of export to the USA, introduced in 1947 and continuing to 1949.

Opel took the role of leader in the medium engine range, followed some lengths behind by Ford, Auto Union and BMW, who specialized in sporty saloons. Mercedes occupied an unrivalled position, dominating the prestige car sector and making their mark with the 300 SL sports car with its "gullwing" doors. The Borgward group also operated in Germany, there producing small cars with the marques Lloyd and Goliath alongside high prestige saloons such as the Borgward Hansa (1950) and the Isabella (1954).

By 1956, Germany was the leading manufacturer in Europe, in the following year producing over a million cars and reaching 1,800,000 in 1960.

Fiat, the largest company in Italy, had suffered badly during the war, but by 1946 had managed to step up production of their pre-war models, the 500, 1100 and 1500. Under the technical direction of Dante Giacosa, the first completely new model to come out was the 1400, a European class saloon with a unitary body slightly American in style and perhaps a little premature for the economic climate of the country. Fiat were, however, successful in anticipating trends and launched models in the early 1950s which brought cars within the reach of the entire nation: two of their earlier successes were the 1100/103, brought out in 1953, and more particularly the 600, introduced in 1955, a small, rear-engine runabout which symbolized the recovery of the Italian economy.

However, national production levels were still well below other European countries, although figures rose from 101,000 in 1950 to 369,000 in 1958. Fiat accounted for 86.7 per cent of production, 90 per cent if we include Auto-

Morris Mini Minor – 1959 (GB) Alec Issigonis's *pièce de résistance* was brought out in 1959 as the Austin Seven or Morris Mini Minor. "Mini" became the marque in 1970. The transverse engine with the gearbox incorporated in block and front-wheel drive meant that there was a lot of passenger space in just 3.05 m (10 ft). The first version had a four-cylinder 848-cc engine.

Ford Anglia – 1959 (GB) Launched at the London Motor Show in 1959, this car was outstanding for the original line of its roof panel and had a four-cylinder 997-cc engine giving 39.5 hp at 5000 rpm. Its top speed was 115 km/h (71.46 mph). More than a million were built, partly because of its modern engine, also much used in racing.

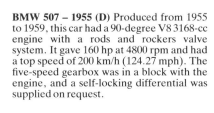

BMW 507 – 1955 (D) Produced from 1955 to 1959, this car had a 90-degree V8 3168-cc engine with a rods and rockers valve system. It gave 160 hp at 4800 rpm and had a top speed of 200 km/h (124.27 mph). The five-speed gearbox was in a block with the engine, and a self-locking differential was supplied on request.

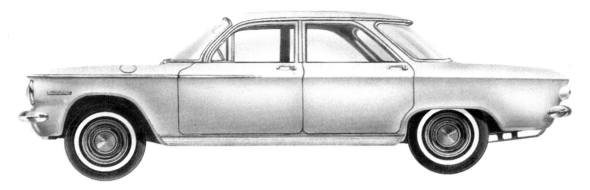

bianchi, who built excellent small runabouts with mechanics from the 500. The remaining 10 per cent was divided between Alfa Romeo's sports cars and the high class vehicles produced by Lancia.

Expansion in the 1960s

In the 1960s, Europe finally became economically strong enough to compete with the USA and this was reflected in the motor industry, where the gap between the two was gradually narrowing. The number of car owners in the USA in 1960 was 320 per thousand inhabitants, as opposed to 76 in the countries which, with the exception of Greece, are now members of the EEC; by 1970, however, the gap had closed, the figures standing at 414 and 203 respectively.

In the USA, only one factor disturbed the peaceful balance of power between manufacturers and this was the continual increase in imported cars, which mounted rapidly after 1965, taking up 13.4 per cent of the market. At the same time, Europe was having to protect itself from attempts by the American motor industry to take over companies in a financially vulnerable position. General Motors already had a strong presence in Germany (Opel) and England (Vauxhall), but their interest in Daimler-Benz was fruitless.

Chrysler also had great difficulty in setting up bridgeheads in Europe, but eventually managed to do so by taking over Simca in 1963 and the Rootes Group in 1967. Volkswagen had previously intervened to prevent them from taking over Auto Union. Ford, on the other hand, showed a particular interest in Lancia, which forced Fiat to intervene and take Lancia over in 1969. Ford had also set their sights on Ferrari, but talks broke down at the last minute when Enzo Ferrari decided that he did not want any interference in the racing division. Once again Fiat stepped in, though on this occasion more discreetly.

The American industry still failed to produce any suitable models to stop the flow of imported cars, even more noticeable in the 1970s. However, signs of greater diversification in the vehicles available were beginning to appear. The new size-groups "compact" and "intermediate" (the former introduced with the Chevrolet Corvair in 1960 and the latter represented by the Ford Fairlane, Rambler and Chevrolet Chevy II) took about 35 per cent of the market in that decade, but at the expense of the "full-sized" cars (standard, medium and luxury) rather than foreign imports.

The 1960s also saw the beginning of a race to cut production costs; this led to General Motors using a common chassis (the external type, which was very popular at the time) on all their intermediates, as did Ford on their full-sized cars, while Chrysler and American Motors began to use unitary body construction. Technically, although there was a proliferation of models with ever-increasing body and engine size, few important innovations were being made. Studebaker began to use disc brakes in 1963 (but other US companies did not use them until the following decade); and more serious research was being carried out into aerodynamics, and was tested on the cabriolet version of the Corvair, which was also fitted with a turbocharger. The majority of American cars, however, were still too closely tied to traditional concepts and a considerable time was to elapse before features which were already standard on European models, such as independent rear suspension, were adopted in the USA. The 1960s also saw the introduction of the first federal laws on pollution and safety, which were to have a considerable effect on the subsequent development of American cars.

Europe, meanwhile, was making great strides forward in the process of popularizing the motor car. The total number of cars on the road in France, Great Britain, Germany and Italy rose from 17,391,000 in 1960 to 58,895,000 in 1973, representing an increase of about 238 per cent. The formation of the Common Market and EFTA (European Free Trade Area), and the resulting relaxation of customs barriers radically altered the situation as regards competition on an international scale. As import restrictions were lightened, operation extended beyond protected home markets, and competition for prices and product improvement became very much fiercer.

Even within the national boundaries, production was becoming more concentrated. Volkswagen took over Audi and NSU, Fiat took over Autobianchi and Lancia, and Panhard came under the control of Citroën. In 1966, BMC became BMH (British Motor Holdings) after swallowing Jaguar, and in 1968 BMH in its turn became BLMC (British Leyland Motor Company) upon taking over the commercial vehicle specialist Leyland.

Production levels were also increasing at a steady pace. In the six original member countries of the EEC, the number of cars rose from 2,645,000 in 1958 to 6,870,000 in 1969, and imported cars began to represent a large share of the market. In France, for example, the number of foreign cars sold went up from 8,706 in 1958 to 298,730 in 1970, while exports surpassed 1,500,000 in the same year. Similar trends were

seen all over Europe, and in their attempts to conquer the continental market, the major companies not only improved and extended their ranges, but also adopted policies of low price "dumping."

Every sector of the market saw the launch of important new cars which were both widely popular and technically advanced. France produced two interesting runabouts, both very spartan yet functional: the Renault 4 in 1961 and the new Citroën 2 CV, which was matched later by two more comfortable models, the Renault 6 and the Ami 6. Simca brought out the rear-engine 1000, and Peugeot introduced the 404 saloon in 1960 and the 204 with a medium-sized engine in 1965.

In England, the rivalry between the Austin Mini and the Hillman Imp became even keener, though the former was to have much greater success. This period was also the heyday of the British roadster, including the Austin Healey Sprite and the MG Midget. Daimler built the eight-cylinder SP 250 using synthetic

Hillman Imp – 1963 (GB)

ROOTES MOTOR

Hillman was part of Rootes Motor Limited, a holding company which controlled various British companies from the 1920s and 1930s onwards. Before the war, the group included Humber, Hillman and Sunbeam, having taken over the first two in 1928 and the third in 1935. Singer joined after the war, in 1956. William Rootes, the brains behind their expansion, died in 1964, and three years later the group passed into the hands of Chrysler, at which point the products from each company lost their individuality. In 1978, the whole European operation of the shaky American giant was taken over by Peugeot, and after this the vehicles produced in Britain carried the Talbot marque. The Imp was brought out in 1963 to combat the success of the Mini. It had a rear-mounted Coventry-Climax 875-cc single overhead camshaft engine with an output of 37 hp at 5000 rpm and a top speed of 130 km/h (80.8 mph). It also featured independent all-round suspension and a four-speed synchromesh gearbox.

materials for the body, while Jaguar brought out the E-Type in 1961 with aerodynamic lines, independent rear suspension and disc brakes, though it also had certain problems with road-holding. The Mk II saloon was also enormously successful, with its 2.4-, 3.4- and 3.8-liter versions.

In Germany, another popular runabout was brought out alongside the Beetle in 1962: the NSU Prinz 4, its successful lines clearly inspired by the Chevrolet Corvair. The Opel Kadett and the Ford Escort enjoyed equal popularity among a large public, and BMW, pulled back from the brink of a serious crisis by their small, successful Michelotti-designed 700, in 1962 brought out the 1500, the first model in the series which was to establish the company firmly on the international market. In 1966, BMW took over Glas, who had begun automobile production in 1955 with the Goggomobil – a small car with engines of between 250 and 400 cc – and the Isar 700 in 1958. In 1961, Glas brought out an interesting

Studebaker Hawk GT – 1962 (USA)
Brought out in 1962, the Hawk Gran Turismo had a V8 4739-cc engine which developed 210 hp at 4500 rpm. A 225-hp version was also available. The gearbox was either a three-speed automatic or a four-speed manual.

Alfa Romeo Giulia – 1962 (I) The Giulia was brought out in 1962 with a four-cylinder twin overhead camshaft 1570-cc engine and an aerodynamic line with a cut off back end. The 1600 Super version of 1969 gave 98 hp at 6000 rpm for a top speed of over 175 km/h (108.74 mph). Production came to an end in 1978.

NSU Prinz 4 – 1962 (D) The Prinz made its début in 1962 with a two-cylinder 598-cc air-cooled engine which developed 30 hp. Its independent all-round suspension and front disc brakes (optional) were not common on a runabout of just 3.4 m (11 ft 2 in). Top speed was 120 km/h (74.5 mph). Versions with a longer wheelbase, the 1000, 1100 and 1200, followed later.

Fiat 1400 – 1950 (I) The 1400 was in production between 1950 and 1958, and was the first Fiat to have a unitary body. The four-cylinder 1395-cc 44-hp engine had a top speed of 120 km/h (74.5 mph). The 1900 version came out in 1952 (60 hp, 130 km/h/80.8 mph), followed by a 1901-cc 43-hp diesel in 1953.

coupé, in 1964 a 1500-cc saloon and in 1965 a 2600-cc model. Glas continued production until 1969 with a large V8 3000-cc saloon and the 1600 GT with a BMW engine.

In Italy, Innocenti appeared on the market for the first time, producing the British Austin A 40 and the Mini under license. In 1964, the Autobianchi Primula came out, a highly innovative four-cylinder 1221-cc with transverse engine, front-wheel drive, sealed cooling system with automatic electric fan, and all-round disc brakes; the body was available in two sizes with a hatchback.

Apart from their usual highly popular runabouts, Fiat brought out two exceptional sports cars in 1966; the Dino coupé and the Spyder, designed by Bertone and Pininfarina respectively. In 1960, Lancia began to produce front-wheel drive vehicles with the Flavia, followed by the Fulvia in 1963, while Alfa Romeo brought out the Giulia in 1962 with its revolutionary cut-off back.

Sweden, which even by 1950

Porsche 356 B – 1959 (D) The first car built by Porsche in 1950, the 356, was the subject of constant improvement. The 356 B, brought out in 1959, had the typical air-cooled flat-four engine displacing 1582 cc and developing 60 hp, and this was increased to 90 hp at 5500 rpm in the S 90 version of 1960. The car had excellent aerodynamic lines, was 4.01 m (13 ft 2 in) long and had a 2.10-m (6 ft 11 in) wheelbase. It weighed 900 kg (1984 lb). The 356 was in production until 1965.

Jaguar E-Type – 1961 (GB) The E-Type, brought out in a roadster and a coupé version at the Geneva Motor Show in 1961, had a tubular trellis chassis, independent rear suspension and front disc brakes. The engine was a classic six-cylinder 3781-cc twin overhead camshaft, developing 269 hp SAE. Its top speed was over 240 km/h (149.13 mph) and its acceleration 0–100 km/h (0–62.1 mph) in just over seven seconds.

Facel-Vega Facellia coupé 2 + 2 – 1960 (F)

FACEL-VEGA

This company was in operation between 1954 and 1964, and produced about a thousand luxury vehicles, mostly with Chrysler engines. One of the most important models was the HK 500, a coupé brought out in 1958 with a V8 4940-cc 260-hp engine, subsequently replaced by a 5907-cc 365-hp version. In 1962, a 6286-cc engine was fitted, giving 390 hp and a top speed of 220 km/h (136.7 mph). The four-door Excellence was also available after 1959. The Facellia had a 1600-cc twin overhead camshaft 120-hp engine, designed by Facel-Vega themselves, and was brought out in 1960 in an attempt to produce a more reasonably priced coupé. The last model produced by this French company was the Facel II in 1962 (5.9 liters, 360 hp) which did up to 240 km/h (149.12 mph). Financial problems led to the company's demise.

Austin Healey 3000 – 1962 (GB) The Austin Healey marque was born in 1955 with the 100 S, produced at the Austin works to a design by David Healey, who had brought it out on his own three years before at the London Motor Show. The engine was the four-cylinder 2660-cc Austin A 90. The 100 Six was launched in 1957 with a six-cylinder 2912-cc engine developing 102 hp that was later uprated to 117 hp. One of its features was the optional overdrive offered on third and fourth. The output was increased with the 3000 Mk II of 1959 and the 3000 Mk III of 1963 to 130 and 150 hp respectively. It finally went out of production in 1970.

▼

Daf Daffodil 750 – 1960 (NL)

Renault 8 – 1962 (F) Taking over from the Dauphine in 1962, the 8 had a four-cylinder 956-cc 48-hp engine. The coupé-cabriolet version was aesthetically very similar to the Floride and was called the Caravelle (below). In 1964, a 1108-cc 50-hp engine was fitted. It had disc brakes on all four wheels. Production of the 8 stopped in 1973.

DAF

The first Daf came out in 1959. It was a small 600 cc and had an original transmission with continual variation of the ratio. Called the "Variomatic," it was later used on all the cars produced by this Dutch company. The first Daffodil had an air-cooled two-cylinder engine developing 22 hp and 90 km/h (56 mph). In 1960, the 750 version (26 hp, 105 km/h / 65.24 mph) was brought out and in 1967, after a few modifications, became the 33.

Meanwhile, in 1965, the 850-cc 44 came out, followed two years later by the 55 with its four-cylinder 1100-cc 47-hp Renault engine. The same engine was used in 1972 on the 66, which was later given a 1300-cc 57-hp version. Volvo took over Daf in 1957 and the marque disappeared a year later. The 66 continued to be produced as one of Volvo's cars until 1978.

▲

Honda Z Coupé – 1970 (J) The Z was brought out on the Japanese market with a two-cylinder 354-cc engine. It had an output of 31 hp, increased to 36 hp on the TS version, and a four-speed gearbox (five-speed and automatic were optional extras). A 599-cc 36-hp engine was used on export models. Its top speed was 120 km/h (74.5 mph).

▼

Mercedes 220 SE Coupé – 1961 (D) Brought out in 1961, together with a cabriolet version, this car had a six-cylinder 2195-cc engine with mechanical fuel injection, developing 120 hp at 5000 rpm. The 220 SE was the first Mercedes to have front wheel disc brakes.

had not managed to produce 10,000 units per annum, reached 100,000 in 1960, a figure which doubled in 1968 thanks to the efforts of Volvo and, to a lesser extent, Saab. The Amazon PV 444 brought Volvo great success in 1946 and was followed in 1958 by the updated P 544 version, of which a total of 440,000 were built over twenty-one years. In 1971, 231,000 vehicles were produced at the Volvo plant. In the meantime, Saab had introduced a series of automobiles with original aerodynamic lines. In 1960, the company was very successful with the 96 in rallies, which naturally had extremely favourable results on sales. By 1971 production had reached 86,000 units.

The Japanese phenomenon

Barely 114,700 cars were on the road in Japan in 1953 and that year 21,300 new cars were registered. Of these, only 8,800 were Japanese vehicles: the remaining 12,500 were American imports belonging to members of the army of occupation, sold as second-hand cars to the Japanese, who were eager to avoid the heavy purchase tax levied on new cars. National production was unable to satisfy the growing home demand with regard to both quantity and quality, and so, instead of adopting an import programme, the Ministry of Commerce and Industry decided to formulate a long-term policy by which the country would eventually become self-sufficient. The first step in the programme was to reduce purchase tax on small capacity vehicles while at the same time offering loans on favourable terms to the companies manufacturing them. In order to bring in the necessary technical expertise, production agreements to build European models under license were also welcomed, in consequence of which Nissan-Datsun obtained a license to build the Austin Ten and Isuzu to build the Hillman Minx.

The 1950s witnessed the first significant growth in production and the appearance on the market of new manufacturers producing, as ever, very small cars. In 1958, Subaru launched the two-cylinder two-stroke rear-engine 360; in 1959, Suzuki marketed the Light Van; and in 1960, Mazda made its appearance with the R 360.

In 1964, over 579,000 vehicles were built, of which 11.5 per cent were exported to developing Asian countries. The increasing number of cars on the road in the 1960s enabled the Japanese automobile industry to reinvest its large profits in new production techniques, and these, together with a near military-style organization of work, very soon led to vastly increased production levels which were considerably higher than those of the Western motor industry.

The golden rule of the Japanese industry was the minimal integration of production: the car companies designed and manufactured the main parts (such as engines and gearboxes) but left

the job of producing about 70 per cent of the component parts to reliable controlled companies. This was financially a very advantageous move, as it enabled the car companies to do away with the stockpiles of components required to cover a few days' production which Western manufacturers traditionally kept in store. Supplies came in continuously as they were required, with the full advantage of reduced production costs. Between 1960 and 1965, sales prices dropped by over 16 per cent, then by a further 7.1 per cent between 1965 and 1970, thus generating a rapidly growing spiral of expansion.

The phenomenal success of small runabouts with a maximum 360-cc capacity on the home market was due to very restrictive legislation, which for example allowed only cars within this range to be parked overnight along the city streets. In order to buy a larger car, a prospective owner had to prove possession of a private parking space.

Small runabouts also accounted for 25 per cent of annual production in 1970. In the 1960s, however, many models appeared of a size more suitable for the new markets. Exports had now reached Australia and the USA, rising from 7,000 in 1960 to 725,000 in 1970 and 1,450,000 in 1972. Even the transport systems were studied with a view to giving maximum returns, and manufacturers also used their own ships.

By the end of the 1960s, Japan had established itself as the third

largest automobile producer in the world, moving into second place in 1971 with 3,717,800 cars. In the same year, Toyota and Nissan-Datsun together accounted for 67 per cent of production, leaving Mazda, Mitsubishi, Honda, Daihatsu, Suzuki and Subaru decreasing shares of the market from 8.1 to 3.1 per cent. Isuzu held only a marginal position.

Although Japanese cars of the 1960s did not present any special features in comparison with those from Europe, they were highly successful because they were both practical and reliable.

After bringing out the small, air-cooled 700-cc Publica in 1960, Toyota enjoyed great success in 1966 with the Corolla, a 1100-cc saloon which celebrated its millionth car only three years after its first appearance. In 1968, the Corona Mk II, a medium car of 1500 to 2000 cc, was brought out, followed in 1970 by the Celica.

The most successful Nissan models included the Bluebird, a 1200-cc which came out in 1961 and had a Pininfarina body on the 1964 version. The Datsun Sunny (1200–1400 cc) was brought out in 1966, followed in 1968 by the Laurel (1800–2000 cc), while the first true Japanese GT, the 240 Z, was launched in 1969: a six-cylinder 2-liter coupé successful in rallying history. It won the 1971 East African Safari and came third in the 1971 and 1972 Monte Carlo Rallies. The 1970 Cherry was the first front-wheel drive car brought out by the company and represented the peak of a long series of highly successful runabouts.

In 1966 Honda produced the small N 360, one of the few Japanese "mini cars" to break into the European market at the time. The small coupé and roadster versions with 600- and 800-cc engines were also of interest, and in 1968 the N 1300, a version with a larger engine, was brought out.

After Mazda's success with the small, two-cylinder models in the 360 series, the 782-cc Familia and the Bertone-designed Luce (1000 and 1400 cc), they brought out the very interesting Cosmo, fitted with a twin-rotor Wankel engine – a feature later to become one of the hallmarks of the company.

Finally, Daihatsu, Suzuki and Mitsubishi concentrated production on small 360-cc cars with a few medium models, while Isuzu produced higher-class vehicles such as the Bellet in 1962, the Florian in 1967 and the 117 coupé with Ghia bodywork in 1968.

The 1973 crisis and new international stability

The sudden leap in the price of oil caught the Western motor industry, which had enjoyed twenty years of continuous expansion, totally unprepared. Despite the fact that the 1973 crisis had repercussions throughout the world and particularly in Europe, unleashing a spiral of inflation and monetary instability, it was the motor industry which felt the effects most markedly.

The effect of the crisis was not to cause drastic cuts in the number of companies, as had happened after

Mazda 110 S Cosmo – 1967 (J) Presented at the Tokyo Motor Show in 1964, the Cosmo went into production in 1967 and was the first car on which they used the Wankel rotary engine. The twin-rotor engine had an overall capacity of 982 cc and developed 130 hp (SAE) at 7000 rpm. Its top speed was 200 km/h (124.27 mph) and it had a five-speed synchromesh gearbox.

the 1929 crash, nor to create a need for total reorganization; instead it brought about a radical change in the way the public viewed and used the automobile. On reflection, it is now clear that, apart from an initial period of disorientation, there was no question of applying the Utopian idea of replacing private motoring with public transport, although people did become more aware of the fact that motoring in the future would become increasingly expensive. The expectations and demands of the motorist therefore changed: economical running and reliability became priorities and buyers were thinking twice before making any purchases. Demand declined considerably, which led to an unprecedented level of competition between the different manufacturing companies.

Recovery was not simply a question of regaining previous production levels and reviving development after a temporary break; long-term programmes were needed to supply a product capable of satisfying a demand that had undergone considerable changes. The most important implication of all was realizing the necessity of reviving technical development, which had been somewhat neglected in the 1960s.

It was undoubtedly the American industry that had to make the most radical changes, on account of the special nature of their products: the majority of cars built in 1970 had eight-cylinder engines which were by no means economical and at least 46 per cent of them were "full-sized" cars measuring over 5.5 m (18 ft) and weighing about two tons. The "intermediates" took up 30 per cent of the market, while the remaining 24 per cent was split between the "compacts" and "sub-compacts." The sub-compacts, which had been brought out between 1970 and 1971 by American Motors with the Gremlin and Ford with the Pinto, were more of an attempt to combat the growing number of imports from Europe and Japan than to lay the basis for the re-establishment of the American car. Their technical features and quality could not compare with the foreign competition and so their success on the market was rather limited.

Ford Capri – 1969 (GB-D) This four-seater coupé was inspired by the American Mustang and was launched in 1969. It was available in a wide range of engines, from the four-cylinder 1300–1700 cc to the six-cylinder 2300 and 2600 cc. The Capri underwent major restyling in 1974.

It was not until after the oil crisis, and particularly after the government in Washington had issued directives on energy conservation in 1975, that the American automobile industry began to realize that the time had come to put a stop to its race to lower production costs (the aim of which was to earn maximum profits), which had led to a rather alarming state of technical stagnation. As late as 1972, there was still no front-wheel drive vehicle on the US market and front disc brakes were still offered as an optional extra that had to be paid for. The most important regulation was the one establishing what was known as the "Corporate Average Fuel Economy". This required the manufacturing companies to respect a top fuel consumption limit based on an average worked out over all the models in production, and it was decided to bring the level down between 1978 and 1985 from 13.1 to 8.55 liters per 100 km (21.6 – 33 mpg). The negative reaction to this by the automobile manufacturers reflected a certain uneasiness on their part. Lighter vehicles were now the order of the day, with four-cylinder engines, more compact body sizes and improved aerodynamic lines, features which brought American cars closer technically to European models.

The Chevrolet Chevette of 1976 was the same as the Opel Kadett City with a 1400-cc engine, while Chrysler in 1977 brought out the Dodge Omni, an American version of the European Horizon but with a Volkswagen engine. In 1980, the Escort was launched and represented the first true "world car," having been designed for both the American and European markets. A similar operation was

concluded two years later with the birth of the Sierra, the product of another international project. General Motors, after having "downsized" their standard and luxury cars, took advantage of European technology to bring their range up to date with the development of new compacts (the X-car), sub-compacts (the J-car based on the Opel Ascona) and front-wheel drive intermediates (the A-car), which were brought out between 1979 and 1982.

In 1981, after the second oil crisis in 1979, the share of the compacts and subcompacts on the American market rose to 38 per cent, while the intermediates accounted for 22 per cent. Since imported cars accounted for 27 per cent, that left only 13 per cent of the market for the traditional standard and luxury models, proving that an era had come to its end.

Production in Europe was better geared towards solving the problem of high energy costs. Smaller engines and bodies, excellent technical records and a traditionally more competitive spirit than in the USA, even before the huge increase in fuel prices, meant that there was no need for a great conceptual revision of the automobile.

One of the first general consequences of the crisis was the interruption of the process by which cars on the road were being brought within an average range of 1500–2000 cc. The home markets in each country maintained their own identity, so the major manufacturers had to extend their ranges in order to guarantee competitiveness in every class of car. The 1000 – 1500 cc range became the most important on average throughout Europe during the 1970s, accounting

for over 40 per cent of the total combined production of France, Great Britain, Germany and Italy.

These four countries suffered their biggest drop in production between 1973 and 1975, when it plummeted from ten million to eight million. The industry managed nevertheless to achieve a certain degree of stability, and after the 1976 crisis made a good recovery. It was consequently better prepared for the effects of the second crisis, in 1979, which so seriously affected the United States. Unlike the USA, however, the European countries lacked clearly defined legislation, both at the EEC level and nationally. In fact, no directives were given to limit fuel consumption, and state intervention often did not extend beyond providing financial support for companies in trouble.

The main problem in France was the difficult situation in which Citroën found themselves, both financially and with regard to their range. Their last new model had been the GS in 1970, with which they had hoped to expand their market, up to then dependent on the rather dated 2-CV/Dyane, the Ami and the DS. In 1968, Fiat made a take-over bid, but in default of government support had to settle for being a foreign partner with a majority shareholding.

In 1974, a plan to restructure the industry on a national level was introduced, and so Peugeot and Citroën merged to form the PSA group. With the subsequent take-over in 1978 of Chrysler's European subsidiaries, whose cars were then produced under the name "Talbot," the group became the biggest Continental manufacturer. However, with three marques all aimed at the same sector of the market, there were inevitable problems as far as rationalization of production was concerned, and they were unable to maintain their position.

Renault, on the other hand, went through a period of great expansion in the 1970s. The great success of the Renault 5, a particularly well-designed and highly reliable runabout, allowed them to stay firmly at the top of the European league of manufacturers, while at the same time a widely based programme established in 1977 enabled them in

December 1980 to buy 46.4 per cent of the shares in American Motors, securing control of the technical direction. Hence began production in the United States of the Alliance and the Encore, corresponding to the European versions, the Renault 9 and 11.

In Britain, British Leyland, in serious difficulties, were nationalized in 1975, but unable to extract themselves from the rather complex situation that had developed partly from financial problems and union troubles, partly from the very varying results from successful and less successful models. The successful cars included the Mini, which won the test of time and exceeded four million units in 1977, and, in the prestige range, the 1970 Range Rover, which was the first and often unsuccessfully copied example of a "luxurious off-road vehicle." The less successful models included the Allegro, brought out in 1973 but replaced ten years later, in 1983, by a more competitive medium car, the Maestro. In addition, marques with an impressive and prestigious history such as MG and Triumph gradually lost their traditional associations. One of the keystones of the continuation of British Leyland was the agreement made with Honda in 1979 for the production of the Japanese car, the Ballade, in Britain, where it was renamed the Triumph Acclaim. Although this first joint venture did not have the desired success, because the model was not one of the most recent produced by the Japanese, the new model brought out in 1984 based on the Honda Civic and sold under the Rover marque has provided British Leyland with an up-to-date product exhibiting the latest in motor technology. With a fall in production levels of 53.8 per cent between 1972 and 1982, Great Britain is the only country in Europe not to have shown signs of an upturn in production since the 1973 crisis.

The German motor industry had already fully recovered its pre-crisis production levels by 1977. Volkswagen had completely updated all their models, introducing the Passat, the Golf and the Polo between 1973 and 1975. At the same time, Audi were relaunched as a major prestige company, offering two series of

Renault 18 Turbo – 1980 (F) This car had a four-cylinder turbocharged engine (1565 cc, 110 hp at 5500 rpm) and was capable of 185 km/h (115 mph). In 1983, its output was increased to 125 hp, giving a top speed of 195 km/h (121.17 mph).

Renault 9 – 1981 (F) The 9 was brought out in 1981 and was also produced, with slight modifications, by American Motors as the Alliance. The series included 1108- and 1397-cc petrol versions giving 48 and 72 hp, and a 1595-cc diesel version which developed 55 hp.

Audi 80 – 1978 (D) In production from 1972, having had a slight facelift in 1984, the Audi 80 range offers a wide variety of different engines, from the four-cylinder 1296-cc 60-hp to a five-cylinder 2144-cc 136-hp, as well as a 1588-cc diesel in an aspirated or turbo version.

Ford Sierra – 1982 (D) The line of the Sierra is the result of intensive research in aerodynamics. Engines available range from four cylinders, 1300–2000 cc, to six cylinders, 2000–2800 cc, and include a Peugeot 2300-cc diesel. The Sierra's layout is classical, with rear-wheel drive.

cars, the 80 and the 100. Development of the range enabled them to offer more than 220 versions in Europe in 1984, based on three families of petrol engines, two diesel engines, four basic beds and eight main body styles. The move to extend their range affected all German companies, sparing not even Mercedes and BMW. Mercedes consolidated its enviable reputation for tradition and quality in the sphere of the large car and tried to introduce the same qualities in a mid-range saloon, bringing out the ultra-modern 190 in 1982, while BMW steadily enlarged the scope of their success from mid-range cars to the top end of the market. The two companies each have two almost parallel ranges of product and are, not unexpectedly, keen rivals.

In 1978, the Auto 2000 programme was launched and, with state backing to the tune of DM 397m., enabled German manufacturers to make full use of their technological capability in building prototypes with the aim of limiting fuel consumption. The programme was completed in 1982 and produced excellent results, notably the interesting Daimler-Benz car, driven by a promising gas turbine, and the unique example on which, with marginal modifications, Audi have based their new 100 model.

In Italy, the crisis resulted in a wave of gloomy pessimism with regard to the future of the motor industry, for which the state authorities had no support plan. The official measures taken were drastic and included banning driving on Sundays and holidays, and a freeze on motorway development, not to mention the traditionally high taxes imposed on running a car. Needless to say, this did not encourage investment in the industry in any way, and the biggest drop in production (-26 per cent) occurred between 1973 and 1975. Fiat was at an enormous disadvantage as a result of an almost total lack of interest in the car. This created a technical impasse which undid all the progress made in previous years with the successful launch in 1969 of the 128 and in 1971 of the 127, both of them several years ahead of European competitors. The launch of the Strada signalled a total modernization of the range

BMW 630 – 1976 (D) BMW's Series 6, launched in 1976, included two two-cylinder models. The 630 had a displacement of 2985 cc and an output of 185 hp, while the 633i fuel-injected version (3210 cc) developed 200 hp at 5500 rpm. The top speeds were 210 and 215 km/h (130.5/133.6 mph) respectively.

Audi 100 – 1976 (D) Produced between 1976 and 1982, this car had a series of available engines, from four cylinders (1588 cc) to five (1921 and 2144 cc). In 1978, a five-cylinder 1986-cc diesel was introduced, and a hatchback, the Avant, was also brought out.

Ford Taunus – 1976 (D) The Taunus series was brought out in 1970 and updated in 1976 with a facelift and further additions to the range, which included four-cylinder 1300-cc 59-hp to 2000-cc 98-hp engines, and two-door, four-door and station wagon bodies.

Lancia Gamma Coupé – 1976 (I) Designed by Pininfarina, the Gamma was introduced in 1976 with two four-cylinder horizontally opposed engines, one of 1999 cc and the other of 2484 cc, output of 120 and 140 hp respectively, and top speeds of 185 and 195 km/h (115 and 121.2 mph). Front-wheel drive.

Alfa Romeo Alfasud Sprint – 1976 (I) The first version of the Alfasud, which remained in production until 1983, had a four-cylinder 1186-cc horizontally opposed engine developing 63 hp at 6000 rpm, with a top speed of 150 km/h (93.2 mph). The body was designed by Giorgio Giugiaro.

Volvo 343 – 1976 (S) Mechanically, the 343 was developed from the 66, of Daf origin. With its capacity increased to 1397 cc, the four-cylinder Renault engine now develops 70 hp at 5500 rpm. The De Dïon rear end and transaxle Variomatic transmission have not been changed. Top speed: 145 km/h (90 mph).

and was followed by the Panda in 1980, the Uno in 1982 and the Regata in 1983. Lancia established themselves as the prestige marque in the group, mainly because of the Delta (1976), Prisma (1981) and Thema (1984).

Alfa Romeo, on the other hand, did not earn the success hoped for when they entered the Fiat competition class with the Alfasud in 1972. They were hampered by production problems, however, rather than the product itself, which was excellent in concept. It was not until 1983 that the 33 and

the Arna took over from the Alfasud, and not until 1984 that the 90 replaced the Alfetta.

In Japan, the 1970s was a period of continuous expansion; by 1980 Japan had become one of the world's major automobile producers. Exports played a vital part in this success, increasing from 22.8 per cent of production in 1970 to 50 per cent in 1976. Imports, on the other hand, were almost non-existent (35,295 in 1982), though this was less a result of any protectionist policy (import tax was completely removed on im-

ported automobiles in 1978), than of very strict legislation on pollution, which made converting European and even American cars to satisfy Japanese requirements too complicated.

This kind of commercial aggression of foreign markets naturally led to defensive moves such as the introduction of quota restrictions, adopted unilaterally in France (3 per cent of the market) and in Italy (about 2,000 vehicles). To prevent other countries from following suit, two strategies were developed. First of all, agreements were

made with the countries involved and export ceilings established, as was the case with Great Britain (10 per cent) and the USA, which takes about half the cars that Japan sells abroad. Secondly, as an alternative, or to offset unilateral cuts, production *in situ* in co-operation with local industries was encouraged: typical examples of this were the Nissan–Alfa Romeo and Honda–BL agreements in Europe and General Motors–Toyota in the USA.

Autobianchi A 112 – 1980 (I) Launched in 1969 with a four-cylinder 903-cc engine developing 44 hp at 6000 rpm, the A 112 has a transverse engine, front-wheel drive and independent all-round suspension. It is just 3.23 m (10 ft 7 in) long. About 1,200,000 have been built in fifteen years.

Alfa Romeo 33 – 1983 (I) Based mechanically on the previous Alfasud, the 33 range launched in 1983 includes a 1350-cc 79-hp, and a 1490-cc 86- or 105-hp version. There is also an interesting version with four-wheel drive, designed and produced in association with Pininfarina.

Fiat 127 – 1980 (I) The 127, Fiat's best-selling model between 1971 and 1982, was launched with a four-cylinder 903-cc engine, later followed by 1050- and 1301-cc engines produced at the Belo Horizonte works in Brazil. The 1301-cc diesel came out in 1981.

Mitsubishi Colt – 1984 (J) Launched in 1983 with a range of 1300- to 1600-cc engines, this car takes over from the 1978 model of the same name, which became one of the most popular world-wide. The top of the range is the 1660 Turbo ECI, with a supercharged four-cylinder 1570-cc engine developing 125 hp at 5500 rpm and an electronic fuel injection system.

From the crisis to the 1980s: a small technological revolution

New resources of energy, new types of engines and new materials seemed destined to make for radical changes in the technical form of the automobile in the aftermath of the oil crisis. In fact, although geared to satisfying the demands of new economic and energy situations, the changes made have been very limited and have essentially respected a certain degree of orthodoxy.

The motor industry once again found itself facing the fiercely competitive situation of the second half of the 1970s, with model designs which could not have taken the sudden crisis into account. Although this had previously proved a serious handicap in the United States, Europe and Japan were already producing cars tailored to the new situation, so that the enormous investment involved in making radical changes was not necessary. A good example of such foresight

was the Volkswagen Golf, which had been brought out in early 1974: its general lines must have been planned at least two years before that. This model was a foretaste of the concept of the "world car" which developed at the end of the 1970s, when demand grew, even in the United States, for more compact and economical cars. Six million were built before the Golf was replaced by a new version in 1983, though no significant changes were made even then.

As a result of this economic and political situation, development went ahead in small stages following a three-line general strategy. On one level, the highly competitive nature of the industry has led the major manufacturers to adopt an aggressive commercial approach which is reflected in the periodic modernization of existing models and the extending of ranges with the use of common components (engines, gearboxes, suspension) on a greater number of product lines: all of which is

achieved through traditional techniques to satisfy motorists' new demands of greater economy, reliability and comfort. Parallel to this development, increasing labour costs, and the need for greater flexibility and therefore a rationalization of production methods, have led to the modernization of production plants. The most advanced are increasingly automated and can memorize and assemble different models, with the great advantage of allowing a faster response to market demand and easy re-tooling of the assembly lines for new models. The Mazda plant built in Hufo in 1982 is one of the most modern on an international scale and can assemble nine different body types (pressing, welding and painting) for three basic models, with just 1,800 men and 155 robots. Final assembly takes place on a single line and a total of over 20,000 units per month are produced. Tests are carried out on each new model and special features are being constantly researched, though these are not considered commercially viable until all reliability tests are passed and the price is right. Design methods were the first to be radically modernized: computerized systems were developed to optimize weight reduction and strength on the basic structure, while giving a better body-suspension assembly to ensure maximum road-holding, comfort and silent running.

Such methods allow for a correlation between the design stage of the car and its production, and also accelerate the development of new vehicles by using mathematically simulated models to replace practical testing whenever possible. As a result, the entire process can now take as little as three years, as opposed to the five years needed with traditional techniques.

The different circumstances surrounding the motor industry in the three main areas of production, the USA, Europe and Japan, fall largely into one of three lines of development. In the United States, plants are being modernized mainly to prepare for technical development of the product; in Europe, the industry's efforts are mainly concentrated on increasing competitive capacity by extending its ranges; and in Japan, where the other two requirements are already satisfied, the emphasis lies on the technical evolution of the automobile itself.

The main preoccupations of those involved in the technical development of the automobile today are basically reduced fuel consumption and toxic emissions, and increased safety. In their attempt to find a way of reducing fuel consumption, companies carried out research into perfecting the petrol engine, into developing new forms of power such as gas turbines, hydrogen engines and electric power, and even into

reviving steam; throughout the 1970s, however, diesel became increasingly popular. In 1972 only Mercedes and Peugeot were offering diesel versions, but the advantages of diesel power were very quickly recognized by nearly all the European manufacturers, and the United States and Japan have also shown a certain degree of interest.

As far as safety was concerned, the concept of the safe vehicle, developed in the early 1970s with the ESV (Experimental Safety Vehicle), proved to be Utopian Cars designed for maximum passive safety were too heavy and expensive, as well as being difficult to make compatible with the "ordinary" cars on the road, so efforts to make cars less dangerous have concentrated on accurate research into the parts of the car which crumple easily, to improve active safety.

Another important factor which has influenced the technical development of the automobile has been the regulations issued in the USA and Japan concerning the reduction of toxic exhaust emissions. On the one hand, this has discouraged many European manufacturers from exporting to the United States, because it has proved unprofitable for them to invest in bringing their products in line with American requirements; on the other, it has meant that Japanese companies have had a consistent technological advan-

tage in the development of anti-pollution systems on small- and medium-capacity engines. A typical example is the stratified charge engine, developed by Honda.

World-wide expansion

If 1956 is remembered as the year when more than a hundred million cars were on the road throughout the world, the motor car celebrated its centenary with more than three times that number.

In fact, by 1982, 330 million cars were on the road, 85 per cent of them in economically more advanced countries, that is the USA, Western Europe and Japan. The automobile industry has developed on a more international scale, one of the contributing factors for which has been the closing of the technological gap between the United States and Europe on the one hand, and Europe and Japan on the other. These developments have led to a new concept of the universally acceptable "world car" and to co-operation on a much wider scale, reflected in a complex network of international commercial and technical agreements.

Spain has also arrived on the scene to take its place among the "great" producers of Europe, having made its entry into the automobile industry with the foundation of SEAT in 1949. The company was first formed to build

Talbot Matra Murena S – 1980 (F) The Murena, a development of the Bagheera, has a mid-rear engine and the unusual arrangement of three seats next to each other. Two versions are produced, one with a 1592-cc 92-hp engine and the other with a 2155-cc 118-hp or 142-hp engine.

Saab 9000 – 1984 (S) The Giugiaro-designed 9000 is built on a base produced in conjunction with Fiat. It has a four-cylinder sixteen-valve 1985-cc engine developing 175 hp with the turbocharger, which works on the APC system to prevent detonation. Its top speed is 220 km/h (136.7 mph).

Opel Corsa – 1982 (D) Three engines are ▶ available on this runabout, which was brought out in 1982 in a two- and three-box version, the latter called the TR: 993 cc, 45 hp, 1196 cc, 55 hp and 1297 cc, 70 hp respectively, with top speeds of 140, 152 and 166 km/h (87, 94.5 and 103.15 mph). The suspension is McPherson strut at the front and interconnected longitudinal arms at the rear.

◀ **Seat Ibiza – 1984 (E)** The first original SEAT project uses a line adapted from Giorgio Giugiaro and Sigma series engines designed by the Porsche engineers. It has two four-cylinder engines, one of 1193 cc (62 hp) and the other of 1461 cc (85 hp). The gearbox-differential unit is also made by Porsche.

93

Fiat cars under license, and in 1951 French capital was invested for the Fasa-Renault. In 1984, SEAT ended their thirty-year association with Fiat and made an agreement with Volkswagen to begin building the German company's cars. At the same time they brought out the Ibiza, the first car to be built on a project that was entirely Spanish: Giugiaro was responsible for its lines and Porsche technicians for its engine.

Citroën and Chrysler have also invested in Spain, where the market is protected by strict import controls, and Ford and Opel opened plants in 1976 and 1982 respectively, completing the escalation of production levels, which by 1983 had reached 970,000 vehicles.

Although often limited by the existing economic system, the motor industry has also developed in Communist countries, largely through agreements with the West. Even before the war, there was production in Eastern Europe from the two excellent Czechoslovak companies Skoda and Tatra, although they were unable to keep up the necessary technical standards in the post-war period of independent development. Fiat blazed the trail into Eastern Europe by making an agreement in 1954 with the Yugoslav company Zastava to build a plant for the production of cars based on the Italian 600, 1300, and the 128 and 127 models, the last using an

Skoda Rapid – 1982 (CS) The four-cylinder 117-cc engine of the Rapid develops 58 hp at 5200 rpm and gives a top speed of 153 km/h (95.1 mph) with 0–100 km/h (0–62.1 mph) in eighteen seconds. It has a four-speed gearbox and front disc brakes.

original body (Jugo 45). In 1967, the Polish company FSO began production of the 125, which later developed into the Polonez, and of the 126 in 1972. The most important agreement, however, was for the VAZ Lada, based on the 124, which was produced on Soviet territory in Tolyatigrad, where 700,000 vehicles came off the assembly lines in 1983. Today Russia is the sixth largest automobile producer in the world. Renault and Citroën have also consolidated their interests in the Communist bloc through their agreements with Romania. Dacia produces the 1310, a Renault 12, while Oltcit builds a cross between the Citroën Visa and the GS. Various Western companies also built a large number of plants during the 1960s in South America, where local governments were becoming hostile to increasing imports. Yet although positive development has been made in

Brazil, where Volkswagen, Ford, General Motors and Fiat are firmly established, and to a lesser extent in Mexico, where Volkswagen, Nissan, Renault and the four American companies all operate, the same is not true of Argentina. The great economic instability caused by the oil crisis has, in fact, forced General Motors and Citroën to close their plants, while Chrysler handed its plants over to Volkswagen in 1980. In the same year, Fiat and Peugeot combined their efforts in Sevel, though the French company pulled out in 1981. Ford and Renault are still in production there. Altogether, the three countries produce about a million cars a year, 70 per cent of which are built in Brazil.

The Far East is another area which, though limited in production capacity, is the object of growing interest from the motor industry. Naturally, the market is

controlled by the Japanese companies, which have many production plants in various countries (Indonesia, Thailand, Malaysia, the Philippines and Taiwan), but several Western companies also have interests in the area, including Ford, who built a plant in 1976 for the construction of bodies for the Laser. This is a version of the Mazda 323 and is the first product of an association which began with the acquisition of 24.2 per cent of the Japanese company's shares. South Korea is also taking on a certain degree of importance with its independent Hyundai company, which started out by assembling British Fords and is now producing a range of original cars based on the 1976 Pony and 1983 Stellar, both of which were designed by Giugiaro with Mitsubishi mechanics.

Unlike the other areas where automobile production is developing basically on the initiative of Western or Japanese concerns, Australia has had a large number of cars on the road since the early years of the post-war period. In 1950, it boasted 98 cars per thousand inhabitants, a figure which was beaten only by North America, and even in 1980 the number was higher than the average in the EEC countries. Automobile production began in Australia in 1948 with Holden, a branch of General Motors, who have held the lead until the present day. Very soon afterwards, other companies set out to build assembly lines, and Ford, Chrysler and British Leyland have taken on leading roles. In the late 1970s, imports began flooding in from Japan, then Mitsubishi, Toyota and Nissan eventually began production in Australia. In 1983, a total of 330,000 cars was built.

In Africa, South Africa is the most advanced country with regard to the motor industry, having produced 250,000 units in 1983. This represented total production from a number of small assembly plants belonging to various companies, mainly of European and Japanese origin. A special feature of these companies is that some have been formed from an association of various manufacturers, for example the Sigma marque covers the marketing of Mazda, Mitsubishi and Peugeot vehicles.

Hyundai Pony – 1982 (ROK) The Pony has a Mitsubishi 1238- or 1439-cc engine (80 and 92 hp respectively) and is designed by the Italian Giorgio Giugiaro. This model, which has put the Korean company on the world market, is 4.03 m (13 ft 3 in) long and has rear-wheel drive.

Gianni Rogliatti THE FORMULA ONE YEARS

Formula 1 racing as we know it today in the 1980s was conceived after the Second World War and is the ideal continuation of the race formulas that governed the great international Grand Prix races from 1906 onwards. Since then, attempts have continually been made to find systems by which the courage of the drivers and the skill of the manufacturers might be evaluated, imposing limits on the weight, engine capacity, fuel consumption and the dimensions of certain parts of the car. The formula in force now will last until 1986 and may be considered the most complex, in that it imposes specific restrictions on practically all areas (capacity, weight, size, consumption and the type of fuel).

In 1947, when the sport was struggling to recover from the stagnation and destruction of the war, a new formula was laid down which took into consideration the materials available and fixed a maximum limit on the engine capacity (1500 cc for supercharged engines and 4500 cc for all normally aspirated versions) leaving all the other aspects open, with the sole condition that the cars were to be single-seaters.

The first races were held mainly in Italy, France and Great Britain, while Germany, which was divided and occupied after the war, was not in a position even to think about motor sport.

The vehicles available consisted basically of the old pre-war cars with 4500-cc aspirated engines such as the Talbot Lago and the lower formula supercharged versions such as the Alfa Romeo 158, the Maserati 4 CLT and the British ERA, as well as the Gordinis and a few other marques.

It was during this period that Ferrari appeared on the scene (1945) as an independent marque destined to become one of the front runners in all world drivers' championships from 1950 onwards. In fact it was in that year that a decision was taken to award points to the various drivers on the basis of their positions in each Formula 1 race. This category was formed because a Formula 2 class had been established in that period for single-seaters with non-supercharged engines limited to two liters, as well as other formula groups such as the Junior and the 3, which were gradually added to create a system by which a wider range of young drivers could take part.

The points system worked as follows: eight points were given to the winner, six for second place, four for third, three for fourth, two for fifth and one for sixth place, and a point was also added for the best lap in the race. This system has remained unchanged ever since, except that the point for the fastest lap has been done away with, and the winner is now awarded nine points.

Another feature of the championship was that two or more drivers could change cars (provided they were in the same team) and split the points won by the driver who crossed the finishing line in that car. This made possible the so-called "team games," by which a team manager could win points for his best driver even if he had problems with his own car, as he was given another team member's car to drive. An attempt was also made to harmonize motor sport on both sides of the Atlantic by including the classic Indianapolis 500 in the racing calendar and making it fully valid in the points system, but no American ever came to race in Europe, and only Ascari and Farina hazarded the Indiana "bowl," without great success. It was only years later that the British car manufacturers brought about a revolution with their rear-engined light cars and changed the face of what had, until then, been the exclusive reserve of the American companies.

Ferrari's influence on the evolution of the formula is also worth noting: starting with supercharged engines (the first model 125 was

Cisitalia D46 – 1948 (I) The four-cylinder Fiat engine fitted on this car had a displacement of just 1089 cc, but it could develop 62 hp at 5500 rpm. The illustration shows the car with which Bonetto took part in the race in 1948 in Florence.

Simca-Gordini – 1948 (F) The main qualities of this car were its lightness and good handling. It had a four-cylinder 1433-cc 105-hp Fiat engine and competed well against much more powerful cars, winning the Grand Prix at both Angoulême and Stockholm.

Maserati 4 CLT – 1949 (I) The 4 CLT was one of the major cars of the post-war recovery period and had a perfectly square 1498-cc supercharged engine that developed 240 hp at 7000 rpm. Many were built and sold to private teams.

Ferrari 125 – 1949 (I) Designed by Gioachino Colombo on the basis of experience he had gained at Alfa Romeo (the Alfetta was also his design), the 125 had a 60-degree V12 1496-cc engine. With a single-stage supercharger, it developed 225 hp at 7000 rpm, with a two-stage, 290 hp at 7500 rpm.

Alfa Romeo 158 Alfetta – 1950 (I) Having won all the races in the 1950 championship, the 158 confirmed the soundness of a project that dated back to 1937. It had an eight-cylinder 1479-cc supercharged engine developing 350 hp at 8500 rpm.

BRM V 16 – 1950 (GB) This was an ambitious project which was not repaid with satisfactory results. The best place obtained by this sophisticated monoposto (135-degree V16 supercharged engine with 475 hp at 11,500 rpm) was fifth in the British Grand Prix 1951.

Talbot-Lago – 1950 (F) Reliability and low fuel consumption (about 4 km/liter/11.3 mpg) were the hallmarks of this car's six-cylinder 4485-cc engine which developed 275 hp at 5000 rpm. It had two sparking-plugs per cylinder and three horizontal carburettors.

Alfa Romeo 159 – 1951 (I) Alfa Romeo won its second championship, thanks to the four wins of the 159, a revised and uprated version of the 158, with 425 hp at 9300 rpm. Alfa Romeo withdrew from racing at the end of the season.

HWM 2000 – 1952 (GB) Driven by men who were later to become famous, such as Collins and Moss, this ex-Formula 2 car had a four-cylinder 1960-cc Alta engine developing 150 hp at 6000 rpm.

Ferrari 625 – 1954 (I) In the two years that this car was competing against the Mercedes W 196, the 625 won only two races: the British Grand Prix in 1954 driven by Gonzales and the 1955 Monaco Grand Prix with Trintignant. The four-cylinder 2498-cc engine developed 240 hp at 7000 rpm.

Ferrari 555 Squalo – 1954 (I) With an original side arrangement of its tanks, this car had a four-cylinder 2480-cc engine giving 260 hp at 7200 rpm. Hawthorn won in Spain in 1954 with this car. The later Supersqualo developed 270 hp at 7500 rpm.

Mercedes W 196 – 1954 (D) The German cars won nine of the fourteen races in the 1954/5 season. The W 196, with exposed wheels, was used on the most tortuous circuits, and came first in Germany and Switzerland in 1954.

Gordini – 1955 (F) The Gordini was one of the first cars to use disc brakes and had an eight-cylinder 2498-cc engine which could develop 245 hp at 7000 rpm. In the 1955/6 season it did no better than two seventh places.

Mercedes W 196 – 1954–5 (D) The W 196 in its streamlined version for fast circuits had an eight-cylinder 2496-cc engine with desmodromic valve gear. Its original output was 257 hp at 8200 rpm, but this was increased to 290 hp at 8500 rpm. It had Bosch direct fuel injection and a tubular chassis.

a supercharged V12), the Maranello works very soon decided to stick to naturally aspirated engines and built a new 4500-cc V12. They managed to beat Alfa Romeo on a few occasions, but failed to win the championship in either 1950 or 1951. Alfa Romeo's decision to withdraw, however, was certainly influenced to a certain extent by the presence of the new Ferrari. The 1952 and 1953 world championships were fought out between Formula 2 machines while everyone waited for the cars to come out that were being built to meet the new regulations, due to come into force in 1954.

Nino Farina, driving an Alfetta 158, won the first world championship title in 1950, coming first in three of the six European races and third in another, thus gaining a slight advantage over the Argentinian Juan Manuel Fangio, who had three wins and a sixth place to his credit with the same car. Fagioli was placed third with another Alfetta, the Frenchman Rosier was fourth with the old Talbot, and the young Alberto Ascari was fifth with the new Ferrari. The tables were turned completely in the following year when Fangio won the championship in an Alfetta, but the Ferrari team won second, third, fifth and sixth places with Ascari, Gonzales, Villoresi and Taruffi respectively driving the 4493-cc V12 Type 375.

The 1952 championship saw the triumph of the Ferrari four-cylinder, 2-liter 500, which not only enabled Ascari to win the title, but placed Farina and Taruffi in second and third places. New English marques such as the Cooper and the Connaught also made their début that year, alongside Maserati, Gordini and Osca (built by the Maserati brothers).

In 1953, Ascari repeated his success of the previous year in a Ferrari, but hot on his heels in a Maserati came Fangio, fully recovered from his terrible accident at Monza.

A new formula came into force in 1954: 2500 cc non-supercharged or 750 cc supercharged (though no car manufacturer took up the challenge, and all the cars were built with naturally aspirated engines), any weight and any fuel (this only lasted until commercial petrol became obligatory in 1958). Of course, all the cars were new. Maserati brought out its six-cylinder 250 F, with which Fangio began piling up points towards the title he then won with the "fabulous" eight-cylinder Mercedes W 196, a car with sensational innovations such as desmodromic valve control and direct fuel injection.

Ferrari held its own with a four-cylinder car developed from the 500, Gordini entered its cars and, at the end of the season, the Lancia D 50 made its début with a very unusual feature in its external side tanks. Ascari had "pole position" in the Spanish Grand Prix, but had to retire. In 1955, the Mercedes cars raced home triumphantly, with Fangio world champion

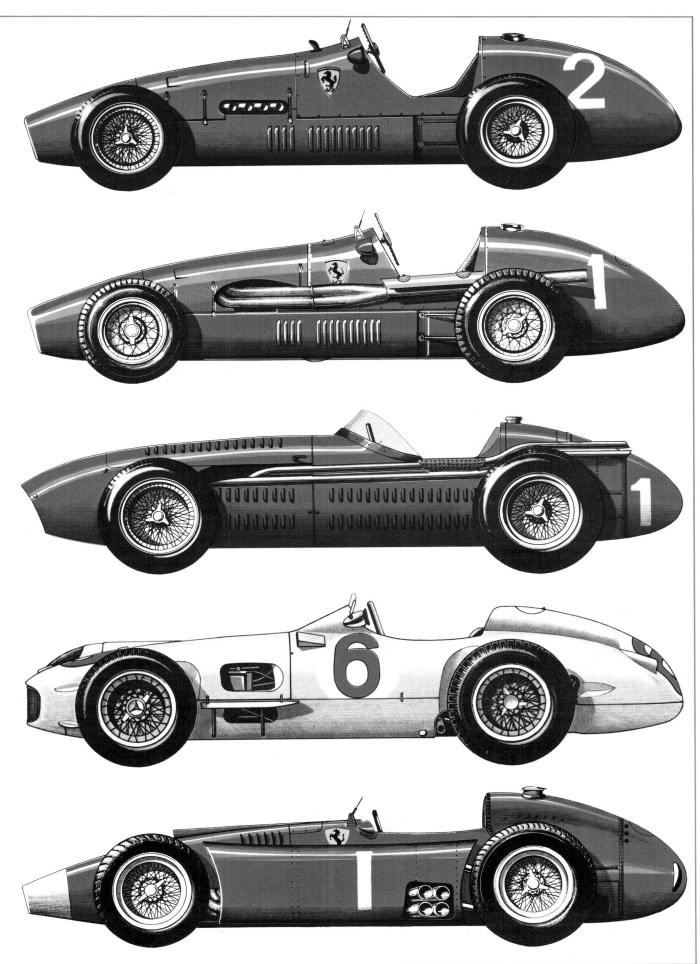

Ferrari 500 – 1952 (I) This car was brought out in 1951 for Formula 2 and had a four-cylinder engine which developed 170 hp at 7200 rpm. It had a tubular chassis and De Dion rear end. With Ascari at the wheel, the 500 won six of the seven races, leaving just one for his team mate, Taruffi.

Ferrari 500 – 1953 (I) Ascari won his second championship in a 500. The output had risen to 185 hp at 7500 rpm. The main feature of this car was its great ease of handling, the result of an excellent distribution of weight, achieved by placing the engine well back and by using transaxle transmission.

Maserati 250 F – 1954 (I) Fangio won the first two races leading to the 1954 championship in this car, which had a six-cylinder 2494-cc engine developing 240 hp at 7200 rpm. It was designed by Gioachino Colombo, but very important contributions were also made by Bellentani and Alfieri.

Mercedes W 196 – 1955 (I) The W 196, built in 1954, was designed to suit all types of circuit and had three different wheelbases; the biggest (2478 mm/98 in) was used throughout 1954 and was reserved for the streamlined version, while the short and intermediate wheelbase were used on the exposed wheel versions.

Ferrari 801 – 1956 (I) When Lancia abandoned racing in 1955 after the death of Ascari, they gave the D 50 to Ferrari, who modified it slightly and renamed it the 801. Vittorio Jano's design included a V8 2485-cc engine developing 250 hp at 8100 nium panels, a feature retained by Ferrari until 1973. The 120-degree V6 1486-cc engine developed 190 hp at 9500 rpm.

once again, followed by Moss. Two Ferrari drivers came in third and fourth places – the young Castellotti and the Frenchman Trintignant.

In 1956, Mercedes disappeared from the scene, having withdrawn fully satisfied from racing, and Fangio won again for the Ferrari team, followed by Moss in a Maserati and Collins in another Ferrari. These Ferraris were a development of the Lancia, tuned up with the help of the grand old master Vittorio Jano, who had designed them. He had returned for the occasion to the "wizard" of Maranello, who had spirited him away to Fiat so many years before and then taken him with him to Alfa Romeo. Lancia withdrew half-way through the 1955 season, stricken with the death of Ascari.

The year 1957 was again Fangio's, this time in a Maserati, proving by his team changes that he could win the title in any car – or was it simply that he always chose the best cars to drive, as Ferrari once maliciously suggested? Moss came second with a British Vanwall, and a certain Jack Brabham made his first appearance, with a strange Cooper car fitted with a motor-pump Coventry-Climax engine. This generated a new philosophy in car construction which led to the domination of the British industry in the Formula 1 arena for many years to come.

In fact, the first race of the 1958 season, the Argentina Grand Prix, was won by Moss in a rear-engined Cooper – the first victory by this type of car since the Auto Union season in the 1930s – but the world championship title went to Hawthorn in a Ferrari 246, an elegant V6 Dino.

In 1959, Brabham asserted his position with the Cooper-Climax and from then on the two names were often seen on the winning car, as the season of the British "assemblers," who made their own cars but bought their engines from others, had begun. Ferrari was second with Tony Brooks.

In 1960, British cars with Climax engines came in like an avalanche: Brabham took the title with a Cooper, followed by McLaren in the same machine, and then by Moss, driving a new Lotus; Ireland came fourth, also with a Lotus, and the American Phil Hill came fifth in a Ferrari.

Meanwhile, in the same year, Formula 2 cars (1500-cc engines) had already taken part by way of experiment and in the following year they became the new Formula 1. They included Ferrari, Cooper and Porsche as well as, after a lapse of many years, the BRM marque – a valiant but unsuccessful British attempt to build a "national" car in the 1950s.

The new formula in 1961 called for non-supercharged engines with a cylinder capacity of between 1300 and 1500 cc, a minimum weight of 450 kg (992 lb) and a series

Vanwall – 1957 (GB) This appeared in the Grand Prix in 1954, but Vanwall could not line up a seasoned team until 1956; in 1957, with Moss, they became Maserati's closest rival. The car had a four-cylinder 2490-cc 262-hp Norton-inspired engine, a tubular chassis and a five-speed gearbox.

Connaught – 1955 (GB) Brooks's victory in the Syracuse Grand Prix in 1955 was the first won by a car with disc brakes. Although it was not valid for the world championship, it was the greatest achievement of this marque. The four-cylinder 2470-cc engine developed 250 hp at 6700 rpm.

Bugatti 251 – 1956 (F) Designed by Gioachino Colombo, the 251 had ultra-modern features such as the transverse mid-rear engine (eight cylinders, 2430 cc, 245 hp) with the drive unit in the center. It made just one appearance at Reims, when it was driven by Trintignant.

BRM – 1957 (GB) Bonnier won the only victory for this car in the Dutch Grand Prix in 1959. It was designed by P. Berthon and was later modified by Colin Chapman. It had a four-cylinder 2491-cc engine which developed 280 hp at 8000 rpm.

Lotus – 1958 (GB) Lotus made its first appearance in the Grand Prix world at Monte Carlo in 1958, when Allison came in sixth and Graham Hill was forced to retire from the race. The four-cylinder 2207-cc Climax engine developed 194 hp at 6250 rpm.

Aston Martin – 1959 (GB) This car was driven by Shelby and Salvadori in the 1959 season, when it was reasonably placed. It had a straight-six 2492-cc engine which gave 280 hp at 8250 rpm.

of safety measures. It was claimed at the time that limiting their cylinder capacity and fixing a minimum weight would ensure that the cars afforded greater protection to their drivers. This was all well and good, but trying to explain why the same men who had advocated a 1500-cc limit in 1961 doubled the engine capacity in 1966, while still claiming it to be in the interests of safety, was slightly difficult. Not only that, but the weight limits were at the same time systematically reduced. While it is difficult to state with any certainty whether safety levels actually decrease with weight, it is a fact that costs increased astronomically because the construction of the chassis progressed from the traditional welded steel structure, to a riveted sheet-aluminium unitary body construction. This was then riveted and glued, and finally composite materials such as honeycomb panels, fiber-glass, carbon and kevlar were used.

In 1961, the championship was won for the first time by an American, Phil Hill, driving a Ferrari. The rear-engined cars from the Maranello works had a triumph at the Belgian Grand Prix, when four set off from the starting grid and won the first four places. In the French Grand Prix, Giancarlo Baghetti won his first race in a Ferrari 156.

The year 1962 saw an important, almost incredible turnabout of events when eight Ferrari executives left the company, including Chiti, the engineer who had designed the rear-engined single-seater. Together they formed a new marque, ATS, which lasted only a short time, though it did make its début in Formula 1. Meanwhile, the engineer Mauro Forghieri came to work for Ferrari as chief designer, a position which he was still holding in the mid-1980s. The British had great success with Graham Hill as champion in his new BRM, Jim Clark came second with the Lotus 25, the first monocoque with a Climax engine, then McLaren in the Cooper-Climax and Surtees in a Lola-Climax. Contrary to popular belief, it was Eric Broadley, the designer of the Lola, who invented the modern monoposto suspension, not Colin Chapman, who adapted it for the Lotus.

The British hold on Formula 1 continued in 1963 with Clark, who won seven out of the ten races and was placed in another two, followed by the BRM drivers Hill and Ginther, with Surtees fourth in a Ferrari. The Climax engine had Lucas indirect fuel injection, which was the only fuel supply system used for twenty years, until in 1983 it was replaced by electronic systems. Porsche also made some occasional appearances before abandoning Formula 1 until 1983, when its participation was limited to its engine.

Surtees became champion in a Ferrari in the difficult 1964 season, with Lorenzo Bandini as his team-mate. By then the teams consisted of

Maserati 250 F – 1957 (I) The 250 F, one of the longest-lived cars in the history of Formula 1, confirmed its absolute superiority when it won the world championship in 1957. The latest modifications included increasing the output to 270 hp at 8000 rpm, fitting a five-speed gearbox and making the body more aerodynamic.

Ferrari 246 – 1958 (I) The 246 was brought out in 1957 for Formula 2 and had a V6 2417-cc engine developing 280 hp at 8500 rpm. Its displacement was increased in the following year to 2497 cc and it became the 256. It won four races with four different drivers: Hawthorn (France, 1958), Collins (Great Britain, 1958), Brooks (France, 1959) and Phil Hill (Italy, 1960). It was the last of the Ferraris to have a front-mounted engine.

Cooper-Climax T 51 – 1959 (GB) This was one of the most important Formula 1 cars in history, as it brought in the rear-mounted engine that has been used ever since on the single-seaters. It made its début in 1957 in Monaco with an engine displacement of just 1960 cc, which in no brought out its enormous potential. In 1959, it was fitted with a Climax four-cylinder 2495-cc engine that developed 240 hp at 6750 rpm, and won the world championship driven by Brabham.

Cooper-Climax T 53 – 1960 (GB) This was a development of the T 51 and had rear coil springs instead of leaf springs as on the earlier version. It still had a tubular chassis, but weighed less. A five-speed gearbox was also fitted. Brabham won five Grand Prix victories and his second championship with this car.

Ferrari 156 – 1961 (I) This was the first car from the Maranello works to have a rear-mounted engine and it enabled Phil Hill to win the world championship. The tubular chassis was covered in aluminium panels, a feature retained by Ferrari until 1973. The 120-degree V6 1486-cc engine developed 190 hp at 9500 rpm.

just two cars per marque, and the "team games" of previous years were no longer possible.

The last year of the 1500-cc formula was another winner for Clark, thanks to his ultra-new Lotus 33, followed by Graham Hill and Stewart in BRMs and Gurney in a Brabham; Honda made their début in Formula 1 and won their first Grand Prix in Mexico at the end of the season.

At Monza, Bandini had also tried out a new Ferrari with a twelve-cylinder, horizontally opposed engine which was later to be used in the Mountain Championship (its engine capacity increased to two liters) and also, of course, in the future 3-liter Boxer. There was even talk of Ferrari conducting research into a fabulous eighteen-cylinder engine with a third bank of six cylinders in between the first two, to make a 3-liter version, but, as far as is known, the idea never got beyond the research stage on the three-cylinder module.

In 1966, a Formula came out due to remain in force until 1986, at least as far as concerns engine capacity: 3 liters naturally aspirated and 1.5 liters supercharged. The weight was originally fixed at 500 kg (1102.3 lb), but was increased to 530 kg (1168.4 lb) in 1969 to allow the car manufacturers to add extra safety measures such as anti-roll bars and fire extinguishers. In 1973, the weight limit was increased to 575 kg (1267.7 lb), again in the interests of safety, to allow leak-proof tanks to be fitted with a unit capacity of 80 liters (17.6 gallons) and a total of 240 liters (52.8 gallons).

These were the years in which a number of aerodynamic changes were introduced to give the cars a better grip for faster cornering – they were fitted with bigger, higher wings which sometimes even overlapped, as on old aircraft. Regulations were, however, eventually changed in order to limit this new development, which was in any case completely illogical if the aim was to maintain some sort of resemblance between racing cars as such and standard series products. In the same period, the two big American tyre manufacturers, Firestone and Goodyear, began research into new types of tyres, following the example of American developments with "dragster" tyres, which were smooth and treadless.

In 1981, new changes were made to the

Porsche 804 – 1962 (D) Porsche were officially involved in Formula 1 for only one season. The car they used had a flat-eight air-cooled engine with output that was increased from its original 180 hp at 9200 rpm to 240 hp at 9300 rpm.

Honda RA 271 – 1965 (J) Japan's entry into Formula 1 took place at the 1964 German Grand Prix with Bucknum. Its only win was with Ginther in Mexico in 1965. The 60-degree V12 1495-cc engine developed 230 hp at 12,000 rpm.

Ferrari 312 – 1966 (I) This car was Ferrari's return to twelve cylinders, in this case with a V configuration and a displacement of 2990 cc. Despite its high output (375 hp at 10,000 rpm), the 312 had only one win, with Scarfiotti in the 1966 Italian Grand Prix.

Ferrari 312 – 1967 (I) Although its output was increased to 390 hp at 10,500 rpm with the adoption of four valves per cylinder, the 312 did not have a successful season, mainly because of the loss of Bandini and the accident which took Parkes out of racing.

Eagle-Weslake – 1967 (USA) This car made its début in the 1966 Belgian Grand Prix with a Climax engine and won the same race in the following year. In 1967 it was fitted with a 60-degree V12 2997-cc engine developing 370 hp at 9500 rpm.

regulations to fix a minimum road clearance of 6 cm (2.4 in) (the cars had to drive over a board of this thickness in the trials) and the weight was increased to 585 kg (1289.7 lb) to allow for side reinforcements to protect both the driver and the tanks. Wankel, diesel and turbine engines were also banned, although they had initially been considered in the regulations with suitable equivalent formulas. Actually, the change in regulations was not necessary, for during the entire period in which the new engines had been acceptable, only Lotus had produced a single-seater with a turbine engine, the 56 B, which raced in 1971.

Lotus also took full advantage of the regulations, for although there was a minimum obligatory road clearance, nothing was said of the side clearances: hence, in 1978, the prolific Chapman invented the famous "sliding skirt" system, which consisted of wings on each side of the center section. These produced an area under the car in which the Venturi principle applied, creating a vacuum which effectively squashed the car on to the track. It was an idea that had already been tried out by Jim Hall on the Chaparral, a sports car with an auxiliary motor that operated a sort of giant vacuum cleaner, whereas in Formula 1 the effect was purely dynamic and created by speed.

The controversial "skirts" were banned in 1982, the year in which the minimum weight began to be reduced as a result of pressure from the British manufacturers, some of whom, not having a supply of more powerful turbocharged engines, tried lightness as a means to remain competitive. The minimum weight had been fixed at 580 kg (1278.7 lb), but in 1983 it fell more decisively to 540 kg (1190.5 lb), though power output continued to rise. In an attempt to increase the efficiency of turbo-engines, which theoretically had unlimited power, it was decided in 1984 to limit the maximum volume of fuel carried on board a single-seater to 220 liters (48.4 gallons) for races over a maximum distance of 320 km (199 miles) (minimum 300 km/186.4 miles). Four-wheel drive was also banned, though it had been tried out by certain manufacturers (Lotus and Cosworth) and was on the programme at BRM. But the alternative was already available to this mechanically complex

Honda RA 302 – 1968 (J) With a 120-degree V8 2987-cc engine (380 hp at 9000 rpm), this car made only one appearance, in the French Grand Prix, which ended tragically with the death of Jo Schlesser and led to the company's withdrawal from racing.

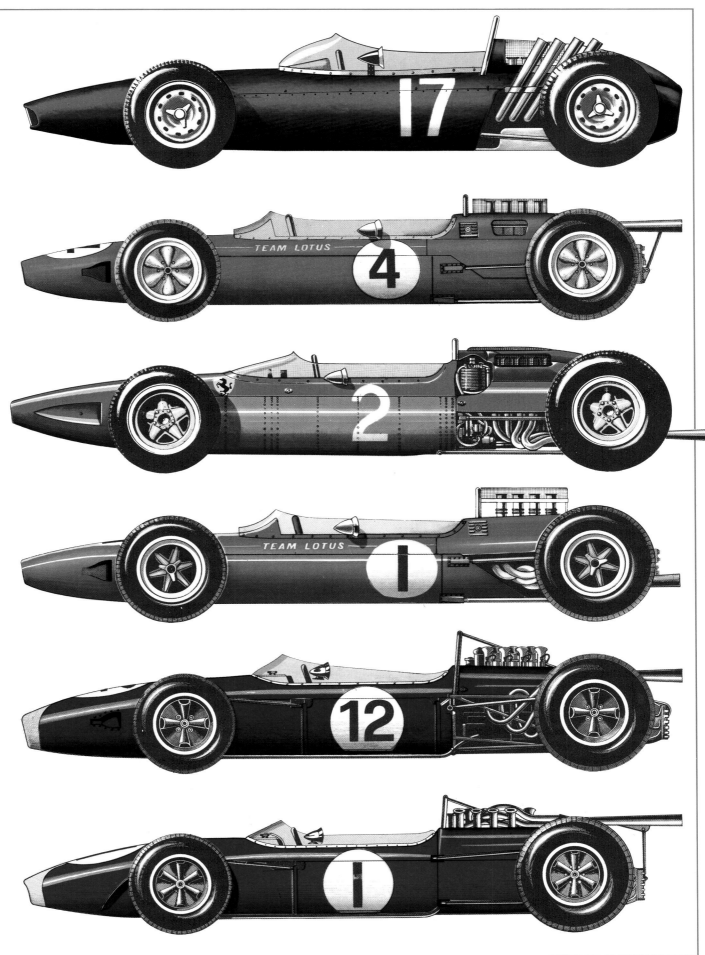

BRM P 56 – 1962 (GB) The P 56 was the winning car of 1962 with a 90-degree V8 1498-cc engine with an output of 190 hp at 10,000 rpm. It boasted sophisticated features such as transistorized ignition, magnesium wheels, triangular arm suspension and coil springs.

Lotus 25 – 1963 (GB) This car rendered all its competitors obsolete at a blow. The monococque frame, aerodynamic line and extremely low weight, combined with a highly reliable Climax eight-cylinder (195 hp at 8200 rpm) engine, made it Jim Clark's winning weapon when he won the world championship in 1963.

Ferrari 158 – 1964 (I) Having changed over to the monococque frame and the V8 engine (1489 cc, 210 hp at 11,000 rpm), the Ferrari 158 enabled Surtees to win the championship. A compact flat twelve was fitted for the 1965 Italian Grand Prix, but the car had no future in Formula 1.

Lotus 33 – 1965 (GB) After a rather unsuccessful start in the 1964 season, this car, a development of the 25, took Jim Clark to the title in the following year. It had a Climax engine which gave approximately 205 hp at 9800 rpm.

Brabham BT 19 – 1966 (GB) The BT 19 was the product of an association between Jack Brabham and Ron Tauranac. It had an Oldsmobile-derived engine built by Repco (90-degree V8, 2996 cc, 315 hp at 7250 rpm) and a tubular chassis. It won the championship, driven by Brabham.

Brabham BT 24 – 1967 (GB) This was another victorious year for Brabham, with Hulme winning another world championship. The engine was again built by Repco, but this time was not based on the Oldsmobile. It developed 335 hp at 8000 rpm, with the same capacity.

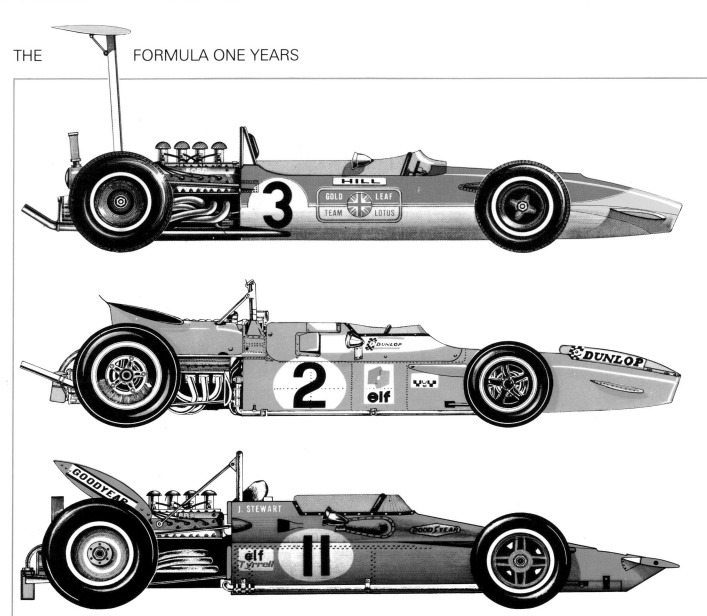

Lotus 49 B – 1968 (GB) This car was built by Colin Chapman and Maurice Philippe around the new Ford-Cosworth engine (90-degree V8, 2995 cc) which was to have a lot of success in Formula 1 up to 1983. It was the first time that the engine (which in its first version developed 415 hp at 9200 rpm) was used also as a bearing part of the structure of the car. Jim Clark won three Grand Prix competitions with this model and also the last win of his career, in 1968, the year that Graham Hill won his second title with a 49.

Matra Ford MS 80 – 1969 (F) Jackie Stewart won the title in 1969 with a good six wins that season in this car. Driven by the increasingly popular Cosworth engine, the MS 80 lasted only a year, because Matra decided to use its own twelve-cylinder engine for the following season.

Tyrrell 003 – 1971 (GB) The structural simplicity and reliability of the Cosworth were the secrets behind the success of this car, which took Stewart to his second world championship. In 1971, Tyrrell won six Grand Prix victories with Stewart driving and another with Cévert at the wheel.

Ferrari 312 B – 1970 (I) The flat-twelve Boxer engine of 2992 cc (445 hp at 11,500 rpm in the original version) appeared for the first time at the début of this car in the South African Grand Prix; it was then used for the next ten years on Maranello cars. The 312 B won the Austrian, Canadian and Mexican Grand Prix races with Ickx driving, and the Italian GP with Regazzoni.

Ferrari 312 B3 – 1973 (I) With ten pole positions and three wins, Ferrari regained their top position in 1974 after a disastrous previous season. Although it had the same name as the former version, this car was substantially different and, with Clay Regazzoni at the wheel, was in a strong position for the title right up to the very last race.

Ligier JS 7 – 1976 (F) This car had a Matra V12 2993-cc engine developing over 500 hp at 12,300 rpm. It achieved good placings in 1977, including Laffite's win in the Swedish Grand Prix, the only win by a car with this French engine.

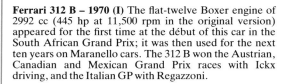

Tyrrell P 34 – 1976 (GB) The original four small-diameter front wheels on this car made no difference one way or the other to the P 34's performance which, with its Cosworth engine, was fairly good. It also had a win in the 1976 Swedish Grand Prix with Scheckter at the wheel.

Brabham BT 45 – 1976 (GB) This was the first product of an association between the British company and Alfa Romeo, who supplied its flat-twelve 2995-cc engine, which developed over 500 hp at 11,500 rpm. Unfortunately, its reliability was uncertain in its first season, when it was raced by Pace and Reutemann. In 1977, it was run with a Cosworth engine.

Brabham BT 46 – 1978 (GB) Brabham went back to using the Alfa Romeo engine on this car, which was driven by Niki Lauda and Watson. It made a name for itself because of its original rear "aspirator," which created an artificial ground effect. The device was later banned, but in the meantime the car won the Swedish Grand Prix with remarkable ease.

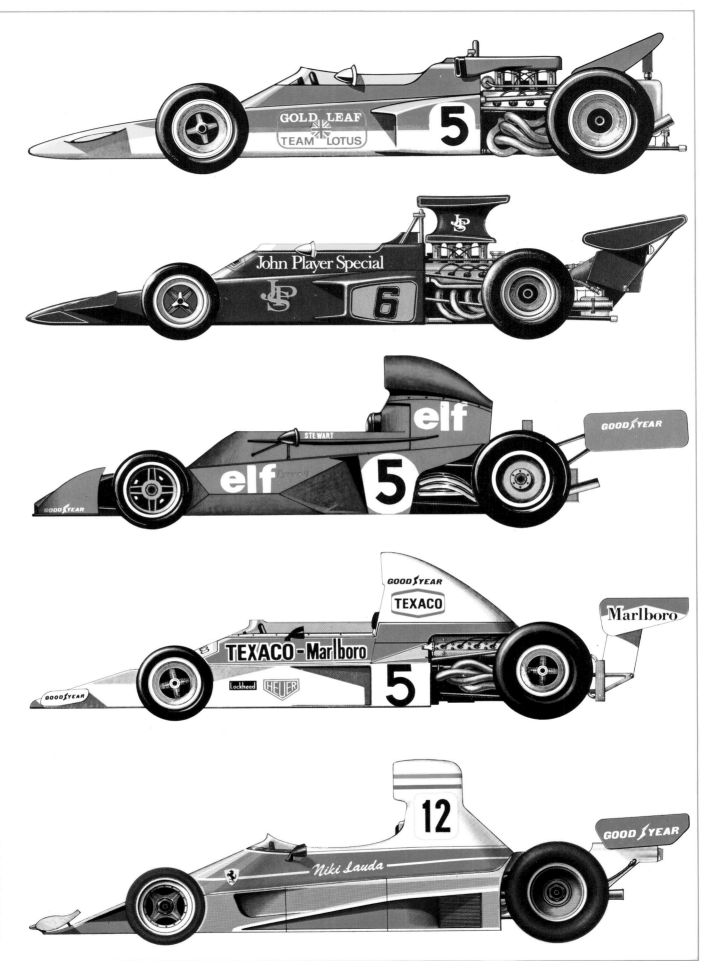

Lotus 72 – 1970 (GB) Raced for six years and with nineteen victories in the world championships, the 72 proved to be the longest-lived of the Formula 1 cars. Chapman and Philippe introduced two important innovations with this car – the wedge shape and side radiators. In 1970, before his tragic accident at Monza, Rindt won five Grand Prix victories, on the strength of which he was awarded the title posthumously.

Lotus 72 (John Player Special) – 1972 (GB) After a relatively quiet season, the 72 became a very keen contender in the following three years. Emerson Fittipaldi drove it to win the championship in 1972, and between 1972 and 1974 it crossed the finishing line first a total of fifteen times. Among its most interesting technical features were inboard front brakes and torsion bar suspension.

Tyrrell 007 – 1973 (GB) The Cosworth had been more or less universally adopted by the British teams; the efficiency of their machines was a result of the improved balance between all the components in the car. The Tyrrell in which Stewart won the championship in 1973 was quite conventional except for its inboard brakes. It was designed by Derek Gardner.

McLaren M 23 – 1974 (GB) This car was used in five seasons from 1973 to 1977, and Fittipaldi and Hunt won the championship with it in 1974 and 1976 respectively. Its long life was also the result of excellent team organization by Teddy Mayer.

Ferrari 312 T – 1975 (I) The adoption of a transverse gearbox and more particularly the overall excellence of Mauro Forghieri's design made this the car responsible for Ferrari's revival. Niki Lauda, who had proved to be an excellent test driver, became world champion with remarkable ease. During this period, the flat-twelve engine developed about 500 hp at 12,200 rpm.

103

McLaren M 23 – 1976 (GB) Distinguishing features of the M 23, apart from the fact that it did away with the aspiration snorkel, were improved suspension geometry, improved aerodynamic line and the adoption of a six-speed Hewland gearbox. The output of the Cosworth engine at the time was about 470 hp at 10,500 rpm.

Ferrari 312 T2 – 1977 (I) This car, which had also been used the previous season, when Lauda missed the title by sheer bad luck, now took him to win the championship for a second time. The T2 was used up to the beginning of the 1978 championship and was driven by Reutemann as well as Lauda.

Lotus 79 – 1978 (GB) Continuing in Colin Chapman's innovative vein, this car was the first to take advantage of the ground effect conveyed by center wings on the body – a feature then copied by all other cars until 1982. Andretti won the title after winning six races, and Peterson took another two for the Lotus team.

Alfa Romeo 179 – 1979 (I) The aerodynamically highly developed 179 had the 60-degree V12 engine (520 hp at 12,300 rpm) that was already in use on the Brabham BT 48, against which it competed very well after its début in the Italian Grand Prix. It was driven by Depailler and Giacomelli in the following year, but although very fast proved too unreliable.

Renault RS 11 – 1979 (F) Although the turbo engine was introduced by Renault in 1977, it was not until the 1979 French Grand Prix that it won a race. The RS 11 had a V6 1492-cc supercharged engine which could develop over 500 hp at 11,000 rpm. It was at its most competitive with a two-stage supercharger.

Ligier JS 11 – 1979 (F) After the Matra engine had been done away with, the Ligier-Cosworth came out and won both the Argentinian and the Brazilian Grand Prix, taking first and second place in the latter with Laffite and Depailler, who also won the Spanish Grand Prix. However, the car was never in the running for the title.

Brabham BT 48 – 1979 (GB) The Brabham-Alfa Romeo association finally ended after the Italian Grand Prix in 1979. In their last season together, their best results were only two fourth places, and they were forced to withdraw from twenty-three of the twenty-nine races they had entered. The 48's only win was with Lauda at the Imola Grand Prix, but it did not count towards the world title.

Tyrrell 009 – 1979 (GB) Designed by Maurice Philippe, the 009 was a good solid car which never achieved more than a supporting role. It was driven by Pironi and Jarier in 1979, coming in third four times, twice for each driver; the two finished joint tenth in the championship placings.

McLaren M 28 – 1979 (GB) The M 28 was one of the first attempts to build a "sandwich" frame instead of the traditional riveted panels. It was never really competitive and was replaced by the M 29, with a conventional frame, half-way through the season.

Fittipaldi F6A – 1979 (BR) Despite a great investment of money and effort on the part of the sponsor, Copersucar, who also gave the car its name, Emerson Fittipaldi never really managed to build a competitive car. The F6 was very conventional and won only one point in the 1979 championship.

Lotus 80 – 1979 (GB) The product of increased research into the ground effect, this car was entered in only three races (Spain, Monte Carlo and France) before it was finally abandoned. Features of the 80 were the overall streamlining of the tail and the extension of the wings right to the back of the car.

Williams FW 07B – 1980 (GB) After winning five times in the 1979 season, the FW 07B helped Jones win the championship in the following year. It was an exceptionally reliable car, which came in the first six places twenty-one times, with five wins by the Australian and one by Reutemann.

Renault RS 01 – 1977 (F) The turbo age began with Renault's début into Formula 1. They entered the RS 01 in the 1977 British Grand Prix, showing a justifiable faith in turbocharging, with an equivalent ratio of 1:2 in comparison with the capacity of reliable, naturally aspirated Cosworths and Ferraris. The V6 1492-cc engine developed about 500 hp at 11,000 rpm in its original version, which had a single turbocharger. Time has shown, however, that there is much room for improvement on this figure.

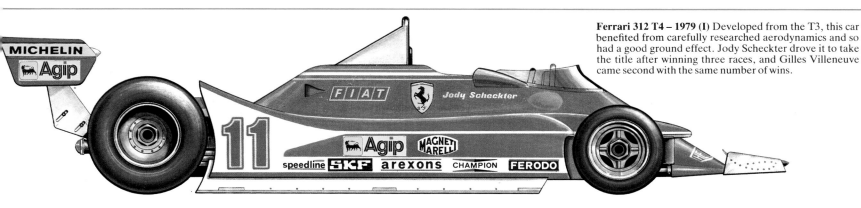

and very expensive system, in that tyres had been perfected to the extent of reaching a traction coefficient of over two, so very high torque could be applied, thus solving the problem of traction with just two drive wheels.

The new formula approved in 1966 has clearly been the longest-lived: it will remain in force until 1986, at least in respect of the engines. It has also led to a proliferation of extremely interesting technical developments. With their wide experience of this engine capacity, Ferrari were immediately in a position to line up a V12 and follow it up with a flat 12 which represented the ultimate in mechanical refinement.

The British, deprived of the reliable Coventry-Climax having decided not to compete in the new formula despite having carried out research into "doubling" the 1500-cc by making a 3-liter V16, were at a loss. Some increased the capacity of their 2-liter engines, while Brabham, with the help of the Australian Repco company, built a V8 based on a standard series engine.

BRM launched into a programme of building a grandiose sixteen-cylinder engine made up of two overlapping banks of eight cylinders, with passages in the cylinder heads for the drive shafts to transfer the drive to the front wheels from a single, rear-mounted box containing the gears and the differential. This engine was used by BRM and Lotus, but the real turning-point came with the entry of Ford, who commissioned Cosworth, already well known for its work in Formula 2 engines, to build a Formula 1 V8 at the cost of £100,000. This engine has led to the success and growth

of a large number of manufacturers, and contributed to wins in over a hundred and fifty Formula 1 Grand Prix races, from the 1967 Dutch GP onwards, won by Clark in a Lotus 49. Their original objective was to have a 3-liter engine, smaller and lighter than the Ferrari twelve-cylinder, which could develop at least 400 hp, and the engine built by designer Keith Duckworth has since developed over the years to produce over 500 hp.

It was Renault, however, who made the greatest innovation. They decided to use the new and more difficult system of supercharging for their return to Formula 1 racing, in which they had played a major role in the pioneer days; for two years, their mechanics battled against all odds, until finally, in 1979, they had their first victory with Jabouille in the French Grand Prix.

The other companies were quick to react and follow suit as soon as it became clear that supercharged engines could produce more horsepower, even though they ran on petrol. Ferrari were the first to use supercharged engines, followed by BMW, who developed their own series block and created an incredible four-cylinder engine, winning a world title in its second year.

Ferrari, Honda and Porsche, like Renault, built six-cylinder engines. Alfa Romeo produced a V8 engine and there may yet be others before the Formula ends.

Maximum output of the turbos has increased gradually from about 500 hp up to the 650–700 hp used in races and the 900 hp used for qualifiers when the battle for pole position is the major problem.

At the start of the 1966 season, a curious thing happened: the traditional manufacturers Ferrari, Maserati and BRM found themselves in difficulties, so Jack Brabham and his car, designed with masterly skill by his friend and fellow Australian Ron Tauranac, won four of the nine races on the programme and took the title with an engine developed from a standard series version with rods and rockers. Then, in 1967, his team mate, the New Zealander Denny Hulme, repeated the feat with an improved engine which had overhead camshafts.

It was only the last race, the Mexico Grand Prix, which decided the hotly challenged 1968 world championship. Graham Hill, in a Lotus Ford 49 B, finished ahead of McLaren and Oliver, and regained the title after six years. The British driver won six Grand Prix victories altogether, as did Stewart, who finished second in a Matra ahead of Hulme (McLaren), Ickx (Ferrari), McLaren (McLaren) and Rodriguez (BRM). In 1969, Jackie Stewart took the lead right from the start in a Matra Ford MS 80, and after Monza (the eighth in the series) the world championship was practically in the bag. Following Stewart, who won six of the races, three consecutively, came Ickx, who classified in a Brabham with two 'wins, McLaren (McLaren), Rindt (Lotus), Beltoise (Matra) and Hulme (McLaren). The Ford-engined cars were unrivalled: eleven wins and good results in all the trials. Then came 1970, a tragic season for the Austrian Jochen Rindt who, after five Grand Prix wins in a Lotus 72/2, was killed in a practise accident on 5 September at the Monza Grand Prix. For his

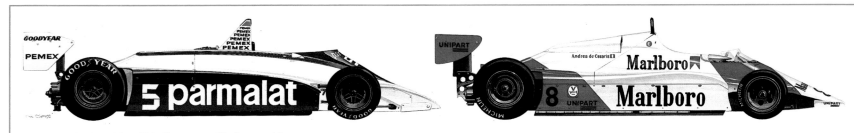

Brabham BT 49 – 1981 (GB) Piquet won his first world championship with the BT 49, with a lead of just one point over Reutemann. The BT 49 was a very sophisticated car with an alloy frame and carbon brake discs. It was also extremely light, just within the permitted minimum, and had an original (and illegal) hydraulic system which lowered the body to ensure contact between the ground and the sliding skirts.

McLaren MP 4 – 1981 (GB) This single-seater, which was the first to adopt highly advanced technology and design in its carbon-fiber frame, was in the running for the 1982 championship for a long time, despite the fact that its engine was still naturally aspirated.

Williams FW 08 – 1982 (GB) With a naturally aspirated engine, a conventional chassis and only one victory to his credit, Keke Rosberg took the last championship to be won with the eight-cylinder Cosworth, whose scant 500 hp was now small beer in comparison with the Ferrari, Renault and BMW turbos.

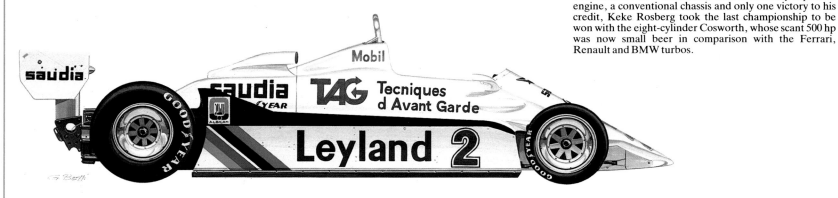

previous victories Rindt was awarded the championship title posthumously. This success for Lotus was completed with Fittipaldi's win in the USA. Ickx came second in the world championship ahead of Regazzoni (both in Ferrari 312 Bs), fourth was Hulme (McLaren) and fifth was Brabham (Brabham) jointly placed with Stewart (Tyrrell).

In 1971, the Ferrari 312 B2 started out as favourite, but only won the opening South African Grand Prix and again in Holland. The title went once more to Stewart who, in a Tyrrell 003, won six of the races. Peterson finished second with the March 711; third was Cévert (Tyrrell); Ickx, the first of the Ferrari team, came equal fourth with Siffert (BRM); and sixth was E. Fittipaldi (Lotus). Regazzoni and Andretti came seventh and eighth with the other two Ferraris.

In 1972, Emerson Fittipaldi won his first world title in a Lotus 72, after three wins at Brands Hatch, Zeltweg and Monza in the second half of the season. Stewart did not gain sufficient points with his wins in the last two races and finished second ahead of Hulme, Ickx, Revson and Cévert-Regazzoni (joint sixth). No other driver before Fittipaldi had ever won the title at only twenty-five years of age.

In 1973, Fittipaldi set off to a good start with two wins, but then Stewart began a relentless race to the top, winning five Grand Prix victories and his third world title before retiring at the end of the season. The Brazilian

finished second in a Lotus 72, third was Peterson, fourth Cévert, fifth Revson and sixth Hulme. Seven outright wins were not enough for Lotus to beat Stewart. The Ford engines continued to dominate.

In 1974, Ferrari made a comeback with the 312 B3s driven by Lauda and Regazzoni. The latter, who was in the lead only four races before the end, battled to the last with Fittipaldi, who pulled off the title in the final moment with his McLaren M 23. Scheckter (Tyrrell) came third, Lauda fourth, Peterson fifth and Reutemann sixth.

No rival succeeded in toppling Ferrari in 1975. The Austrian Niki Lauda regained the title for Maranello after eleven years, winning five of the Grand Prix races (another was won by Regazzoni, the second in the Ferrari team), and came in ahead of Fittipaldi and his McLaren at the end of the season. Third was Reutemann (Brabham), fourth Hunt (Hesketh), fifth Regazzoni and sixth Pace.

Lauda also looked set to carry off the laurels in 1976, but after five wins he had a terrible accident at the Nürburgring. He missed the next two Grand Prix races, but later returned to Monza with his Ferrari 312 T2 to challenge James Hunt, who had six wins to his credit with his McLaren M 23. The title was decided at the last race in Japan, where Lauda was forced to retire because of the rain. Hunt won the title by one point and Scheckter came third ahead of Depailler, Regazzoni and Andretti.

In 1977, Niki Lauda regained the title,

winning three Grand Prix events in his Ferrari 312 T2 and becoming certain of victory two races before the end of the season (in which he overtook Villeneuve). The Italo-American Andretti in his Lotus 78 had four wins, but this was not enough to oust the Austrian; he was also beaten to second place by Scheckter in a Wolf WR3. Reutemann was fourth, Hunt fifth and Mass sixth.

Mario Andretti was unrivalled in 1978, winning six races in his elegant black "ground-effect" Lotus 79, to take the title ahead of his team mate Peterson, who died tragically at Monza. Reutemann, with the Ferrari 312 T3, won four Grand Prix victories and finished third ahead of Lauda in a Brabham; fifth was Depailler (Tyrrell) and sixth Watson (Brabham).

In 1979, Ferrari regained its position at the top through the efforts of Jody Scheckter, who won the title, and the performance of Villeneuve, who finished second. With three wins each, these two Ferrari drivers confirmed the superiority of the 312 T4. Jones came third in a Williams FW 07, Laffite fourth (Ligier), Regazzoni fifth (Williams) and Depailler sixth (Ligier) jointly with Reutemann (Lotus).

The year 1980 saw the triumph of the Williams FW 07B, with which Alan Jones won the championship and Carlos Reutemann came third. Piquet finished second with a Brabham BT 49 which won three races. Jones won five of the races (the last two being the decisive ones) and Reutemann had one victory

McLaren MP 4/2 – 1984 (GB) The MP 4/2, star of the 1984 season with Lauda and Prost, has a V6 Porsche-designed engine with a displacement of 1499 cc, two KKK turbochargers and Bosch electronic fuel injection. It develops about 670 hp. The chassis is made entirely of composite materials and is built by the American Hercules Company which specializes in aerospace.

to his credit. Laffite came fourth ahead of Pironi and Arnoux, while Ferrari only managed tenth place with Villeneuve, with no outright wins.

The 1981 world championship was decided at the last race in Las Vegas, where Piquet came fifth with his Brabham BT 49C and took the title by just one point from Reutemann who came eighth in a Williams FW 07C. The Argentinian had started off the season in grand style, but trailed back at the end, unable

to beat Piquet. Jones was third in another Williams followed by Laffite (fourth in a Talbot-Ligier), Prost and Watson.

In 1982, a Williams FW 08 came first, driven by the Finn Keke Rosberg, who won only one Grand Prix but was the most consistent driver of the season. Ferrari paid dearly that season, first with the tragic death of Villeneuve (Zolder) and then with Pironi's accident at Hockenheim. He was finally placed second in the championship, followed by Watson

(McLaren), Prost, Lauda and Arnoux.

The 1983 championship was one of the most exciting, decided on the last race at Kyalami, where three contenders were competing for the title: Prost (Renault RE 40), Piquet (Brabham-BMW) and Arnoux (Ferrari 126 C3). Piquet (the third to cross the finishing line) was crowned world champion (the first in a turbo) ahead of Prost, Arnoux, Tambay, Rosberg, Watson and Cheever (joint sixth). Ferrari won the manufacturer's title.

Ferrari 126 C4 – 1984 (I) The 126 C4 is a logical development of the C3 of 1983. It is distinguished by a chassis which is the product of the most advanced composite material technology, using a nomex honeycomb with carbon fiber and kevlar panels. The engine has also been improved: it is about 15 kg (33 lb) lighter and has been fitted with a Weber-Marelli electronic injection system.

THE EVOLUTION OF DESIGN: THE COACH-BUILDERS

Between the wars, America, France and Great Britain were the main coachbuilders, designing bodies for the most prestigious cars of the time; after the Second World War, automobile design developed as a phenomenon that was almost exclusively bound up with the work of Italian designers, who over a period of thirty years radically altered the concept of what was beautiful. Cars with extraordinarily rich and sumptuous lines were ousted by those incorporating the latest features of new technology. The nature of the work of the coachbuilder has evolved from a concern with mainly aesthetic aspects to a more integrated view of the car, taking into consideration production methods and the application of new materials. Besides producing marvellous show prototypes in their design studios, displaying the full range of their talents, designers have more often than not been closely involved in the development of everyday cars, which have the same, though less spectacular, aesthetic value as the prototypes. It is no coincidence that many of the world's major manufacturers have used Italian designers and built up relationships which have established long-standing traditions: an example of such a union is the thirty-year association between Peugeot and Pininfarina, not to mention the importance of Giorgio Giugiaro's designs to the success of Volkswagen in the 1970s and Fiat in the 1980s. The father of the Italian school of design was Battista "Pinin" Farina. After leaving his brother Giovanni's company in 1930, Farina founded the Carrozzeria Pininfarina, which produced a series of bodies incorporating highly innovative features such as the angled windscreen and the horizontal radiator grille. The Cisitalia coupé, brought out in 1947, was the first expression of his highly personal style, one that was both simple and functional, in contrast with current trends which sought to "amaze" everyone with lines that were as complex as they were irrational. In 1952, Pinin Farina was employed by the American company Nash for the design and production of a small run of Healey coupés and roadsters. The same year also saw the start of his highly successful association with Ferrari, the first fruit of which was the Cabriolet 212 Inter. In 1953, production started on the Fiat 110 TV coupé, the first in a long line of custom-built cars sold through the Turin company's network. Two fascinating new roadsters, the Alfa Romeo Giulietta and the Lancia Aurelia B 24, came out in 1954 and 1955 respectively.

From 1955 onwards, Peugeot also began a regular association with Pinin Farina, while BMC employed him for two very successful cars, the Austin A 40 in 1958 and the 1100 in 1962. In 1963, the Sigma, a new car designed with passenger safety in mind, went on to the drawing board. Battista Farina's work has received official recognition on many occasions, including his nomination as an honorary member of the Royal Society of Arts in London and the conferment of the *Légion d'honneur* by the French president, Charles de Gaulle.

"Pinin" died on 3 April 1966, but his son Sergio and son-in-law Renzo Carli have continued his leading role in the evolution of motor car design. In November 1967, the aerodynamic BMC saloon was unveiled and, although only one was built, it started a general trend towards this type of body, which has since been used on countless successful motor cars. In 1975, the Camargue was the first of the Rolls-Royce's series-produced cars to be designed by a foreign designer.

The first body designed and produced by Giovanni Bertone was the Spa 9000 in 1921. Before the war, close connections had already been established with the major Italian companies, particularly Lancia; after the war, the company went into operation on an international scale under the direction of Giuseppe Bertone, who had taken over from his father. In 1952, Arnolt in Chicago commissioned Bertone to design the body for their own coupé on an MG chassis, but it was not until two years later that his reputation was firmly established with the Alfa Romeo Giulietta Sprint, for which 40,000 bodies were built in thirteen years. This was followed by the series-production of other highly successful bodies such as the NSU Prinz coupé, the Alfa Romeo Giulia GT, the Fiat Dino

Cisitalia 202 (Pininfarina) – 1947 (I) This car, built on Fiat 1100 parts, introduced a new style which was to set the standard for post-war sports cars, and itself won recognition with a place in the Museum of Modern Art in New York. Its aerodynamic lines enabled it to reach a top speed of 160 km/h (100 mph) with an output of only 50 hp.

coupé, the Fiat 850 spyders, the Simca 1200 coupé, the Alfa Romeo Montreal, all the Lamborghinis, the Fiat X1/9, the Dino 208 GT 4 and the Lancia Stratos.

Also produced were futuristic prototypes characterized by a completely functional design. These included two Chevrolets: the Testudo, built in 1963 on a Corvair Monza base; and the Ramarro, built in 1984 on a Corvette base. Bertone also designed a number of highly popular cars including the Volkswagen Polo of 1975 and the Citroën BX of 1983.

In 1968, Giorgio Giugiaro founded Ital Design, who besides creating prototypes have supplied major manufacturers with new model designs backed up by a full cost analysis and outlines for the necessary production tools. Among their designs are the Alfasud and the Alfetta GT for Alfa Romeo; the first versions of the Passat, the Scirocco and the Golf for Volkswagen; the M1 for BMW; the Panda, the Uno and the Lancia Delta, Prisma and Thema for the Fiat group, as well as the Ibiza for Seat. The Korean company Hyundai commissioned Giugiaro to design the Pony and the Stellar, while Isuzu in Japan series-produced the Piazza, originally designed as a show prototype – the "Ace of Clubs."

An important design feature in Giugiaro's estimation is passenger space. The Lancia Megagamma of 1978, for example, gave rise to the concept of the "space wagon," immediately taken up by many of the Japanese manufacturers, who have produced normal-sized cars, but with a generous amount of headroom to make the best possible use of space.

Before creating Ital Design, Giorgio Giugiaro had begun work

Cadillac (Pininfarina) – 1954 (USA) The association of Cadillac and Pininfarina, which dates back to the early 1950s, was made official in 1984 with a production agreement for the building of a prestige cabriolet body by Pininfarina in Turin. This particular two-seater, with its distinctive circular radiator grille, was built in 1954.

109

Aston Martin DB4 GTZ (Zagato) – 1959 (GB) A small production run of this car, based on the DB4, was built with an aluminium body which reduced its weight to only 1250 kg (1.25 tons), 200 kg (441 lb) less than the original. Acceleration was staggering, thanks to the 314 hp developed by the British six-cylinder 3670-cc engine: 0–100 km/h (0–62.14 mph) in only 6.5 seconds.

Chevrolet Rondine (Pininfarina) – 1964 (USA) The soft lines of this two-seater coupé conceal the powerful mechanics of the Corvette Sting Ray, possibly the best known of the American sports cars. The V8 5346-cc engine developed 250 hp SAE at 5500 rpm. The car was a one-off model.

Fiat 2300 S (Pininfarina) – 1964 (I) This one-off by Pininfarina was built on Fiat 2300 S mechanics with a six-cylinder 2279-cc engine which could develop 150 hp SAE. It was a highly elegant vehicle with features that are still used today, for example the arrangement of the secondary light bank under the bumper.

Alfa Romeo Carabo (Bertone) – 1968 (I) Launched at the Paris Motor Show in 1968, the Carabo used Alfa Romeo 33 mechanics with a V8 1944-cc engine. Particularly innovative features were the wedge shape, accentuated by the continuous bonnet–windscreen line, and side windows following the line of the body.

Maserati Boomerang (Ital Design) – 1972 (I) Designed by Giorgio Giugiaro, this one-off model was brought out at the Geneva Motor Show in 1972. The base mechanics were from the Maserati Bora, an eight-cylinder 4.7-liter mid engine. Characteristic features of this car were the very drawn-out square lines, with large areas of glass.

Ferrari 250 P5 (Pininfarina) – 1968 (I) This was a one-off competition model based on the line developed through the prototypes of the 1960s, starting with the 250 P in 1963. The engine was the classic Ferrari V12 of 2953 cc. An original feature was the casing of the headlamps in a single light bank on the front. The same line, slightly simplified, was used for an Alfa Romeo 33 brought out in 1969.

in 1956 at the Fiat Design Center; in 1959 he joined Bertone and then went on to Ghia. Originally founded as a coachworks in 1915 by Giacinto Ghia, this company has belonged to Ford since 1972. Ghia's greatest successes were to come after the Second World War, when Chrysler, Ford and Packard commissioned various "dream cars," together with designs for a number of production vehicles such as the Chrysler 300 in 1958 and the luxurious 6.4-liter model of 1960, of which about fifty were built. Various European companies have also used Ghia: for example, for the Renault Floride of 1958, the Volvo P 1800 of 1959, the two Volkswagen Karmann-Ghia coupés and the Fiat 2300 coupé. In 1967, the American company Rowan bought out the holdings and made Alessandro De Tomaso président. The Mangusta (1967) and the Pantera (1970) were the only new models brought out during this

Mazda MX-81 Aria (Bertone) – 1981 (J) Built on Mazda 323 Turbo mechanics (1490 cc, 130 hp), the MX-81 was the product of a joint venture between the Japanese company and Bertone of Italy, and was introduced at the Tokyo Motor Show in 1981. Its major innovations included an original driver's position with a "track" steering wheel (a band made up of rubber blocks sliding around the instrument panel). The instruments were also replaced by a colour monitor.

period, both with Ford V8 engines and designed by Giorgio Giugiaro. Since the acquisition of Ghia by Ford, many experimental cars have been produced, including the "Probe III" on which the Sierra was modelled.

Other Italian coachbuilders have also earned themselves a place in the history of automobile design. The Milanese company

Zagato, in operation since 1929, is famous for its sports cars: these include the Aston Martin DB4 GT of 1958 and the Alfa Romeo TZ and TZ2, which combined many important sporting features, as well as many GTs, which have been produced in small series on the more common Lancia and Alfa Romeo mechanics. The interesting Alfa Zeta 6 prototype

came out in 1983 on Alfa 6 mechanics with a long, streamlined aluminium body.

Having gained valuable experience with Giovanni Farina, Giovanni Michelotti set up for himself in 1949 and has designed many series-produced cars for companies all over the world. Among them are the 1960s BMWs, from the small 700 to the 1602–2002 saloons, including the original touring version; and Japanese cars such as the Isuzu Skyline Sport and the Hino Contessa. Michelotti was also responsible for the designs of the Triumph Herald, the TR 5 and the Fiat 850 coupé, and has produced a number of one-offs on Ferrari mechanics, for example the Meera S in 1983, which was based on the 400i.

The Milanese company Touring, which went out of operation in 1966, also made a substantial contribution to the evolution of automobile design. The company was founded in 1926 and produced

Lotus Esprit (Ital Design) – 1972 (GB) Introduced as a one-off in 1972, the Esprit went into regular production in 1976, entering its third series in 1983. It is available in a four-cylinder 2174-cc 160-hp version and also supercharged – as the Esprit Turbo, launched in 1980 – developing 210 hp with the same engine.

Audi Quartz (Pininfarina) – 1982 (D) This prototype combined the sophisticated four-wheel drive mechanics of the Audi Quattro with a futuristic body built with totally new materials: the bumpers, for example, use the technique of the sandwich structure in kevlar; the bonnet, roof and side panels are aluminium, the door panels are steel sandwich, the rear window is polycarbonate, and the seat and steering wheel frames are carbon fiber.

The need for further progress in the economical running of cars and increasing demands on the part of the customer for improved comfort and safety have urged the major companies to probe more deeply into the applications of new technology. The early 1980s have been characterized by the launch of a great number of prototypes designed for new materials and new methods of series production.

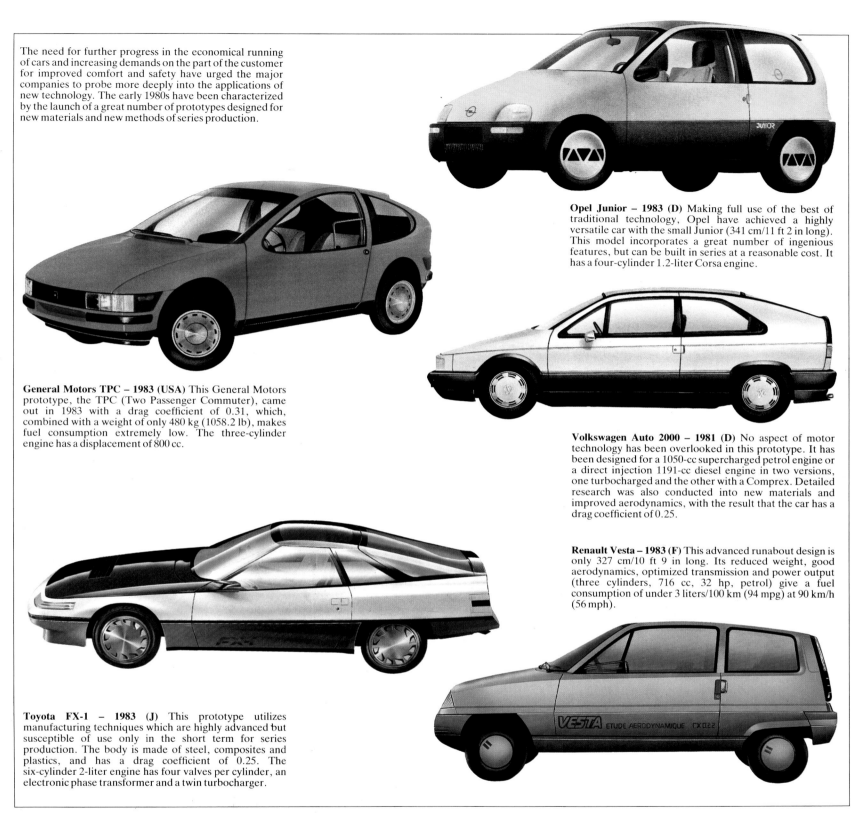

General Motors TPC – 1983 (USA) This General Motors prototype, the TPC (Two Passenger Commuter), came out in 1983 with a drag coefficient of 0.31, which, combined with a weight of only 480 kg (1058.2 lb), makes fuel consumption extremely low. The three-cylinder engine has a displacement of 800 cc.

Toyota FX-1 – 1983 (J) This prototype utilizes manufacturing techniques which are highly advanced but susceptible of use only in the short term for series production. The body is made of steel, composites and plastics, and has a drag coefficient of 0.25. The six-cylinder 2-liter engine has four valves per cylinder, an electronic phase transformer and a twin turbocharger.

Opel Junior – 1983 (D) Making full use of the best of traditional technology, Opel have achieved a highly versatile car with the small Junior (341 cm/11 ft 2 in long). This model incorporates a great number of ingenious features, but can be built in series at a reasonable cost. It has a four-cylinder 1.2-liter Corsa engine.

Volkswagen Auto 2000 – 1981 (D) No aspect of motor technology has been overlooked in this prototype. It has been designed for a 1050-cc supercharged petrol engine or a direct injection 1191-cc diesel engine in two versions, one turbocharged and the other with a Comprex. Detailed research was also conducted into new materials and improved aerodynamics, with the result that the car has a drag coefficient of 0.25.

Renault Vesta – 1983 (F) This advanced runabout design is only 327 cm/10 ft 9 in long. Its reduced weight, good aerodynamics, optimized transmission and power output (three cylinders, 716 cc, 32 hp, petrol) give a fuel consumption of under 3 liters/100 km (94 mpg) at 90 km/h (56 mph).

a few Weymann-type bodies and a series known as the "Flying Star," an exceptional speedster on Isotta Fraschini and Alfa Romeo chassis. It then developed a special "superlight" structure consisting of a tubular steel frame covered with aluminium panels. This was used for many of the Alfa Romeo sports cars of the 1930s, including the 6 C 1750 GT which won the Mille Miglia of 1932 in the Tourer

class. In 1940, BMW won overall first in the Mille Miglia with a 328, also by Touring, who had produced the body for the Ferrari 815 Superlight for the same event. The most important post-war cars included the Lancia Flaminia convertible of 1959, the Maserati 3500 GT which was produced with great success between 1957 and 1964, and the Lamborghini 350 GTV, brought out in 1963.

In 1974, the name "Vignale" was another to disappear from the sides of prestige cars after a very active existence inaugurated twenty-eight years before by Alfredo Vignale who had gained valuable experience with Pininfarina. The Ferraris of the early 1950s were among the most important cars he produced, including the model built for the Panamerican race of 1953. Many

people commissioned Vignale to design bodies for their own Ferraris (of which 140 one-offs were produced), Rolls-Royces, Cadillacs, BMWs and Mercedes.

Various companies including American Motors and Daihatsu also commissioned Vignale to design prototypes for cars that later went on the assembly lines. The company was taken over by Ghia in 1969.

Michele Fenu THE MANUFACTURERS' CHAMPIONSHIP

The manufacturers' or constructors' championship has been for many years the most important alternative to the drivers' world championship. It has become an inseparable blend of spectacular competition, with rivalries between companies that have passed into history and legend, suspense-filled duels between great drivers, and, inevitably, tragic accidents.

In the thirty-one years of its stormy but fascinating history, the championship has brought into the limelight both small manufacturers and the giants of the European and American industry – Ferrari, Mercedes, Aston Martin, Jaguar, Porsche, Ford, Matra, Alfa Romeo, Maserati, Lancia, Cobra and Abarth. It has also encouraged – particularly in the early days, when computers and simulators were still part of science fiction – the development of specific features of the motor car such as aerodynamics, tyres, brakes, electrical systems and electrically operated accessories.

The competition was first held in 1953, three years after the birth of Formula 1, and was inspired by races of the 1920s and 1930s, particularly the Le Mans 24 Hours. Its aims were not dissimilar: to contribute to the recovery of an industry that had been weakened by war, and to stimulate technical progress and public interest. The idea was to race cars which were similar to standard series products or developed from them.

The competition is today coloured by the notion of a trial of endurance and has often confused the public because it has brought together cars very different both in appearance and also performance, and has countless times modified and altered its already obscure

regulations. For example, it has sometimes used the same classification to cover cars which are in fact markedly different from each other. From 1953 to 1961, the manufacturers' championship was limited to sports cars; from 1962 to 1965, it accepted only GTs in three classes (up to 1000 cc, 2000 cc and over 2000 cc); in 1966, it was for two-seater racing cars; from 1967 to 1971, for sports cars and prototypes; from 1972 to 1975, for sports cars only; from 1976 to 1981, for silhouettes (with a parallel world championship for sports cars in two of those seasons); and finally, since 1982, it has been open to group C cars, which are effectively prototypes.

A total of 288 races were run between 1953 and 1983, equivalent to approximately half a million kilometers (300,000 miles). Ferrari and Porsche have won most races and titles, and have been the most consistent participants. Ferrari withdrew in 1974, as they were unable to concentrate on both Formula 1 and the manufacturers' championship at the same time; however, Porsche still takes part.

The story of the world championship began on 8 March 1953 with the Sebring 12 Hours and, after seven races, Ferrari finally won ahead of Jaguar and Aston Martin. The cars had front-mounted engines and rear-wheel drive, very long bonnets and narrow tyres. Jaguar caused a stir at Le Mans by fitting disc brakes. The drivers were Fangio, Farina, Villoresi, Taruffi, Castellotti, Hawthorn and Collins, but it was Giannino Marzotto who won the first victory for Maranello at the Mille Miglia on 26 April in Brescia.

In 1954, Ferrari retained the championship, having battled against Lancia, Osca and Jaguar. No limits had been imposed on engine

capacity, and Ferrari lined up both 3- and 5-liter cars (twelve cylinders, 350 hp).

The year of the Le Mans tragedy, 1955, seemed to toll the end of the championship. Mike Hawthorn, coming down the grandstand straight, decided to pull into the pits with his Jaguar. To do this, he braked and swerved, blocking Macklin's Austin Healey, into which Levegh's Mercedes hurtled at 250 km/h (155.34 mph). The engine split off and the car crashed into the crowd, killing many spectators. The race, however, continued, and Hawthorn came first. On the wave of reaction that followed the accident, it seemed that racing would be banned, but the clamour eventually died down and Switzerland was the only country in fact to prohibit the sport. The title went to Mercedes, who were one point ahead of Ferrari, mainly thanks to the efforts of Stirling Moss. After their victory, Mercedes withdrew the splendid eight-cylinder 2979-cc 300 SLRs, which they had based on their Formula 1 cars, and retired from motor sport altogether. Ferrari's star began to shine again and the company went on to win the championship in three consecutive seasons, beating Maserati after a series of duels.

Another tragedy shook the racing world in 1957, when the Marquis de Portago's Ferrari came off the road and ploughed into a group of spectators. De Portago, his co-driver Nelsen and ten other people died. For the Mille Miglia, won by Taruffi, this was the end.

In 1958, the Maranello works had no rivals and won four out of the six races (the other two went to Aston Martin), making famous the name of the splendid 3-liter 300-hp Testa Rossa. The rules limited the engine capacity to 3000 cc, and so put the big Maseratis and

Ferrari 375 Plus – 1954 (I) This car had a V12 4954-cc engine with a maximum power of 350 hp at 6000 rpm. Gonzalez and Trintignant won with it at Le Mans, and Maglioli drove it to win the Panamerican. The engine was developed from the 4523-cc engine fitted on the 375 MM and the 375 America in 1953.

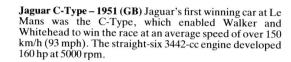

Ferrari 166S – 1949 (I) The 166S driven by the Chinetti-Seldson team won the first of the nine Ferrari victories at Le Mans. The V12 1995-cc engine developed 150 hp at 7000 rpm with a single shaft valve gear and one Weber carburettor. The average speed of the winners in the 24 Hours was over 132 km/h (82 mph).

Jaguar C-Type – 1951 (GB) Jaguar's first winning car at Le Mans was the C-Type, which enabled Walker and Whitehead to win the race at an average speed of over 150 km/h (93 mph). The straight-six 3442-cc engine developed 160 hp at 5000 rpm.

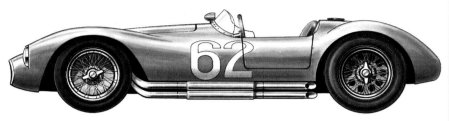

Cunningham C4R – 1952 (USA) Briggs Cunningham was one of the stars of the Le Mans 24 Hours from 1950 to 1953. The C4R was used in 1952. It had a Chrysler V8 5425-cc engine developing 300 hp at 5200 rpm, and came in fourth, driven by its builder and Spear. In 1953, it won the Sebring 12 Hours.

Maserati A 6 GCS – 1953 (I) This car was entered mainly by private teams and was used in various versions from 1947 onwards. It won races both as a sports car and in Formula 2. The straight-six 1978-cc engine developed 130 hp at 6000 rpm.

Ferrari 750 Monza – 1954 (I) This car had a four-cylinder 2999-cc engine (260 hp at 6400 rpm), but is mainly remembered for the accident at Monza in 1955, in which Ascari was killed, and for Gendebien's negative comments about its roadholding. It had a De Dion rear end and transaxle transmission.

Alfa Romeo 6C 3000 – 1953 (I) This was the last of the Alfa Romeo sports cars until the company went back into racing in the 1960s with the 33. It came second in the Mille Miglia, but all three cars entered in the Le Mans were forced to retire because of mechanical trouble. The six-cylinder 3495-cc engine developed 246 hp at 6500 rpm.

Jaguar D-Type – 1955 (GB) Brought out in 1954, this model won the 1955 Le Mans 24 Hours with Hawthorn at the wheel, at an average speed of 172 km/h (107 mph), and repeated its success in 1956 and 1957. The six-cylinder 3442-cc engine developed 295 hp at 5750 rpm. The tubular chassis was reinforced with sheet panels.

115

Lancia D24 – 1954 (I) This car was designed by Jano and was particularly successful in road races such as the Panamerican, which it won in 1953 with Fangio at the wheel, and the Mille Miglia, won in 1954 with Ascari. The V6 3284-cc engine (reduced to 3099 cc for the Panamerican) developed 265 hp at 6200 rpm.

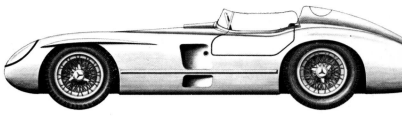

Mercedes 300 SLR – 1955 (D) Mercedes won its only World Manufacturers' Championship with this car. The 300 SLR came first in the Mille Miglia, the Tourist Trophy and the Targa Florio with Stirling Moss driving, while Fangio won the Nürburgring and the Swedish Grand Prix. It had an eight-cylinder 2979-cc engine (310 hp at 7500 rpm).

Ferrari 290 MM – 1956 (I) The 290 MM made its début with a V12 3490-cc engine (32 hp at 7300 rpm) and won the Sebring 12 Hours with Fangio and Castellotti driving. It also won two consecutive Mille Miglias, the 1956 with Castellotti and the 1957 with Taruffi. Ferrari took the World Manufacturers' Championship in both those years.

Maserati 450 S – 1957 (I) The star of the 1957 season, this car won the Sebring 12 Hours with Fangio and Behra driving, and the Swedish trials with Moss. It was entered at Le Mans with a closed body designed by Mike Costin. It was in the running for the title, but then had to withdraw at the last race in Venezuela. The V8 4477-cc engine developed 400 hp at 7000 rpm.

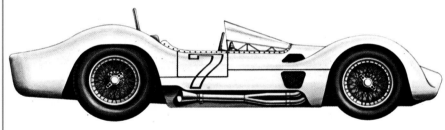

Maserati 61 (Birdcage) – 1960 (I) The Birdcage had an original chassis made up of reduced-diameter tubes which made it possible to cut the weight down to just 585 kg (1290 lb). It was brought out in 1959 with a four-cylinder 1989-cc engine (mod. 60) developing 200 hp at 7800 rpm, but then had a 2890-cc engine (mod. 61) fitted which developed 250 hp at 6500 rpm. It won its first race at Rouen and was extremely successful in the USA.

Rover-BRM – 1963 (GB) Driven by a turbine engine developing about 150 hp, the Rover-BRM took part unofficially in the 1963 Le Mans 24 Hours, driven by the Graham Hill–Ginther team. If it had been classified, it would have been placed eighth, after covering the 4172.91 km (2592.92 miles) at an average speed of over 173 km/h (107.5 mph). In 1965, a closed version came tenth in the same race.

Jaguars out of the running. However, Porsche, who were producing small sports models, began to appear in the placings.

In 1959, Aston Martin managed to break into the Ferrari era. They won three races out of five, as against Ferrari's single win, while Porsche won its first championship race at the Targa Florio. Stirling Moss amazed everyone at the Nürburgring when, in an epic chase, he "burned off" the Ferraris of Gendebien and Brooks.

Aston Martin retired after this, though Ferrari continued and won the 1960 championship ahead of both Porsche and Maserati, who gave a thrilling performance with the Type 61 in spite of poor reliability. As the sports cars were about to make way for the

GTs, Ferrari won again in the following season, in three groups based on their engine capacities. It was a parade of Ferraris, with the 3-liter V12s and the Dino 246 – the first Ferrari to have a rear-mounted engine. Phil Hill, von Trips, Bandini and Gendebien had nothing to fear from Porsche – nor from the fragile Maseratis.

The GTs had a free run in 1962 when, according to the organizer's intentions, the competing cars should have been production models. But, although sports cars had been thrown out through the door, they came back in through the window so to speak, when the hybrid class of prototype or experimental GT was born. The necessary hundred models of these built to gain homologation had slightly

higher windscreens and a better interior finish than the sports car, although the sound of the engine at full revs was the same. Ferrari used V6, V8 and V12 engines, mounted both at the front and the rear, with 2–4-liter capacities (the limit had been raised) and came first in its class (over 2000 cc). The same happened again in 1963, when the confusion surrounding the championship was increasing. The GT calendar included rallies and hill climbs, and attention therefore centered mainly on the prototypes. Ferrari dominated in this group with the 250 P, a car which was ahead of its time with a 3000-cc V12 engine, independent front suspension and a rear-mounted engine. Ferrari used a series version of the prototype, the 250 Le Mans, at the end of a successful

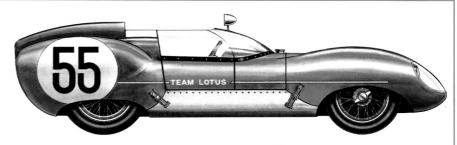

Aston Martin DB3S – 1955 (GB) The DB3S was built both in a roadster and a covered version, and came second in the fifty-fifth and fifty-sixth editions of the Le Mans 24 Hours, with Frère–Collins and Moss–Collins respectively. It had a six-cylinder 2922-cc engine developing 210 hp at 6000 rpm and a four-speed gearbox, and could reach almost 230 km/h (143 mph).

Lotus Mk II – 1956 (GB) This Lotus, designed by Mike Costin and Colin Chapman, should be remembered among the small-capacity prototypes which raced in the 1950s. It had a 1098-cc Coventry-Climax engine developing 75 hp at 6500 rpm, and came first in its class in 1956 and 1957, among other places at Le Mans.

Ferrari 250 TRS Testa Rossa – 1958 (I) With a displacement of 2953 cc, this twelve-cylinder Ferrari could develop 300 hp at 7500 rpm. In 1958, it won the Sebring 12 Hours, the Targa Florio and the Le Mans 24 Hours, and repeated its success in the following year with a double in the American race. It was used in competitions until 1960.

Aston Martin DBR 1/300 – 1959 (GB) Derived from the 1/250 which had raced at Le Mans in 1956, this car won the World Manufacturers' Championship when Stirling Moss won three of the five races. It came in first and second at Le Mans. The six-cylinder 2922-cc engine developed 265 hp at 6400 rpm and had transaxle transmission.

Ferrari 246P – 1961 (I) This was the first rear-engined sports car to be produced at Maranello and had a V6 2417-cc engine developing 280 hp at 8500 rpm. It made its début at and won the Targa Florio, with von Trips and Gendebien. In the 1961/62 season, Ferrari used both twelve-cylinder front-mounted engines (developed from the Testa Rossa) and also V6, V8 and V12 rear-mounted engines in their cars.

AC Cobra – 1964 (USA) The AC Cobra won the GT category of the World Manufacturers' Championship in 1964 and 1965 with a V8 4727-cc engine that gave almost 380 hp at 7000 rpm. A coupé version was also built which had one of its best results when it was placed fourth in the Le Mans 24 Hours, with Gurney and Bondurant.

Ferrari GTO – 1962 (I) The Gran Turismo Omologata was the last front-engined car used by Ferrari in the endurance trials. Driven by a V12 2953-cc engine, it won many victories in the GT category, winning in its class at Sebring in 1962. Outright wins included Daytona and the Tourist Trophy in 1963.

Ferrari 250 P – 1963 (I) Brought out in 1963 with the classic V12 2953-cc engine (300 hp at 7800 rpm), this car was later fitted with increased-capacity engines of 3286 cc (275 P), 3967 cc (330 P) and 4390 cc (365 P). It achieved good results up to 1965, winning the Le Mans 24 Hours in two consecutive years, 1963 and 1964.

Ferrari 330 P2 – 1965 (I) In 1965, Ferrari used this car driven by two V12 engines, either a 3967-cc (330 P2) developing 410 hp at 8200 rpm, or a 3286-cc (275 P2) developing 350 hp at 8500 rpm.

Alfa Romeo 33.2 – 1968 (I) Derived from the spyder that had done so well in the previous year, particularly in hill climbs, the 33.2 made its début at the Daytona 24 Hours where it came fifth with the Andretti–Bianchi team. It had a V8 1995-cc engine (a 2510-cc version was also entered in the Targa Florio and at Brands Hatch), developing 270 hp at 9000 rpm. It was used with a short- or long-tailed body, depending on the type of circuit. It gained an excellent fourth place at Le Mans with Giunti–Galli.

Alfa Romeo TZ2 – 1966 (I) The star of the GT category, Alfa Romeo achieved excellent results first with the TZ (1963) and then the TZ2, winning in its class at Sebring, Nürburgring, Le Mans and the Tour de France in 1964. A feature of the TZ was its tubular chassis. The engine was the classic four-cylinder 1570-cc used on the Giulia, which at first developed 112 hp but was later increased to 170 hp at 7500 rpm.

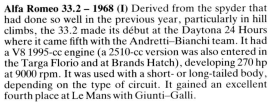

Ford GT 40 – 1968 (USA) The début of the GT 40 (V8, 4262 cc, 350 hp approx.) saw Phil Hill make second best time at the Nürburgring 1000 km in 1964. Although it proved to be very fast, the car obtained no other important results for the rest of the season. It was modified under Shelby and, with the 4728-cc 385-hp engine also fitted in the Cobra, won its only victory, in 1965 at Daytona, with Miles and Lloyd. The World Manufacturers' Championship was won in 1966 with the 6997-cc Mk II, which came first at Daytona, Sebring and Le Mans. When the 5000-cc limit was imposed for the Sports class, the car was abandoned, although it was later used by semi-official teams such as John Weyr's Gulf-Mirage. It was given new Weslake heads and a displacement of 4942 cc, and in the 1968/69 season won important races such as the 1968 Le Mans 24 Hours with the Ickx–Redman team.

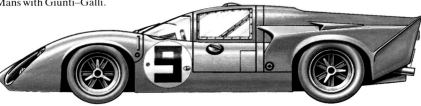

Lola T70 Mk III – 1969 (USA) Admitted to the Sport category in 1968, the T70 had a V8 4990-cc Chevrolet engine with rods and rockers, and developed 430 hp, later increased to about 500 hp. The only significant win it had came with a Mk III prepared by Roger Penske, with Donohue–Parsons, in the 1969 Daytona 24 Hours.

▼

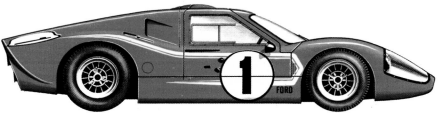

◄ **Ford Mk IV – 1967 (USA)** From 1965 to 1967, there were no limits on cylinder capacity, and so Ford built seven-liter cars based on developments of the GT 40. The Mk IV was used in their final year of direct involvement in racing. With its V8 6980-cc engine, developing 530 hp at 6200 rpm, it won the Sebring 12 Hours with McLaren and Andretti, as well as the Le Mans 24 Hours with the Gurney–Foyt team at a record average of over 218 km/h (135 mph).

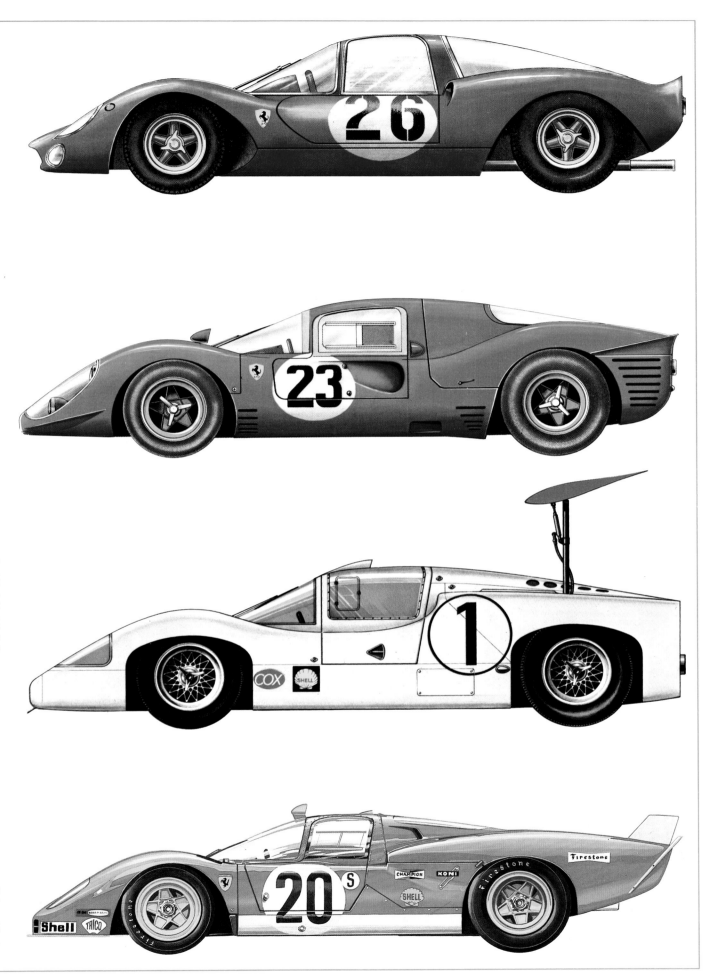

Ferrari Dino 206 S – 1965 (I)
The V6 Dino prototype series was brought out in 1965 with the 166 S and the 206 S. The former had a 1592-cc engine giving 175 hp at 9000 rpm, and won fourth place at the Nürburgring with Bandini–Vaccarella (the track officials wanted to check its displacement at the end of the race). The 206 S (1987 cc, 205 hp at 8800 rpm) was used in the European Hill Climb Championship, won by Scarfiotti.

Ferrari 330 P4 – 1967 (I)
Between 1966 and 1967, Ferrari was involved in a historic duel with Ford, and although the American company beat the Ferrari 330 P3 (V12, 3968 cc, 420 hp) in 1966, the 330 P4 (V12, 3989 cc, 450 hp at 8200 rpm) regained the title the following year. At their début, the Bandini–Amon and Parkes–Scarfiotti P4s won first two places in the Daytona 24 Hours (third was the P3/4 of Rodriguez–Guichet). Bandini–Amon then won at Monza, followed by a series of excellent placings, including second and third at Le Mans behind the Ford Mk IV. Both the P3 and the P4 were available in closed and open top versions.

Chaparral 2F – 1967 (USA)
The 2F had a V8 6997-cc Chevrolet engine which could develop about 570 hp at 6500 rpm, and was noted for its rear variable-angle wing connected to the suspension and its three-speed automatic gearbox. It won the Brands Hatch 500 in 1967 with the Phil Hill–Spence team.

Ferrari 512 S – 1970 (I) The 512 S had a V12 4993-cc engine developing 550 hp at 8500 rpm (later increased to 585-600 hp at 8800 rpm) but won only the 12 Hours at Sebring in 1970 with Andretti–Giunti–Vaccarella. The fact was that Ferrari could do nothing against the Porsche 917, which, although not more powerful, was better balanced. In the following year, with the improved 512 M given to private teams, nothing changed, although some models, such as Roger Penske's 512 M Sunoco, did prove competitive.

Porsche 908.03 – 1970 (D) Porsche brought out this flat-eight 2997-cc prototype, which developed 350 hp at 8400 rpm in its original form, in 1968 and a year later it was the car that won the World Manufacturers' Championship. It was raced that year in both an open-top version (908.02) and a closed one with a long tail. The ultra-light 908.03 was launched in 1970 and entered by Porsche on the most winding tracks, as these were not really suitable for the big 917s. With it they won both the 1970 Targa Florio and the 1970–1 Nürburgring 1000 km.

Porsche 917 LH –1970 (D) Although Porsche had prepared long-tail versions of the 917 which could do up to 400 km/h (248.5 mph), it was a short-tail (Kurtz) version which won at Le Mans in both 1970 and 1971. The 1971 season was in fact another period in which the company clearly demonstrated its superiority, with seven wins, three of them by the Rodriguez–Oliver team, while Marko and Van Lennep won the 24 Hours in France at an average speed of over 222 km/h (138 mph).

Porsche 917 – 1970 (D) After a test season in 1969 when the car showed great problems of handling, Porsche passed the 917 over to private teams including John Wyer's, who had suggested major aerodynamic changes. In 1970, this German sports car totally dominated the World Manufacturers' Championship and won four races with Rodriguez–Kinnunen, two with Siffert–Redman and one at Le Mans with Attwood–Herman. The flat-twelve air-cooled engine with central drive take-off was increased from 4494 cc in 1969 to 4907 cc. It was uprated from 540 hp at 8400 rpm to about 600 hp at 8400 rpm.

▼

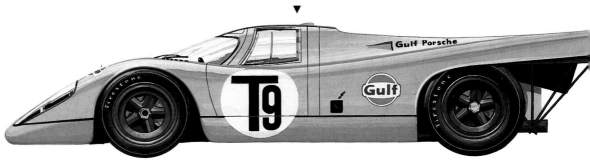

Alfa Romeo 33 TT 3 – 1972 (I) After the 33.3 had won a good three races in 1971, the new version with a tubular chassis did very well against the Ferrari 312 Ps. The V8 Alfa Romeo had a displacement of 2994 cc and developed 440 hp at 9800 rpm. It came fourth at Le Mans with the Vaccarella–De Adamich team.

Ferrari 312 P – 1972 (I) After an amazing test season in 1972, the 312 P won all the races it entered. The flat-twelve engine was developed from the F1 (2991 cc, 450 hp). Ickx, Andretti, Regazzoni, Redman and Peterson were the drivers who contributed to its winning the World Manufacturers' Championship.

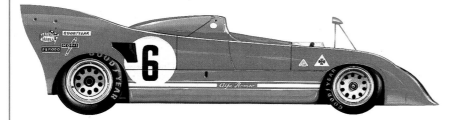

Alfa Romeo 33 TT 12 – 1974 (I) The 33 TT 12 had been unable to compete with the better-tested Matras in the 1974 season (and company policy also intervened), but in the following year Alfa won the title with seven wins out of nine races. The flat-twelve 2995-cc engine developed 470 hp (later increased to over 500 hp) at 11,000 rpm.

Matra Simca 660 – 1970 (F) Matra entered both the 650, brought out the year before, and the new 660 in the 1970 season's races. The V12 engine developed from their F1 had a 2999-cc displacement and an output of 430 or 450 hp, depending on the race. Its best results were two fifth places at Monza and Brands Hatch. The 660 was also raced in 1971 and 1972, but without much success.

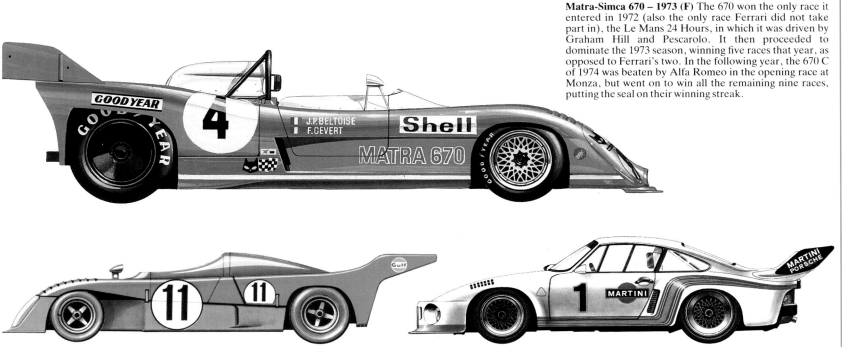

Matra-Simca 670 – 1973 (F) The 670 won the only race it entered in 1972 (also the only race Ferrari did not take part in), the Le Mans 24 Hours, in which it was driven by Graham Hill and Pescarolo. It then proceeded to dominate the 1973 season, winning five races that year, as opposed to Ferrari's two. In the following year, the 670 C of 1974 was beaten by Alfa Romeo in the opening race at Monza, but went on to win all the remaining nine races, putting the seal on their winning streak.

Gulf-Ford GR 8 – 1975 (GB) A new regulation was introduced for the 1975 Le Mans 24 Hours (not valid for the World Manufacturers' Championship) based on precise fuel consumption limits with a minimum of twenty laps between any two refuelling stops. The leader from the second hour onwards was the John Wyer team's Gulf-Ford, driven by Ickx and Bell, who crossed the finishing line first after having covered over 4594 km (2855 miles). The GR 8 was fitted with the classic Ford Cosworth V8 2995-cc engine developing about 370 hp.

Porsche 935 – 1976 (D) Developed from the 911 series, this car had a flat-six, 2857-cc turbocharged engine developing 630 hp at 8000 rpm. The 935 won the title in Group 5 of the Silhouettes championship, while another Porsche, the 936 Turbo (2142 cc), won the Group 6 Sports class title in the same year.

season for Scarfiotti, Surtees and Bandini.

The ever-successful Ferrari factory which, though small, had become quite a legend, created other problems, particularly for those who tried in vain to buy it out, as was the case with Ford. On 20 May 1963, Ford were on the brink of taking over Ferrari, until second thoughts at the last minute on the part of Enzo Ferrari brought the whole thing to a halt, and Henry Ford swore revenge. The first moves in what was to become known as "the battle of David and Goliath" began in 1964. A new Ford GT, based on a British car, the Lola, and driven by a V8 engine, appeared at the Nürburgring 1000 km, but the championship was restricted to GT prototypes and Ferrari's model was homologated. Porsche led in the 2-liter class and an American team associated with Ford, A.C. Cobra, was going strong with its roadsters and GTs.

Cobra actually won the manufacturer's trophy, which was once again limited to the usual three groups of GTs, but Ferrari won the

prototype trophy. The battle proved to be an exciting one between Europe and the USA: it was a fight between Ferrari – still independent at the time and not in the Fiat group – and Ford, aided by a futuristic car, the Texan Jim Hall's Chaparral, which had a Chevrolet (General Motors) engine and automatic transmission. Ferrari lined up with its 330 P2 3300-cc and 4000-cc prototypes, and Ford with its GT 40s (semi-monocoque frame, 4200 cc). The Americans wanted to prove that it was possible to beat Ferrari, who reigned supreme over the sport, with "souped up" series engines giving improved performance. However, at the Le Mans 24 Hours, where the challenge reached its peak, the Maranello works had an incredible triumph with the 250 Le Mans, while the official cars withdrew, together with the 7-liter monsters put on the track by Detroit.

Ford did not give in, however, and finally succeeded in beating Ferrari in 1966. After a series of very inconclusive trials, they reached

Le Mans with Ferrari ahead in the championship with thirty-six points while Ford was second with twenty-six. The winner in France would take the title, and this time the powerful GT Mk II, giving about 500 hp, won the contest, with three cars taking the first three places in the hands of McLaren–Amon, Miles–Hulme and Bucknum–Hatchesson. The 330 P3s of Scarfiotti, Rodriguez and Bandini were knocked out and Ford won the championship by two points.

Ferrari recovered the title in 1967, though Ford won at Le Mans. Porsche continued to increase their engine capacities, and Alfa Romeo appeared on the scene with a 2-liter V8 33, as did Matra, with its small-engined Alpine Renault coupés.

In 1968, the rules of the championship were changed. The competition was opened up to sports cars up to 5000 cc and prototypes up to 3 liters. Ferrari left, and Ford beat Porsche, who had brought out the 3000-cc 908. Alfa brought out its 2500-cc 33.

Renault-Alpine A 442B – 1978 (F) The Renault Alpine only just missed winning the Le Mans 24 Hours in 1977, after being in the lead for nineteen and a half hours, but in the following year it won at the hands of Pironi and Jaussaud. The A 442B had a V6 Garrett turbocharged engine with a displacement of 1997 cc and an output of 500 hp at 9900 rpm.

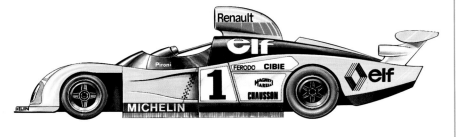

In 1969, the Porsche era began when the German company won its first outright title ahead of Ford and Lola, winning seven out of seven races with the Siffert–Redman champion team in a 908. The most impressive model, however, was the 917 sports car, which was destined to create an era. It made its début at Spa with its flat-twelve 4500-cc 540-hp engine. The season registered its first win with the Belgian Jackie Ickx at Le Mans, the début of the 3-liter 332 and an unsuccessful Ferrari prototype, the 312 P.

The years 1970 and 1971 were also triumphant ones for Porsche, who succeeded in fending off Ferrari's attack and its 512 S. They also amused themselves at the Targa Florio by bringing out a special version of a lozenge-shaped 908, soon nicknamed "the Bicycle." In 1971, Ferrari concentrated on the development of a 3-liter car for the 1972 championship, which proposed 3000-cc sports cars. This presented no problems for Porsche, despite the fact that Alfa Romeo had come back into the limelight with three wins.

The year 1972 saw Ferrari's swan song. Porsche's 917 having been finally pensioned off, they withdrew from the championship, and neither Alfa nor Matra-Simca could outclass the Maranello works, which won ten of the eleven races with the 312 P and a formidable team of drivers (Andretti, Ickx, Regazzoni, Peterson, Redman, Pace, Merzario and Schenken), although for French national honour Matra won at Le Mans.

Porsche 956 – 1984 (D) This car dominated the 1982, 1983 and 1984 seasons. The 956 Group C has a flat-six 2650-cc engine with a mixed cooling system – air for the cylinder barrels and water for the heads. It also has two KKK turbochargers and a fully electronic injection system. Its output is in the order of 600 hp.

Then like a bolt from the blue came the turn of the French in the championship. In 1973, Ferrari had not developed the 312 P sufficiently, and union trouble also slowed down their operation. The same applied to Alfa Romeo. Matra-Simca secured their position at the last race in Watkins Glen, when the Pescarolo–Larrousse 670 came in ahead of the red spyders of Ickx and Merzario. In 1974, Maranello retired completely from the world manufacturers' championship to concentrate exclusively on Formula 1. The oil crisis struck, Daytona was skipped, and the Nürburgring and Le Castellet 1000 km were cut to 200 km. Matra won again, but the championship struggled under the weight of rising costs and competition from Grand Prix racing.

The last year of the 3000-cc sports was 1975. Alfa Romeo seized the advantage and their efforts were crowned when they won the title with seven races out of nine. The Porsche

Lancia LC 2 – 1984 (I) Porsche's greatest rival, this car has an engine developed from the Ferrari V8 with a displacement of 2599 cc. Its two KKK turbochargers give an output that varies from 600 to 700 hp depending on the pressure, and it also has Weber-Marelli electronic injection.

Carrera Turbo, however, was a fearsome rival, and Renault also experimented with supercharging on the A 442.

Another Porsche era began in 1976 with the silhouettes championship, together with a world championship for sports cars over shorter distances – the minimum in the manufacturers' trophy was 1000 km (621.4 miles) or six hours. Porsche won the former with the 935 T and the latter with the 936 T. The silhouette was a formula based on the simple idea of an outward appearance similar to that of normal production models, with ample mechanical modifications. In 1977, Porsche won the silhouettes again, but Alfa Romeo took the sports cars title. In the 1978/9 season, the competition was limited to silhouettes and became a German jamboree, although Lancia appeared on the scene at Silverstone on 6 May 1979 with their Montecarlo Turbo.

In the following season, Lancia became world champion. They repeated their success in 1981 in a championship that was called an endurance trial, while Porsche consoled themselves at Le Mans. The German company hit the top again in 1982 with the 956 Group C car and won all the races in 1983.

Progress was discussed in terms of limiting fuel consumption and introducing sophisticated electronic systems, but, as far as the championship was concerned, the golden years of the 1950s and 1960s seemed well and truly over.

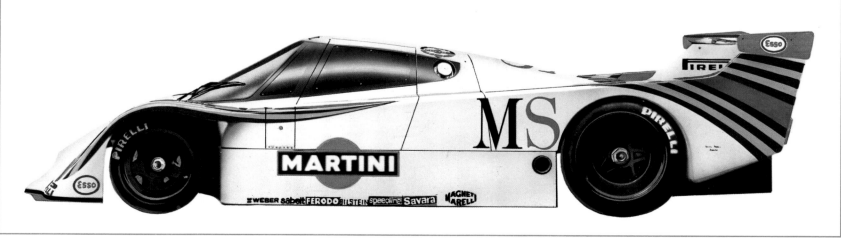

RALLIES

Lancia Fulvia HF – 1971 (I) The HF engine, ahead of the front axle, was a V4 1584-cc twin overhead camshaft version developing 160 hp at 7200 rpm. It had front-wheel drive, with the gearbox in a block with the differential. The Fulvia HF was active from 1966 onwards, but its greatest year was 1972, when it won the title, and the Morocco, Monte Carlo and San Remo rallies.

This type of competition dates back to 1911, when the first Monte Carlo Rally (won by a Turcat-Méry) was organized. Between the two wars, other rallies followed the Monte Carlo, among them the Liège–Rome–Liège in 1931, the Moroccan Rally in 1934 and the Alps Cup in 1938. But it was not until after the Second World War that they really became popular, as a result mainly of the introduction of a valid formula which seriously tested the everyday car. Until the 1950s, those who took part in the Monte Carlo Rally were, on the whole, private individuals, winning with cars such as the Delahaye, Hotchkiss, Allard, Ford, Lancia and Jaguar. However, the promotional value of the rallies also attracted many companies, which entered official cars that had been specially modified. Slowly but surely, therefore, they strayed further and further from the principle of "strictly series" cars that had been rigidly observed for so long.

In order to win now, an *ad hoc* machine and a highly efficient organization were needed, involving costs so high that private teams were effectively excluded. The first official car to win a rally was the Renault Dauphine in 1958.

The 1960s were dominated by Scandinavian drivers, the first to win with the easy-to-handle Mini Cooper, outclassing cars with even twice its 100 hp, in 1964, 1965 and 1967. These successful, small, front-wheel drive British cars were followed by the powerful "all behind" Porsche 911, which won in 1968, 1969 and 1970, when the manufacturers' international rallies championship was established to extend public interest to other races.

The early 1970s was a period of alternating success for Alpine and Lancia. The former was declared champion in 1971 and 1973; the latter, with the Fulvia coupé HF, in 1972, and with the Stratos – the first "made-to-measure" rally car – in 1974, 1975 and 1976. The Fiat 131

Abarth won the championship in 1977, 1978 and 1980, the Ford Escort RS in 1979 and the Talbot-Lotus in 1981. In the same year, the Audi integral-traction Quattro made its début and went on to win the title in 1982, inspiring nearly all the other companies to bring out their own four-wheel drive models. In 1983, however, victory went to the new but more traditional four-cylinder 2-liter, 300–310-hp supercharged Lancia Rally.

Among the most important cars to appear over the fifteen years of the World Rally Championships (which became its official title in 1973) were the Datsun 240 Z and the Mitsubishi Colt, which both won various East African Safaris between 1971 and 1976; the Datsun Violet, which won the same race from 1979 to 1982; the Saab 99, which was the most frequent winner in Sweden; the Renault 5 Turbo, winner at Monte Carlo in 1981; and the Opel 400, which won the title in 1982 and 1983.

Alpine 1600 S – 1971 (F) The Alpine 1600 S weighed just 760 kg (1675.5 lb) and used the Porsche rear overhanging engine layout, proving to be one of the easiest to handle cars of the 1970s. The four-cylinder 1565-cc engine had valve gear with rods and rockers, and was fed by four carburettors. It developed 160 hp at 7200 rpm and had a central five-speed gearbox. In 1971 it won the Acropolis, Austrian Alps, Monte Carlo and San Remo rallies.

Lancia Stratos – 1974 (I) Winning the World Championship in 1974, 1975 and 1976, the Stratos was the first car to be designed specifically for rallying. The engine was centrally mounted with a very short wheelbase and independent all-round suspension. The V6 2418-cc engine was developed from the Ferrari Dino, and the original version developed 245 hp at 8500 rpm. The plastic body weighed just 890 kg (1962 lb).

Renault 5 Turbo – 1981 (F) The 5 Turbo has won two World Rally Championship races, one at Monte Carlo in 1981 and the other in Corsica in 1982. It has very little in common with the normal 5: the mid-rear engine displaces 1397 cc and, with turbocharger and fuel injection, has a "basic" output of 160 hp at 6000 rpm.

Audi Quattro – 1982 (D) The first car to bring four-wheel drive to the Rallies Championship, the Quattro has permanent integral traction with three differentials. The front-mounted, overhanging, five-cylinder 2199-cc engine has Pierburg injection and a KKK turbocharger, with an air–air heat exchanger. With an output of 360 hp at 7000 rpm, it won the title in 1982 and came second in 1983.

Gianni Rogliatti # THE WORLD LAND SPEED RECORD

The World Land Speed Record began as a bet as long ago as 1898, when the nobleman Gaston de Chasseloup-Laubat covered a measured distance for the first time in his electric Jeantaud, covering the standing-start kilometer in fifty-seven seconds, an average of 63.158 km/h (39.244 mph). His feat was immediately copied by the Belgian Jenatzy in *La Jamais Contente*, breaking the 100-km/h (62.137-mph) barrier and exploding the myth that a man's lungs would burst at that speed.

After the electric car came Serpollet's steam car and finally the first petrol car, the American billionaire Vanderbilt's Mors, which took the record in 1902. In 1906, Marriott, an American, hit 200 km/h (124.27 mph) in a steam car – the last time a record would be set by steam. The mile distance over which this was measured was not considered valid, however, so officially the first car to exceed 200 km/h was Hémery's Benz.

New records set at 100-km/h (62.137-mph) intervals were taken by Segrave in 1927 at 327.981 km/h (203.797 mph); Malcolm Camp-

Jeantaud – 1898 (F)
Driver: Chasseloup-Laubat
Electric motor with Fulmen battery – 63.158 km/h (39.24 mph)
Achères, France.

Jenatzy *La Jamais Contente* – 1899 (F)
Driver: Jenatzy
Two electric motors with Fulmen batteries – 105.904 km/h (65.805
Achères, France.

Serpollet – 1902 (F)
Driver: Serpollet
Four cylinder steam engine – 120.771 km/h (75.043 mph)
Nice, France

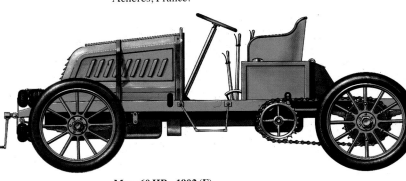

Mors 60 HP – 1902 (F)
Driver: Fournier
Four cylinders, 9200 cc, 60 hp – 123.249 km/h (76.583 mph)
Dourdan, France.

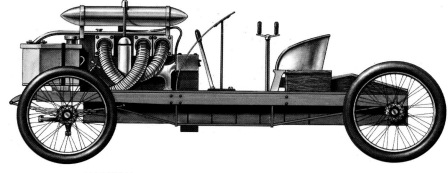

Ford 999 Arrow – 1903 (USA)
Driver: Henry Ford
Four cylinders, 15,700 cc 72 hp – 147.014 km/h (91.35 mph)
Lake St Clair, USA.

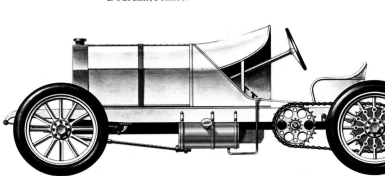

Mercedes Simplex 90 HP – 1904 (D)
Driver: Vanderbilt
Four cylinders, 11,900 cc, 90 hp – 148.510 km/h (92.280 mph)
Daytona Beach, USA.

bell in 1932 at 408.621 km/h (253.905 mph); Eyston in 1937 at 501.374 km/h (311.539 mph); and then Cobb in 1947 at 634.267 km/h (394.114 mph).

After the war, a new phase began with the arrival of jet engines. At first, reaction to these was hostile, because they did not conform to regulations (a car is a vehicle with four wheels, at least two of which are drive wheels), but they were finally accepted after a change in the rules which now stipulated only that there had to be four wheels.

Donald Campbell brought the record back to England with the last of the Bluebirds, which was turbine driven but also had drive wheels. He died later in an attempt to break the water speed record. Turbines and rocket engines have made it possible to break the 1000-km/h (621.37-mph) barrier with ease, and at times the torpedo-shaped cars have even broken the sound barrier on open tracks.

Two Americans, the Summers brothers, captured the ultimate dream with the fastest car of all time: the Goldenrod, built with four modified series engines, which sped along at 658.527 km/h (409.189 mph) in 1965. Only jets on wheels can break this record even today. No wheel with or without a tyre could provide sufficient thrust to take a car over 1000 km/h (621.37 mph).

Some may ask why these men do it. With the land speed record, it is simply a case of covering a kilometer in a few tenths of a second less than the previous record-holder. For this an incredible amount of tenacity is required, first to convince sponsors to finance the undertaking, then to solve the many problems that arise during construction of the car and finally to get into the driving seat and, concentrating on the black line down the center of the track, slam the accelerator to the floor. The whole thing is over in seconds; but, for the record to be valid, the same distance must be covered in the opposite direction within an hour of the first run.

After the triumph and the congratulations, there is simply the wait for someone to do better: then the race begins again.

Gobron-Brillié – 1904 (F)
Driver: Rigolly
Four cylinders, 13,600 cc, 130 hp – 166.628 km/h (103.538 mph)
Ostend, Belgium.

Darracq – 1904 (F)
Driver: Baras
Four cylinders, 11,259 cc, 100 hp – 168.188 km/h (104.507 mph)
Mongeron, France.

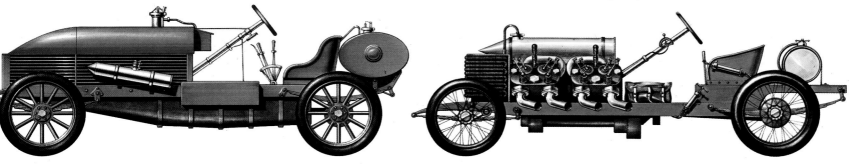

Napier Six – 1905 (GB)
Driver: Macdonald
Six cylinders, 15,000 cc, 90 hp – 168.381 km/h (104.627 mph)
Daytona Beach, USA.

Darracq V8 – 1905 (F)
Driver: Héméry
90-degree V8, 22,500 cc, 200 hp – 175.422 km/h (109.002 mph)
Arles–Salon, France.

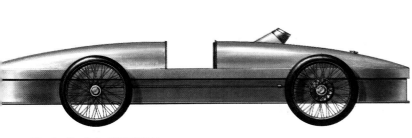

Stanley Rocket – 1906 (USA)
Driver: Marriott
Two-cylinder steam engine, 120 hp – 195.606 km/h (121.544 mph)
Daytona Beach, USA.

Blitzen Benz – 1910 (D)
Driver: Oldfield
Four cylinders, 21,500 cc, 200 hp – 211.500 km/h (131.420 mph)
Daytona Beach, USA.

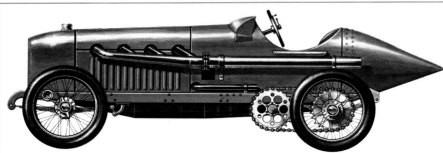

Benz – 1914 (D)
Driver: Hornsted
Four cylinders, 21,500 cc, 200 hp – 199.676 km/h (124.073 mph), average
over both directions
Brooklands, GB.

Packard 905 – 1919 (USA)
Driver: De Palma
V12, 9900 cc, 240 hp – 241.148 km/h (149.842 mph)
Daytona Beach, USA.

Duesenberg Double Duesey – 1920 (USA)
Driver: Milton
Two sets of eight cylinders, 10,000 cc in all, 184 hp – 251.052 km/h (155.996 mph)
Daytona Beach, USA.

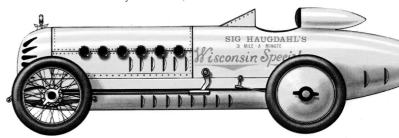

Wisconsin Special – 1922 (USA)
Driver: Haugdahl
Six cylinders, 12,500 cc, 250 hp – 260.658 km/h (161.965 mph),
unconfirmed
Daytona Beach, USA.

Sunbeam 350 HP – 1922 (GB)
Driver: Guinness
60-degree V12, 18,300 cc, 350 hp – 215.250 km/h (133.750 mph), average
two runs
Brooklands, GB.

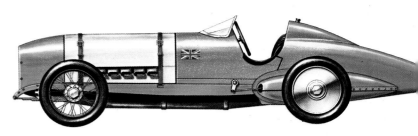

Sunbeam – 1924 (GB)
Driver: Campbell
60-degree V12, 18,300 cc, 350 hp – 235.217 km/h
(146.157 mph)
Pendine Sands, GB.

Delage – 1924 (F)
Driver: Thomas
60-degree V12, 10,600 cc, 280 hp – 230.634 km/h (143.309 mph)
Arpajon, France.

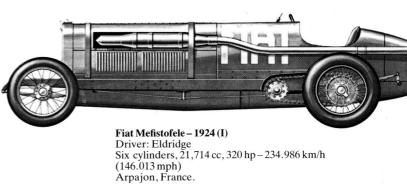

Fiat Mefistofele – 1924 (I)
Driver: Eldridge
Six cylinders, 21,714 cc, 320 hp – 234.986 km/h
(146.013 mph)
Arpajon, France.

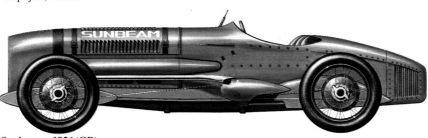

Sunbeam – 1926 (GB)
Driver: Segrave
65-degree V12 supercharged, 4000 cc, 306 hp
Southport, GB.

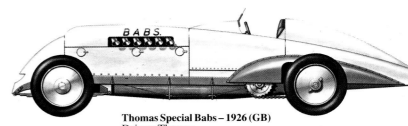

Thomas Special Babs – 1926 (GB)
Driver: Thomas
45-degree V12, 26,900 cc, 400 hp – 275.229 km/h
(171.019 mph)
Pendine Sands, GB.

Napier-Campbell Bluebird – 1927 (GB)
Driver: Campbell
Twelve cylinders, 22,300 cc, 450 hp – 281.447 km/h (174.883 mph)
Pendine Sands, GB.

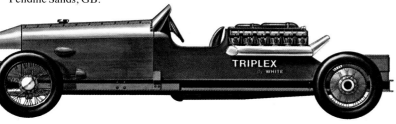

White Triplex – 1928 (USA)
Driver: Keech
Three sets of twelve cylinders, 81,000 cc in all, 1200 hp – 334.022 km/h
(207.551 mph)
Daytona Beach, USA.

Napier-Campbell – 1928 (GB)
Driver: Campbell
Twelve cylinders, 22,300 cc, 450 hp – 333.062 km/h (206.955 mph)
Daytona Beach, USA.

Rolls-Royce Campbell Bluebird – 1933 (GB)
Driver: Campbell
V12, supercharged, 36,500 cc, 2300 hp – 438.123 km/h (272.236 mph)
Daytona Beach, USA.

Railton Mobil Special – 1938 (GB)
Driver: Cobb
Two sets of twelve cylinders (Napier), 26,900 cc in all, 1250 hp
– 536.471 km/h (333.347 mph)
Bonneville, USA.

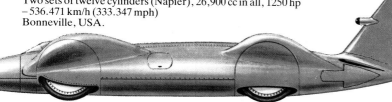

Bluebird – 1964 (GB)
Driver: D. Campbell
Bristol-Siddeley Proteus turbine engine, 4100 hp – 648.728 km/h (403.100 mph)
Lake Eire, Australia.

Sunbeam 1000 HP – 1927 (GB)
Driver: Segrave
Two V12s, 45,000 cc in all, 870 hp – 327.981 km/h
(203.797 mph)
Daytona Beach, USA.

Stutz Black Hawk – 1928 (USA)
Driver: Lockhart
V16, 3000 cc supercharged, 385 hp – unsuccessful attempt
Daytona Beach, USA.

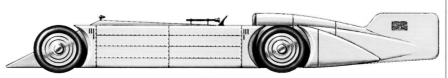

Irving Napier Golden Arrow – 1929 (GB)
Driver: Segrave
Twelve cylinders, 26,900 cc, 925 hp – 372.340 km/h
(231.361 mph)
Daytona Beach, USA.

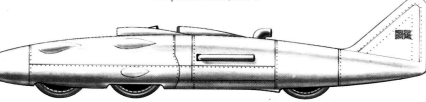

Thunderbolt – 1937 (GB)
Driver: Eyston
Two V12s, supercharged (Rolls-Royce), 73,000 cc in all,
4700 hp – 501.374 km/h (311.539 mph)
Bonneville, USA.

Wingfoot Express – 1964 (USA)
Driver: Green
Westinghouse J 46 three-stage reaction engine – 664.950 km/h (413.180 mph)
Bonneville, USA.

Spirit of America – 1964 (USA)
Driver: Breedlove
General Electric J 47 reaction engine – 665.151 km/h
(413.305 mph)
Bonneville, USA.

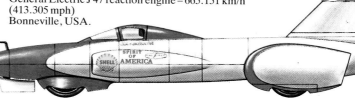

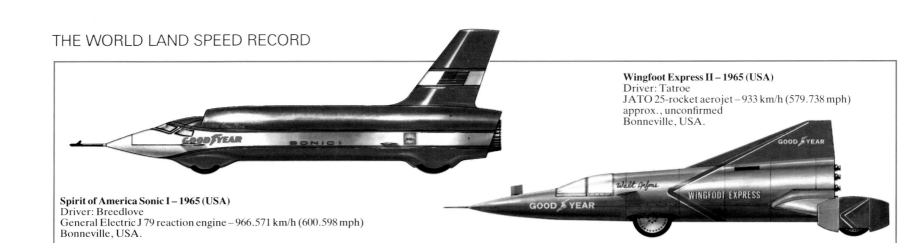

Wingfoot Express II – 1965 (USA)
Driver: Tatroe
JATO 25-rocket aerojet – 933 km/h (579.738 mph)
approx., unconfirmed
Bonneville, USA.

Spirit of America Sonic I – 1965 (USA)
Driver: Breedlove
General Electric J 79 reaction engine – 966.571 km/h (600.598 mph)
Bonneville, USA.

Goldenrod – 1965 (USA)
Driver: Summers
Four Chrysler V8s, 29,400 cc in all, 2432 hp – 658.527 km/h (409.189 mph)
Bonneville, USA.

The Blue Flame – 1970 (USA)
Driver: Gabelich
Reaction Dynamics reaction engine – 1001.667 km/h (622.406 mph) unconfirmed
Bonneville, USA.

◀ **Green Monster – 1965 (USA)**
Driver: Arfons
General Electric J 79 reaction engine – 927.829 km/h
(576.525 mph)
Bonneville, USA.

Thrust 2 – 1983 (USA)
Driver: Noble
British Electric reaction engine – 1019.700 km/h
(633.611 mph)
Black Rock, Nevada, USA.
▼

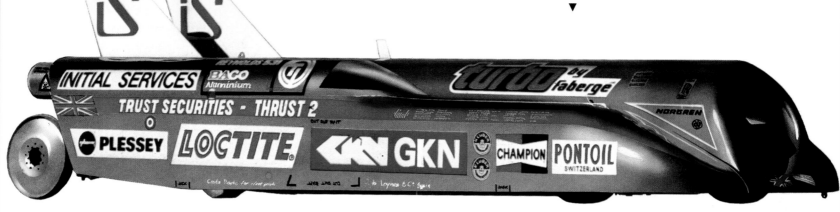

THE GREAT INVENTIONS

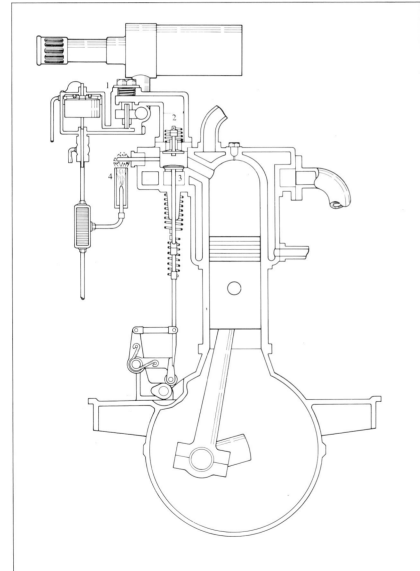

Cross-section of the Daimler engine which has formed the basis for all subsequent versions – it already had a Maybach constant-level carburettor. 1 – Maybach carburettor with float; 2 – automatic inlet valve; 3 – controlled exhaust valve; 4 – incandescent tube ignition.

The two Germans, Daimler and Benz, independently developed a real automobile engine in 1885 and 1886 respectively. It was light, powerful and reliable, and was either used directly or built under license by the first automobile manufacturers. It was then copied and perfected, and gradually developed greater power, faster rotation speed, a higher number of cylinders and a bigger engine capacity. Daimler had previously built other engines, but these were stationary and consequently heavier. It is interesting to compare the specifications of Daimler's light engine, fitted on to a bicycle in 1885 – 0.5 hp, 20 kg (44 lb), 0.264 liters, 700 rpm – with the average small car engine today. The latter has a unit cylinder capacity similar to that of the Daimler engine, but, as it usually has four cylinders, its total capacity is 1100 cc, its weight approximately 100 kg (220.4 lb) and it develops about 60 hp at 5000–6000 rpm.

Yet the most extraordinary result of progress in this area is the total performance of racing cars today: with the aid of turbochargers, it is now possible to obtain an output of over 600 hp from a 1500-cc engine weighing 160 kg (352.74 lb) at 12,000 rpm.

Once they had their engine, the car builders of those pioneer days looked around for the other components they needed to "make" an automobile. Obviously the vehicle had to be easily maneuverable; it would have to cope with bad roads; it must be able to stop quickly when necessary; and finally it must not present problems on starting.

This required components which later became standardized such as a correct steering system, tyres, a differential, ball bearings, brakes, suspension, a gearbox and clutch, and also a suitable position for the power unit. The closed body and all its accessories did not become necessary until later, when the automobile had developed into a real means of transport as opposed to the curiosity it had represented in its early days.

The gear change was developed by Daimler, then Benz, followed gradually by others, using the only system considered reliable at the time – chains working on sprockets of different diameters.

As this system had an idler to take up the slack, they almost inadvertently invented the clutch, which was indispensable for starting the engine in neutral and then connecting it progressively to the transmission. As power outputs increased, manufacturers began to use gearwheels and went on to create the clutch as we know it today, a metal plate (which could also be a cone or cylindrical drum) driven by the engine with another similar part covered in leather (later asbestos) to transfer the drive to the gearbox.

In-line gear change, that is direct gear change without loss of power, to give maximum speed, is generally accredited to Louis Renault's shaft drive at about the turn of the century.

The problem of steering also had to be dealt with. At first, the whole front axle turned, mounted on leaf-springs in the same way as the carriages before it. Then it was realized that, although this system may have been good enough for the speeds at which carriages ran, it was not suitable for the ever-increasing speeds of automobiles. It was at this point that the work of a certain Rudolph Ackermann was remembered: a German coachbuilder who had died in 1834, Ackermann had while working in London in 1818 applied and patented a steering system based on an idea by another German, Lankensperger. As is often the case, the name of the original inventor was immediately forgotten and parallelogram steering has since been known as "Ackermann steering."

However, it was not only the non-drive front wheels which gave problems on cornering; also to be considered were the rear wheels, which, at least in the early days, were usually the drive wheels. Whether they are at the front or the rear, the drive wheels cannot be fixed rigidly to an axle because, when taking a bend, the inner wheel has to turn more slowly than the outer wheel as it travels less distance. This is where a mechanism came in useful that had been invented in 1700 by master watchmakers, who had devised "differential wheels," a system of gears which could invert the drive or change the ratio. In 1828, a French watchmaker, Onesiphore Pecqueur, who took a great interest in

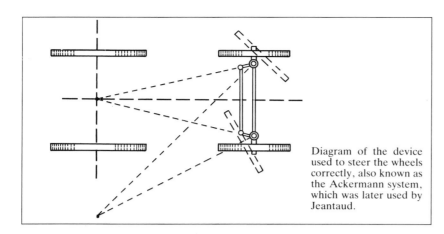

Diagram of the device used to steer the wheels correctly, also known as the Ackermann system, which was later used by Jeantaud.

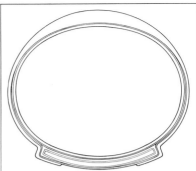

Cross-section of the pneumatic tyre developed by the Scotsman Dunlop in 1888.

Cugnot's steam carriage, designed one of his own with a differential mechanism on the rear drive wheels to make cornering easier. Although his design was not taken up at the time, the Englishman Roberts in 1831 found that the mechanism could be used on motor carriages, and so the device was rediscovered and finally fitted on the first motor cars.

Ball bearings, that is the insertion of rotating elements between two surfaces to reduce friction, are based on a concept that is even older than the wheel. Ball bearings have been found on Roman ships which had sunk in Lake Nemi in Italy. Leonardo da Vinci also mentions them, but it was a British mechanic, Joseph Hughes, who studied them in their modern form and they were produced in series from 1878 by another Englishman, William Brown. Multiple-row ball bearings, cylindrical and conical rollers, and so forth, are simply variations of the same idea.

Pneumatic tyres were less important to the development of the automobile (which in fact works just as well without them) than to the development and improvement of the speeds that could be reached, but they have made the automobile virtually unbeatable as a means of transport over short or middle distances (and even over long distances, too, until the advent of the aeroplane).

The idea of pneumatic tyres was first conceived by the Scottish inventor John Boyd Dunlop, who in 1888 applied the notion to his son's bicycle, inventing the tubeless tyre at the same time, since he used a garden hose for the job. His work was then improved upon by a system for "vulcanizing" rubber, patented by Charles Goodyear in 1844, though he was not finally granted the patent until 1852, after a long court battle with another inventor, Robert William Thompson, who claimed the idea as his.

In 1891, the Michelin brothers invented the detachable tyre with its own inner tube, which improved the car's performance enormously. Conclusive proof of the superiority of pneumatic tyres was provided by Comte Chasse-loup-Laubat in 1897, when he demonstrated that resistance to forward movement was 35 per cent greater on a car with solid rubber tyres than on one with pneumatic tyres, and this at 25 km/h (15.5 mph). Two years later, the Belgian Jenatzy reached 100 km/h (62.137 mph) with Michelin tyres on his celebrated electric car, *La Jamais Contente*.

The problem of stopping a moving car has grown at the same pace as the development of improved engines allowing vehicles greater speeds. Manufacturers have therefore had to move from the normal carriage or bicycle type of brake, fitted on the rear wheels, to drum brakes, first with outer shoes, then with a band wound around the drum (which gave a great "servo" effect if the band was wound in the same direction as the movement of the drum) and finally with inner shoes. For a long time, the brakes were fitted only on the rear wheels, partly assisted by a brake on the transmission.

At the beginning of the century, despite much indecision, brakes began to be fitted on to the front wheels. One of the pioneers in this field was the engineer Giustino Cattaneo, who designed the Isotta Fraschini and fitted front-wheel brakes in 1910. A curious innovation was adopted by the Scottish marque Argyle in 1911, consisting of diagonal control of one front and one rear brake by means of a pedal, the other two being operated by the hand lever. This predated by some sixty years the dual triangular-split hydraulic circuits used today on Volvos and other marques.

Another significant development was made in 1911 by the American Charles Kettering, who put the final touches to a complete electric starter system with a small, battery-operated electric motor recharged by a dynamo driven by the engine. This system, which was used at the time on Cadillacs, is still used today by all manufacturers.

The last, but far from being the least important, development was a power-plant arrangement which incorporated various features still seen on modern motor cars: the transverse engine with front-wheel drive and independent front suspension. The pioneer of this system was the American Walter

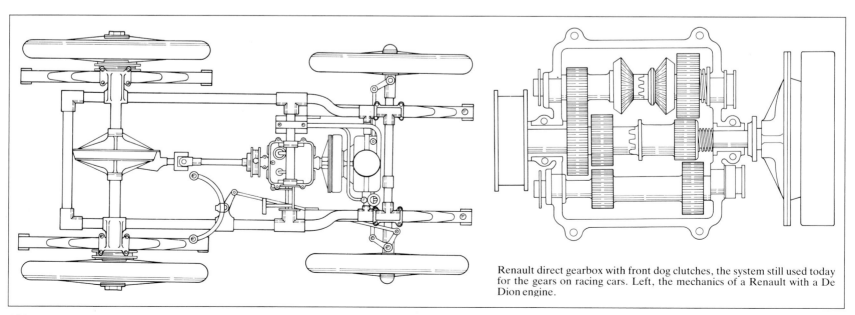

Renault direct gearbox with front dog clutches, the system still used today for the gears on racing cars. Left, the mechanics of a Renault with a De Dion engine.

Christie, who began to build a series of racing cars with a front-mounted engine with four cylinders, arranged either in line or in a V, and front-wheel drive. The suspension used a system which later became famous as "Lancia suspension" – a telescopic strut served as the steering-pin for each wheel at the same time. The transmission incorporated half-axles with universal joints at the ends, all enclosed in a one-piece cast-bronze casing. The racing models had only direct gear, or in certain cases a reduced gear for starting.

On the basis of experience gained with these cars, a small production run of taxis was built in 1909 with transverse four-cylinder engines of approximately 2.5 liters capacity, the gearbox in line with the engine and the drive transmitted to the differential through a pair of cylindrical gears. They also had front-wheel drive and the telescopic suspension system coupled to the steering.

In the first twenty or thirty years of its life, the automobile engine underwent constant modification until it included many of the features we now recognize today, particularly the use of four cylinders in line – one of the longest lasting and most popular. Naturally the improved materials used today were not available then, but they were gradually put on the market as the specialized car industry developed them.

Examples of such refinements are bi- and tri-metallic bearings, light alloys, iron alloys for thin-walled castings, high-resistance steel alloys and powder-sintered metals. These are just some of the materials which have led to the refinement of automobile design, increasing the specific power output and reducing the weight. At the end of the first hundred years, it can be said that unsupercharged series petrol engines today can reach power outputs of approximately 50–60 hp per liter and weights of 1.5 kg (3.31 lb) per hp. As for supercharged racing engines, such as those used on Formula 1 cars, the results are staggering: over 400 hp/liter and less than 250 g (8.8 oz) per hp. In fact, a typical six-cylinder Formula 1 engine in 1984 develops approximately 650 hp with a 1.5-liter capacity (even up to 700

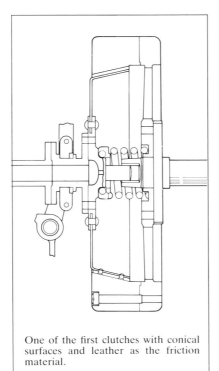

One of the first clutches with conical surfaces and leather as the friction material.

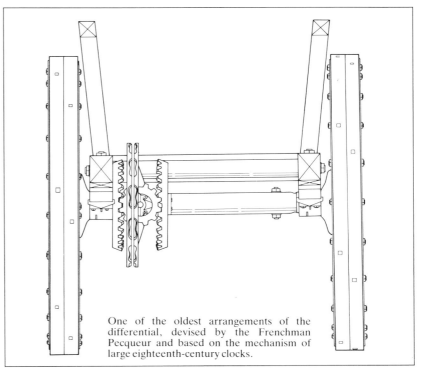

One of the oldest arrangements of the differential, devised by the Frenchman Pecqueur and based on the mechanism of large eighteenth-century clocks.

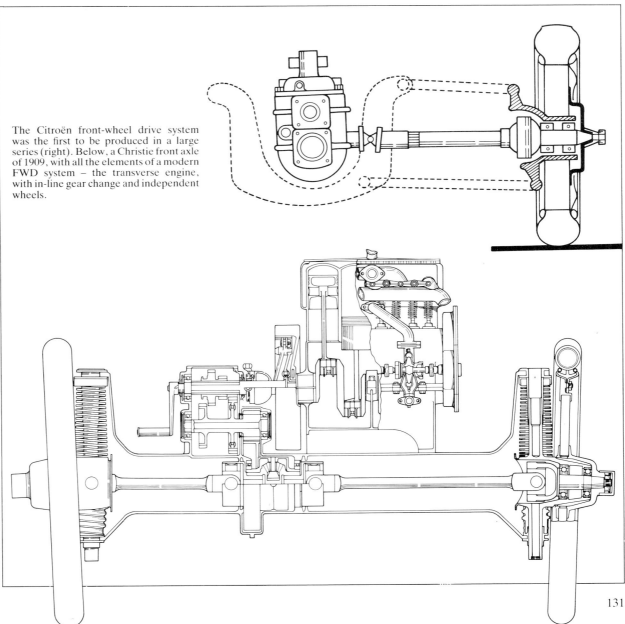

The Citroën front-wheel drive system was the first to be produced in a large series (right). Below, a Christie front axle of 1909, with all the elements of a modern FWD system – the transverse engine, with in-line gear change and independent wheels.

hp for qualifiers) and generally weighs less than 160 kg (352.7 lb).

Two important innovations were adopted before and after the Second World War. The value of overhead valves and cams had been confirmed when, in 1914, the Lautenschlager Mercedes, by winning the Automobile Club de France Grand Prix, proved the superiority of this system beyond a shadow of doubt. An ever-increasing number of manufacturers began to use them between the two wars, even on their touring cars, and Fiat launched the 509 runabout with a single-liter capacity using this kind of system. The other great step forward, particularly from the sporting point of view, was the adoption of superchargers. Mercedes were the first to try this system, and Fiat also had great success with it, followed by Alfa Romeo and all the other companies. For forty years, the Roots-type supercharger reigned supreme wherever supercharging was allowed by the sports regulations, and it was not until the 1970s that the turbocharger, operated by exhaust gases, was rediscovered, although it was widely used on the big diesel engines and led to the performances of today's cars.

The late 1920s and early 1930s saw progress in other parts of the automobile: front-wheel drive had been proposed by various manufacturers, but did not really begin to become popular until the industrialist André Citroën was brave enough to launch it on a large-series model. Many other manufacturers tried front-wheel drive, mainly on special or luxury cars – Bucciali, Audi, Cord are among the makes – and it was used experimentally on various competition cars. Until Issigoni's legendary Mini was born in 1959, however, the Citroën was the only large-series car produced with front-wheel drive. After this, a new trend was set: the more it was used and the more the advantages of front-wheel drive became apparent, especially when combined with a transverse engine, the greater the number of manufacturers who began to use it. Today, with the exception of very few companies, the whole motoring world is using front-wheel drive. One potentially interesting

The classic hydraulic brake arrangement consists of a small cylinder with two pistons which push out the shoes; with disc brakes, on the other hand, the pistons push the pads on to the disc.

The first successful compressor was the Wittig-type vane supercharger used by Fiat (A), but it was then replaced by the Rootes blower type (B) still in use today (under the name "Volumex") as an alternative to the turbocharger.

A   B

phenomenon which could be developed further is that of four-wheel drive on normal cars, as opposed to off-road vehicles, introduced in the 1960s by the British company Jensen and brought out very authoritatively by Audi in 1981.

The four-wheel drive arrangement is used on the track and the road mainly for the transmission of power. However, as it is known to improve road-holding, especially in bad conditions, it also introduces the question of safety which, together with pollution, has become an issue of increasing importance over the last twenty years.

Mechanical improvements to the car have been accompanied by developments in the bodywork, with regard both to structure and to line, and the Citroën Traction Avant of 1934 introduces another innovation, in the form of sheet steel unit-body construction. In fact Lancia had already pointed the way to this type of construction with their Lambda in the mid-1920s, but the Italian version was a structure that only went as far as the waistline, since the Lambda was an open-topped car, whereas the Citroën also used the roof as a strengthening element.

At the same time, manufacturers began to develop an interest in aerodynamics on both sides of the Atlantic. Various European models, from the Lancia Aprilia onwards, and certain American cars, such as the Chrysler Airflow with its evocative name, showed that research had begun. The intuitive Pininfarina had also worked on the problem of improving the shape of the automobile without losing sight of aerodynamic efficiency. However, the problem only began to be tackled in a truly scientific way in the 1970s, with the increased use of wind-tunnels. Once again, Pininfarina (not the founder himself, but his successor) was the first coachbuilder to have his own wind-tunnel, one of the first in the world, for research purposes.

Although Bugatti once said that cars were made to run, not to stop, brakes have for obvious reasons always been considered important. The greatest innovation (after the application of front brakes, as already discussed) was the adoption of hydraulic brakes, which were developed during the 1930s. The hydraulic system transmits the braking force exactly as desired, smoothly and reliably; but in the interests of safety the

double hydraulic circuit was later adopted, separating the wheels into pairs to ensure that the car would stop even when a pipe was leaking. Power brakes have also taken a great deal of the effort out of braking.

The last stage in the evolution of brakes was the development of disc brakes – although these had been used by Lanchester in the early 1900s. Already well known in aviation for their resistance to overheating, disc brakes were tested on racing cars with excellent results and then fitted on series cars from the 1960s onwards. They were perhaps *too* effective and there was a return to drum brakes on the rear wheels for nearly all cars except the biggest and fastest. The final touch was the invention of an electronically operated anti-skid system allowing the driver to brake even on slippery surfaces.

The most notable advance of the 1970s and 1980s has been made by the diesel engine. Although tried out in passenger cars by Mercedes in the 1930s, the diesel engine was not fully accepted until it lost its traditional image of being slow and heavy in relation to its power output, and it was realized that one could be made which weighed only slightly more than a petrol engine yet with the aid of a turbo could give the same performance. Research in the motor industry is at present concentrated on reducing fuel consumption, and here, at least for the moment, the diesel engine leads.

As for the petrol engine, there have been highly successful developments with a wide-scale application of electronics. This particular type of advanced technology was slow to be applied to the automobile, perhaps because early attempts were rather clumsy and discouraged manufacturers. The most important uses of electronics in recent years include electronic ignition with pre-programmed advance, fuel injection integrated with the ignition and, eventually, with the gear control, anti-skid brakes, control systems for the main functions, suspension adjustment, the operation of occasional systems such as indicators and windscreen wipers, and – the latest additions – driver-assistance systems with recorded "spoken" instructions.

ONE HUNDRED YEARS OF DIFFERENT MARQUES

ALFA ROMEO

The automobile is a hundred years old and Alfa Romeo "only" seventy-five. Since its late start, Alfa has made a name for itself in its own particular way, scoring firsts on many occasions. From as early as 1923, when Alfa won first, second and fourth place in the Targa Florio, it is difficult to find any other motor company manufacturing in series which has collected as many competition successes.

On thinking back to the early days of Alfa, I see the sophisticated, demanding pioneers of motor sport, who relied on their Portello cars to meet the challenge of conquering time and space, sharing in the unequalled excitement of new technology, sure of a winning performance. When Henry Ford exclaimed, "I lift my hat when I see an Alfa Romeo go by," he confirmed our role in world motoring.

Subsequent development, from a semi-craftsman skill to series and mass production, has been nurtured by the same spirit, for these cars still have that extra special quality in terms of technology, performance and safety; their characteristic mechanics are the tried and tested fruits of experiments on the race track.

A visit to the Alfa Romeo Museum in Arese, one of the most important and prestigious single-marque museums in the world, reveals that many of the technical innovations considered to be recent developments were, in fact, already widely used on old Alfa Romeo models. The victorious marque of the great racing drivers has now also become the unmistakable marque of countless Alfa enthusiasts.

But the secret behind the long and happy union between Alfa Romeo and the automobile does not end there. The standard of technology and performance associated with Alfa Romeo complement the special quality of its design to create a style which now, as yesterday, we still strive to make unique.

ETTORE MASSACESI   President, Alfa Romeo S.p.A.

Alfa Romeo went into large-series production with the Giulietta, at the same time keeping its traditional sporting image. The saloon brought out in 1955, just one year after the Sprint, had the classic four-cylinder twin-shaft light alloy 1290-cc engine in the version which developed 53 hp at 5500 rpm. The TI model of 1961 developed 74 hp at 6200 rpm, with a top speed of 155 km/h (96.31 mph). A total of 178,000 were built between 1954 and 1965.

One hundred 24 HPs were produced between 1910 and 1911 to a design by Giuseppe Merosi. The particular brilliance of the engine was due to the lightness of the flywheel. Lubrication was full pressure.

The 20/30 HP, a development of the 24 HP, was launched in 1914. It had a four-cylinder 4084-cc engine with an increased output of 49 hp, giving a top speed of 115 km/h (71.45 mph). A total of 380 were built up to 1920.

The RL six-cylinder series was in production between 1922 and 1926. The most powerful version was the Super Sport, with a 2994-cc 83-hp engine. A four-wheel braking system was fitted in 1923.

The 6C 1750 Gran Sport had innumerable racing successes, including the 1930 Mille Miglia with Nuvolari–Guidotti, who exceeded an average 100 km/h (62.14 mph) for the first time. The six-cylinder 1752-cc engine developed about 100 hp.

The 6C 1900 was in production for only one year, 1933, during which 197 were built. The engine was derived from the 1750 engine and had a displacement of 1917 cc, developing 68 hp, with a top speed of 130 km/h (80.8 mph).

The 6C 2300 (2309 cc) was in production between 1934 and 1939, with a power ranging from 68 to 95 hp. The Mille Miglia model had a Touring superlight body, and Guidotti and Boratto took it to fourth place in the 1937 Mille Miglia.

The last pre-war Alfa Romeo, the 6C 2500 – the illustration shows the SS version – reached rare levels of technical perfection. It had all-round independent suspension, with a torsion bar on the rear axle. It was in production from 1939 to 1943.

Alfa Romeo production was resumed after the war with the 6C 2500 *Freccia d'Oro* ("Golden Arrow"). It was one of the first Italian cars to have column change. A total of 2,717 were produced, all with a displacement of 2443 cc, developing between 87 and 110 hp.

The first car to be produced in series (21,089 were built between 1950 and 1959) was the 1900, which had a four-cylinder 1884-cc 90-hp engine. In 1954, the 1975-cc 115-hp Super was launched. The 1900 was also the first car on which Alfa Romeo used a unitary body construction.

The origins of Alfa Romeo date back to the move by Darracq to set up an assembly and sales point for some of their models in Italy, for which they founded the Società Anonima Italiana Darracq in Naples in 1906. It was transferred almost immediately to Milan, to a new and up-to-date covered plant occupying 8000 sq m (86,111 sq ft) in the Portello area of the city.

The production programme was for six hundred cars a year, but Darracq cars had a very lukewarm reception on the Italian market, mainly because they could not cope with the difficult road conditions of the time: by 1909, the French company, which was also in trouble back home in France, decided to sell off its Milan branch. The majority holdings were bought by a group of industrialists from Lombardy with the financial backing of the Milan Agricultural Bank, which put up half a million lire. The company name was changed a year later to ALFA

(Anonima Lombarda Fabbrica di Automobili – the Lombardy Automobile Factory Ltd) and Giuseppe Merosi, who had previously been at Fiat and Edoardo Bianchi, where he was chief engineer, was called upon to plan production on a radically new basis. The 24 HP was the first car to bear the new insignia, which has remained unchanged over the years (two typical Milanese heraldic symbols – the red cross on a white background representing the city of Milan, and the snake of the powerful Visconti family). The 24 HP was brought out in 1910 with a four-cylinder 4084-cc engine, which had an L-shaped head and unilateral valves. It was capable of 100 km/h (62.1 mph) and already had the features which were later to be associated with the image of Alfa Romeo: brilliant performance combined with excellent braking and road-holding, and a distinctive blend of tourer-cum-sports car, features which won the 24

HP a lead over its adversaries in the 1911 Targa Florio before it was unfortunately forced to retire. In the same year, the 12 HP, 2413 cc, came out, followed by the 40/60 HP, 6082 cc, in 1913. Alfa production was divided between these three models which were continuously updated until just before the First World War, when the major shareholder, the Banca di Sconto (Discount Bank), decided to ask the Nicola Romeo Company to take over the administration. In 1912, automobile production was temporarily suspended to make way for military orders – munitions and Isotta Fraschini aeroplane engines were supplied under license – just as the company had reached two hundred cars per annum.

At the end of the war, ALFA went into liquidation and the Portello works became part of SA Italiana ing. Nicola Romeo & Co., who built, among other things, railway engines in Saronno and aeroplanes in Naples. From 1919 onwards,

The 1900 Super Sprint, like the saloon, was built under the technical direction of D'Alessio and was brought out in 1954. The body was a Touring Superlight, as on its predecessors, the Sprint and the Disco Volante ("Flying Saucer"), both built on the same base mechanics.

Designed by Bertone in 1953, the Giulietta Sprint (above left) went into production in the following year with a four-cylinder 1290-cc engine that developed 80 hp at 6300 rpm. In 1962, the same body was used for the 1570-cc Giulia Sprint (92 hp at 6220 rpm). The Giulietta Spider (above right) was designed by Pininfarina, but its technical specifications were the same as the Sprint. This open-topped version also took the new Giulia name and engine in 1962.

The Giulia, which came out in 1962, had a particularly well-researched aerodynamic line and remained in production until 1978. The original 1570-cc 92-hp engine was later uprated to 98 hp for the Super version; it was replaced in 1964 by a 1290-cc engine, and in 1976 by a Perkins 1760-cc diesel.

Alfa Romeo went back to using six-cylinder engines with the 2600 in 1962. It had a 2584-cc engine with an output of between 130 and 145 hp, depending on the version. The saloon was accompanied by the Sprint, designed by Bertone (illustrated), the Spider Touring, and the Sprint Zagato.

The Spider first came out in 1966, when it was known as the Duetto. This name was subsequently abandoned. It originally had an engine of 1570 cc, but later versions were also fitted with 1290-, 1779- and 1962-cc engines. This was another original design by Pininfarina.

The Montreal was in production from 1970 to 1976. Its eight-cylinder 2593-cc engine (200 hp at 6500 rpm) was developed from the 33 prototype, and it had Spica fuel injection and dry sump lubrication. The design was by Bertone.

The 1750 came out in 1968 with a 1779-cc engine developed directly from the 1600 Giulia, giving 132 hp SAE at 5500 rpm. In June 1971, the 1962-cc 2000 came out, with a top speed of 190 km/h (118 mph).

The Bertone-designed Giulia Sprint GT was brought out in 1963, followed by the GT 1300 Junior (1966), the 1750 GTV (1968) and the 2000 GTV (1971), although the name "Giulia" was not used for these models.

The first car produced at the Pomigliano d'Arco works was the Alfasud, which went into production there in 1972 with a flat-four 1186-cc engine (63 hp at 6000 rpm). Subsequently, 1296-, 1350- and 1490-cc engines were also used. The bodywork was designed by Giorgetto Giugiaro, as was that for the 1976 Sprint version, which had 1300- and 1500-cc engines.

The Alfetta came out in 1972 with a 1779-cc 118-hp engine (increased to 122 hp in 1981); 1570-cc and 1962-cc engines were fitted in 1975 and 1977 respectively. The 1982 model was a 1962-cc 130-hp with fuel injection. The 1994- and 2392-cc turbodiesel models came out in 1980 and 1983.

The Alfetta GT 1800 made its début in 1974, followed two years later by the GTV 1600 and 2000, the latter being available in a 150-hp turbo version after 1979. The V6 2492-cc Alfa 6 engine, developing 160 hp, was fitted in 1980. Giugiaro designed the body.

The 1978 Giulietta, with a 1357-cc 95-hp engine, and also a 1570-cc 109-hp version, had similar mechanics to the Alfetta, with transaxle transmission and a De Dion rear end. The 1800 came out in 1979, the 2000 in 1981, the 2000 Turbodelta and the 2000 Turbodiesel in 1983.

Launched in April 1979 with a 2492-cc V6 engine developing 160 hp at 5800 rpm, the Alfa 6 was given a complete restyling in 1984, and the range was extended with the addition of the 2-liter V6 (135 hp) and the five-cylinder 2494-cc turbodiesel with a VM-built engine.

The Spider was restyled in 1971 and finally lost its distinctive receding tail, which was replaced by the more modern cut-off tail. The most powerful version, the 1962-cc 2000 Spider Veloce, develops 130 hp at 5400 rpm, assisted by Spica electronic injection. In 1983, the front and tail ends were slightly modified by the addition of a wrap-around spoiler.

the cars were built under the name "Alfa Romeo." Merosi further developed the old 24 HP and the 20-30 ES, and in 1921 built the first of the six-cylinder cars, the GI 6330 cc, although only fifty-two were made. The first really new car to come out was the six-cylinder RL which later enjoyed a long series of racing successes; 2,600 of them were built between 1922 and 1926. The RM was a four-cylinder version which came out in 1924.

Increasing involvement in competition racing led to the creation of a specialist section, which was placed under the direction of Vittorio Jano in September 1923. After he had designed the famous Grand Prix P2 with Luigi Fusi, his influence began to be extended to the series-produced cars, and this resulted in Merosi's handing in his resignation. The period between the wars was characterized by the 6C, of which 7,960 were produced including the successive 1500, 1750, 2300 and 2500 versions; these models firmly established Alfa Romeo among the most skilled sports car builders, a reputation which was consolidated with a steady stream of racing victories. The year 1931 saw the launch of the 8C, a prestige car for which Castagna, Touring and Zagato produced excellent bodies. In 1933, Alfa Romeo was nationalized, the majority holdings

passing from the Banca di Sconto to the IRI (the Institute for Industrial Reconstruction), and, on the eve of the Second World War, it became more and more apparent that the company should move out of the limited field of sports car specialization. With a production total of only 12,745 vehicles in thirty years, the company clearly needed to boost its profitability, and it was clear that a significant increase could only be achieved by the introduction of a more popular style of car. After the break in production during the war years, Alfa Romeo reappeared in its traditional role as winning marque on the most important circuits, thanks also to Orazio Satta. In 1950, the first series-produced saloon, the 1900, was brought out. Because of the remarkable features of D'Alessio's design, this car served to promote the image that the Portello company had built up on the race track, extending it to the family car. The year 1954 saw the birth of the Giulietta, 178,000 of which had been produced by 1965, confirming the industrial growth of the company. The Giulietta first appeared in the Sprint version – a 2+2 coupé with the highly successful lines of Pininfarina – which mechanically set the standard for all later Alfa Romeo models from the 1962 Giulia to the 1750 in 1968, the 1972 Alfetta and the new Giulietta in 1978.

Between 1962 and 1972, a six-cylinder 2600-cc model was brought out in various versions, and 1968 saw the launch of the Duetto – a successful Pininfarina roadster still in production today.

As a result of the continual rise in production levels (208,000 in 1973), a new plant was opened in Arese. In 1972, Alfasud was formed, marking the company's entry into the lower end of the market, with the construction of the new Pomigliano d'Arco works near Naples.

The oil crisis, management problems and union disputes made the 1970s a very difficult period for Alfa Romeo. With the exception of special cars such as the Montreal (with its prototype 33 V8 engine used in the Manufacturers' Championship from 1968 to 1972) and the Alfa 6, a prestige vehicle the intrinsic features of which reflected a design that was already outdated, no completely new car was brought out until 1983, when the successor to the Alfasud 33 was launched. This was the first step in a systematic programme to update the range which included agreements in 1983 with Nissan to produce the ARNA, an average runabout with an Alfasud engine and a Nissan Cherry/Pulsar body, and with Fiat to produce a common bed for the Alfa Romeo, Fiat and Lancia high-fascia saloons.

Mechanically the same as the earlier Alfasud, the 33 was brought out in 1983 with a 1350- or 1490-cc engine. In 1984, the range was extended to include a model with optional four-wheel drive, designed in association with Pininfarina.

The product of an agreement with the Japanese company Nissan, which supplies the body, the Arna uses Alfasud mechanics and the Alfasud flat-four 1186-cc engine. The model came out in 1983, followed by the 1350-cc TI in 1984.

Based on the previous Alfetta, the Alfa 90 was brought out in 1984 with a four-cylinder 1779- or 1962-cc engine, or a 2492-cc V6 engine. The diesel version has a VM 2393-cc 110-hp supercharged engine.

AMERICAN MOTORS

RAMBLER – JEFFERY – HUDSON – NASH – KAISER – JEEP

American Motors as a corporation is little more than thirty years old, but its family tree is deeply rooted and has many branches.

One of our ancestors – the Thomas B. Jeffery Company – began building cars before the turn of the century and sold its first Rambler at the Chicago Auto Show in March 1902. Another ancestor – the Hudson Motor Car Company – built and sold its first automobile in the summer of 1909.

Some of the other important names in AMC's genealogy include Charles W. Nash, who bought the Jeffery firm in 1916 and renamed it Nash Motors, and John North Willys, whose company gave birth to the famous workhorse Jeep at the start of the Second World War.

American Motors and its predecessors have indeed contributed important chapters to the history of our dynamic industry through the years. We are confident that the solid foundation American Motors has built will enable the company to grow and prosper as the industry moves into its second century.

W. PAUL TIPPETT   Chairman and Chief Executive Officer

The Eagle is produced in a two-door, four-door or estate version and one of its special features is its original four-wheel drive system, which has three differentials, the center one being lockable. It has a Pontiac four-cylinder 2471-cc 89-hp engine, although a V6 4235-cc 118-hp engine is also available, with a top speed of 165 km/h (102.5 mph). The steering is based on a circulating ball bearing system with a variable power-assisted reduction box.

In 1904, the Rambler was brought out as a goods vehicle of 2 cu yd or 500 lb capacity, according to the catalogue of the time. This Type 1 cost $850.

On 4 April 1905, President Theodore Roosevelt took part in the Louisville parade in this Type 2 Surrey, another product from Rambler.

The Model 36 of 1908 was sold at $3,250. The company offered a silver clock to any owner who could do over 24,000 km (15,000 miles) in six months – more than two hundred people came forward.

This 1909 Hudson cost $900 and was known as the Model 20. It was the first commercial success for the company, founded by eight Detroit businessmen.

The Rambler 63C of 1911 was very similar to the electric cars of the time and could carry four passengers. The height of the steering tiller was adjustable.

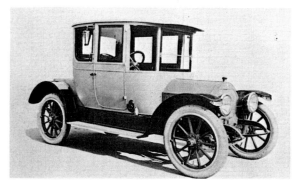

In 1913, the Hudson Model 37 coupé came out, with a finish that was well above average, offering a leather interior and "Richelieu blue" for the body (grey was optional). The wheels and chassis were blue and black.

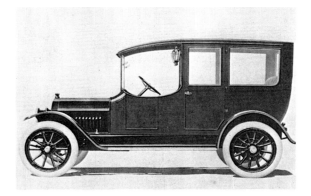

This three thousand-dollar limousine was called the Jeffery (dropping the name "Rambler," which had been in use for twelve years) in honour of the founder, who had died four years previously. It appeared on the market in 1914.

The Model Six-54 was the top of the Hudson range in 1914 and cost $3,100. At the time, only five years after the company had been founded, Hudson was the sixth most important automobile producer in the USA.

The 96-2 of 1915 was one of the few Jeffery cars to be produced; the factory concentrated more on commercial vehicles, selling 7,600 as opposed to 3,100 cars. It had a straight-six engine.

What may be seen as the origin of present-day American Motors dates back to 1902, when the first single-cylinder Rambler was built in Kenosha, Wisconsin, by the Thomas B. Jeffery Company. Jeffery was a bicycle constructor with a burning desire to get into the new world of motor propulsion, who subsequently built many different automobiles and lorries, specializing in integral traction vehicles. His four-wheel drive lorries were the most reliable on the market at the outbreak of the First World War, and the company was therefore commissioned to supply integral traction vehicles to send to the front.

In 1916, Charles W. Nash left the board of General Motors, where he had been managing director, to buy Jeffery's company and his Kenosha plant, which then became known as the Nash Motor Company. The arrival of Nash was a determining factor in the restructuring of the company, which very soon became the leading manufacturer. Two years later, the company's industrial supremacy was established with a total of 11,000 units, including cars and lorries. This figure was to rise over the following years as a result of supplies produced for the army during the First World War.

Nash, Lafayette and Ajax reached a production figure of 138,000 units in one year (1928), but it was not until 1937 that an important step was taken, with the merger agreement between Nash and the refrigerator manufacturer Kelvinator, leading to the formation of the Corporation for American Motors. The two companies were dependent on each other from the financial point of view, but entirely separate with regard to their two lines of production, cars and fridges. In 1950, the Rambler came out under the double name of the new company. It was the first "compact" American car, and introduced the concept of the

The V8s and V12s were tested for two years before the 76-hp version used in the Super Six of 1916 was developed. This car offered the driver no protection from the elements.

In 1916, the 104S was brought out as part of the Chesterfield series. This Jeffery had a body built by the Seaman Body Corporation of Milwaukee.

As early as 1918, when more than 10,000 were sold, the Nash 681 had a six-cylinder overhead camshaft engine, first brought out in late 1917.

This 1918 Hudson had all the luxuries available at the time as standard fittings: automatic heating, courtesy light, footrest and speaking tube.

The Phaeton five-seater of 1919 was one of the most popular models produced by Essex. One of this marque's road records was the fastest time on the Cincinnati–Indianapolis.

Sold in 1922 at $985, this four-cylinder Nash Model 41 was one of the contributing factors to the company's holding first place among American automobile manufacturers.

In 1923 this car was built and put on sale as the Model 134 for $5,500. A year later, Nash bought the car and the marque from the Lafayette Motor Company, founded in 1920.

In 1924, a new six-cylinder engine was introduced on this Essex Touring in place of the previous one of four cylinders. The car cost $8,850.

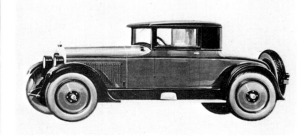

In 1926, Nash had twenty-four different models in their range. This is the Special-Six coupé, of which 135,000 were sold that year, taking sales over the 100,000 mark.

In only one year, Nash built a record 138,137 cars, the Model 338 of 1928 being a major contributing factor to the company's success. The record was unbroken until 1949.

The 1928 Hudson coupé was one of the many body versions available on a shorter chassis (only 9 ft 10 in, or about 3 m). The back seat was known as the "mother-in-law's seat."

Essex brought out this speedabout in 1929, the year of the Wall Street crash. From 1930 onwards, it was also available in identical form but with the Hudson marque.

The Essex town sedan of 1932, one of the last cars with the Essex marque, because their assembly lines were taken over half-way through that year by the Hudson Motor Car Co.

In 1933, Nash production dropped to fewer than 150,000 units. However, the Model 1194 remained one of the most important cars that year. It cost $1,955.

The 1933 Hudson Super Six coupé was fitted with a straight-six engine. The cars in the series were also available with eight-cylinder engines.

The AMC Pacer was put on the market in 1975, with an unusual design for the United States. Its rounded bodywork enclosed passenger space for four people in a coupé body shell. Initially it was fitted with a six-cylinder 4.2-liter engine.

smaller car to the American car market. Four years later on 1 March 1954, the merger between Nash-Kelvinator and Hudson combined all the companies under the new title of "American Motors Corporation."

The Hudson Automobile Company was set up in 1909 by Roy D. Chapin, who managed to produce 300,000 units in twenty years; he reached this figure in 1929, the year of the Wall Street crash, and production suffered as a result of its repercussions.

In 1958, the Nash and Hudson marques were abandoned and production continued under the name "Rambler." In the following year, the AMC produced 401,000 vehicles, exceeding half a million in 1963. Meanwhile, the Corporation had diversified its range a good deal, and offered both conventional motor cars and lorries, as well as many versions of four-wheel drive vehicles, a "speciality" of American Motors. In fact, the American group which had begun building lorries to supply the army during the First World War was never to abandon this line completely.

In 1968, AMC sold off the Kelvinator division to concentrate exclusively on the production of automobiles. New models were added to the Rambler: the Rebel, Matador, Javelin, AMX and the Hornet appeared on the market and enjoyed a certain degree of popularity in America, all following the philosophy of the compact car. In 1970, immediately after the AMC had taken over control of the Kaiser-Jeep company, the Rambler was replaced by the Gremlin.

The connection between the AMC and Kaiser-Jeep stems from John Willys, who had built plants in Toledo in 1911, barely three years after taking over Overland. In 1915, Willys

In 1934, Nash brought out the popular 110, with Lafayette lines, at a list price of $585 – 745. It had a 75-hp engine and 12,691 were built.

The 1937 Hudson Victoria coupé was built for export, with right-hand drive. This was unusual for the United States, but in 1937 Hudson was concentrating on exports.

Two different body styles were available for the 1939 Hudson Brougham Convertible. Each had a six- or eight-cylinder engine, giving 110 and 122 hp respectively.

One of the cheapest Lafayette cars of 1936 was this three-seater coupé. Lafayette produced 27,498 of them that year, and Nash earned a million dollars.

The 1940 Nash was a four-door saloon, the flagship of the home range. It had an eight-cylinder engine and sold at $1,195. It was later replaced by the Nash 600.

The 1941 Nash 600 was the only completely new car that year. Its petrol consumption was very low, giving 600 miles for only 20 gallons of petrol (about 14 km/liter).

141

In 1941, while still under the name of Nash-Kelvinator Corporation, Nash brought out the Ambassador, at $1,030 the most expensive car in their range.

The first convertible "compact" from Nash-Rambler appeared on the market in March 1950 and had a six-cylinder engine. The Rambler marque reappeared for the occasion.

The Hornet Sedan of 1954 had a six-cylinder engine that could develop 160 hp. With a twin camshaft fitted, the output increased by 10 hp.

The model 5829-2, better known as the Rebel (1958), had a V8 engine. Rambler adopted a more effective rustproofing immersion system the same year.

While the popularity of the American series was increasing, American Motors brought out a four-door estate and a convertible fitted with a six-cylinder engine.

In 1970, the Hornet Sedan (saloon) arrived. The new two- and four-door compact was available with six- or eight-cylinder engines. In all, 92,458 were built in the year of launching.

In 1970 American Motors put the Gremlin on the market as the first of the subcompacts. More than 26,000 were produced that year. In the September, AMC bought Windsor Plastics.

The coupé version of the Matador, a five-seater brought out in 1974, was added to the saloon and estate versions that were already in production, and to the sporty X.

From its very first appearance in September 1983, the Renault Alliance was an immediate success. The four-cylinder 1.4-liter/1397-cc engine has electronic injection.

The Renault Encore offers a high degree of comfort in the American Motors subcompact range. It has five doors and the rear seat folds down to give ample luggage space.

The CJ-7 jeep of 1984 has the new four-cylinder 2.5-liter engine, the same as that used on the Cherokee range. It is also available with an optional six-cylinder 4.2-liter engine.

Overland became the second most important manufacturer in the United States, specializing in four-wheel drive vehicles. This specialization proved useful in 1941, when they were called upon to present the American Army with a prototype vehicle which became known as a General Purpose vehicle. This was immediately abbreviated to GP and then changed to Jeep, the name which Willys patented, winning the commission and becoming the official Jeep manufacturer for the army.

After the war in 1953, Willys were taken over by Henry J. Kaiser and the new company became known as the Kaiser-Jeep Corporation. Six years later, a series of developments led to Kaiser-Jeep being ready to join the AMC; Kaiser-Jeep sold IKA in Argentina to Renault, and Willys in Brazil to Ford.

In 1971, the AMC, which had taken over Kaiser-Jeep the year before, set up a separate division to group the military vehicle and post van production plants together under the name American Motors General.

In 1979, an association began with Renault, which had acquired 46.6 per cent of AMC shares; the American company also became the Renault agent in the United States and Canada.

A general look at the current situation of AMC shows that the Kenosha (Wisconsin) plant is producing the Alliance (Renault 9) and the Encore (Renault 11), while the Toledo plant in Ohio produces civilian jeeps with the CJ5, Wagoneer and Cherokee models. There are factories in another seven cities producing spares. In Brampton (Ontario, Canada), on the other hand, they produce the AMC Eagle 4 × 4, and two other factories produce engines and interior upholstery. Jeeps are also assembled in Australia, Bangladesh, Egypt, Indonesia, Israel, Japan, Mexico, Morocco, Pakistan, the Philippines, Portugal, South Korea, Spain, Sri Lanka, Taiwan, Thailand and Venezuela.

ASTON MARTIN

The Aston Martin company was founded in London in 1922 by Lionel Martin, who decided to use his own surname plus a name taken from the Aston-Clinton hill climb, which he had won in 1913 in an Isotta Fraschini with a 1400-cc Coventry-Simplex engine.

Up until 1925, when the old Coventry-Simplex side-valve engine was used, Martin was financed by the amateur racer, Luis Vorov Zborowski, but after the talented Pole was killed in an accident at Monza in 1924, the company was taken over by Augustus Bertelli in 1926. Under his guidance, the famous 1.5-liter engine was brought out, which was to win a great number of races, particularly on the International and Le Mans models of 1932 and the Mark II and Ulster of 1935. In 1936, Aston Martin changed hands again, and the new owner, Gordon Sutherland, brought out a four-cylinder 2-liter overhead camshaft model. When the war ended, the company was taken over by David Brown, who brought about a definite change for the better on the technical and commercial fronts. In 1949, Aston Martin began fitting the DB series cars with a six-cylinder, twin overhead camshaft engine designed by Lagonda, another company taken over by Brown in the same period. The original displacement of 2.58 liters (DB2) was increased in 1952 to 2.9 liters. In 1959, a 3.7-liter engine was used for the DB4, later increased to 4 liters for the Lagonda Rapide (a prestige saloon built between 1961 and 1963), the DB5, DB6 and DBS.

A V8 5340-cc version came out in 1969 which was used on all later Aston Martins, as well as the futuristic Lagonda saloon of 1976. The Volante convertible came out in 1978.

Brought out in 1927 with a 1495-cc single overhead camshaft engine, the first 1.5-liter series included the International, Tourer and Sport models, and was in production until 1932.

During the war, Claude Hill, the chief designer under the Sutherland management, had built a new four-cylinder 2-liter engine with rods and rockers which was used on the first Aston Martins of the period 1948-50. This series was officially known as the DB1.

The DB2/4 Mk III, with a 2.9-liter engine, was in production between 1957 and 1959. This version developed 186 hp at 5500 rpm.

After the second series, produced from 1932 to 1934 and including the New International, Le Mans and Standard models, the Mk II and the Ulster were brought out, each of them capable of 80 hp at 5250 rpm.

In 1949, the six-cylinder series was launched with the DB2, which had a six-cylinder (2850 cc, 195 hp) twin overhead camshaft engine designed by W. O. Bentley for Lagonda. The body was made in aluminium by Tickford, another company in the David Brown group.

The DB4, brought out in 1958, had a Touring superlight body and a 3670-cc engine that developed 240 hp at 5500 rpm. The output was increased in the later Vantage and GT versions. The GT was capable of reaching 240 km/h (150 mph).

The DB5 made its début in 1963 with a 3995-cc engine developing 286 hp at 5500 rpm. The same engine was used on the DB6 of 1965 (illustrated above) and the DBS of 1967, setting the pattern for all later Aston Martins. The DB6 had all-round disc brakes and a five-speed gearbox.

The 5340-cc V8 engine was used for the first time on the DBS V8 of 1969, which had a De Dion type rear axle and a top speed of 272 km/h (170 mph). The soft-top cabriolet Volante was brought out in 1978 (306 hp at 5000 rpm, with a top speed of 240 km/h or 150 mph).

Brought out in October 1976, the Lagonda is a luxurious high performance saloon with the same mechanical features as the DBS V8. It has a top speed of 225 km/h (140 mph). The extremely large body is 528 cm (17.3 ft) long and weighs over two tons.

AUDI HORCH – DKW – AUTO UNION – NSU

"Audi" is the Latin translation of the surname of August Horch, the founder of the other German company that bears his name. Horch left this company because of irreconcilable differences with its board of directors in 1909 and created a new company, for which he was forbidden to use his own name – hence the formation of Audi Automobilwerke GmbH. The first car he built was the 10/28 HP, a four-cylinder version with an original valve-gear system that used opposed side valves. From the very start, the company was active in competition racing, and Audi won a great many races including the Tour des Alpes in 1912, 1913 and 1914. The 14/35 HP came first on the two latter occasions and was subsequently known as the Alpensieger. When the war ended, the G 8/22 HP runabout was launched on to the market, but it was not very successful and was followed by a number of prestige cars. However, as a result of competition from Mercedes and Horch, and the company's own precarious financial situation, it merged in 1928 with DKW, which had brought out its first automobile, the small, two-stroke P15, in the same year.

DKW took almost entire responsibility for design in the two companies. Audi's was the prestige name in the new group, which built a few large cars such as the Dresda six-cylinder and the Zwickau eight-cylinder, both of which had American Rickenbaker engines. In August 1932, Horch and Wanderer also joined the group, thus forming Auto Union AG, although the four marques all maintained their own independence on the market. The Wanderer marque was the second most popular of the group after DKW until the Second World War, after which it was no longer used.

During this period, Audi's production was characterized by the Front model which had front-wheel drive and was built in the Horch plant from 1934 onwards, the last pre-war Audi being the Front 225 with an overhead valve engine. After the war, Auto Union moved to Ingolstadt (the original Horch and Audi plants

One of the last Horch cars, the 853 A of 1938 belonged to the eight-cylinder series of 1930. The straight-eight single-shaft engine had a displacement of 4944 cc on this model.

With a two-stroke three-cylinder 900-cc engine capable of 30 hp, the 3-6 was derived from the F9 prototype, production having been delayed by the outbreak of war. The models illustrated are a 1953 soft-top and a 1956 saloon.

The small front-wheel drive F1 cabriolet of 1931 had a two-cylinder 584-cc engine developing 18 hp, and a chassis made up of two central beams and transverse supports.

The 1000 was launched at the 1957 Frankfurt Motor Show, the only car to have the Auto Union name. It was available in saloon, coupé and roadster versions. The three-cylinder 980-cc engine developed 50 hp. It was an automatic mixture two-stroke model with a thermosiphon water-cooling system. The four-speed gearbox had synchromesh on all speeds.

In production from 1959, the DKW Junior had a typical two-stroke three-cylinder 741-cc engine with an output of 39 hp SAE at 4300 rpm. Its top speed was 115 km/h (71.5 mph).

After the war, the Heilsbronn plant produced Fiat-derived cars. These included the Weinsberger, descended from the Nuova 500 (above left), and the Jagst Riviera Coupé (above right), which was built on the mechanics of the 600.

The NSU Prinz, brought out in 1958 with a two-cylinder rear-mounted air-cooled transverse engine (above), had a displacement of 598 cc and an output of 20 hp. In 1962, the Prinz 4 (below) came out with a more powerful 30-hp engine and Corvair-inspired lines. Two years later, a four-cylinder, 996-cc 43-hp engine was also used (Prinz 1000). The year 1965 saw the appearance of a version with a longer wheelbase and a 1117-cc engine, the 110, which became the 1200 in 1967 (bottom). The 1000 was also available in a TT and TTS sports version.

were in Zwickau in East Germany) and from 1949 to 1966 only the DKW marque was used, continuing with the traditional two-stroke engine. In 1958, Daimler-Benz took over control of the group. The first move by the new management was to launch the Audi at the 1965 Frankfurt Motor Show. It was a four-cylinder version of the F 102 designed by the Stuttgart company, who also developed the 100 model in 1969. In 1963, Volkswagen joined Daimler-Benz in running Auto Union and took complete control two years later. When NSU (Neckarsulmer Strickmaschinen Union) joined the group in 1969, the name of the company was changed to "Audi NSU Auto Union AG" and remained so until 1984, when "Audi AG" began to be used.

Directly derived from the Audi prototype built as part of the Auto 2000 programme, the new 100 was brought out in 1982 with a range of petrol engines (1800, 1900 and 2200 cc) and a 2000-cc diesel engine in both normally aspirated and turbo versions. The peak of the range is the 1983 200 Turbo which has a five-cylinder 2144-cc engine boosted by a turbocharger with an output of 182 hp at 5700 rpm and a top speed of 230 km/h (143 mph). The four-wheel drive version came out in 1984.

The very modern design of the 1967 Ro80 was combined with a twin-rotor Wankel engine having a total displacement of 994 cc and an output of 130 hp SAE at 5500 rpm. It was a front-wheel drive model and had semi-automatic, three-speed transmission with a hydraulic torque converter. Top speed was 180 km/h (112 mph). It had power-assisted disc brakes with a brake regulator. Production ceased in 1977.

Brought out in 1966, the Super 90 was the most powerful of the mid-range saloon series until 1972. The 1760-cc engine developed 90 hp at 5200 rpm and gave a top speed of 163 km/h (101.3 mph).

The Audi 50 came out in 1974, a full year before the Volkswagen Polo, which had exactly the same body. The 1093-cc engine developed 50 hp on the LS version and 60 on the GLS. It was in production until 1978.

The first of the Audi 80 series came out in 1972 with a four-cylinder engine of either 1296 or 1471 cc, developing 60 and 85 hp respectively. In 1976, the displacement of the more powerful model was increased to 1588 cc. The second series came out in 1981 with the addition of a 1588-cc 54-hp diesel, followed by a turbodiesel (70 hp), a four-cylinder 1781-cc (85- or 112-hp) version, and two five-cylinder engines of 1900 (2000 after 1983) and 2144 cc. Four-wheel drive versions have also been available since 1983. It is sold in the USA as the Audi 4000.

The Audi range was completed in 1968 with the 60 and the 75. The first of these (above left) was a 1496-cc model which could develop 60 hp at 5200 rpm and had a top speed of 144 km/h (90 mph). The 75, on the other hand, had a 1697-cc 75-hp engine, giving a top speed of 150 km/h (93.2 mph). Each was available in a two- or four-door version, and there was also an estate model known as the Variant.

The Audi 100 made its début in 1969. The four-cylinder 1760-cc engine came in two versions, with an output of 85 or 100 hp. A 1871-cc 112-hp coupé was also produced which could reach 185 km/h (115 mph) and had a standard four-speed synchromesh gearbox. A three-speed automatic version was also available.

In September 1980, the coupé was built on the 80 floorpan and is now available in various models: the GL (1781 cc, 75 hp), GT (1921 cc, 115 hp) and GT 5E (2144 cc, 130 hp).

The Audi Quattro, brought out in March 1980, heralded a whole series of cars, not only Audis, with four-wheel drive. Its five-cylinder 2144-cc engine has a turbocharger. A lighter version came out in 1983 with a shorter wheelbase.

In 1976, the 100 series (above) was completely updated and extended with the Avant model, which had a rear hatchback and different new engines: a four-cylinder 1600-cc and three five-cylinder versions (a 1900- or a 2200-cc petrol version, and a 2000-cc diesel). In 1982, the third series came out, with a much more powerful aerodynamic line. The Avant model is illustrated below. It is sold in the USA as the Audi 5000.

NSU had begun building automobiles in 1905, under license from the Belgian company Pipe, and specializing in small capacity cars. In 1926, a new plant was opened in Heilsbronn which was taken over two years later by Fiat for the production of Italian-derived cars. In 1958, the company went back to building original cars with the new Prinz, a very successful little runabout, particularly with the Prinz 4 series of 1962. In 1964, NSU was the first company to market a car with a Wankel engine and, since the Prinz had gone out of production in 1972, the ultra modern Ro80 rotary-engined saloon, which had been brought out in 1967, was the only car keeping the marque alive up to 1977. With the exception of the small 50, built from 1974 to 1978, Audi production from the 1970s onwards was split into two lines, the 80, launched in 1972 and completely updated in 1981, and the 100 which, apart from the original series in 1969, also came out in two totally new series in 1976 and 1982. In 1980, the original Quattro came out, a four-wheel drive sports model which has enjoyed a string of successes in rallies and set the trend towards four-wheel drive on all Audi products.

AUSTIN ROVER

AUSTIN – MORRIS – ROVER – MG – TRIUMPH

The car companies which today make up BL can trace their history back to the beginning of motor manufacture in Britain, and their development is closely tied to the development of the UK motor industry during this century. Pioneers such as Herbert Austin, William Morris and the Rover company, started by John Starley and William Sutton, contributed radical and innovative ideas which moved the industry forward in quite different ways.

Austin is probably best remembered for his Austin Seven of the 1920s, which brought popular family motoring within reach of ordinary people; William Morris injected new manufacturing ideas as well as creating a rich heritage of Morris and MG models, while the Rover name was associated from the start with stylish motoring based on engineering innovation. Yet, of all the models produced by BL, the Mini, the brainchild of Sir Alec Issigonis, must rank in any definitive list of cars which have changed the direction of the industry and brought a new motoring dimension to millions of people.

RAY HORROCKS   Group Chief Executive – Cars, BL Public Limited Company

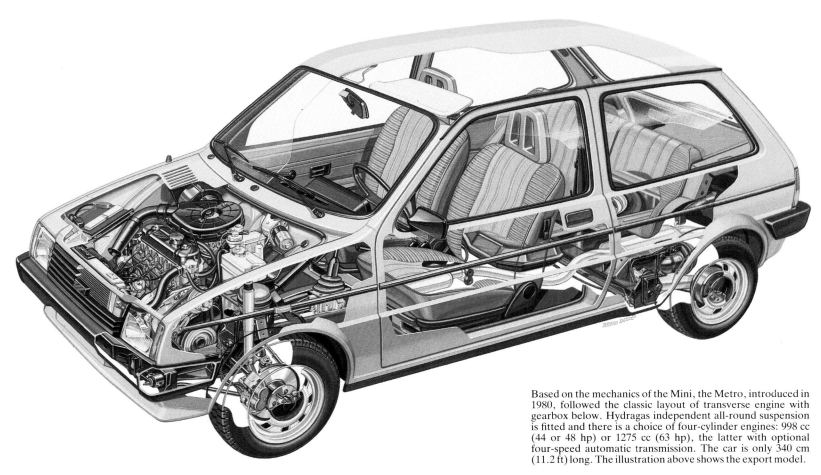

Based on the mechanics of the Mini, the Metro, introduced in 1980, followed the classic layout of transverse engine with gearbox below. Hydragas independent all-round suspension is fitted and there is a choice of four-cylinder engines: 998 cc (44 or 48 hp) or 1275 cc (63 hp), the latter with optional four-speed automatic transmission. The car is only 340 cm (11.2 ft) long. The illustration above shows the export model.

Herbert Austin at the wheel of his first car, a 32-hp four-cylinder, in 1906.

This 7 HP came out in 1909 with a single-cylinder engine and bodywork which prepared the way for the Seven.

This 1913 tourer had a four-cylinder 45-hp engine which could reach 80 km/h (50 mph).

The 12 HP came out in 1922 and was an immediate success. It had a four-cylinder 1661-cc engine.

The Seven of 1922 was a runabout with a four-cylinder 696-cc (later 747-cc) engine. Production totalled 300,000.

In 1931, a new version of the Twenty came out, with a six-cylinder 3400-cc engine.

The new soft-top A 90 Atlantic was launched at the London ▶ Motor Show of 1948.

Brought out in 1932, the Ten-Four remained in production until 1947 when it was replaced by the A 40. The four-cylinder 1125-cc engine was water-cooled.

The A 35 of 1957 was also called the Seven and was a four-cylinder 800-cc runabout with overhead valves and a ▶ four-speed gearbox.

Austin

The prototype of the first car with the Austin name was exhibited at the London Motor Show in 1905, but the company did not really take off until a year later. Herbert Austin was already known at the time for having popularized another make, the Wolseley. In just five years, Austin expanded to employ a thousand men and in 1920 was producing a hundred cars a week. The Austin Seven, of which 300,000 were produced, was one of the most famous. The Seven also takes the credit for saving the company from financial difficulties in the 1920s. The chassis was used by many other coachbuilders and even by some major car manufacturers such as Morgan and Datsun, who used it with their own bodywork.

The plant was in Longbridge in Birmingham, and many aeroplanes were built there during the Second World War. Herbert Austin was made a peer of the realm and took on Leonard Lord to ensure that he would have a successor to take over the company. Austin died in 1941. In 1952, when Lord had already been president for some time, Austin joined the Nuffield (Morris) group and formed BMC, the British Motor Corporation.

In 1959 the Mini arrived. Over five million were built from a design which came off the drawing-boards at Longbridge. This small car

The A 40 Devon (left) came out in 1947 and proved one of the most popular models of the post-war period. The 1958 Mk II (above) had a four-cylinder 1098-cc 48-hp engine. It had a unitary body, hydraulic pedal-operated brakes and was water-cooled. This model marked the beginning of the company's association with Pininfarina.

The Austin Healey Sprite, a roadster with completely innovative lines, had a 948-cc engine capable of 140 km/h (87 mph); it made its mark in both rallies and competitions.

The Austin Healey 3000 Mk II of 1959 had a six-cylinder 2912-cc 130-hp engine; top speed 173 km/h (107.5 mph).

The Allegro came out in 1973 with a two- or four-door body, front-wheel drive and an engine of 1.1, 1.3, 1.5 or 1.7 liters. In 1983, it was replaced by the Maestro (below), a hatchback with an engine of 1.3 or 1.6 liters and a five-speed Volkswagen gearbox.

The 1963 A 60 Cambridge was fitted with a four-cylinder 1622-cc 63-hp engine. It had a unitary body and rear-wheel drive.

The A 110 Westminster (six cylinders, 2912 cc, 126 hp) was a four-door, six-seater with a unitary body, rear-wheel drive, front disc brakes; power-assisted steering optional extra.

The name "Princess" returned with this new saloon in 1975. It had a transverse engine and front-wheel drive, with Hydragas suspension, a four-speed gearbox and power-assisted brakes.

The ultra-modern 1984 Montego is available in eight models with three different engines (1.3 to 2 liters). It also has a new electronic instrument panel, perfected since the Maestro.

The 1961 Vanden Plas Princess was a high-class limousine with a six-cylinder 3993-cc engine.

In the summer of 1959 appeared the Mini, designed by Alec Issigonis. This small, four-seater runabout (3.05 m/ 10 ft long) introduced the transverse engine with front-wheel drive. The Mini (this became the marque) is still in production, after minor improvements to its bodywork. The original 848-cc engine of 1959 was upgraded to 998 cc in 1984. An estate version, the Clubman Estate, is also available. Above, a 1959 model; below, the 1984 Mayfair.

was fitted with engines which ranged from 848 to 1300 cc, and one special car built for the Targa Florio in Sicily even had two different power plants, one a 1300-cc engine mounted at the front and the other an 1100-cc engine connected to the rear wheels. The car did not manage to reach the finish under its own steam, but it was nevertheless an interesting experiment.

In 1966, the company merged with Jaguar/ Daimler and in 1968 with BLMC, which had been formed by a merger between the Leyland Motor Corporation and BMH (British Motor Holdings). Today it is known as the Austin Rover group which, apart from Rover and Morris, also includes MG and Triumph, Jaguar having been reconstituted as a separate public company.

Rover

After several years in operation as a bicycle factory, Rover built their first car, the 8 HP, in 1904; in 1919 another 8 HP was brought out, of which a total of 18,000 were built, setting a record for the time. The company survived the recession of the next decade with relative difficulty and

The first four-wheel Rover came out in 1904. It had a single-cylinder engine which developed 8 hp. It remained in production until 1912.

The 8 HP of 1922 had a twin-cylinder, air-cooled engine. It remained in production until 1925.

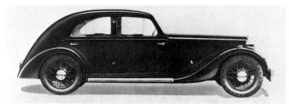

Various versions of the 14 HP of 1935 were available. It had an engine of six cylinders, 1.6 liters, and hydraulic brakes.

The Jet 1 Turbocar appeared in 1950 and was the first car to have a gas turbine engine.

Brought out in 1963, the P6 or 2000 had a unitary body, independent front suspension with horizontal coil springs, and a De Dion rigid rear axle. The four-cylinder engine had a displacement of 1975 cc.

The 12 HP came out in 1912 as a four-cylinder 2.2-liter model.

The 14-45 HP of 1925–8 had a four-cylinder 2.1-liter engine, and brakes front and rear.

This 1939 model, the 20 HP, also had a six-cylinder engine, with an increased engine displacement of 2512 cc.

The 1950 Pininfarina-designed 75 had a six-cylinder 2103-cc engine and Girling hydraulic brakes.

The P5B, on the market from 1967 to 1973, had a V8 overhead valve engine of 3.5 liters with central camshaft, and rear-wheel drive. It was fitted with an automatic Borg-Warner three-speed gearbox and all-round disc brakes.

approached the Second World War with its production based mainly on quality. The war kept the Rover plants near Birmingham fully occupied building aeroplane engines; after the war, Rover's activities were centered on the Solihull plant, where the P3, P4 and P5 luxury saloons were built, as well as the first car to be powered by a gas turbine engine. Large areas of the plant lay unused at the time, so in order to make them profitable Rover responded to a government call and in 1948 built the Land Rover, an off-road vehicle of which over a million had been produced by the mid-1970s.

The 2000, a classic saloon with an overhead camshaft and De Dion rear axle, came out in 1963. In 1966, the company merged with BMH. Rover also obtained a license from General Motors to build its light-alloy, 3.5 liter engine, which was used in the new Rover saloon and in the Range Rover, an off-road vehicle which brought a combination of elegance and practicality to the market. At the beginning of the 1980s, production began on a 2400 diesel with an Italian VM engine.

This smart Sport Tourer body was used on the 12 HP mechanics in 1947.

The 100, part of the P4 series, had a six-cylinder 2.6-liter engine, disc brakes on the front wheels, and overdrive.

The result of a joint venture between Austin Rover and Honda, the Rover 213 of 1984 has a new suspension system, a 1342-cc engine developing 70 hp at 6000 rpm, and a five-speed gearbox. The 1600-cc 216 was brought out in 1985.

This off-road model has been universally known as the Land Rover since it first appeared in 1948 (above). Over the years, production has increased dramatically, and from time to time its mechanics and body have been improved. Until 1979, the Land Rover was available with three different engines (2.3 liters, petrol or diesel, and 2.6 liters); in 1979, a V8 engine of 3.5 liters was added to the range. In 1984, the new Ninety, with a short wheelbase, was introduced. The illustration below shows President Peron of Argentina with one of the first Land Rovers. The Range Rover (bottom) is a four-wheel drive estate with a 3.5-liter V8 engine and power-assisted all-round disc brakes.

MG

The story behind this marque dates from the 1920s, when William Morris owned a company in Oxford known as the Morris Garage, the initials of which became the name of the sports car. The first MG was produced by putting a personalized body on to the Morris Cowley Bullnose. With the launch of the Midget, which was built on a Morris Minor chassis, the company expanded rapidly and production was transferred to Abingdon. Very soon, MG became famous for small sports cars with a reputation for sturdiness and reliability. At the beginning of the 1930s, new sports models with four- and six-cylinder engines came off the production lines and won a number of races, but after reorganization by the Nuffield Group in 1935, the sports programme was called to a halt. In the middle of the Second World War, Cecil Kimber, who from the beginning had made a great contribution to the company's remarkable success in his capacity as Director of the Morris Garage, left the company. The new management policy dictated that sports cars and saloons were to be built side by side, so the popular TF was built at the same time as the YA or Magnette. In 1955, production began on the MGA (100,000 units) and in 1962 the MGB roadster and coupé were launched. In 1968, BLMC and the Leyland group merged. The MG name was only to reappear in 1982 with the MG Metro.

The year 1976 saw the launch of the new 3500 as part of the fast tourer range, with a design that broke completely with Rover tradition. The five-door saloon had the usual V8 engine, but was later joined by the 2600 and the 2300 six-cylinder models. In 1982, these were followed by a 2400-cc turbodiesel version and the Vitesse, another 3500 with fuel injection. ▼

This sporty MG 14/28 HP was brought out in 1924 on the Morris Bullnose chassis with a 1548-cc engine.

The first Midget appeared in 1928. The 1929 Type M had conventional mechanics (four cylinders, 847 cc) and a two-seater body with the typical boat-shaped rear-end. It was followed by the 18/80 Mk I (below) with twin carburettors, power-assisted brakes and a four-speed gearbox.

The 1936 TA Midget had an engine of 1.3 liters. It was followed after the war by the TC (the last of the MGs to have a rigid axle) and the TD, which had independent front wheels.

The 1939 Type WA saloon had a six-cylinder 2.6-liter engine. It was followed after the war by the 1.25-liter Y type.

The classic four-cylinder 1489-cc 60-hp Magnette, which came out in 1956, was the first MG to have a unitary body.

The 1955 MG A had the same engine as the previous Midget, but was uprated to 69 hp. The Twin Cam model (above left) was in production from 1958 to 1960 (2,000 units in all). The MG A was replaced in 1962 by the MGB roadster and coupé (1965). The illustration above right shows the 1.8-liter MGB GT of 1980 with its new grille and bumper.

Developed from the Austin model, the MG Metro has a more powerful, 1300-cc 73-hp engine. A turbo version came out in 1983 with an increased output of 94 hp.

Triumph

Triumph started up last century as a bicycle factory and later branched out into the construction of motor cycles. More than twenty years were to elapse before they assembled their first car, which had an engine designed by Ricardo. After 1936, the company began to use Triumph engines on their cars instead of Coventry-Climax. In 1939, the company was declared bankrupt and was bought by T. W. Wards; he sold it in 1945 to Sir John Black, who already owned Standard. In 1950, the Mayflower came out on the market, with 32,000 units built on a tubular chassis and with a Standard 10 engine. It was not until 1952, however, that Triumph achieved real success with the launch of the TR 2, the first of the post-war Triumph sports cars, consolidating its position with the Herald, built with a Michelotti body. This formula seemed to work and the TR 5, the Spitfire and the 2000 were all built with bodies designed by Michelotti. These were followed by the fuel-injected 2.5 PI roadster and the V8 Stag. Meanwhile, Triumph-Standard was taken over by Leyland in 1961 (later to become British Leyland), thus adding credibility to the marque. BL went into production with the TR 7 at the Speke plant near Liverpool, although this car was very quickly dropped. The Triumph name reappeared with the Acclaim, which was brought out after an agreement with Honda.

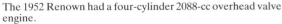

The first Triumph was the Super Seven of 1927 which came out in competition with the Austin Seven. It had a small, 893-cc engine. A total of 15,000 were built.

The 1952 Renown had a four-cylinder 2088-cc overhead valve engine.

The 1939 Dolomite, shown in the saloon version, had a six-cylinder 1991-cc engine.

The 1959 Herald was highly successful and remained in production until 1971. Designed by Michelotti, it had a 948-cc engine, later increased to 1147 cc and 1300 cc.

This small 1946 roadster had the 1800-cc engine and transmission of the Standard Vanguard.

The 1966 GT 6 was a small hardtop built on the Spitfire Mk IV chassis. The six-cylinder 1998-cc engine developed 95 hp at 5000 rpm and gave a top speed of 172 km/h (107 mph).

152

Developed from a prototype based on the pre-war Standard Nine frame, the 1952 TR 2 was the first of a long series of successful roadsters, the last of which was the TR 7 in 1975. The first version had a four-cylinder 1991-cc engine developing 90 hp at 4800 rpm, with a top speed of 170 km/h (106 mph). It had a steel chassis with coil springs at the front and semi-elliptic leaf-springs at the back. After a successful career, with many race wins to its credit, the TR 2 was replaced by the TR 3 in 1955.

The TR5 had a new six-cylinder 2498-cc engine developing 150 hp at 5500 rpm, and disc brakes on the front wheels.

In an attempt to standardize production, Triumph brought out several different versions of the Dolomite in 1972, with engines ranging from 1300 to 1850 cc.

The 1970 Stag had a 2997-cc V8 engine developing 147 hp at 5500 rpm. The bodywork was designed by Michelotti.

A new coupé, the TR 7, was brought out in 1975. With a conventional 2-liter engine, it was aimed particularly at the American market. A soft-top model was also available from 1979.

The 2500, launched in 1968, was available in a saloon or estate version. The six-cylinder engine later had fuel injection.

The Spitfire, came out in 1962 and continued to be built until the 1980s. The original 1.2-liter engine was increased to 1.5 liters. It had a top speed of 160 km/h (100 mph).

BMW

For more than seventy years, the BMW marque has been an integral part of the development of the automobile technology which has characterized this century. BMW aircraft engines made a significant contribution to the progress of modern air flight and the BMW engineers also deserve credit for the first touring motor cycle which, more than sixty years later, is still a precise and valid point of reference for the two-wheel industry today.

In the 1930s, BMW cars and motor cycles were reserved exclusively for a few privileged sports lovers who appeared at all the European circuits, and it was, in fact, enthusiasts like these who recognized the potential of the compact BMW saloons which were to distinguish themselves for their excellent performance and sporty lines. As a result of the introduction of this modern concept of the automobile on to the market, BMW has now become an international company operating in over a hundred countries and having three million cars on the road.

BMW is one of the few companies of the Western world to have made a profit every year for the past twenty years, and to have expanded during this period at a greater rate than any other car manufacturing company.

BMW's success as a result of their continuous technical innovations has been tried and confirmed in their racing wins, bringing the company to a level where it is no longer sufficient to limit development to the present, but essential to be actively engaged in research for the future.

In the years to come, BMW will maintain their tradition of producing cars of the highest quality and performance.

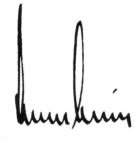

EBERHARD VON KUENHEIM   President and Managing Director of Bayerische   Motorenwerke AG

The year 1978 saw the beginning of a small series of the mid-engined M1 with a body designed by Giorgio Giugiaro. It had a straight-six 24-valve twin overhead camshaft engine of 3453 cc, developing 277 hp at 6500 rpm. Weighing 1290 kg (1.27 tons), the M1 was capable of reaching 262 km/h (163 mph).

The updated Series 3 range brought out at the end of 1982 includes two- and four-door models. These are available in two four-cylinder versions, the 316 and the 318i, both of which have the same 1767-cc engine, one carburetted and the other with fuel injection; and two six-cylinder versions, the 320i (1990 cc, 125 hp) and the 323i (2316 cc, 150 hp).

Bayerische Motorenwerke was set up in 1916 by a merger between Rapp Motorenwerke and Gustav Otto Flugmaschinenfabrik. They immediately went into production with aircraft engines and later with motor-cycle engines; they began producing cars in 1928 when the company took over Dixi, a small company building Austin Sevens under license. The British car continued to be produced under the BMW marque. A sports version won the team prize in the 1929 Alpine Cup and the class prize in the 1930 Monte Carlo Rally, the year when the two-seater 748-cc Wartburg was brought out. The first original tourer was the AM 4, brought out in 1934 with a 975-cc 20-hp engine.

Fritz Fiedler, who became chief engineer in 1933, was responsible for the first six-cylinder engine, fitted that same year on the 303 (1173 cc, 30 hp), which was to herald a long series of sporting cars. The most famous of these was unquestionably the 328 of 1937. The 3485-cc 335 was brought out just before the outbreak of the war; after the war, in 1952, production was resumed with the 501. This was developed from the earlier 326 and continued the tradition of large capacity engines such as the 502 of 1954, which had a 2580-cc 100-hp V8 engine. The same engine was used on the 507, an exceptional 3168-cc (160-hp at 4800 rpm) sports car, of which only two hundred and fifty were built between 1955 and 1959.

Production in the 1950s was clearly not suited to the post-war recovery period, and in 1959 BMW found themselves on the verge of bankruptcy. One of their first attempts to produce a more popular car was the Italian Isetta, built under license; this was a very small runabout which had a reasonable degree of success between 1955 and 1962. The company finally achieved its aim in 1959 with the 700, a two-cylinder with a Michelotti-designed body. Over

The 3/15 CV built in 1928 was a version of the Austin Seven, the license for which had been acquired by Dixi, a small company taken over by BMW in the same year.

Designed by Fiedler, the 315 had six cylinders, with a capacity of 1490 cc, and developed 34 hp. It was also available in a sports version, the 315/1, which had an output of 40 hp.

The 326, in production from 1936 to 1940, had a 1971-cc 50-hp engine with twin Solex carburettors and all-round hydraulic brakes.

Between 1937 and 1939, 462 of the celebrated 328s were built. ▶ This sports car won the 1940 Mille Miglia at an average speed of over 166 km/h (103 mph) with Von Hanstein at the wheel.

The first six-cylinder engine was used on the 303, which came out in 1933 in both a limousine and a soft-top version. The engine had a displacement of 1173 cc and an output of 30 hp.

The six-cylinder 1911-cc engine designed in 1934 formed the basis for all pre-war production. In 1936, it was used on the 319, which came in a sports version developing 55 hp.

The 327 came out in 1937 in both a coupé and a soft-top version. It had the 2-liter engine from the 326, which developed 55 hp at 4000 rpm.

The outbreak of war ruined chances of success for the 335, the largest-engined and most prestigious model produced by BMW before the war. It had a six-cylinder 3485-cc engine.

The 501 was launched at the 1952 Frankfurt Motor Show. It had a displacement of 1971 cc and developed 65 hp at 4400 rpm. In 1955, a 2077-cc engine was fitted.

The series of prestigious V8 engines was inaugurated in 1954 on the 502, which had the body of the 501 and a displacement of 2580 cc. A 3168-cc version was later used, which developed 140 hp at 5400 rpm.

The last V8 BMW, the 3200 CS of 1962, had a displacement of 3168 cc and an output of 160 hp at 5600 rpm. Its top speed was 200 km/h (124.2 mph). Servo-assisted disc brakes were fitted at the front.

Brought out in 1959, the 700 had a light alloy, two-cylinder 697-cc engine with an output of 35 hp at 5200 rpm, a top speed of 120 km/h (75 mph), and independent all-round suspension. It was also available in soft-top and coupé versions.

Total modernization of the BMW range began with the 1500 of 1962. The 1800 came out in 1963: 1766 cc, 90 hp at 5800 rpm and a top speed of 160 km/h (100 mph). In 1966, a 1990-cc engine was also used, with outputs of 100 and 130 hp.

The largest engine in the successful two-door saloon series inaugurated in 1966 by the 1602 (1573 cc, 85 hp) was the 1990-cc 2002, brought out in 1968, which developed 100 hp, later increased to 130 hp on the 2002 Tii. A tourer and a soft-top were also available, the latter only in the 2002 version.

The six-cylinder 2494-cc 150-hp 2500 saloon came out in 1968, followed by the 2.8 L (2788 cc, 170 hp), the 3.0 S (2985 cc, 180 hp), the 3.0 Si (195 hp) and the 3.3 Li (3210 cc, 200 hp).

Modernization of the six-cylinder saloons began in 1972 with the 520, and ended with the 525 and the 528, as well as a cheaper, four-cylinder model, the 518. The series was restyled in 1981, and in 1984 appeared the M 535i (3.5 liters, 218 hp). The 524 TD turbodiesel version came out in 1983.

Launched in 1978, the 628 CSi and the 635 CSi (2788 and 3430 cc, 184 and 218 hp respectively) were joined in 1984 by the M 635 CSi, which had a six-cylinder 3453-cc 286-hp engine developed from that used on the M1. Its top speed was 255 km/h (158.5 mph).

The Series 7 cars, the most prestigious six-cylinder saloons produced by BMW, made their début in 1977 with the 728 (2788 cc, 170 hp), 730 (2986 cc, 184 hp) and 733i (3210 cc, 197 hp). Two years later, the range was updated with the addition of the 728i and 735i, which had the same engines as the Series 6 models, and the 732i (3210 cc, 197 hp). The 745i came out in 1979 with a 3430-cc 252-hp turbocharged engine.

180,000 were produced up to 1965. BMW finally became firmly established on an international scale in 1962 when it brought out the 1500, a car that heralded a successful series of four-door (1800 and 2000) and two-door (1602 and 2002) saloons. A series of large, six-cylinder saloons with 2500- and 3300-cc engines were built between 1968 and 1977, from which the famous CS coupés were developed. In 1966, BMW took over the Glas company and was involved in build-

ing their eight-cylinder 3000 and a 1600 coupé.

In the 1970s, BMW gradually updated and rationalized their own range into three basic product lines: the Series 3, brought out in 1975, which included the compact four- and six-cylinder 1800–2300 saloons; the Series 5 of 1972, which included the four- and six-cylinder 1800–3500 saloons; and the Series 7, which was made up of more prestigious six-cylinder cars from which the Series 6 coupés were developed.

In association with its Austrian affiliate, BMW-Steyr Motoren GmbH, the Munich company developed a supercharged diesel engine (six cylinders, 2443 cc, 115 hp at 4800 rpm) in 1983, which has since been fitted on the BMW 524 TD and is supplied to Ford in America for the Lincoln Continental. The development of BMW has brought about a growth in production, increasing the total output of cars from 140,000 in 1963 to 410,000 in 1983.

CHRYSLER

DODGE – PLYMOUTH

The invention of the automobile changed the social history of mankind. It gave masses of people the power of individual mobility never before available to them.

The automobile gave men, women and children the ability to explore beyond the horizon of their native villages and towns. And what they saw with the automobile changed their way of thinking and feeling about themselves, their families and their livelihoods. It expanded their hopes, expectations and realizations for a better life.

On this centenary of the motor car, I pay tribute to an invention which became a gift to the people. It provided them with an infinite number of personal benefits. It began the never-ending love affair between the people and their automobiles.

LEE A. IACOCCA   Chairman of the Board and Chief Executive Officer of the Chrysler Corporation

The Imperial – typically American in both size and mechanical layout – was introduced in September 1980. The 5210-cc V8 engine has an output of 142 hp SAE at 4000 rpm. The valve gear is operated by rods and rockers, with hydraulic valve-play recovery. The Imperial's top speed is 180 km/h (112 mph) and it has automatic three-speed Torque Flite transmission.

The first Chrysler car, the Six of 1924, was also the first mid-range American car from the point of view of engine displacement and price. Around 32,000 were sold in 1924.

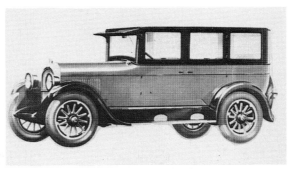

In June 1925, the four-cylinder Chrysler Four Series 58 was introduced. The 1926 models had six-cylinder engines.

An Imperial 80 of 1928 with a specially designed one-off body. Note the small door at the rear for easy access to the dicky.

In 1928, Chrysler introduced two new cars, the De Soto and the first Plymouth. The latter had a four-cylinder 45-hp engine, and cost $670–725.

Chrysler took over Dodge in 1928 when their sales had suffered a sudden drop. The 1930 Eight had an eight-cylinder 75-hp engine.

The 1930 77 was further vindication of the Chrysler policy of increasing investment in research and new models. The 77 cost $1,495.

Introduced in late 1932, this Plymouth had a six-cylinder engine designed by Zeder. Production of Plymouths increased between 1930 and 1932.

When the Chrysler and De Soto Airflow models were brought out in 1934, they introduced a new concept in body design, being more smoothly contoured, with a new distribution of weight. Despite the fact that many of its design features were subsequently adopted on post-war cars, the Airflow was not a great commercial success.

From 1934 onwards, Dodge cars were fitted with overdrive, independent front suspension and center-point steering. Automatic clutch was offered as an extra. Above, a 1935 saloon; below, a 1938 model.

The 1939 Imperial had an eight-cylinder 3235-cc 135-hp engine with hydraulic coupling. It sold for $1,198, the Custom Imperial costing $2,595.

A rare 1946 Town and Country Hardtop Coupé, of which only seven were built. The shooting brake body had wooden side panels.

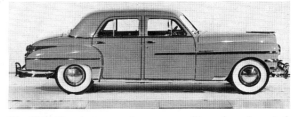

Plymouth Special De Luxe, 1948. The wheel diameter was bigger than on pre-war models, and the car weighed less, though the body design was unchanged.

The 1949 Chryslers were given a new grille and an elongated tail, a foretaste of the "fins" that were to become popular in the 1950s. The illustration shows the New Yorker.

Launched in 1979, the Gran Fury is a front-engined, rear-wheel drive saloon with a unitary body. It has automatic Torque Flite transmission and a circulating ball bearing steering system. It is available in two versions, the 3.7 with a straight-six 3678-cc engine, and the 5.2 with a 5210-cc V8. Neither of these versions is for export.

It was Walter P. Chrysler who in 1925 founded the automobile company that bears his name. The company started out with the Six, a car that was considered impossible at the time, which combined excellent road features with a very low price. The car was so well made and designed that 32,000 were sold in the first year of production (1924), a real success story. The Six was the result of a design produced by a team of three engineers, Zeder, Skelton and Breer, who were largely responsible for the early commercial success of the newly born company. In June 1925, a few months after the appearance of the Six, the Four was designed and launched. One of the technical reasons for the high degree of comfort of the Six and the Four was the introduction of rubber silent-block mountings, which reduced vibration. In 1926, four models were put on the market, the four-cylinder 50 series, the six-cylinder 60 series, the 70 – a new version of the Six – and the 80, which was known as the Imperial. The numbers of the series reflected the top speed in miles per hour of each model. In 1927, Chrysler was in fifth place among the other American automobile companies, with 192,000 units produced. Just before the great depression, Chrysler, which was making rapid progress, had built the first vehicle in the Plymouth line (at the low price of about $700) and the De Soto, which was a line of four-cylinder vehicles. At the same time, the company merged with Dodge, who also specialized in lorry construction. In 1934, the Chrysler and De Soto Airflow series was brought out. These cars offered a great deal more comfort than the other models available at the time, because the engine was positioned very far forward on the front axle, a design feature which was taken up in Europe by Citroën with their Traction Avant.

Over the years, Chrysler has expanded its interests, working in all fields of technology, particularly those connected with transportation.

The 1957 Dodge Royal had a V8 245-hp engine with fuel injection. Note the four front headlamps, used for the first time that year.

In 1955, the design of the Plymouth body was also changed, resulting in this 1958 Belvedere with its elongated tail and the long fins that were so typical of the period.

Brought out in 1960, the Dodge Dart was available in three versions, the Phoenix, the Pioneer and the Seneca. The first two had V8 engines, the Seneca a straight-six.

The 1961 Plymouth Fury two-door hardtop. The 5907-cc four-stroke V8 engine developed 309 hp at 4600 rpm and was capable of reaching 180–200 km/h (112–125 mph).

The Chrysler Newport had a unitary body and a 90-degree V8 engine of 5916 cc. Its market price in 1962 was $2,964.

The Chrysler Turbocar came out in 1963, after six years of research. The aerodynamic line was very pleasing, despite the heavy rear end. The lighting clusters were set in the bumpers.

The Plymouth Valiant compact, which was introduced in 1962, had a unitary body and was rustproofed. The six-cylinder engine developed 101 hp at 4400 rpm. The 1967 Signet model (below) was a four-door version, available with a six- or eight-cylinder engine.

A two-door hardtop, the 1966 Plymouth Sport Fury was a V8 version of the Fury. It had a slightly longer body and weighed about 1735 kg (1.7 tons).

Competition from the "small" European and Japanese cars led American companies to reduce the size of their own. Illustrated is the Dodge Coronet.

The elegant and sophisticated Dodge Custom 880 fell into the middle price range. Six different models were available; illustrated above is the four-door hardtop of 1962.

The Chrysler 300 of 1967, shown here in the two-door hardtop version, was a luxury car which had disc brakes, a 7.2-liter 350-hp V8 engine, and a four-speed synchromesh gearbox.

The Dodge Monaco was a six-seater with a 6286-cc V8 engine developing 279 hp at 4400 rpm. Its top speed varied from 175 to 185 km/h (110–115 mph).

One of Plymouth's "mid-range" cars was the Satellite Sebring coupé hardtop. It had a six-cylinder 3.7-liter engine, and drum brakes. An automatic Torque Flite gearbox was available on request.

The two-liter made by Chrysler France was brought out in 1973. It had power-assisted all-round disc brakes.

◄ The New Yorker, an American luxury car, was still in production in 1973. In the following year, the bodywork was modified and five different engines were offered.

◄ Produced in Great Britain, the Chrysler Alpine GL was brought out in 1975 with the same engine as the Talbot Simca 1510: four cylinders, 1294 cc, 68 hp at 5600 rpm, and a top speed of 150 km/h (93 mph).

The 1983 Fifth Avenue forms part of the Chrysler luxury range. It comes with many optional extras, from electric windows to air conditioning, reclining seats and cruise control. Its basic price was $13,990.

The 1967 Dodge Coronet 500, shown here in the hardtop version, was available with six different V8 engines, with displacements ranging from 4490 to 6974 cc.

In 1966 appeared the new Dodge Charger, with a cut-off rear end. The 1968 version (above) was fitted with V8 engines and had a unitary body.

The Duster was a compact Plymouth available as a coupé or coupé hardtop, with a six-cylinder 3.7-liter or an eight-cylinder 5.2-liter engine.

The 1971 Dodge Polara series had either a six-cylinder 3.7-liter engine or a 5.9-liter V8. The three-speed synchromesh gearbox had column change.

The Chrysler 180 was distributed by Chrysler France. It came out in 1970 with a 1.8-liter 100-hp engine, all-round disc brakes and a top speed of 170 km/h (105 mph). ►

Brought out in 1981 in coupé and soft-top versions, the Dodge 400 has a four-cylinder 2213-cc engine developing 85 hp SAE at 4800 rpm. A 2555-cc version produced by Mitsubishi is also available, with an output of 93 hp SAE at 4500 rpm. The same engines are used on the Chrysler LeBaron, which is practically a four-door version of the 400. Its top speed is 155–165 km/h (96–102 mph).

As well as cars and lorries, Chrysler produces marine engines and has built armed cars and missile parts in all corners of the world. In the early 1980s, Chrysler survived the recession in the American market, emerging victorious, thanks to its president Lee Iacocca.

Chrysler headquarters is in Michigan and the Corporation as a whole provides work for over 90,000 people. In typical North American style, a monument has been erected in front of the head office to Walter P. Chrysler, in memory of his qualities both as a man and as a businessman. In 1984, Chrysler made an agreement with Maserati in Italy, part of the De Tomaso group, and bought 5 per cent of the company, in preparation for the production in the near future of an American car with Italian styling. The agreements reached with the Italo-Argentinian Alejandro De Tomaso were made with a view to producing a new Chrysler model, not an American-built Maserati, although the Italian Biturbo is proving very successful on its own account in the USA.

Though similar to each other, Plymouth's 1984 Gran Fury and Chrysler's New Yorker are aimed at different markets. Both are four-door saloons, but the Gran Fury has a 5.2-liter V8 as opposed to the New Yorker's four-cylinder 2.2-liter engine.

Chrysler brought out this new Laser coupé, with a 2.2-liter turbo engine, in 1984. Together with the Dodge Daytona coupé, it is aimed at the sports enthusiast. Its top speed is 180 km/h (112 mph).

A 2.2-liter turbo engine is used on the 1984 Dodge 600. This front-wheel drive car is also sold in a soft-top version.

CITROËN

It is impossible to talk about the Citroën company and its influence on the history of the automobile without first mentioning the man who created it. In 1919, André Citroën launched the first European car to be built in a large series, intending to build a hundred units a day of that particular model.

André Citroën was one of the first to believe in the international role of the automobile and demonstrated this by taking part in such great adventures as the marathon across the Sahara and a similar trek across Asia.

From 1919 to 1934, Citroën was again at the forefront in the diffusion and popularization of the automobile. In addition, André Citroën published a repair manual, launched the idea of a "year's guarantee," free servicing and payment by instalments, perfected new methods of market research and set up schools for his salesmen. At the same time, he also developed his company's image and had 185,000 road signs erected. From 1924 to 1934, the Citroën name shone from the Eiffel Tower. He also invented industrial tourism by opening his factories and providing guided tours for the public. In addition, André Citroën organized a fast transport bus service, launched his own motor insurance company and opened branches in Belgium, Switzerland, Italy, Spain, Germany, Great Britain, Sweden and Poland.

Finally, and most important of all, it is because of its products and technology that the Citroën company has revolutionized the world of the automobile. The Traction Avant, brought out in 1934, was the first model of a range which lasted until 1957 and conquered the world: from 1934, Citroën has built sixteen million cars, all with front-wheel drive. The Traction Avant opened up the main avenues along which Citroën was to conduct its research. Hydro-pneumatic suspension, high-pressure power-assisted brakes, power steering and the use of new materials have all resulted from developments made since 1934. A new philosophy in private transport appeared with the 2 CV. The DS, nicknamed "La Bombe" at the Paris Salon, was also revolutionary for its aerodynamic lines and innovatory features. The GS and the CX have both benefited from this technological progress; the BX is likewise an original product, its body made in synthetic materials – materials of the future, characterized by their high performance and lightness.

The marque of the double chevron has influenced the automobile world with its avant-garde technology. It still keeps this role today, developing the manufacture of diesel and turbo engines, and light aerodynamic and economical cars.

JACQUES CALVET   President of Automobiles Citroën

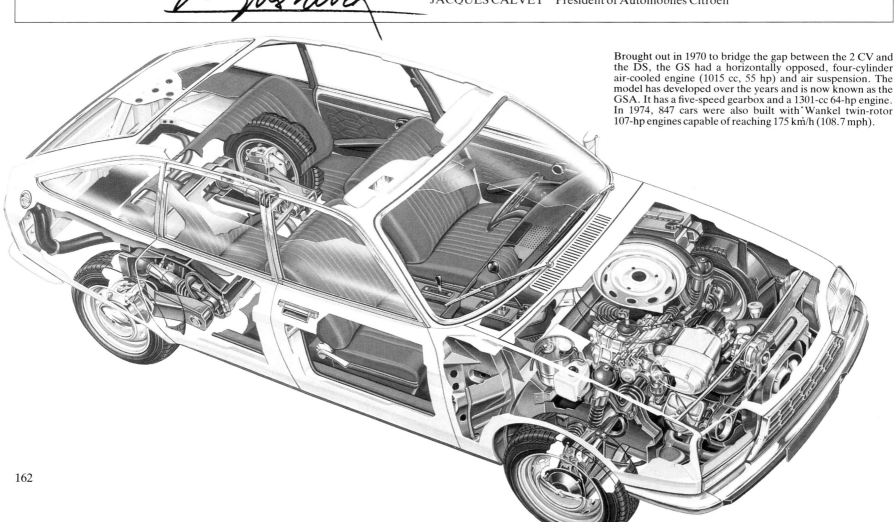

Brought out in 1970 to bridge the gap between the 2 CV and the DS, the GS had a horizontally opposed, four-cylinder air-cooled engine (1015 cc, 55 hp) and air suspension. The model has developed over the years and is now known as the GSA. It has a five-speed gearbox and a 1301-cc 64-hp engine. In 1974, 847 cars were also built with Wankel twin-rotor 107-hp engines capable of reaching 175 km/h (108.7 mph).

162

When the first Citroën in history, the A, came off the assembly line in Quai de Javel in May 1919, André Citroën was forty-one years old; he had, however, already gained valuable experience both as an industrialist and a manager. Shortly after leaving the Ecole Polytechnique, he set up a factory with a couple of partners to manufacture industrial gears with bevelled teeth, which were stronger and quieter than the traditional straight-tooth gears. As a result, the "points" or inverted "V"s which graphically represented the bevelled gears became the symbol of the marque, known in French as the *double chevron*.

Citroën's association with automobiles had begun as early as 1907, when the company took over the management of Mors, which was going through a difficult period after an initially successful launch at the turn of the century. Citroën, however, was above all a great industrial organizer, and while Europe was on the verge of the upheaval of the First World War, he bought land on the Quai de Javel to the south-west of central Paris, where he set up a munitions factory with excellent production systems to supply the hard-pressed French army. When the plant was complete, it was producing up to 55,000 grenades and shells a day.

On this wave of industrial success, the dynamic André Citroën was commissioned by the French government to supervise the power supplies to the army factories, to organize provisions for the workers in those industries and to manage the Roanne arsenal. With the benefit of this experience, Citroën realized that the industrial revolution would also lead to the increased popularity of the automobile and so gave a team of engineers the task of designing and building a car that would be relatively luxurious and powerful. By 1917, a dozen or so prototypes had been tested in "service" between Roanne and Javel. Meanwhile, in the depths of the factory and with the utmost secrecy, André Citroën had dismantled and seen how certain very famous American cars – Buick, Nash and Studebaker – were put together in order to study the application of large-series production methods to the automobile.

In fact the first Citroën was also the first European car to be built in a large series. It was the Type A, a roadster also known as the 10 HP, 8/10 and driven by a four-cylinder in-line 1327-cc engine developing 18 hp at 2100 rpm. Light and easy to handle, the Citroën A had extremely soft, comfortable suspension (which was later to become a feature of all Citroëns), left-hand drive, a centrally positioned gear lever directly connected to the gearbox, and engine, clutch and gearbox all housed in a single unit.

All this gave the car an illusion of being very simple, light and easy to drive, contributing greatly to its success with the public. The first A was delivered on 4 June 1919 to a certain M. Testemolle for a sum of 7,950 f. A total of 18,291 were built in the *conduite intérieure* version, as well as a small number of "sports roadsters" after 1921 which could do 90 km/h (56 mph) and give on average 11.5 km/liter (32.5 mpg).

The first Citroën – and also the first European car to be built in a large series – was the A. Brought out in 1919, it was a 1327-cc 18-hp roadster with a top speed of 65 km/h (40 mph).

The B 2 was developed from the A, and had a 1452-cc side-valve engine with fan as opposed to thermosiphon cooling.

Having overcome the teething problems with the B 10, Citroën used a steel body for the first time on the B 12.

The 10 was a 1932 model with a wheelbase of 315 cm (12 ft 4 in), obtained by fitting the 36-hp engine of the 15 on to the frame of the 8.

Launched at the 1921 Paris Motor Show, the 5 CV – built from 1922 onwards as the Type C, also known as the *Citron* ("Lemon") – was a mid-range, 856-cc 11-hp model.

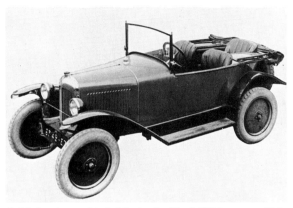
A third seat was added at the back of the 5 CV; because of this seating arrangement the car was known as the *Trèfle* ("Trefoil," i.e. clover-leaf).

The C 4 (an abbreviation of the AC 4, i.e. André Citroën, four-cylinder), shown here in the closed body version of 1929, was similar to the C 6, but with a shorter bonnet.

The 10 A, the last development of the 10, had independent torsion bar front suspension.

The *Petite Rosalie*

Between 15 March 1933 and 27 July of the following year, a modified 8 (nicknamed *Petite Rosalie*) covered a record distance of over 300,000 km (186,411 miles) at an average speed of 93 km/h (57.8 mph) on the Montlhéry circuit. Justly proud of *Petite Rosalie*'s result (left), Citroën offered three million francs to anyone who could better this performance; no one could. Right, the 8 CV Rosalie with a standard saloon body.

This is the first official photograph of the 7 CV, the legendary Traction Avant of 1934, which was produced in various versions up to 1957.

Between September 1934 and July 1957, more than 10,000 units were built of the 11 Light, a more powerful version of the 7 S, capable of reaching 120 km/h (74.5 mph).

Brought out in 1949 (although the first prototypes were on the road as early as 1939), the legendary 2 CV is still in production. This is the Special, with three side lights.

The unforgettable DS (6 October 1955–24 April 1975) had air suspension, making it one of the most advanced cars of the post-war period.

Brought out in April 1961, the Ami 6 used the base of the 2 CV with a flat-two 602-cc 20-hp engine and had a top speed of 105 km/h (65.25 mph).

The Dyane is another spin-off of the 2 CV: it had the standard 602-cc engine but developed 30 hp (as opposed to the 29 hp of the 2 CV) and could reach up to 121 km/h (75 mph).

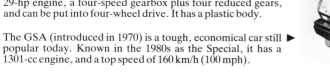

Brought out in 1979, the Mehari 4 × 4 has the standard 602-cc 29-hp engine, a four-speed gearbox plus four reduced gears, and can be put into four-wheel drive. It has a plastic body.

The GSA (introduced in 1970) is a tough, economical car still ▶ popular today. Known in the 1980s as the Special, it has a 1301-cc engine, and a top speed of 160 km/h (100 mph).

The "break" version of the big CX has ample goods or passenger space, a top speed of 151 km/h (94 mph) and a high degree of comfort.

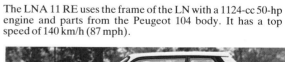

This is a Citroën built in Romania. Launched by Oltcit on 15 October 1981 at the Bucharest Exhibition, it is sold in Western Europe as the Axel.

The LNA 11 RE uses the frame of the LN with a 1124-cc 50-hp engine and parts from the Peugeot 104 body. It has a top speed of 140 km/h (87 mph).

The BX (illustrated here is the 14 RE) is the new Citroën mid-range car. It is also available with a diesel engine and has hydropneumatic suspension.

The CX TRD turbodiesel is unquestionably one of the fastest and most comfortable diesel saloons today. Its 2.5-liter 95-hp engine gives a top speed of over 170 km/h (105.6 mph).

Available only since Summer 1984, the Visa diesel has a PSA 1769-cc 60-hp engine, a top speed of 154 km/h (95 mph), and a fuel consumption of 16 km/liter (45.2 mpg).

In June 1921, the A was followed by the B 2, which had an engine displacement of 1452 cc and very few points in common with the previous model. Then in 1923, in a small series, came the sporty 300 B 2 "Caddy" – an elegant three-seater which was in great demand both with the motorists of its day and with collectors today.

The popular 856-cc two-seater C roadster was also in production from the spring of 1922. It was normally a light yellow colour and so was affectionately nicknamed "*Petit Citron*" ("Little Lemon"). The cabriolet version followed, featuring the typical prow-shaped tail.

As early as June 1924, Citroën were producing more than 250 cars a day; the Javel plant had extended itself over the whole 15th *Arrondissement* and branches had been opened in Belgium, England, Italy, Holland, Switzerland and Denmark. Citroën was the first company in Europe (as well as being one of the first in the world) to use an all-steel body instead of wood. This led to the launch of the B 12 and B 14, the best-equipped of the series-produced cars with a splendid dashboard and adjustable seats. In only two years, 132,483 "indestructible" B 14s came out of the Citroën plant.

The AC 4 and the AC 6 (A and C are the initials of the manufacturer and 4 and 6 the number of cylinders) were developed from the B 14; in 1931, the CGL (Citroën Grand Luxe) was brought out, based on the prestigious C 6F but with a 2650-cc 53-hp engine, and very high-class bodywork and interior finish. The AC 4 and the AC 6 also gained a lot of prestige after the famous "Asian Crossing," which took it as far as the Himalayas. In 1932, a spartan version of the C 4, the C 4 IX, was brought out with a 1628-cc 30-hp engine, but was not well received by the public.

In the 1933 Paris Salon, Citroën exhibited five different models (8, 10, 15, 10 light and 15 light), representing a whole range, but it was not until April 1934 that the revolutionary new 7 – the famous Traction Avant – was brought out. It remained in production for twenty-three years (until 1957), during which time 750,000 were built. The Traction, Citroën's first truly revolutionary car, opened the way to front-wheel drive (more than two-thirds of the cars on the road throughout the world today have front-wheel drive, and Citroën themselves have built more than sixteen million cars, all with front-wheel drive, in the fifty years from 1934 to 1984).

However, the Traction also changed the face of Citroën, for it signalled the company's move into the technology of the future and ambitious new techniques.

The first prototype of the 2 CV, a veritable legend of a car which is still in production, came out in 1939 (though the first studies into the "people's car" began in 1936), but it was not put on the market until 1949, partly because of the war. The unforgettable DS was launched in 1955, with its highly advanced air suspension and aerodynamic lines, followed in 1961 by the small but distinctive Ami 6. In 1970, Citroën tried out the Wankel rotary engine on the M 35, and in the same year brought out the GS, which had an air-cooled, 1-liter flat engine and air suspension, and the SM coupé, which was produced in collaboration with Maserati, using the latter's six-cylinder 2670-cc engine. The CX came out in late 1974 as the successor to the DS, followed in 1976 by the LN, which shared certain mechanical parts with the Peugeot 104 ZS.

The Visa came out in 1978 and the BX in 1982; both these cars, plus the CX, are now available with diesel engines, completing the wide Citroën range.

This unusual version of the unbeatable 2 CV is known as the 2 CV 6 Charleston. Initially produced as a limited series, it is still in production today.

FERRARI

When Ferrari Automobili was founded in 1945, the marque was already well known alongside the names of other motor manufacturers, and its history dates back still further, as its founder had been working in the motor industry since 1919 and consequently had accumulated a wealth of experience.

Enzo Ferrari had already built cars before, when the Scuderia Ferrari used Alfa Romeo material (the Alfa Bimotore and the Alfetta 158 were his creations). These were followed by two models of a sports car, the Auto Avio Costruzioni, Type 815 of 1940, which he built after he had left the Milan company. The first true Ferrari, however, was the 125 Sport, which was announced in late 1946 and made its début in Piacenza on 11 May 1947.

In the meantime, Ferrari continued developing sports cars and GTs, producing the 166, 212 and 250 (Ferrari models were identified for a long time by the unit displacement of one cylinder in his twelve-cylinder engines, so that, for example, 125 meant a 1500-cc engine while 250 indicated a 3-liter) and an F 1 monoposto was also fitted out which made its début at the Italian Grand Prix in Turin on 5 September 1948.

Development in the sports sector continued with the adoption of naturally aspirated 4500-cc engines – Ferrari's first cars had been supercharged 1500-cc versions – followed by four-cylinder 2-liter models for the F 2, then by six-cylinder 2.5 liters, and 1.5 liters unsupercharged six- or eight-cylinder versions, before returning to twelve-cylinder 3-liter versions. When the Ferrari name was combined with Pininfarina bodywork the production of tourers took off on a truly international scale. Until then, Ferrari bodies had been built by the best coachbuilders, from Vignale to Michelotti; after 1952 almost all were designed by Pininfarina.

The scale of Ferrari's development on an industrial basis can be seen from the production figures of cars destined for the market: 7 cars were produced in 1947 (including racing cars); by 1950 this figure had risen to 70, then to over 300 in 1960, nearly 1,000 cars in 1970 (in 1969 they joined Fiat), reaching 2,000 cars a year in 1979 and stabilizing at 2,500 a year in the 1980s. The Ferrari plants include two factories, one for bodywork at Modena (formerly the Scaglietti coachbuilders) and one for the production of mechanical parts and final assembly at Maranello which has a surface area of 148,000 sq m (177,008 sq yd), 68,000 sq m (81,328 sq yd) of which are covered. The racing section was transferred to a modern, independent unit next to the Fiorano

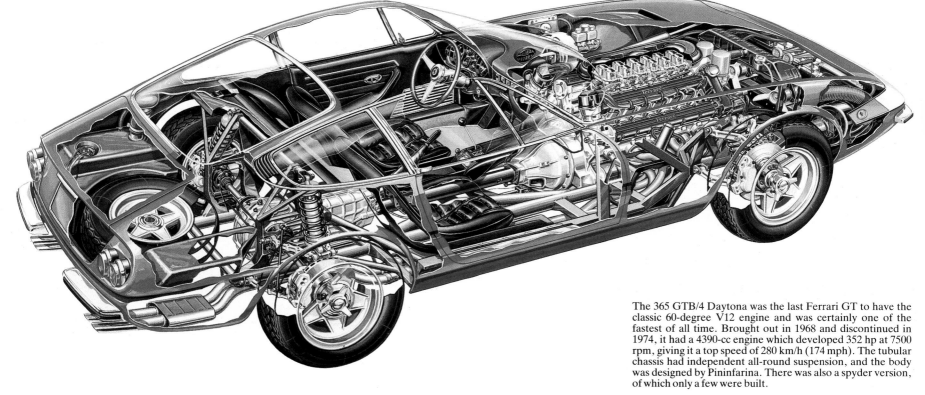

The 365 GTB/4 Daytona was the last Ferrari GT to have the classic 60-degree V12 engine and was certainly one of the fastest of all time. Brought out in 1968 and discontinued in 1974, it had a 4390-cc engine which developed 352 hp at 7500 rpm, giving it a top speed of 280 km/h (174 mph). The tubular chassis had independent all-round suspension, and the body was designed by Pininfarina. There was also a spyder version, of which only a few were built.

Brought out in 1984, the GTO represents the application of the most sophisticated competition technology to production cars. The 2855-cc V8 engine is entirely made of light alloy, with four valves per cylinder and electronic fuel injection. It has two turbochargers (one for each bank of cylinders), each with an air-to-air heat exchanger which increases the output to 400 hp at 7000 rpm. Its top speed is 302 km/h (188 mph) and it can reach 0-100 km/h (0-62 mph) in 4.9 seconds.

circuit, and in 1984 an engine test section was completed which has test rigs capable of measuring power outputs in the order of 1000 hp. Ferrari employ approximately 1,600 people, 100 of them in the racing section. Ferrari's continuing involvement in racing is clearly seen from the number of titles they have won: the company's drivers took the Formula 1 world championship title in 1952, 1953, 1956, 1958, 1961, 1964, 1975, 1977 and 1979, while the marque took the world

title for the company in 1982 and 1983. The Manufacturers' Championship, which is competed for in endurance races, has seen Ferrari take the title every year from 1953 to 1967 (with the exception of 1955, 1959 and 1966), and in 1972, although more recently they have not competed in the Championship, preferring to concentrate on Formula 1. The experience gained in racing has enabled the company to transfer valuable developments such as fuel injection, electronic

ignition and synthetic materials (carbon fiber, honeycomb panels, and so forth) to production models.

Ferrari's production concentrates on GT models with large capacity V12 engines and, more specifically, sports cars with 2- and 3-liter V8 engines, including the GTO, a version with twin turbochargers. A four-door model, a completely new venture for Ferrari, is on the drawing-board for the near future.

The 212 Inter was brought out in 1952. The V12 engine had a displacement of 2562 cc and an output of 160 hp at 7000 rpm. Its weight of 850 kg (1874 lb) allowed excellent acceleration and a top speed of 220 km/h (137 mph).

Built mainly for the American market, the 342 America had a 4102-cc V12 engine developing 230 hp at 6000 rpm and was capable of 186 km/h (115 mph). As the 375 America, in 1953, it had a 4523-cc engine developing 300 hp at 6500 rpm.

The first 410 Superamerica made its début in 1956. The single shaft 4962-cc V12 engine developed 340 hp at 6500 rpm. The series remained in production until 1959. In 1958, Pininfarina built the two-seater coupé, illustrated above.

FERRARI

The classic Ferrari V12 had an engine of 2953 cc. Used for the first time in 1952, it was a characteristic feature of the 250 GT, in production from 1955 to 1963. The 1958 version (illustrated above) developed 235 hp at 7200 rpm, with a top speed of 240 km/h (150 mph).

The 365 GTC/4 was brought out in 1971 with a 4390-cc V12 engine that developed 340 hp at 6800 rpm. Its top speed was 260 km/h (161.5 mph). The body, designed by Pininfarina on a tubular chassis, had retractable headlights plus two extra double-function patented lamps (long distance and fog lamps).

The 1962 version of the 400 Superamerica developed 340 hp at 6750 rpm, with a 3967-cc engine. The four-speed gearbox also had overdrive. The top speeds in the different ratios were 109, 163, 220 and 287 km/h (68, 101, 137 and 178 mph). It was 430 cm (14 ft 1 in) long.

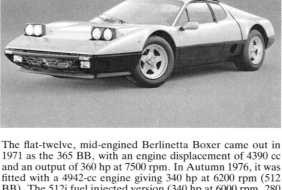

The flat-twelve, mid-engined Berlinetta Boxer came out in 1971 as the 365 BB, with an engine displacement of 4390 cc and an output of 360 hp at 7500 rpm. In Autumn 1976, it was fitted with a 4942-cc engine giving 340 hp at 6200 rpm (512 BB). The 512i fuel injected version (340 hp at 6000 rpm, 280 km/h [175 mph]) came out in 1981.

Having introduced the first 2 + 2, the 250 GT in 1960, Ferrari brought out the 330 GT 2 + 2 in 1964. It had an engine displacement of 3967 cc and could develop 300 hp at 6600 rpm. The gearbox originally had four speeds plus overdrive, but this was changed to five speeds in 1965.

The mid-engined Dino series was introduced in 1967 with the 206 GT, a 1968-cc V6 giving 180 hp at 8000 rpm. In 1969, the displacement was increased on the 246 GT (above) to 2418 cc, with an output of 195 hp at 7600 rpm. In 1974, the six-cylinder engines were replaced by the V8 on the 208/308 GT4 (below), which had a Bertone body and was in production until 1980.

The 308 GTB (above left), which made its début in the 1975 Paris Motor Show, was followed two years later by the open GTS version (right). The 2962-cc V8 engine developed 230 hp at 6600 rpm. In 1980, a fuel injection system was fitted which reduced the output to 214 hp; but in 1982, when the head was replaced by one with four valves per cylinder, the output rose again to 240 hp at 7000 rpm. A 1991-cc version (155 hp) was brought out in 1980, forming the basis for the 208 Turbo of April 1982 (220 hp).

The last Ferrari to have the V12 engine, the 400i, was brought out in 1976. Its 4823-cc engine developed 315 hp at 6400 rpm and gave a top speed of 235 km/h (146 mph). A five-speed manual or a General Motors' Turbo-Hydramatic three-speed automatic gearbox was available.

The Mondial, introduced in 1980, has the same fuel-injected engine as the 308 series and is the first four-seater Ferrari with a mid engine. The tubular chassis is reinforced with pressed steel and can be dismantled at the back together with the engine. The cabriolet version was brought out in 1984 (above right). The Quattrovalvole ("Four-valve") of 1982 has a top speed of 240 km/h (150 mph).

The 1984 Testa Rossa has the twelve-cylinder engine of the BB with four valves per cylinder and electronic injection; 400 hp, top speed 290 km/h (180 mph).

FIAT

A history and analysis of the succession of models brought out by Fiat, from 1899 – the year of the company's foundation – until the present, is the best and most accurate way of outlining our technical and technological contribution to the development of the motor car, which is directly reflected in the cars we have produced and the objectives we have reached over the years.

From the first car built, the two- to three-seater 4 HP with its horizontal engine, separate gearbox with no reverse, chain drive and top speed of 35 km/h (21.75 mph) to the Zero, the first Fiat to be produced in a large series, with it modest engine capacity and top speed of 70 km/h (43.5 mph); from the 509 (the popular Topolino) to the Balilla; from the 1400, the first Fiat with a unitary construction, to the 1100 and the 500; from the 124, 128 and 127, each of them chosen car of the year (1967, 1970 and 1972), to the Panda: all represent solid contributions to the history of the motor car.

And finally, the Uno: its selection as car of the year in 1984 has rewarded the dedication and skill of the men who work at Fiat and the vast investment our company has ploughed into creating this highly innovative model. The forward-looking design of the Uno involved the use of computers at both design and test stages, and of automated and flexible production systems including robots.

These advanced methods are consistent with the history of Fiat, whose range of models is among the most modern and up-to-date in the world.

An essential quality of today's car is naturally its market appeal; in addition, however, and perhaps more important still, the product must respond perfectly to ever more specific demands with regard to fuel consumption, comfort and safety.

UMBERTO AGNELLI   President, Fiat Motors S.p.A.

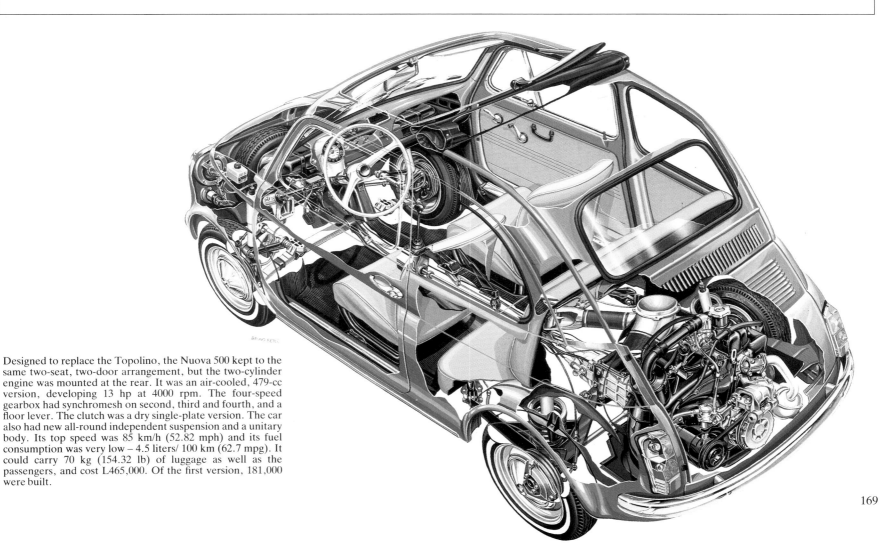

Designed to replace the Topolino, the Nuova 500 kept to the same two-seat, two-door arrangement, but the two-cylinder engine was mounted at the rear. It was an air-cooled, 479-cc version, developing 13 hp at 4000 rpm. The four-speed gearbox had synchromesh on second, third and fourth, and a floor lever. The clutch was a dry single-plate version. The car also had new all-round independent suspension and a unitary body. Its top speed was 85 km/h (52.82 mph) and its fuel consumption was very low – 4.5 liters/ 100 km (62.7 mpg). It could carry 70 kg (154.32 lb) of luggage as well as the passengers, and cost L465,000. Of the first version, 181,000 were built.

The first Fiat, the 3½ HP of 1899, was an open-topped car with a top speed of 35 km/h (21.75 mph) and fuel consumption of 8 liters/100 km (35.31 mpg). The rear-mounted two-cylinder 679-cc engine developed 4.2 hp at 800 rpm.

In 1901, the front-engined 8 HP (1082 cc, 10 hp at 1100 rpm) was brought out, with mechanical brakes on the transmission and rear wheels, a three-speed gearbox with reverse, and a top speed of 45 km/h (28 mph).

The first four-cylinder model, the 12 HP, was brought out in 1902. The front-mounted 3768-cc engine developed 16 hp at 1200 rpm; its top speed was 70 km/h (43.5 mph) and fuel consumption was 20 liters/100 km (14.12 mpg).

Three engines, 6371, 6902 and 7363 cc respectively, were fitted in the three series of the 24/32 HP, all with four cylinders. Output was 32 hp at 1200 rpm. The cars had pneumatic tyres and carried four to six passengers.

The 18/24 HP of 1907 had a front-mounted four-cylinder 4502-cc engine developing 24 hp at 1400 rpm. It also had a four-speed gearbox with reverse, a mutli-plate clutch and mechanical band brakes on the transmission. Its top speed was 60–70 km/h (37.28–43.50 mph).

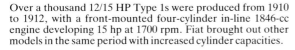

Over a thousand 12/15 HP Type 1s were produced from 1910 to 1912, with a front-mounted four-cylinder in-line 1846-cc engine developing 15 hp at 1700 rpm. Fiat brought out other models in the same period with increased cylinder capacities.

A front-mounted four-cylinder in-line 3052-cc engine developing 20 hp at 1200 rpm gave the Fiat-Ansaldi 10/12 HP (from 1906 known as the Brevetti) a top speed of nearly 60 km/h (37.3 mph). Its fuel consumption was 14 liters/100 km (20.18 mpg).

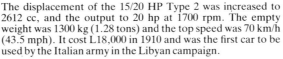

The displacement of the 15/20 HP Type 2 was increased to 2612 cc, and the output to 20 hp at 1700 rpm. The empty weight was 1300 kg (1.28 tons) and the top speed was 70 km/h (43.5 mph). It cost L18,000 in 1910 and was the first car to be used by the Italian army in the Libyan campaign.

The Fabbrica Italiana Automobili Torino, known by its initials, FIAT, was set up in Turin on 1 July 1899 by a group of founding partners headed by Giovanni Agnelli.

The founding partners belonged to the Piedmontese nobility and business circles, and all shared a great enthusiasm for the then infant means of transport, which had already taken off on an industrial scale in France and Germany.

The new company made rapid strides in its first few months of existence· even before formalizing the title deeds, a plot of land had been found near the River Po with a surface area of 12,000 sq m (14,352 sq yd), where the factory was later built. Meanwhile, work was under way in the small workshop of the Ceirano brothers to get the first cars ready. These were based on earlier experiments by Ceirano & Company on a voiturette designed by Aristide Faccioli.

When Fiat (as they came to be known) were founded, they bought Ceirano outright, so the voiturette became the first Fiat, a 3.5-hp model with a two-cylinder, rear-mounted engine and an open four-seater vis-à-vis body. The first commercial and administrative director of Fiat was Enrico Marchesi, and the young company also had the benefit of the talent and experience of men such as Lancia and Nazzaro.

In its first year of existence, the company built roughly fifty cars of the 3.5-hp type (also known as the 4 HP), which was then joined by a second, 6-hp model. By 1984, eighty-five years later, the production capacity of Fiat in its various plants in Italy and abroad cleared a million and a half cars.

Fiat operations are not limited to motor cars, however; the company has branched out into all sectors of transport – its motto in the 1930s was "Land, Sea and Air" – and technology, involving dozens of component manufacturing companies, producing ball bearings, carburettors, plastics and electronics. Apart from motor cars, Fiat operation is divided into: commercial vehicles, metallurgical products, components, production systems, civil engineering, railway systems, aviation, telecommunications, bio-engineering, tourism, transport and financial services.

The groundwork of this success was laid down by the founder, Giovanni Agnelli, and by his equally famous successor Vittorio Valletta. Agnelli decided right from the start to reject originality for its own sake and to opt for a solid programme of production of models not too advanced for the public taste.

However, Agnelli's policy on motor racing was altogether inspired: he was quick to realize its importance and Fiat had a brilliant history in that field until 1927, after which the company decided to retire from competition racing. In recent years, however, Fiat's new directors have begun to participate actively in all forms of motor sport again, taking full advantage of the technological advances and publicity it can provide today.

Another important reason for Fiat's success has been a sound financial policy, including a programme of self-financing that has enabled the company to withstand the impact of major economic crises over the years whereas less

The 20/30 HP (above, the Landaulette version) was known as the Type 3 (1910–12). The four-cylinder in-line 3967-cc engine developed 32 hp at 1600 rpm. Top speed 80 km/h (50 mph); fuel consumption 22 liters/100 km (12.84 mpg).

The Fiacre of 1909 had a 2009-cc engine with 16 hp at 1400 rpm. Over 1600 were built, designed specifically for public transport. Top speed 60 km/h (37.3 mph); fuel consumption 10 liters/100 km (28.25 mpg).

The Zero of 1912 had a 1847-cc engine with 19 hp at 2000 rpm and a top speed of 70 km/h (43.5 mph). It could carry four passengers and 50 kg (110.23 lb) of luggage. The electrical system was 12 volts after 1915 and the car sold at L8,000.

The 70 had a 2001-cc 21-hp engine giving a top speed of 70 km/h (43.5 mph), and on this account was supplied to the Italian Army in the First World War. It was equipped with mechanical brakes on the rear wheels.

The 501 roadster of 1919 had a 1460-cc engine developing 23 hp at 2600 rpm. It had an 80 W dynamo and a 39 Ah accumulator. Front brakes were also available as an optional extra on the last series.

The 510 had a straight-six 3446-cc engine developing 46 hp at 2400 rpm. Its top speed was 85 km/h (49.7 mph), its fuel consumption 18.7 liters/100 km (15.1 mpg). Front brakes were an optional extra.

The saloon version of the 1919 505 had a top speed of 80 km/h (50 mph). Mechanical shock-absorbers were fitted. It had a capacity of 2296 cc and developed 30 hp at 2300 rpm. The version illustrated is the roadster.

The 519 of 1922, had a straight-six 4766-cc engine developing 80 hp at 2600 rpm and a top speed of 115 km/h (71.46 mph). It carried six passengers and 50 kg (110.23 lb) of luggage, with a fuel consumption of 22.5 liters/100 km (12.5 mpg).

In 1925, a four-cylinder in-line 990-cc 509, capable of 22 hp at 3400 rpm, cost only L18,500. Its top speed was 78 km/h (48.5 mph), fuel consumption was 9 liters/100 km (31.4 mpg), and it could carry four passengers and 50 kg (110.23 lb) of luggage.

solidly based companies have been swept away. Such prudence also went hand in hand with an enlightened vision of the future: a notable example is the Lingotto works, built in 1915 when the First World War was in full swing. It was the biggest plant in Europe at the time and boasted many forward-looking features, including a test track on the roof.

From a technical point of view, production has evolved in harmony with the times. After the first two models, which had rear-mounted engines, a front-engine two-cylinder car was brought out in 1901; a year later, the first four-cylinder model was unveiled, the 12 HP, which had a front honeycomb radiator and wheels still made of wood, although practically the same both front and back. The 24/32 HP followed in 1904, then the 60 HP in 1905 and the 24/40 HP in 1906. In 1908, the four-cylinder monobloc engine represented a new technical feature; in 1912, the Fiat Zero was launched. This model may be considered the forerunner of the runabout and remained in production until 1915.

The period leading up to the First World War

was also a time during which Fiat were having great success in racing. Apart from the series models that were taking part, there were also specially built competition cars such as the 75 HP, built in 1904 for the Gordon Bennett Cup, with a 14,112-cc engine, and the 130 HP of 1907, which won the Automobile Club de France Grand Prix.

There were also models with enormous capacity engines such as the 574 and the 576 record versions, the latter with four cylinders and a 28-liter capacity.

After the First World War, others began to learn from Fiat's racing technology: Jano and Bertarione, two of the first specialists successfully to apply the supercharger to racing engines, moved to Alfa Romeo and Sunbeam respectively, helping to spread the advanced theories and methods behind Fiat's achievements.

After pioneer experiments with the supercharger, an extraordinary car was brought out with a twelve-cylinder engine in two parallel banks of six which, with a capacity of only 1500 cc, developed 187 hp and a top speed of 240 km/h (149.13 mph). Fiat made their début at and won

the Monza Grand Prix des Voiturettes in 1927, after which the company practically retired from racing until the 1960s.

Throughout this period, production levels began to reach dizzying heights: after only 35,000 vehicles manufactured during the war, the industry began to show signs of recovery. Over 40,000 cars were produced in 1925 thanks to highly advanced assembly lines at the ultra-modern Lingotto works.

All the series models were given a number, starting with the 501 and finishing, although not in strict numerical order, with the 525; the 520, also called the Superfiat, appeared in 1921, with a twelve-cylinder engine, although only five were built; the 519, a six-cylinder model, was brought out in 1922 and remained in production until 1927; the 502 of 1923 used the same engine as the 501, but on a bigger body; the 509, a classic of its type, was the first "thousand" built in a large production series (over 90,000 from 1925 to 1929) with a highly refined overhead camshaft engine typical of Cappa design. The 503 of 1926 was a development of the 501 and 502, while the 512 of

Brought out as a replacement for the 510, the 512 of 1926 had a straight-six 3446-cc 46-hp engine which could take the saloon up to 80 km/h (50 mph) with a fuel consumption of 19.7 liters/100 km (14.4 mpg). It carried six passengers and their luggage, and cost L65,000.

Standard left-hand drive (for the first time) and coil ignition were the most innovative features of the 520 of 1927. It had a straight-six 46-hp engine which could reach 90 km/h (56 mph) and cost L31,000.

In the two years following its introduction in 1926, 42,000 of the Model 503 were built. The car had a 1.5-liter engine (1460 cc, 27 hp), carried four passengers at 75 km/h (46.6 mph), had all-round brakes and weighed 1535 kg (1.5 tons) fully laden.

The 525 of 1928 was 5 m (16.4 ft) long and had an unladen weight of 1875 kg (1.84 tons). At a top speed of 97 km/h (60.3 mph), it could carry six to seven passengers and their luggage. The mechanical shock-absorbers were later replaced by hydraulic dampers.

Production figures for the 514 of 1929 ran to 37,000. It had a front-mounted four-cylinder 1438-cc engine developing 28 hp at 3400 rpm, and a top speed of 82 km/h (51 mph). Its electrical system was 6 volts, 105 A h. The two-door version cost L18,500.

The 508 Balilla (1932-4) represented the runabout class and over 41,000 were built in three years. It had a four-cylinder 995-cc engine developing 20 hp at 3400 rpm, a three-speed gearbox and all-round hydraulic brakes. It had four seats and cost L10,800.

The 518 Ardita of 1933 was brought out to replace the 522 and the 524. The four-cylinder 1758-cc engine developed 40 hp. It had a four-speed gearbox with synchromesh on third and fourth. Top speed was 100 km/h (62.14 mph).

The "Topolino" ("Little Mouse") 500 had a 569-cc 13-hp engine, top speed of 85 km/h (52.82 mph) and fuel consumption of 6 liters/100 km (47.1 mpg). It had a four-speed gearbox with synchromesh on third and fourth.

The main feature of the 1500, launched at the 1935 Milan Motor Show, was its independent front suspension. The six-cylinder 1493-cc 45-hp engine had overhead valve gear and a top speed of 115 km/h (71.5 mph) carrying five people.

the same year was a big car with a six-cylinder engine.

Fiat went into the 1930s with the 514, 515 and 522 models (all produced in various versions), but during that decade there was a change in direction on the technical front with the arrival of Fessia and the début of the young engineer Dante Giacose, the "father" of modern Fiats.

The 508, still in the old style with a side-valve engine, was also called the Balilla and had a four-cylinder 995-cc engine with a 65-mm (2.56-in) bore and 75-mm (2.95-in) stroke. It was from this, after a slight modification to the bore, that the legendary 1100 (68 × 75 mm/2.7 × 2.95 in) engine was developed. This was to be one of the longest-lived in the history of the motor car, for it remained in production until 1962 and then, with a further increase in the bore to 72 mm (2.83 in), until 1966.

Two more models which also had names as well as numbers in line with the times, the 518 four-cylinder Ardita and the 527 six-cylinder Ardita, came out in 1933 and 1934 respectively. The 1500 of 1935 had a straight-six overhead valve engine with a capacity of only 1493 cc that

developed 45 hp, the same as the 2000-cc Ardita. It also had a tubular chassis, independent front suspension and an aerodynamic body.

A year later, the legendary Topolino 500 was launched, the first true runabout, with a four-cylinder engine of only 569-cc capacity, developing 13 hp. It was built for two passengers, but could carry up to four or five and had independent front wheels; bumpers were an optional extra.

After the 500, the 508 C Eleven Hundred appeared in 1937, and finally the luxury six-cylinder 2800 was launched in 1938. After that, production concentrated on military vehicles until 1945.

Post-war recovery was not easy: substantial repairs had to be carried out and customers found. Senator Giovanni Agnelli died on 16 December 1945, his son Edoardo had been killed in an aircraft accident on 14 July 1935 and his grandson Gianni was too young. But Giovanni Agnelli had been right to choose Vittorio Valletta as his associate, for it was he, assisted by men such as Gaudenzio Bono, Gayal de la Chenaye and others, who made Fiat great after

the Second World War. The foundations for success were already laid, and as well as the vast Lingotto works, an even bigger plant was built at Mirafiori, this time developed on one level as opposed to the five at the Lingotto plant.

Mirafiori had been conceived in the 1930s and was to be extended on many occasions in the 1950s and 1960s. Just a few kilometers from Mirafiori, the big new Rivalta complex was built, and it was not until later that the operation was decentralized with the opening of important new installations in southern-central Italy.

The models in production were obviously pre-war versions suitably updated, for example the 500 B and C, the 1100 B and E and the 1500 D and E. In 1950 a completely new car was brought out: the 1400 had a unitary body and a design inspired by the new aesthetic criteria established by Pininfarina with his Cisitalia berlinetta (which was developed on Fiat 1100 parts with enormously valuable new technical and design features).

The 1400 was followed by the 1900 (by this time Fiats were referred to by their engine capacity). In 1955 a new runabout – the 600 – came out

In June 1936, Fiat brought out the 500 – the Topolino – a car that was produced in a very large series. Initially designed as a two-seater (but also used to seat four), its rear suspension was later modified to incorporate semi-elliptic leaf-springs instead of the quarter-elliptic springs of the first series. It was therefore also known as the "short spring" or the "long spring." The last version, the B, came out in 1948 with a more powerful overhead-valve engine. Over 120,000 Topolinos were built.

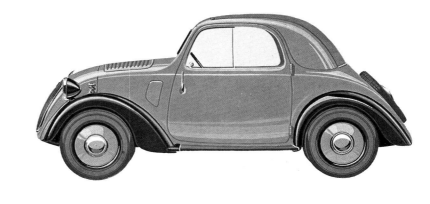

The 1100 of 1939 differed from the 508 C, particularly in its "windbreaker" front end. It remained in production until 1948, when the 1100B came out, using the same body but with a more powerful engine and variable flexibility rear leaf-spring suspension. The car could reach 110 km/h (68.3 mph) with four passengers and 50 kg (112.5 lb) of luggage.

The Spider was launched at the 1966 Turin Motor Show as the open version of the 124, with the 1438-cc 90-hp engine of the S. It was also produced with a 1600-cc, 1800-cc and 2-liter engine, the latter having fuel injection on the current model. With two seats and 40 kg (88.1 lb) luggage capacity, it could reach over 170 km/h (105.63 mph), even with the 1438-cc engine. The five-speed gearbox had synchromesh and a floor lever, and the body was entirely designed by Pininfarina, who are now producing the Spidereuropa 2-liter.

The 2800 was the flagship of the Fiat pre-war range and had a six-cylinder 2852-cc, 85-hp engine capable of 130 km/h (80.8 mph). The limousine carried six passengers and 50 kg (110.23 lb) of luggage, and weighed 2340 kg (2.3 tons) fully loaded.

The 8 V was a GT with a 1996-cc V8 engine developing 105 hp at 6000 rpm. It had a top speed of 190 km/h (118 mph) and a fuel consumption of 17 liters/100 km (16.6 mpg). A two-seater, it was the first Fiat to have independent wheels.

The new 1100 of 1953 was also known as the 103. In production until 1956, by which time over 250,000 had been built, it had a front-mounted four-cylinder 1098-cc engine giving 36 hp at 4400 rpm. Top speed: 116 km/h (72.1 mph).

The 1400 of 1950 was the first Fiat with unitary body construction and air conditioning. It had a four-cylinder in-line 1395-cc engine developing 44 hp at 4400 rpm; the gearbox had synchromesh on second, third and fourth.

The 600 of 1955 had a 635-cc rear-mounted engine developing 21.5 hp at 4600 rpm; it had a top speed of 95 km/h (59 mph) and a fuel consumption of 5.7 liters/100 km (49.6 mpg). There was a floor gear lever, rather than column change.

The 1800/2300 was brought out at the Geneva Motor Show in 1959. The front-mounted six-cylinder 1795- or 2054-cc engine developed 75/82 hp at 5000 rpm. It had a four-speed fully synchromesh gearbox and a booster on the braking system.

The 1200 cabriolet of 1959 was built by Pininfarina, who produced over 15,000. Its top speed was 145 km/h (90 mph); it had two seats, a 1221-cc engine (the 1100 D), developing 58 hp at 5300 rpm, and a floor gear lever.

Production of the 1960 500 went to Autobianchi in 1968. With its rear-mounted 449.5-cc 17.5-hp horizontal engine, it could carry four passengers and 40 kg (88.2 lb) of luggage. The gearbox had rapid engagement.

Around 600,000 of the new 1961 1300/1500 were built, with engines of 1295/1481 cc, 65/72 hp and a top speed of 140/150 km/h (87/93.2 mph), a single-plate hydraulic clutch and front disc brakes.

which brought motoring within the reach of all Italians. It was completely new in concept (rear-mounted engine and four independent wheels) and marked a turning-point; the 600 was followed in 1957 by the new 500, which also had a rear-mounted engine, but in a two-cylinder air-cooled version. Both models enjoyed a long life with successive variations and versions. In 1964, the 850 was brought out as a development of the 600, while in 1961 new models appeared to replace the traditional ones – the rear-wheel drive 1300–1500 four-cylinder series saloons and the 1800–2300 six-cylinder series with a family of new engines designed by Aurelio Lampredi, ex-technical director of Ferrari.

Fiat went into the 1970s with these models and their sports derivatives, as well as with the 124 and the 130, the latter a luxurious V6 saloon and coupé.

A further change on the technical front came about in 1969, when the 128 was brought out, the first Fiat to have a transverse engine and

front-wheel drive. The system had already been fully tested by Autobianchi, part of the Fiat group, and was yet another of Giacosa's creations. In fact, Giacosa had been one of the pioneers of the fully forward (engine and final drive) system for runabouts (which was later used on all sizes), but doubts about the effective "tightness" of the indispensable universal joints ensured that Fiat kept to their prudent tradition of not innovating too rapidly.

The 128 was followed by the 127, one of the most successful cars in the world from 1971 onwards. A final rear-engined runabout, the 126, appeared in 1972, followed by the Strada in 1978, the Panda in 1980 and the Uno in 1983. Throughout this period, the company kept hold on the market for medium-to-large front-engine rear-wheel drive cars with the 131 and 132 Argenta, until these were replaced in 1984 by the Regata and the Tipo Quattro, or Type 4.

The diesel engine had been put to one side for a while, after having been tried experimentally in

the 1400, but began to play an important role from the end of the 1970s onwards.

The 1960s and 1970s saw a certain concentration of the motor industry as a result of increased research costs and as a result of difficulties faced by small and medium-sized firms trying to compete with the big companies. As a result, Fiat became a pole of attraction for other Italian companies, which were either amalgamated or taken over. The first was Autobianchi in 1964 – though the agreement was not formalized until 1967 – followed in 1969 by Lancia and Ferrari.

An attempt to make an international agreement to take over Citroën did not bear fruit, and in 1982 Fiat also dropped out of Seat, in Spain, which had originally been established as one of its branches.

The company's interest in sports cars has risen over the last twenty years, from the 1500 and 1600 cabriolets of 1962 to the 850 spyders and coupés of 1965, from the 124 coupé of 1967 to the 124

Launched on 20 January 1983, the Fiat Uno was chosen car of the year for 1984. It comes in two versions and has front-wheel drive, based on the engines of the 127 family. The 45 uses the 903, the 55 the 1050, and the 70 the 1300 cc. The diesel engine is the 1300-cc Brazilian engine from Fiat Automoveis, which has a precombustion chamber in the sparking-plug housing. The Uno has a four- or five-speed gearbox, and a fully automatic gearbox is also available. The body comes with three or five doors, and a variety of optional extras. There is also an ES (Energy Saving) version with improved fuel consumption.

The 1964 850 had a two-door, four- to five-seater body, rear-mounted 843-cc 34-hp engine, top speed of 125 km/h (77.7 mph), fully synchromesh four-speed gearbox and fuel consumption of 6 liters/100 km (47.1 mpg). It had independent suspension.

The 1967 125 had a 1608-cc 90-hp engine with belt-driven twin overhead camshaft, four-speed gearbox, independent front wheels and rigid back axle. Speed: 160 km/h (100 mph).

The Dino Spider, the first Fiat with four overhead camshafts, was developed from the 2-liter Ferrari of the same name; 1987-cc 160-hp engine, 210 km/h (130.5 mph); hydraulic clutch, five-speed gearbox and self-locking differential.

The 128 of 1969 was front-wheel drive; its engine capacity was 1116 cc, developing 55 hp, with a top speed of 135 km/h (83.9 mph). It had overhead valves and camshafts and a four-speed synchromesh gearbox.

The 124 saloon of 1966 had a front-mounted 1197-cc 60-hp engine which gave over 140 km/h (87 mph). It had a synchromesh four-speed gearbox, independent front wheels and a rigid back axle.

The 130-2800, the flagship of Fiat's range, had a V6 engine developed from the Dino producing 140 hp and 180 km/h (111.8 mph). It had all-round independent suspension and an automatic three-speed Borg-Warner gearbox.

The four-cylinder 1995-cc engine of the new Campagnola was developed from that of the 132. Its output was 80 hp, and it had a four-speed gearbox with a reduction unit, a self-locking rear-differential (optional on the front) and a unitary body.

The 126, with a capacity of 600, later 650 cc, is a development of the 500. Fitted with a two-cylinder air-cooled rear engine and four-speed gearbox, it can carry four passengers and 40 kg (88.1 lb) of luggage at over 105 km/h (65.24 mph).

The Maratea is a luxuriously finished estate, built on the 131 base, with a chrome-plated roof-rack. It is available in a petrol (1995 cc) or a diesel (2445 cc) version.

The new Strada is available with engines of 1116, 1301 and 1485 cc, in ES, 60, 70 and 85 versions, and automatic with a three-speed gearbox. The manual gearbox is four-speed (five-speed optional). A 1700-cc diesel version is also available.

This second series of the 131 Supermirafiori has engines with displacements of 1367, 1585 and 1995 cc, with outputs of 75, 97 and 113 hp, giving top speeds of 155, 170 and 175 km/h (96.3, 105.6 and 108.7 mph). Five-speed gearboxes and electric windows are standard.

Several series of the Panda, launched in 1980, have been brought out: the 30 with a 652-, the 34 with an 843-, and the 45 with a 903-cc engine. The Panda 4 × 4 is a 968-cc version developed from the A112.

The third series of the 127 has 903- and 1049-cc engines, a four- or five-speed gearbox, front disc brakes and a limited slip differential on the rear axle. Three- or five-door version.

The Regata Super, supplied with a 1500 or 1600 petrol engine, and also with the new 1929 diesel engine, differs from the Regata in that it has a more luxurious interior finish, including a central locking system and electric front windows.

The executive saloon of the Fiat range, the Argenta, comes in various versions – the 100 (1600), 120 (2000, carburettor), 120 ie (injection) and Sx (plus accessories and a supercharger). There are also diesel and turbodiesel versions with SOFIM 2445-cc engines.

Abarth Spyder of 1972, and ultimately to the 128 coupé and the X1/9 "five-speed" of 1978, together with the sports versions of the Strada and the 127.

However, the company has taken active part in competition racing with the 124 spyder and the 131 rally, two cars developed from series models with performances worthy of world rally championships.

After a period in which both the Fiat and the Lancia teams co-existed, racing organization was unified with the result that both rallies and prototype track races are now run by the cars from a single team based in the Abarth workshop, also taken over by Fiat.

Of course Ferrari are the jewel in the crown of the whole sporting operation, in that they not only compete in Formula 1, but also supply engines for the Lancia prototypes for the endurance trials. Finally, it should also be remembered that Fiat's technical involvement in motor sport has been expressed both by their experimenting, like all other companies in the 1980s, with turbocharged engines, and by their use of traditional superchargers, fitted on a whole range of cars. This policy is vindicated by the good results obtained with the Lancia Rally, the only modern competition car to have a supercharger.

Among the very varied activities of Fiat, aviation also plays an important part. From 1908, when the first aircraft engine was designed, at least 65 different engines have been produced, 33,000 of which have been built in various series (with piston engines).

Special power-plants have also been built for world record attempts, including the height record (6435 m/21,112.2 ft), set in 1917 with the A 12 engine, to the duration and distance records, set in 1928 with the A 22 T engine, which did 50 hours and 7666 km/4763.42 miles. The most interesting record, still unbroken in 1985, was the speed record for seaplanes set in 1934 by Agello with the 24-cylinder 3100-hp engine fitted on the Macchi racing seaplane. More recently, interest has been turned towards turbine engines, from the Orpheus type brought out in 1960 under license from Rolls-Royce, to the big JT 10D 232 turbofans for civil aircraft which came out in 1980.

Interest in diesel engines began in 1909 with a two-stroke 300-hp model for a submersible; by 1915 this had already increased to 2300 hp with the 2 C 176. Countless engines for land and sea use have been produced, and the first Italian diesel electric locomotive came out in 1922, with the first experiments in dual-effect two-stroke engines. These later became a Fiat speciality and were used for big marine engines with outputs of 32,500 hp from the 9012 type engine (twelve cylinders with a 900-mm/35.4-in bore). Of course there have also been diesel engines for lorries since 1931 and for cars since 1953. Fiat now produces 1300-, 1700-, 1900- and 2400-cc capacity diesel engines both in normally aspirated and turbocharged versions.

FORD

LINCOLN – MERCURY

Ford Motor Company's founder, Henry Ford, played a pivotal role in the early stages of development of the automobile industry. In the short space of about six years, he conceived three ideas that set the stage for the expansion of the industry. First, he developed the Model T, the first really practical automobile. Second, he established the moving assembly line to produce it in volume. Third, he instituted the $5 day, with which he made it possible for his employees to buy his product and expand the market. Any one of these concepts would have assured him an honoured niche in history. To have developed all three was indeed an amazing feat that provided the basis for expansion of Ford Motor Company into a multinational enterprise with production and sales facilities on six continents.

PHILIP CALDWELL   Chairman of the Board, Ford Motor Company

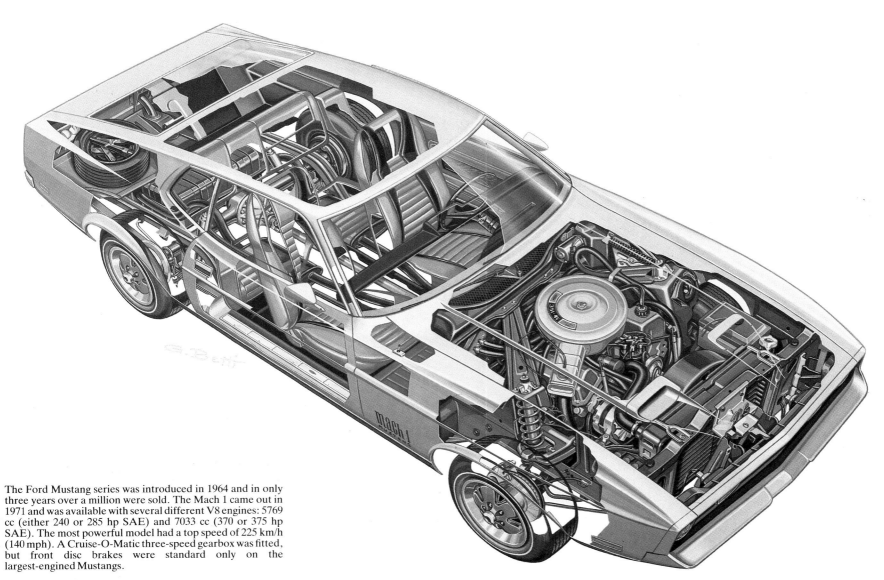

The Ford Mustang series was introduced in 1964 and in only three years over a million were sold. The Mach 1 came out in 1971 and was available with several different V8 engines: 5769 cc (either 240 or 285 hp SAE) and 7033 cc (370 or 375 hp SAE). The most powerful model had a top speed of 225 km/h (140 mph). A Cruise-O-Matic three-speed gearbox was fitted, but front disc brakes were standard only on the largest-engined Mustangs.

The Model A of 1903, shown here in the convertible tonneau version, was the first Ford to be produced in a small series. It had a two-cylinder engine and sold at $850.

The Model R came out in 1907 and was offered with a four-cylinder 15-hp engine at $750.

In October 1908, the first T came out of the Ford plant. More than fifteen million were built in nineteen years, in various versions. It was available with a four-cylinder in-line 2892-cc 21-hp engine and the first Model T tourer of 1908 sold at $850. Over the years, however, the price of the car dropped to $260 (for the roadster) despite gradual improvements in design and mechanics. This enormous difference in price was made possible by the new production methods which Ford introduced. Above: the Ford Model T tourer of 1912 with the Ford family on board. Above right: the 1921 runabout ($319). Right: the 1927 Fordor, which cost $545. The four-door body was first introduced in 1923.

In late 1927, the new Model A replaced the T, which had by then gone out of production. The four-cylinder engine came in either a 2- or 3-liter version. The 1929 Standard Phaeton model cost $460.

Five million Model As had been sold by the end of 1931, when nineteen versions were available. The illustration shows the De Luxe Fordor, which cost $630.

The revolution of 1932 was embodied in the new V8, which came in fourteen different body styles. Here we have the De Luxe Three Window, which cost $540.

This new 1937 coupé (De Luxe Five Window Club coupé) also had a V8 engine. The body had up-to-date styling, with recessed headlights.

The factory which was to mass-motorize the Americans can trace its origin directly back to 30 July 1863, when Henry Ford, considered by many to be the father of the automobile, was born of an Irish immigrant and his wife, the adopted daughter of another Irishman. In fact, while research and early experiments in the automobile were being conducted in Europe, parallel trains of thought were taking place in America, where the belief was also firm that the transport of the future lay in vehicles independent of animal power. Henry Ford was one of the stoutest supporters of this opinion: so strong, indeed, was his conviction that, at the age of sixteen, he left the farm where he was born, knowing that he was not cut out for country life. From there, he went to Detroit, where he became an engineer, taking on a variety of jobs which provided him with a wealth of experience and brought him even closer to his objective of acquiring as much technical knowledge as possible on the subject of engines. Ford worked in a tram factory for a week, and then moved to the James Flowers & Brothers workshop, where he stayed for nine months before moving on to the largest shipyard in Detroit. While moving around from one job to another, the young Henry learned of the existence of the German Nikolaus August Otto's engine from articles in specialist magazines. Meanwhile he married Clara Bryant and they went to live on a plot of land in Dearborn; soon after, however, in 1891, the couple moved to the city, where Ford had found a job as an engineer (for $45 a month) at the Edison Illuminating Company in Detroit. Ford straightaway built a workshop in a hut behind the house, where he set about studying how to build an internal combustion engine: his first prototype was fixed to the kitchen sink for its initial tests towards the end of December two years later. Having proved that the engine worked to his satisfaction, Ford then turned his time and attention to the

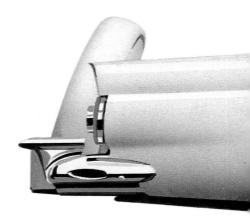

construction of a vehicle in which to install it. Thus, on 4 June 1896, the Quadricycle made its first appearance on the road, with Thomas Alva Edison's encouragement for Ford to continue his early experiments. Ford then left his job at Edison's to devote himself entirely to the development of the automobile, starting off in a company with other financiers. His great moment finally arrived in 1903, when the Ford Motor Company was officially founded on 16 June. The entire property of the newly opened factory consisted of a large number of patents and $28,000 capital put up by twelve shareholders. The others involved in the company with Ford were a coal merchant and his accountant, a banker, two brothers (the owners of an engine factory), a carpenter, two lawyers, a clerk, a jeweller and an air-rifle salesman.

The first series-produced car to be put on sale with the slogan "even a fifteen-year-old can drive it, it is so simple," was bought for $850 by a Chicago dentist, Doctor Pfenning. This first sale, at a time when the company capital had dropped to a mere $223, was an occasion to celebrate among Ford's shareholders. In little over fifteen months, over 1,700 Model As were produced, bringing in close to $100,000 for the company. At this point in the company's history, it moved its main factory to much bigger premises on the corner of Piquette and Beaulieu Avenues. These were the years of the battle against the syndicate which protected Selden's patent rights to reserve control over "carriages with non-animal traction." After a long fight in the courts, however, Ford emerged victorious.

Meanwhile, in the Detroit Motor Show of 1904, a four-cylinder 3.5-liter Malcolmson-Ford was brought out. The cars of that period already had breaking systems, unlike the first Quadricycle, which did not. By the middle of 1906, Malcolmson was removed and he sold his shares to Ford for $175,000. Ford became president of

the company and started production of the small Model N, a light four-cylinder car which went on sale for $600. In two years, Ford sold almost 9,000 Ns and other models directly derived from it. His greatest achievement, however, was the presentation on 1 October 1908, at the Olympia Motor Show in London, of the Model T, the car destined to change the course of the history of the American automobile. The Model T symbolized an era in American motoring history – it was a car which you could have "in any colour provided it was black," the only colour in which it was produced, in order to maximize savings in production time, since paints in those days did not dry quickly enough for the rate of production of Ford's assembly lines. With the Model T, Ford also gave millions of Americans a symbol – "the universal automobile" – which was immediately nicknamed "Lizzie." It was a four-wheeler to which the roads of the time and their terrible surface conditions presented no problem, as the Lizzie's reliable mechanics easily withstood the mud and bumps. After 1910, the cars came off the assembly lines of the Highland Park Factory in Michigan, and by that time the rate of production had reached one car every ninety minutes. Another development resulting from the assembly line was Ford's announcement on 5 January 1914 that the worker's pay was to go up to $5 a day, an increase of 100 per cent. This enabled Ford workers to become customers of the company and buy their own cars; in this way, the circle of potential customers was widened and sales naturally increased.

In nineteen years, over fifteen million Model Ts were built, and in that period the company gradually changed its structure. In 1917, production of trucks and tractors began, together with construction of the giant Rouge plant in Dearborn; the company also began to build the Eagle anti-submarine ships as part of its contribution to the First World War. Immedi-

This 1939 De Luxe Fordor Sedan had a modified new front-end design and was also available as a soft-top. It cost $790.

Brought out in 1940, the Lincoln Continental convertible was one of the most beautiful cars of its day. It was produced in limited numbers because of the outbreak of war.

The immediately post-war cars had only slightly modified bodies compared with the 1942 models. Illustrated is the Super De Luxe Fordor of 1946.

The 1955/57 Thunderbird was a luxury two-seater with a five-liter 193-hp V8 engine, either a manual or automatic gearbox and all-round drum brakes. Sixteen thousand were sold in the first year of production. The basic model cost $2,700; with all optional extras – e.g. electric windows, automatic gearbox, and power-assisted brakes and steering – the price rose to $3,500.
▼

In 1949, Ford's products underwent radical alteration – the bodies were much more aerodynamic than before. The engine was still a V8, but with a displacement of 3916 cc. The illustration shows the Custom Convertible.

The new front end of the Mercury of 1952, shown here on the Custom Hardtop Sport coupé. In this year, the company's range of cars was totally revised. ▶

The first Ford sports car, the Thunderbird, came out at the end of 1954 and was Ford's answer to the General Motors Corvette. It was a small two-seater, with a 4785-cc V8 engine.

In 1955, the Ford range, apart from the Thunderbird, consisted of the Mainline, the Customline and the Fairlane – economy, mid-range and luxury lines respectively. The illustration shows the Fairlane Crown Victoria.

Limited numbers of the luxurious 1956 Lincoln Continental Mk IIIs were built for the few clients who could afford to spend $9,540.

The Mercury Hardtop Colony Park, of which 5,929 were sold in 1959, was the most expensive estate in the range at a price of $3,932.

One of the most successful Ford models, the Fairlane 500, was on the market with a six- or eight-cylinder engine. When it came out in 1958, its four headlights were symbolic of its new body design. The 1962 model (right) was very similar.

The ultra-modern 1960 Falcon was designed to compete with the European compacts. It had a six-cylinder engine and a unitary body. Its market price of $1,975 guaranteed its success.

The 1962 Mercury Meteor was the perfect compromise between the large car and the compact. It was available with a straight-six or a V8 engine, in a two- or four-door version.

The six- or eight-cylinder Galaxy replaced the Fairlane 500 in the powerful, high-priced car range in 1959. The illustration shows the 1962 Galaxy 500 Club Victoria.

ately after the war, in 1919, the presidency of the company passed to Henry's son Edsel, and in 1922 Ford acquired the Lincoln Motor Company. Three years later, production began on the first three-engine 196 (affectionately known as the Tin Goose) which was built for the first scheduled flights. On 31 May 1927, the car plant closed down for six months; on re-opening, the Model T was replaced by the Model A of which five million were built in 1931. It was not until 1 April 1932 that the first Ford eight-cylinder V-engine saw the light of day, Ford being the only company in the world which had succeeded in casting this highly complex engine in one single monobloc piece. The adoption of the V8 engine on the new Fords did, however, create problems, as transversal leaf springs were already out of date

by then, or rather they had been technically improved upon, so the chassis had to be updated for the engine. This resulted in the launch of the 40, which had a longer wheelbase than its predecessor, the 18, and had a cruising speed of around 128.75 km/h (80 mph). A 10,000-mile endurance rally was covered with the 40, demonstrating its reliability and low fuel consumption. In the same month as the rally, a 40 won the Elgin Road 203 miles (in a lightened two-seater sports version), exceeding 165.75 km/h (103 mph) on the straight. In 1935, the 48 was brought out, and with it the V8 engine rapidly reached its second million. In 1939, seven years after the introduction of the first V8, Ford went into the mid-range automobile class with the Mercury series. The company found itself

producing cars to satisfy the most popularly demanded features under the Ford name, with the Mercury as the average family car and the Lincoln (of the Lincoln Motor Company, bought in 1922) as their luxury version. The development of V8-engine models continued for another four years, by which time the company was fully involved in supplying materials for the troops at the front. As well as supplying land vehicles to the army, Ford also produced 8,600 B 24 bombers and 57,000 aeroplane engines.

At the height of the war, the company suddenly lost Edsel, who died in 1943, and Henry was obliged to take over again until 4 September 1945. After the war he handed over the position to his grandson, Henry II, who took over the presidency with the finances in a precarious state,

Brought out in late 1970, the Pinto was the first of Ford's subcompacts. The engines were developed from European versions and came in a 1599-cc 75-hp SAE or 1998-cc, 100-hp SAE. It had a four-speed synchromesh gearbox, independent front suspension and a rigid rear end with semi-elliptic leaf-springs. Its top speeds were 150 and 160 km/h (93.2 and 100 mph) respectively.

while Henry I retired with his wife Clara to the farm in Fair Lane, Dearborn, where he remained until his death on 4 April 1947.

As a result of the younger Henry's successful campaign to put the company back on its feet, Ford were in a position to bring out their first vehicle of the post-war period two months before Japan surrendered; on 3 July 1945, Henry Ford II personally delivered a Super De Luxe Tudor with its 100-hp engine to President Harry Truman.

The company then entered a period of rejuvenation, thanks to the efficiency of those with whom the new president surrounded himself. In this period, the Super De Luxe Sportsman coupé was launched on the market in

The 1962 Comet had a new front end and new sides, a six-cylinder 85-hp engine and an optional automatic gearbox.

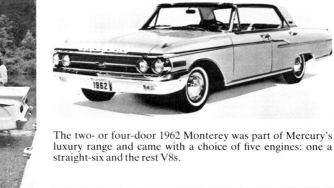

The two- or four-door 1962 Monterey was part of Mercury's luxury range and came with a choice of five engines: one a straight-six and the rest V8s.

The 1962 Thunderbird had a restyled rear end and came in a hard- or soft-top version. Its top speed was 200 km/h (125 mph).

The Falcon Futura compact of 1962 was a new departure. It had a unitary body which underwent few modifications to the body design over the years.

The new Ford sports model, the Mustang, came out in 1964 and was Ford's biggest post-war success. Over 500,000 had been sold by the end of 1965.

The 1969 Fairlane 500 combined an attractive design with a relatively low price of $2,325.

The 1969 Mercury Cougar four-seater coupé had a 4.7-liter V8 engine with a twin-body carburettor and developed 200 hp at 4400 rpm.

The Lincoln Continental was Ford's luxury car and was offered as either a sedan or a coupé hardtop. It had a unitary body, a 7.5-liter V8 engine and disc brakes. Below: the MK III had a floorpan with cross-members. Bottom: the 1975 version.

New models from 1969 and 1970 were the Cobra in the sports range, and the Maverick in the subcompacts. Above: the Shelby Cobra, a Shelby-modified Mustang with a Cobra 428 Jet Ram engine. Below: the 1970 Maverick with a unitary body and six- or eight-cylinder engines.

The luxury Thunderbird model was developed from a sports car and had a 7.5-liter V8 engine which developed 223 hp at 4000 rpm.

The 1978 Fairmont subcompact was brought out to replace the Maverick. In 1980 it was fitted with a 2.3-liter turbocharged engine.

The 1979 LTD also had modified bodywork and was a smaller size overall. It had a 4.9- or 5.8-liter V8 engine.

◄ The new Thunderbird series, the Heritage, went on the market in 1979 with a two-door body and either a 4.2- or 4.9-liter engine.

The Torino was brought out in 1968 as a development of the Fairlane series. It came in different versions: sedan, hardtop and estate.

The 1972 two-door LTD coupé hardtop had a 5.8-liter twin carburettor V8 engine that developed 165 hp at 4200 rpm. Its top speed was 170/180 km/h (105.6/112 mph).

The 1974 Ford Pinto had a larger 2- or 2.3-liter engine than before, a unitary body and an automatic gearbox.

First brought out in July 1974, this Granada compact was available with either a two- or four-door body, and either a 3.2- or 4-liter straight-six engine.

The Mercury Bobcat (similar in style to the Ford Pinto) came out in 1975. The bodywork was modified over the years.

The Mustang II was brought out in 1974. It was a two-door four-seater coupé with a sporty, elegant line that was more compact than any of the previous series. The bodywork was restyled in 1978, and as a result the overall dimensions were increased. Various versions were available, with engines from 2.3 up to 4.9 liters with a four-body carburettor. The version illustrated above came out in 1982.

The Mercury Marquis, one of the range of American luxury cars, was available with a 4.9- or 5.8-liter V8 engine. An automatic gearbox with overdrive was an optional extra from 1980 onwards. From 1983, the basic engine was a 4.9-liter with fuel injection. Above: the 1979 Brougham coupé. Below: the four-door 1981 saloon.

September 1945. At a list price of under $2,000, it had wooden outer door panels, and also boasted an electric hood and leather seats. The post-war economic recovery was meanwhile well under way, and industrial production was continually on the increase. In 1948, models were brought out for the following year with semi-elliptic rear leaf-springs and a new gear change with overdrive. This technical development was not modified in any particular way in 1950, and the new type of suspension remained on all three makes, which continued to use the 95- and 100-hp V8 engines – only police cars were made with an extra 10 hp.

One significant achievement in terms of production was the rate of over 9,000 units per day in 1950: this was the highest since the Wall Street crash of 1929. The outbreak of the Korean War meant that limits were imposed on the allocation of raw materials, while a new law was introduced which fixed list prices; both factors contributed to a certain extent to the drop from a million and a half units per year to less than a million between 1951 and 1952.

In 1954 appeared the famous Thunderbird, with the new 4800-cc engines – a two-seater convertible true to the American ideal of a sports car. It enjoyed considerable success on the

The 1979 Lincoln Continental had also been modified: the bodywork was more compact, it had fuel injection and an automatic gearbox with overdrive.

The Ford LTD Crown Victoria. This four-door saloon came out in 1981 with a 4.9-liter 140-hp V8 engine.

The new Escort was brought out in 1980 with a four-cylinder 1.6-liter engine. In 1984, a 1.6-liter turbocharged engine and a 2-liter diesel were also available.

The Mercury Lynx range was given a new 1.6-liter engine in 1983. The RS model (above) developed 80–84 hp. Below: the LN 7 coupé.

The 1983 Mustang, a soft-top two-door four-seater with a 5-liter V8 engine, had a top speed of 210 km/h (130.5 mph).

The compact LTD is a luxury model. Left: the four-door saloon that came out in 1983. Above: the Crown Victoria of the same year.

This EXP coupé was brought out on an Escort base in 1981 with a four-cylinder 1.6-liter engine. A turbocharger with fuel injection was added in 1983. It also had a five-speed gearbox.

A new aerodynamic design was used on the 1983 Thunderbird coupé, brought out in direct competition with the European sports models. It had a 2.3-liter turbocharged engine.

The Mercury Capri coupé came out in 1978 to compete with the Ford Mustang. The range was completely changed in 1983/84 with the addition of 2.3-, 3.7- and 4.9-liter engines as well as a 2.3-liter turbo version with fuel injection.

The Mercury Topaz of 1984, shown here in the LS four-door version, is a smaller car which has sacrificed nothing in the way of comfort. The Topaz comes with either a four-cylinder 2.3-liter petrol or a 2-liter diesel engine.

market and inspired a new breed of Ford cars, whose lines grew longer and longer over the following years until they became excessive in length – even for the USA – making entry for the smaller European cars into the American market easier. Compact American cars came on to the market in the early 1960s, and included the Ford Falcon, one of the most popular by far, followed by the Tudor and the Fordor. In the meantime, important developments were taking place in the sports car field: the Mustang, a car with six or eight cylinders and speeds of up to 190 km/h (120 mph) came out in 1964 and proved even more successful than the Thunderbird, selling over a million in just two years.

Meanwhile, Ford had ventured into other related areas of activity and formed several associated companies, among them Ford Motor Credit, a finance company which also helped in the purchase of their own cars; American Ford Insurance; the Ford Parts Division, which handled spares; and the Philco-Ford Corporation, which was involved in electronics, computers, space technology and domestic appliances. An important change took place on the company front in 1956 when Ford became a joint-stock company with over 40,000 shareholders. The following figures give a brief idea of Ford's development over the last few years. In 1972, 2,399,584 cars came off the Ford Motor Company assembly lines (including Mercury and Lincoln) out of a total 8,802,175 cars produced in the USA. In 1978, out of a total of 9,220,240 cars, Ford accounted for 2,511,888. In 1982, Ford produced 1,104,074 cars from a total of 4,942,600.

Ford-Europe

The Ford Motor Company Aktiengesellschaft, as Ford-Germany was originally known, is perhaps the only company which was not bought as part of the expansionist policy of the mother company (as was the case when General Motors bought Opel). It was founded in Berlin in 1925 at the express request of Henry Ford, who wanted a European plant (or plants, since he also founded Ford-Britain), where he could easily build and sell the Model T at competitive prices.

In 1926, fifty Model Ts were coming off the Ford assembly lines a day in Berlin, and in 1928 the Model A went into production. On 2 October 1930, Ford-Germany began the construction of a new factory in Cologne which is still the headquarters of the company. One month after work began on the new plant, the twenty-five thousandth A came off the production lines in Berlin, and on 4 May the Ford factory, employing 458 men, was officially transferred to its new site. At the outbreak of the Second World War, Ford-Werke AG (the new company name), which produced 35,000 vehicles in 1939, began to turn out war supplies. The year 1939 saw the appearance of the first Taunus, which was followed by a new model in 1948; the 12 M came out in 1952, followed by the 15 M and the 17 M,

In 1961, Ford-Britain brought out an original saloon which echoed the characteristic lines of the smaller Anglia. The Consul Classic 315 came in a two-door, four-door or coupé version, the latter known as the Consul Capri. The four-cylinder 1498-cc engine could develop 59.5 hp SAE at 4600 rpm, and gave a top speed of 135 km/h (84 mph). It had front disc brakes and a steering system based on circulating ball bearings. The rear end had a rigid back axle with semi-elliptic leaf-springs.

Two Model As were originally brought to England in 1903 by an Englishman who had obtained permission to sell them in Europe. Illustrated is the 1928 saloon.

Brought out for the first time in London in 1905, the Model B, fitted with the 24-hp engine optional on the A, was after 1932 assembled also in Germany.

The Model Y, launched in 1932 at the Royal Albert Hall, was the first original British Ford. In 1933, 32,958 were built. The photo shows the Type 18.

Introduced in 1932, a great many versions of the V8 were on the market. The photo shows the Spezial of 1937–41.

◄ In 1932, Ford-Germany launched the Köln, which was very similar to the British Y or Popular. It had a British-built four-cylinder 933-cc engine.

The Eifel was brought out in 1935 with a more powerful four-cylinder 1157-cc engine.

In 1939, the first Taunus (left) came off Ford-Germany assembly lines, and the models brought out after the war (right) set the seal on the popularity of this successful series. The 12 M came out in 1952 and remained in production until the 1970s, although it was constantly modified and improved. In 1957, the 17 M was added to the 12 M and the 15 M, which had come out in 1955. The series was fitted with a four-cylinder 1698-cc 60-hp in-line engine. In 1960, the 17 M was completely redesigned, becoming bigger and more curved, and proved very successful. The 12 M of 1962 had front-wheel drive.

1952-Taunus 12 M

1955-Taunus 15 M De Luxe

1957-Taunus 17 M De Luxe

1962-Taunus 12 M

1960-Taunus 17 M P3

1968-Taunus 15 M P6

1966-Taunus 12 M

1967-Taunus 17 M P7

1968-Taunus 15M RS P6

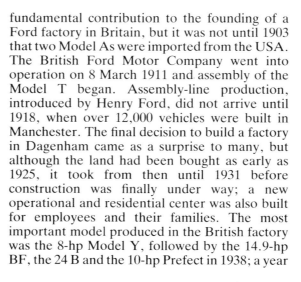

while in May 1961, in Cologne, production figures reached a million. The previous year had seen the first engine coming off the assembly lines in the new plant. An important new development came about in 1965 with the introduction of the Transit, the commercial vehicle which conquered the European market. The next significant date was 27 August 1968, when the first series of Escorts was introduced; this was followed by the Capri in 1969 and the Consul/Granada in 1972. Production of the Taunus was abandoned with the introduction of the Sierra, but the new Escort and the Orion remain on the assembly line at Ford-Germany, which now has another plant in Saarlouis.

The origins of Ford-Britain date back to 1890, barely twenty years after the European depression of 1870. Percival Perry's enthusiasm made a

fundamental contribution to the founding of a Ford factory in Britain, but it was not until 1903 that two Model As were imported from the USA. The British Ford Motor Company went into operation on 8 March 1911 and assembly of the Model T began. Assembly-line production, introduced by Henry Ford, did not arrive until 1918, when over 12,000 vehicles were built in Manchester. The final decision to build a factory in Dagenham came as a surprise to many, but although the land had been bought as early as 1925, it took from then until 1931 before construction was finally under way; a new operational and residential center was also built for employees and their families. The most important model produced in the British factory was the 8-hp Model Y, followed by the 14.9-hp BF, the 24 B and the 10-hp Prefect in 1938; a year

later, the Anglia went into production. The V8-engine models underwent many changes, culminating in the 1948 Pilot. During the war, Ford-Britain's efforts were directed towards the production of tractors, 4 × 4 vehicles and gun carriers. In 1947, a total of 115,000 vehicles came out of the Dagenham works, increasing to 300,000 in 1953. The 1950s saw the rise in popularity of the 997-cc Anglia, followed by the Zephyr, Zodiac, Cortina, Consul, Granada, Capri and Escort. New factories appeared at Halewood (also for commercial vehicles), Basildon, Langley and Southampton. In line with its policy of decentralization, Ford-Britain also opened a plant at Swansea in 1965 for the construction of axles and bodies. In 1974, more than half a million vehicles were built, bringing in over £400 million in exports.

Brought out in 1976, the Fiesta was restyled in 1983. The original 957-cc 45-hp and 1117-cc 53-hp engines were augmented by 1297-cc 66-hp and 1608-cc 54-hp engines in 1977 and 1984 respectively. The diesel version has a top speed of 148 km/h (92 mph).

Launched in 1953, the Zodiac was over the years produced in several versions. The 1962 model was fairly similar to the Zephyr Four of the same year (above).

Ford-Britain brought out a new small-engined model in 1959. The Anglia had the four-cylinder 997-cc engine of the pre-war model and was sold as a saloon or an estate.

The Cortina (the British version of the German Taunus) came out in 1962, and over a million were sold in four years. It was the first of the cars with medium-capacity engines, ranging from 1.3 and 1.5 to 1.6 liters. The bodywork was modified in 1970/74, and in 1979 it had the same structure as the Taunus.

In 1968, Ford-Britain built 543,611 cars. The Escort came out that year as a replacement for the Anglia and proved very successful. The GT version had a four-cylinder 1098-cc engine developing 75 hp at 6000 rpm. The displacement was later increased to 1298 cc. The car was fitted with power-assisted front-wheel disc brakes.

The Taunus 20 M of 1964-7 was a two-door saloon fitted with a 1998-cc 85-hp 60-degree V6 engine giving a top speed of 160 km/h (100 mph).

The Capri came out in 1969 with a 1300-cc 57-hp engine. British and German versions were identical.

The Granada GXL (left) and XL coupé (right) came out in 1972. Both had the same 2.6- or 3-liter V6 engines, a four-speed gearbox with reverse, front disc brakes and a top speed of 182 km/h (113 mph). The coupé body was discontinued in 1974.

Production of the Consul, first brought out in 1950, reached 350,000 units in the next six years. The 1972-74 L (above) was available with a choice of three engines: 2, 2.5 or 3 liters.

The Taunus has undergone continuous modification. The 1976 GL model (left) had the same mechanics as previous models, but a completely new body which proved just as popular. Another successful Taunus design was brought out in 1981 (right: the L version) with a choice of engines from 1.3 to 2.3 liters. The front end was restyled, with a new grille and wrap-around bumpers, and new rubber side strips.

The 1977 Escorts had four-cylinder engines ranging from 1.1 to 1.6 liters and redesigned bodywork. Illustrated is the 1300-cc Escort Sport.

In 1979, this Granada Ghia joined the mid-range compacts. It was available with either a 2.3- or a 2.8-liter V6 engine.

This 1982 Granada had a 2.8-liter engine with fuel injection, a five-speed gearbox and a top speed of 190 km/h (118 mph). It was also available with a 2.5-liter diesel engine.

The new three-box Orion has a 1.3- or a 1.6-liter engine and wider market appeal.

The Fiesta is a small but roomy front-wheel drive compact with low fuel consumption. The XR-2 of 1981 has a four-cylinder 1.6-liter engine with a top speed of 180 km/h (112 mph).

A new version of the Capri was launched at the 1981 Geneva Motor Show. The 2.8-liter engine had fuel injection and a top speed of 210 km/h (130.5 mph).

Available with a wide range of bodies, the 1982 Escort has been very well received by the public. It also offers a choice of engines, from 1.1 to 1.6 liters.

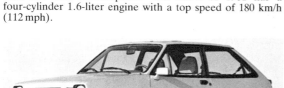

Launched in 1982 with 1.3- to 2.8-liter engines, and a diesel, the Sierra has already appeared on the market in different versions. In Autumn 1983, the new three-door saloon came out, followed immediately by the sporty XR 4, which combines the comfort of a saloon with the performance of a sports car. The Sierra is aimed at a wide range of the market and replaces the Taunus/Cortina. It has independent all-round suspension, energy-absorbing bumpers and power-assisted, dual-circuit brakes.

GENERAL MOTORS

BUICK – CADILLAC – CHEVROLET – OLDSMOBILE – PONTIAC

As with all new undertakings, the advent of the automobile began with doubt and confusion, and its early days created a vortex which dragged thousands of industrial giants to financial ruin.

In fact the entire history of the automobile is the story of an arduous struggle for survival, a struggle which began for General Motors with the work of R.E. Olds, who built the first Oldsmobile car in 1897 with 5 hp and a top speed of 24 km/h (15 mph).

With the takeover of the Cadillac Automobile Company, which concentrated on building a limited number of high quality, prestige vehicles, the Buick Motor Company, the Oakland Motor Company and the Pontiac Motor Division, the great William C. Durand, better known as "Fabulous Bill," founded the General Motors Corporation on 26 September 1908 and began a great challenge. Chevrolet and the Dayton Engineering Laboratories Company (Delco) also came into General Motors at a later date.

In the late 1920s, General Motors led the world's automobile manufacturers in abandoning the single product policy and adopting a range policy, for which a slogan was coined: "A car for every wish and every pocket."

General Motors came out of the great crash in a strong position as a result of changes that had been made, and won over 50 per cent of the entire American motor market. The company takes part in major public initiatives with its own permanent representatives and large financial contributions, and has made important contributions to medical science. It also organizes training and further courses at university level for its own employees.

To space research, General Motors made a great contribution by supplying the Apollo 8 guidance and navigation system, which was designed and built by the AC Electronics Division.

One in every two cars sold in America today comes off the Corporation's assembly lines.

On that distant 6 September 1908, not even fabulous Bill himself could have predicted that the company he founded would one day grow to such a size.

GENERAL MOTORS

The 1965 version of the Cadillac Fleetwood had a 7033-cc V8 engine with an output of 345 hp SAE at 4600 rpm. It had a top speed of about 200 km/h (124.25 mph) and a Turbo-Hydramatic three-speed automatic gearbox. This classic luxury car was 4.70 m (18.7 ft) long and weighed 2165 kg (2.13 tons). The Calais, a pillarless hardtop, was also produced.

The first car built by the Olds Motor Vehicle Company came out in 1897 with a single-cylinder 5-hp engine. It is now in the National Museum of History and Technology, Washington, DC.

The first Buick, the Flint, came out in July 1904 with a twin-cylinder 22-hp engine.

Launched in 1903, the Cadillac Model A had a removable tonneau which converted it from a two- to a four-seater. It had a single-cylinder horizontal engine.

The Curved Dash was the first car to use the Oldsmobile name. It was built between 1901 and 1907, and had a single-cylinder 7-hp engine.

The Buick Model D came out in 1907 with a four-cylinder 30-hp engine. The Touring five-seater model originally cost $2,500.

In 1909, Oakland was taken over by GM, but its first car (two cylinders, 20 hp) had been launched in 1907.

Brought out in 1908, the Oldsmobile Model M was a large, four-cylinder car also available in the Palace Touring and Flying Roadster versions.

The Cadillac Thirty was brought out in late 1906 and remained in production for eight years. The 1912 model (above) used a four-cylinder engine of 32.4 hp.

The Oldsmobile Limited came out in 1910 with a new, six-cylinder 60-hp engine, giving a top speed of over 100 km/h (62.14 mph).

This American motor industry giant began in 1892 when R. E. Olds collected all his savings to convert his father's naval and industrial engine factory in the new Olds Motor Vehicle Company, where the new horseless carriages known as automobiles were to be built. For five long years, however, the Oldsmobile (as their product came to be known) did not get beyond the experimental stage. In 1895, the first model, a four-seater with a petrol engine that could develop 5 hp and reach 30 km/h (18.6 mph), went for its trial run.

Olds proved himself not only an excellent inventor, but also a good businessman and was very successful with his first model, of which only a few were built. As a result of his success, he founded the first American factory in Detroit (the original and present-day heart of the American automobile industry) which was devoted exclusively to the production of automobiles. The first car was a luxury model costing $1,250, but the second model came out at a list price of just $650 and was very successful on the market. Two years later, at the turn of the century, Olds had sold over 1,400 of this economical car. In 1902, Oldsmobile was the first factory to produce 2,500 vehicles, proving itself a true pioneer in the history of the series-produced motor car.

The same year, the engineer David Buick (who had likewise been previously involved in the construction of marine engines) founded a factory under his own name in Detroit. While these developments were taking place in the industry, a third factory was also built in Detroit – the Cadillac Automobile Company. This was founded by Henry Leland, who was already building car engines with experience gained in the Oldsmobile factory, where he worked until 1901, when the factory was partially destroyed by fire. At the end of 1902, the first Cadillac was brought out – a car distinguished from the very beginning by its luxurious finish – although at the time "luxury" meant having a horn and oil lights included in the price. In the following year, tiller steering was replaced by the steering wheel, the reduction gearbox was introduced and some cars were fitted with celluloid windscreens. Oldsmobile reached a target of 4,000 cars in one year.

In 1907, the Oakland Motor Car Company was also founded. This later became the Pontiac

The first Chevrolet, the Six, was a five-seater produced by the Detroit factory in 1912. That year, 2,999 of the Classic Six were built.

The 1916 Buick D-55 was a large seven-seater tourer with a six-cylinder engine giving 25.3 hp. It cost $1,485.

The Cadillac Series 51, which came out in 1915, introduced the new V8 engine, whose output subsequently underwent few modifications.

The Chevrolet FA-4 Sedan of 1918. The door on the right side opened in the center to give access to the rear seats, while the one of the left gave on to the driver's seat.

The 1923 Oldsmobile Model 37 B four-door Sedan had a six-cylinder engine giving 40 hp.

The first Pontiac, the 6.27 Landau Coupé, was launched at the 1926 New York Motor Show. In twelve months, 76,742 were sold. It had a six-cylinder engine of 40 hp.

The 1926 Cadillac Series 314 had a new engine – a 90-degree V8 developing 86 hp at 3000 rpm.

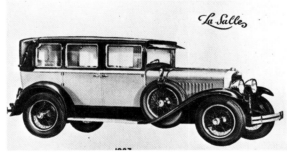

The 1927 Cadillac La Salle was an instant success. In the first three years, 54,000 were sold.

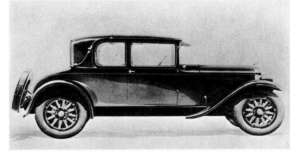

The 1928 Buick Master 6 Model 28-58 five-seater coupé had a six-cylinder 75-hp engine and cost $1,850.

Motor Division, on the initiative of Edward Murphy, who converted his factory where horse-drawn carriages had been produced.

In 1904, many technical improvements were made to the cars including magneto and flywheel ignition, and full-pressure lubrication; in response to public demand, a four-cylinder engine was made available. It was not until 1906, however, that Buick launched the first series-produced four-cylinder car.

By 16 September 1903, so many different manufacturers were operating, at a time of great market instability, that the weakest disappeared and the stronger companies were forced to form a consortium. General Motors was thus formed, bringing together Oldsmobile and Buick, joined in 1909 by Cadillac and Oakland. Positive results

were immediately seen from this union.

Cadillac won the Dewar prize in London for having built their cars with interchangeable parts, an important factor in making series-production possible. The "Caddy," as it was familiarly known among Americans (by association with the golf caddy), was also the first car to have a standard accumulator and thus an independent source of electrical energy. The Dewar prize was awarded a second time to Cadillac in 1912, when they made the electric starter motor a standard accessory – an innovation which helped popularize the motor car among American women too, as it meant they could use one more easily. In 1912, the electric motor appeared, built by the Delco Company, which is still part of the Corporation today.

The General Motors Truck Company was formed from the merger between Reliance Motor and the Rapid Motor Vehicle Company, whose commercial vehicle, launched in 1902, could be considered the first American truck. After two years' preparation, the first industrial vehicle was sold under the name GMC-Trucks. In 1908, the Fisher Closed Body Co. evolved from an idea of the coachbuilder Fisher's. He believed that it was both unreasonable and uncomfortable to have to drive an open car in the rain or over dusty roads, and so designed and built completely closed car bodies. Cadillac ordered 150 in 1910 and, very soon after, many other GM makes were using the same coachbuilder. General Motors eventually bought a 60 per cent share in the Fisher Body Corporation.

The six-cylinder F-31 roadster came out of the Oldsmobile Lansing plant in 1931. A very high daily rate of production enabled 47,279 Oldsmobiles to be built that year.

The V 16 Cadillac was launched in 1931. Above: the 1932 model, with air-cooled engine. Disc brakes were available as an optional extra.

Officially known as the Eagle, but also called the Master, the Chevrolet of 1933 was completely redesigned. It cost a mere $565 and was immediately popular.

The six-cylinder engine on this 1935 Pontiac Standard Six Sedan was directly derived from the eight-cylinder version. It developed 80 hp at 3800 rpm and had hydraulic brakes.

The Buick Series 40 Special Victoria coupé of 1936 had an eight-cylinder 30-hp engine and cost $885–905 depending on the model.

The 1940 Series 60 estate. Oldsmobile had Hydramatic automatic gearboxes fitted for the first time that year.

In 1940, Chevrolet had three different lines on the market – the Master 85, the Master De Luxe (above: a Town Sedan) and the Special De Luxe; 895,734 cars were built that year.

The 1946 Oldsmobile Series 60 Special Convertible coupé had a six-cylinder engine developing 100 hp at 3400 rpm and cost $1,657 for the basic model; 194,755 cars; in 1946.

Cadillac was still offering Hydramatic gearboxes as an optional extra in 1947, when 59,436 cars were built. Above: the Series 62 coupé.

In 1948, Chevrolet production increased although very few changes were made: 775,982 cars were built and 715,992 were sold. Above: the Fleetmaster coupé.

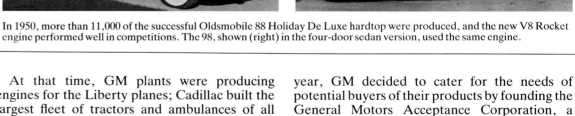

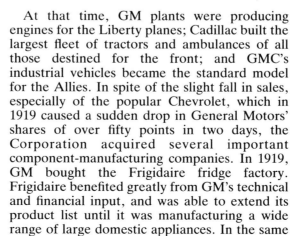

In 1950, more than 11,000 of the successful Oldsmobile 88 Holiday De Luxe hardtop were produced, and the new V8 Rocket engine performed well in competitions. The 98, shown (right) in the four-door sedan version, used the same engine.

In 1911, Luis Chevrolet, a driver of Swiss origin, brought out a car entirely designed and built by himself. W. C. Durant, one of the founders of GM, liked his idea, so that year the Chevrolet Motor Company was formed. Also operating out of Detroit, the new company produced cars that were technically highly innovative for their time, a fact that contributed significantly to their commercial success, which was such that, in a very short time, "Chevy" led the market in their field. In 1918, just before the Armistice in the First World War, the Chevrolet Company was also incorporated into the General Motors Company. During the war years, production at General Motors was concentrated on supplying military vehicles.

At that time, GM plants were producing engines for the Liberty planes; Cadillac built the largest fleet of tractors and ambulances of all those destined for the front; and GMC's industrial vehicles became the standard model for the Allies. In spite of the slight fall in sales, especially of the popular Chevrolet, which in 1919 caused a sudden drop in General Motors' shares of over fifty points in two days, the Corporation acquired several important component-manufacturing companies. In 1919, GM bought the Frigidaire fridge factory. Frigidaire benefited greatly from GM's technical and financial input, and was able to extend its product list until it was manufacturing a wide range of large domestic appliances. In the same

year, GM decided to cater for the needs of potential buyers of their products by founding the General Motors Acceptance Corporation, a finance company which offered easy terms of repayment.

In the years immediately following, other factories were founded directly by GM to guarantee a store of components for their assembly lines. Other companies, too, were taken over by this American group, by now well on the way to becoming an industrial giant, capable of branching out in all directions. In 1925, the merger between the GM Truck Company and the Yellow Cab Manufacturing Company took place, with the aim of building both taxis and trucks at the same time (the

In 1934, Buick cars were completely redesigned and fitted with independent front suspension and an eight-cylinder engine. The version illustrated is the 29/31, which cost $925.

company was incorporated into General Motors in 1943, by which time the Corporation had already acquired most of its shares).

In those years, technical advances went ahead hand in hand with new developments on the financial side, such as the foundation of insurance companies. In 1928, Cadillac introduced a synchronized ratio gearbox; in 1933, the GM engineers solved the problem of independent front suspension; and in the following year, the two-stroke diesel engine designed by GM drove the first diesel-powered series. In 1939, Oldsmobile introduced automatic gear change on their models for the following year – the first in which GM's sales reached the 25 million mark. In 1941, GM like everyone else became involved in the war effort, turning out great quantities of arms and supplies for troops at the front. Production included 119 million bombs and grenades, 206,000 aeroplane engines, 190,000 cannon, 1.9 million machine-guns, over 3 million rifles, 13,000 aeroplanes, 854,000 trucks and amphibious vehicles, 38,000 assault and other vehicles, at a total cost of 12.3 billion dollars. This represented an immense effort, not only for that particular period, but for any economy at any time. Because of it, recovery was slow in the years immediately after the war, hampered by lack of raw materials. Nevertheless, production

The redesigned 1953 Buick Roadmaster Riviera, with a V8 engine and Dynaflow automatic transmission (first introduced by Buick in 1948).

The Pontiac Star Chief Custom Catalina of 1954 had its air-conditioning unit fitted under the bonnet for the first time, instead of in the boot.

The year 1955 was a good one for GM, whose production increased by 50 per cent. Chevrolet also contributed to this success with the Bel Air.

The Chevrolet Corvette, launched in 1953, was the first American sports car and the first car in production to have a fiberglass body. Illustrated below is the 1956 model.

Introduced in 1957, the Cadillac Eldorado Brougham was a dream car, offered with a stainless steel roof, air suspension and twin front headlamps.

This Chevrolet Lakewood estate, launched in 1961, had a bigger loading area than any other model of the time.

The famous Pontiac Catalina was updated in 1962 and given a unitary body, a new front end, a redesigned rear end and new front suspension.

The first Oldsmobile compact, the F 85 (shown above in the 1961 Cutlass Sport coupé version) had a unitary body and a front-mounted, 3523-cc 155-hp V8 engine.

The 1962 Oldsmobile Starfire coupé had a chassis with side members, power-assisted drum brakes and a 6456-cc 345-hp V8 engine.

The Chevrolet Biscayne series came out in 1958 as part of the company's more economical range. It had a six-cylinder 3851-cc engine. Above: a 1962 model.

The 1962 Oldsmobile 98 sports sedan combined aerodynamic lines with the comfort and convenience of a four-door body. It had a Skyrocket 330-hp engine and Hydramatic transmission as standard.

The Chevrolet Bel Air, shown above in the 1962 two-door version, was part of the big six-seater range and had a six-cylinder 3.8-liter engine.

In 1960, Buick applied to its models a series of technical improvements. The 1962 Invicta Hardtop had a chassis with cross-members and an automatic gearbox.

Very few changes were made to the design or mechanics of the 1962 Cadillac Series 62. It had a four-speed plus reverse automatic gearbox.

The 1962 Oldsmobile Starfire coupé had a chassis with side members, a manual, three-speed gearbox with reverse and a 6.5-liter V8 engine.

The 1965 V8 Pontiac Grand Prix coupé was the forerunner of a new body design without rear fins.

The compact Pontiac Tempest, shown here in the 1965 Custom Coupé version, had a four-cylinder supersquare engine (1961). A choice of six- or eight-cylinder engines was in 1965 available on request.

Immediately recognizable because of the moulding which ran down the whole side, the Chevrolet Chevelle Malibu four-door saloon had a six- or eight-cylinder engine.

With the aim of increasing sales, the Chevrolet Chevy II Nova of 1965 was built with a choice of engines.

The first Chevrolet Caprice to come off the assembly lines in April 1967 was also the hundred millionth GM car.

The Cadillac Calais of 1966 had a new Turbo-Hydramatic gearbox and boxed side members.

The sporty lines of the 1967 Pontiac Firebird were echoed on this Chevrolet Camaro available with a six- or eight-cylinder engine.

After many years of research from 1959 onwards, the Oldsmobile Tornado was launched in 1966 and proved an instant success. It had a new line with a fastback body and retractable headlights. The front end was also new, with a very narrow radiator grille. A particularly efficient air-conditioning system was designed in 1967, with the vents in the boot.

One of the most successful models of the Chevrolet range was the Impala, available in six different models: cabriolet, sport coupé, sport sedan, four-door saloon and two estate models.

The Buick Le Sabre of 1967 had a new chassis with boxed side members. Front disc brakes and automatic transmission were available as extras.

The 1967 Pontiac Le Mans had a new body design with either a six- or eight-cylinder engine, rear-wheel drive and manual gearbox. Front disc brakes were optional.

The Chevrolet sports car, the Camaro, was brought out at the end of 1966. It had a unitary body, an adjustable steering wheel, central gear lever and individual front seats.

Pontiac also has its sports version – the 1968 GTO, which came with varying outputs. Optional were power-assisted steering and a Turbo-Hydramatic automatic gearbox.

The Buick Electra 225, available with several different body types, was part of the GM luxury range. It had a seven-liter V8 engine.

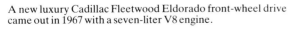

A new luxury Cadillac Fleetwood Eldorado front-wheel drive came out in 1967 with a seven-liter V8 engine.

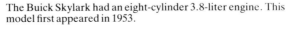

The Buick Skylark had an eight-cylinder 3.8-liter engine. This model first appeared in 1953.

The medium-sized Chevrolet Chevelle Malibu was one of Chevrolet's best sellers in 1969 (367,100 units).

The lines of the Chevrolet Corvette have been altered many times since its first appearance in 1953. It has a fiberglass body, independent rear suspension and all-round disc brakes. Illustrated here is the 1969 Sting Ray coupé with the new seven-liter V8 engine.

The "top" class Chevrolets were redesigned in 1969. Above: the Impala.

Part of the Buick sports range, the GS was given a new front end in 1971. It was driven by a 5.7-liter V8 engine.

In 1970, the Buick Riviera was fitted with a new 7.5-liter V8 engine. In 1971, the body was completely redesigned with a fastback tail.

The Monte Carlo came out in 1970 as one of Chevrolet's prestige models. It differed in line from the company's other cars and had a choice of five different engines.

The 1971 Cadillac Sixty Special Brougham was a four-door saloon which belonged to the company's prestige range.

The Vega, the new "small" Chevrolet, came out in 1971. It had a four-cylinder 2.3-liter engine, with an aluminium block.

Oldsmobile engines suffered a reduction in power in 1971. Above: the Cutlass Supreme.

The 1972 front-wheel drive Oldsmobile Tornado had a 7.4-liter engine and a rigid-axle rear suspension.

The Camaro range was completely updated in 1972 with the Type SS, which had a new front end, headlamps and grille.

The Chevrolet Impala was one of the best sellers in the United States. Above: the Custom coupé of 1972.

The Delta 88 Royale belonged to Oldsmobile's luxury range. It had a 5.7-liter V8 engine.

The 1973 Pontiac Grand Prix coupé had a 6.6-liter V8 engine and automatic gearbox. A 7.5-liter engine was also available.

In 1972, President Nixon presented the Russian Premier Brezhnev with a front-wheel drive Cadillac Eldorado.

The 1973 Century Luxus was a Buick compact with a more streamlined design. It had an eight-cylinder 5665-cc engine.

The 1974 Chevrolet Monza sports car was derived from the Vega. It had a choice of engine, ranging from 2.5 to 3.8 liters.

The 1975 Cadillac Seville had front-wheel drive and independent suspension. A diesel version was also available.

was geared to the demands of the market and made steady progress.

Public interest in automatic gear change led to GM's concentrating research in this field, so that, by 1950, all the models built in the United States were available with an automatic gearbox: the Hydramatic was used on the Oldsmobile, Pontiac and Cadillac, the Dynaflow on the Buick, the Powerglide on the Chevrolet. Contouring of the bodywork was proceeding at the same time, resulting in a greater surface area of glass and improved aerodynamic lines. A hardtop was introduced in 1949, with a two-door open body on to which an all-steel roof could be fitted as required.

The outbreak of the Korean war meant that part of production was diverted into providing

supplies for the front (although to an almost negligible extent in comparison with the Second World War). The percentage thus reallocated reached 19 per cent and then levelled off at about 5 per cent from 1956 onwards. General Motors is still one of the major suppliers of military vehicles to the American army.

In 1951, GM built a revolutionary new model, the XP Sabre, which had a new engine and new suspension, as well as a completely redesigned steering box. It was a prototype designed for the race track, but it gave birth to the Chevrolet Corvette Sport, produced in series with huge success from 1953 onwards. In 1954, great celebrations greeted the production of the fifty millionth car, a Chevrolet cabriolet hardtop (1955 model): the car was painted gold both

inside and out, and was exhibited in sixty-five American cities. At the same time, all works belonging to GM and their associates were opened to the public, who were invited to see for themselves the degree of rationalization reached in the group's production plants.

Between 1951 and 1955, the five makes which still today form General Motors – Buick, Chevrolet, Pontiac, Oldsmobile and Cadillac – were given a standard new V8 engine with a higher compression ratio; the electrical supply was also changed from 6 to the much more reliable 12 volts. Power-assisted steering and brakes appeared on all the cars and the glass area was increased to improve visibility and safety. Interior comfort was improved by the installation of the first air-conditioning systems.

The sporty Pontiac Firebird is a four-seater with a unitary body which comes in a variety of models. The range was completely updated in 1981 with the adoption of new 2.5-, 2.8- and 5-liter engines. The last of these was uprated again in 1984 (190 hp). The Trans Am Turbo with aluminium alloy wheels, illustrated below, came out in 1982.

An experimental new version of the Chevrolet Corvette was launched in 1974, with a twin-rotor or a four-rotor engine. These precursors of rotary-engine cars also incorporated design features which were considered to be well ahead of their time.

The 1974 Pontiac Trans Am four-seater sports coupé had a unitary body and a new reinforced bumper. It remained in production until 1980. ▶

The compact 1974 front-wheel drive Oldsmobile Omega remained in production until the 1980s, with constant updating of the range.

Introduced in 1976, the Chevrolet Chevette had the lowest fuel consumption of any American car. It had a 1.6-liter engine.

The Chevrolet Caprice Classic of 1977 had a smaller and consequently lighter body. It had a six-cylinder 3.7-liter engine.

The 1978 Oldsmobile Starfire was a 2 + 2 coupé with a four-cylinder 2.5-liter engine. Derived from the Monza, it also came with a 3.8-liter V6 engine.

The Buick Skylark (above: the 1977 model) has been part of the GM X-cars range since 1979. It is a front-wheel drive compact with a four- or six-cylinder engine.

Despite the new trend towards smaller and more economical cars, Buick brought out this luxury front-wheel drive Riviera in 1978, with a V6 turbo or a V8 engine.

In 1981, Chevrolet, Pontiac and Cadillac introduced a completely new concept with a range of cars known as "J cars," based on smaller bodies which sacrificed nothing in terms of comfort, and minimized running costs. They were front-wheel drive, with four-cylinder transverse engines of 1800 cc. Top: the Chevrolet Cavalier. Above: the Pontiac J 2000. Below: the Cadillac Cimarron.

The Buick medium-sized cars include the Regal, which has been in production since 1981 and comes with a 3.8-liter V8 or turbo engine, or in a diesel version with an injection pump.

The Chevrolet Chevette sold in Germany as the Opel Kadett and in Great Britain as the Vauxhall Chevette, and was part of the company's mid-low range of cars. It had a six-cylinder 1.6-liter engine.

The 1980 Pontiac Phoenix was a compact car with a four-cylinder 2.5-liter engine and front-wheel drive.

Brought out in 1979, the Chevrolet Citation was a small, front-wheel drive compact with a four-cylinder 2.5-liter engine.

One of the GM mid-range cars, the 1982 Pontiac 6000 had a four-cylinder 2.5-liter engine, front-wheel drive and an automatic gearbox.

In 1982, the Buick Electra still had rear-wheel drive. The automatic gearbox and overdrive were standard. In 1984, it was changed to front-wheel drive.

Thirty years separate the first Corvette from this 1983 version, which has a 5733-cc V8 engine developing 205 hp at 4300 rpm. Its top speed is 225 km/h (140 mph) and it accelerates from 0–100 km/h (0–62 mph) in 7.5 seconds. The plastic body is mounted on a steel and aluminium chassis and has a total weight of 1415 kg (1.4 tons). There is a choice of gearbox, either four-speed automatic or four-speed manual with overdrive.

During this period, GM replaced their classic sedans with the four-door hardtop, a series of cars with completely new bodywork; the first "safety measures" were also introduced, including front safety belts. The decade between 1950 and 1960 was particularly prosperous in the United States, seeing a rise in demand for a second car in the family. Over the same period, the proportion of estates sold rose from less than 2 to 10 per cent of the market, while the demand for smaller European cars also increased. It was then that GM decided to produce a compact version with the Pontiac Tempest,

The Chevrolet Camaro Z 28 was brought out in January 1982, at the same time as the new Pontiac Firebird. The five-liter V8 engine has a manual gearbox.

which also came out with the Buick Special and the Oldsmobile F 85, cars which were an immediate success. The market hit a plateau in the 1970s, remaining in this state for ten years, when it suffered dangerous drops in production levels. The "crisis," however, has now found its own solution, with a return to the traditional models to which the Americans have been accustomed since the early days of motoring. In fact, the reduction in size of cars coincided, perhaps by coincidence, with the slump in the market, while the return to larger cars marked the beginning of the recovery.

◄ The Oldsmobile Firenza of 1982 was part of the GM "J car" range and had a four-cylinder transverse engine.

The new Pontiac coupé is called the Fiero and is the first ► American mid-engined two-seater. It has a 2.5-liter engine and independent all-round suspension.

The two-door Cadillac Eldorado (left) and the four-door Seville (right) of 1984, two of the company's luxury cars, have a front-mounted engine and all-round independent suspension.

The 1984 Cadillac Fleetwood Brougham Sedan has classic lines and a 4.1- or 5.7-liter V8 engine.

OPEL
VAUXHALL

In the mid nineteenth century, Adam Opel from Rüsselsheim decided to settle down after a number of jobs which had taken him as far as Paris. He started production of the world's first sewing-machine in his uncle's stable – his uncle, a locksmith, not permitting him to set up in his workshop. At first, most tailors were violently opposed to Opel's invention, seeing the machine as something that would take away their jobs. It was finally accepted, however, and continued to be produced until 1911, when a good part of the Rüsselsheim factory was destroyed by fire. At this point, the Opel brothers decided to abandon the sewing-machine business and concentrate entirely on manufacturing cars and bicycles. Making use of the new methods employed in England – the leader at the time in two-wheel transport – the Opel factory went through a period of expansion, particularly after the invention of the pneumatic tyre by the Scottish inventor John Boyd Dunlop and its application to the motor car by the Frenchman Michelin.

Production of the first Opel began in Rüsselsheim in 1898. It had been launched on its career by Lutzmann, who in Berlin had won a race, specially organized to mark the foundation of the first Automobile Club, with a four-wheel vehicle that he had built himself. After they had seen the race and taken note of the main technical features of the car, which included the abundant use of ball bearings on the wheels and the drive shaft, the Opel brothers decided to go into business with him. In early 1899, there appeared on the market the first examples of the Opel Patent Motorwagen – the first eleven cars in a long series which continues to the present day. Fitted with a 1500-cc 4-hp rear-mounted engine which could take it up to a maximum speed of 20 km/h (12.4 mph), the Opel was a small, light two-seater, although some four-seaters were also built, as well as a delivery van.

In 1899, the Opel brothers and Lutzmann built a larger car which could reach 40 km/h (24.9 mph) with four passengers. At that time, however, Opel cars were unable to compete with the more advanced vehicle technology of the French, and, since manufacturing automobiles was eating up all the capital that had been made from the sewing-machine business, the car section was closed and they returned to bicycles, but in an engine-driven version: the motor cycle. Meanwhile, on a trip to Paris, the Opel brothers took on the concession for the sale of Renault cars in Germany and, since Renault was not big enough to supply sufficient numbers of cars to justify the organization of a sales/service system in economic terms, the Opel brothers arranged another agreement to sell the Darracq throughout Germany, too. The Darracq was a small French car, with a cardan shaft transmission system and an 8-hp twin-cylinder engine, which was a great commercial success in Germany. By the following year, however, the Opel brothers had uprated it from 1100 to 1360 cc, and an Opel-Darracq model came out with a 9-hp engine.

Opel had earned a good reputation as builders of automobiles, largely as a result of their wide range of models, which underwent modification at a rate that would prove impossible for the present-day industry. Production levels rose from 358 units in 1905 to 3,519, including cars and lorries, in 1914. Thanks to advertising campaigns and racing successes, Opel had managed to secure a firm foothold in the market. By their fiftieth anniversary, they were simultaneously producing lorries, agricultural tractors and even aeroplane engines. At the time, technology was

The first post-war Kadett brought out in 1962 had a 993-cc engine and was followed by 1078-cc, 1196-cc and (on the Rallye 1.9 S) 1897-cc 90-hp versions. The series was completely updated in 1973, although it kept to the classic arrangement, with the engine mounted at the front and rear-wheel drive. A two- or four-door saloon and a Caravan version were also available, with 993- or 1196-cc engines. The series went out of production in 1979, when the front-wheel drive Kadett D was launched.

The first patented Opel was built with the Lutzmann system, but very few were built before more successful engines were adopted.

The 1902 10/12 PS tonneau had a two-cylinder, vertical, 1884-cc engine. It was the first to arrive in Frankfurt on 31 August 1902 in a race restricted to voiturettes.

A four-cylinder engine was used in 1908 on the 10/18 PS, shown here in the phaeton version.

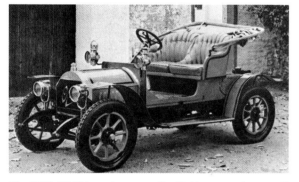

The 1909 4/8 CV was known as the Doktorwagen because it was the doctors' most popular choice for getting around. It had a two-seater open body with a small hood.

The 1924 Laubfrosch ("Frog") was the first series-built German car. It had a four-cylinder 4/12-hp engine. The 4/4 (above) came out in 1925.

In production from 1931 to 1933, by which time Opel had already joined General Motors, this 1.8-liter saloon had a six-cylinder side-valve engine.

The 1935 P4 was the cheapest Opel and cost RM1,450 in 1937. It was built without modifications until 1938, with a four-cylinder 1074-cc engine.

The Olympic Games were held in Germany in 1936 and so the new Opel was called the Olympia. It had a steel unitary body and cost only RM2,500.

◄ The Kadett came out in 1937 and was in production until 1939 with the same four-cylinder 1.1-liter side-valve engine.

clearly still in its early stages, as Opel's production schedules show: it took upwards of six weeks to build the chassis for a small saloon and up to three months for a larger vehicle, while painting the bodywork could alone take up to five weeks, this being the time required for the paints then in use to dry.

Of all the models designed in that period, two worthy of mention are the Volksautomobil ("the People's Car") with its single-cylinder engine, and the open Doktorwagen, the small two-seater soft-top favoured by doctors. Opel models were meanwhile competing in many races and won several victories – in fact the whole period was one of races and records.

Immediately after the First World War, Opel began to concentrate once more on automobiles, the flow of which had been interrupted during the war by the production of military vehicles. During the post-war recovery period, the sales network they had developed during sixty years of

business experience in the most varied types of products, ranging from sewing-machines to bicycles and motor cycles, proved extremely useful. At the 1921 Berlin Motor Show four- and six-cylinder engines and roadsters were presented.

Germany, meanwhile, was suffering the effects of inflation and instability on the eve of Hitler's rise to power: only 910 cars were produced in 1923. Yet, only two years later, the figure reached five figures and exceeded 100,000 in 1935. A significant factor in this success was Wilhelm Opel's visit to America, where he saw and admired the Ford system of series production. Opel subsequently changed over to the production of a single car, which was very similar to the Citroën 5 CV. With a four-cylinder engine with side valves, 12 hp and a three-speed gearbox, the car was often painted green and was therefore known as the Laubfrosch or "Frog"; its French counterpart was similarly given the

nickname "Le Citron" ("The Lemon") because of its bright yellow colour. The Opel "Frog" cost RM 400 and the interest it aroused immediately boosted sales. In 1928 alone, production reached 42,771 units and accounted for 26 per cent of all the cars sold in Germany.

As American automobile companies began to invade the European markets, importing complete cars and also building factories on the Continent, Opel's fortunes were to change yet again. The first step towards such expansion was taken by GM, who bought Vauxhall Motors for $2.5 million. On 18 March 1929, the foundation of a partnership between GM and Opel was announced, part of the shares being sold for $30 million. As a result, management by the Opel family came to an end when the remaining shares were sold in 1931 and the running of Rüsselsheim was handed over to Reuter, a director of GM who had already run Oldsmobile with great success.

Beginning with the small 1200-cc P4 Opel in

The Admiral came out in 1937 and was an extremely elegant four-door model with a six-cylinder 3620-cc 95-hp engine. It cost RM6,500.

Changes were made to models within the same range at a tremendous rate in the post-war period. The 1959 Kapitän had an increased output of 80 hp.

A new design was also used for the 1963 Rekord. The car was a little longer, but also lower, and for the first time had optional power-assisted front disc brakes.

The 1962 Kadett was built at the new Bochum plant. It was completely redesigned and had a supersquare single-liter engine with a displacement of 933 cc. The 1983 Kadett GTE (above) has a sporty streamlined shape which is very different from the sober two-door bodywork of the 1962 model.

Developed from the Kadett, the GT coupé was launched in 1967 with a 1.1- or 1.9-liter engine. It had a two-seater body with retractable headlamps that could be driver-operated.

The Commodore was a new model brought out at the 1967 Geneva Motor Show with a six-cylinder engine of 2.5-liters, developing 115 hp. A rear anti-roll bar and power steering were available on request.

Opel brought out coupé versions of the Kadett and the Olympia in 1967. The choice of engine was 1.5 or 1.9 liters. Above: the Olympia coupé.

The Ascona, brought out in 1970 to occupy the position between the Kadett and the Rekord, was available with four different engines and three body styles. Above: the 1976 L. The 1980 Ascona series also has a two-liter injection engine.

Another 1970 model, the sporty two-door Manta coupé had no front grille (the air intake was concealed behind the bumpers) and a choice of engine from 1.6 to 2 liters. The GT/E model had electronic fuel injection.

The Opel Corsa comes in a two- or three-box model. The basic engine is 45 hp, 993 cc, but 1200- and 1300-cc engines are also available, with top speeds of 140, 152 and 166 km/h (87, 95 and 103 mph) respectively.

The Monza (above) and the Senator (below) came out in 1978 and are part of Opel's luxury range. The first is a coupé and the other a saloon, and they share the same 2.8- or 3-liter engines, floorpan and independent rear suspension.

1935, the company went on to bring out the first Kadett in 1937. It had a longer wheelbase than the P4 and cost RM 2,100, a figure that people could still afford at the time; a total of 107,000 were built before the war. Meanwhile, new engines were made for the Kadett and the Olympia, the latter being given a new 1.5-liter engine which could develop 37 hp. The Kapitän, with a six-cylinder engine and a unitary body similar to that of the Kadett, came out in 1939; two years previously, the Admiral had been launched which, with a 3620-cc 95-hp engine, was the most opulent car of the pre-war period. This four-door luxury vehicle was a veritable flagship for the range. Production figures continued to increase until 1940, when they reached the million mark; almost at the same time, however,

production came to a halt because of the war. The economic disaster which followed as a result of Germany's defeat also affected Opel, whose factories were destroyed by the Allied bombers. Getting production off the ground again proved difficult, both from the technological point of view and also because of the problems created by foreign occupation. By 1946, however, the 1½-ton lorry, the Blitz, was already coming off the production lines with a Kapitän 2.5-liter engine. In 1950 it was the turn of an updated Olympia, and in 1953 modifications to the Kapitän sent production levels soaring to over 100,000 units for the first time since the war. The Kapitän and the Olympia remained the pillars of support for Opel until the introduction in 1958 of the Rekord, a car which filled the gap between the two existing models. Following the American tradition, Opel changed the grilles and the lines of their cars almost every year. In 1962, the reintroduction of the new Kadett 1200 (all the production plans for the previous ones had gone to the Russians by way of war reparation – hence the launch of the Moskwitch) boosted Opel's production levels with a European-size car. Opel cars of the 1960s began to resemble those of today, with their square lines and horizontal front radiator grilles. More and more powerful engines

Europe's best selling model in its category in the 1970s, the Rekord was radically modified in 1977 and restyled in 1983. In its latest form, the range includes 1796-cc, 90-hp and 1979-cc 110-hp petrol engines, and a 2260-cc diesel, available in a naturally aspirated 65-hp or an 86-hp turbo version.

were introduced, and a 1900-cc diesel engine, the same as the one that has now been uprated to 2.3 liters, was also brought out. Parallel developments took place as Opel returned to the world of racing with the Commodore, Kadett and Ascona, with pleasing results, particularly in rallies.

Vauxhall

The growth of British Vauxhall, bought in 1925 by General Motors, was mainly due to American investment. In fact, when the company was bought, it was still a comparatively small factory. It was taken over by GM, who aimed to improve their chances of expansion into the European market through the use of local industries, although directed from the USA. A few years later, GM also bought the Opel company in Germany (1931). Vauxhall has always produced cars designed specifically for the British market, making use of small changes to Opel models in a tradition closely inspired by the Opel philosophy. The twin copies of the Opel Kadett and the Vauxhall Viva (1963) and the Rekord-Carlton are both recent. In the case of the Rekord Facelift, the new German car was remade for the first time along the lines of the Carlton, adopting its whole front end.

Vauxhall's role, as a division of General Motors in Europe, is to produce cars with a German flavour (Opel), but designed to suit the particular requirements of the British market.

The Cresta was brought out in 1954 with a six-cylinder Velox engine. The front end was modified in 1956.

The new style Viva of 1971 had a more spacious interior and improved soundproofing.

The cheap Vauxhall Cadet had a 17- or 26-hp engine and cost £280–295.

◀ The first Vauxhall car, the SCV, came out in 1903 with a single-cylinder 5-hp engine. Forty were built.

The Vauxhall Victor Type F came out in 1975 and 390,745 were produced.

The Carlton came out in October 1978 with the same body design and mechanics as the Opel Rekord. It had a two-liter 100-hp engine.

HONDA

The largest motor-cycle manufacturer in the world, Honda began building automobiles in 1962. The first Honda cars were very clearly influenced by the design of the motor cycle and had small passenger compartments. The four-stroke engines were often air cooled.

The very first car produced was a 531-cc 44-hp roadster with an engine speed of up to 8000 rpm. It had a front-mounted engine and rear-wheel drive, and its motor-cycle ancestry was evident from the twin chain transmission (one chain per wheel). The small Honda first appeared at the 1964 Geneva Motor Show. Two years later, the

car was joined by a coupé version with an increased engine displacement of 800 cc.

Honda cars did not meet with much success on the world market, however, at least not compared with their results in the two-wheel sector. In 1966, after their car sales had dropped even further, they brought out the N 360, a small, two-seater two-box car which closely resembled the British Mini and was immediately christened by the public the Mini Honda. It had a two-cylinder air-cooled 354-cc 31-hp engine, front-wheel drive and a transverse engine mounted in a body that was 2.5 m (8.2 ft) long and

The two-door N 360 was presented in 1966 in Tokyo with a two-cylinder 354-cc 31-hp air-cooled engine and front-wheel drive. The N 500 (below), which had a slightly more powerful engine (500 cc, 40 hp), was the export version.

The S 600 coupé, which also came in a soft-top version, was a two-cylinder model with a four-cylinder in-line engine of 606 cc, which developed 57 hp at 8500 rpm and had a top speed of 150 km/h (93.2 mph).

Brought out in 1970, the Z had a two-cylinder water-cooled engine and front-wheel drive. Its engine displacement was 354 cc, developing 36 hp at 9000 rpm (in the TS version). It had a unitary body, and drum brakes on all four wheels.

The N 1300 saloon had a front-mounted 1298-cc straight-four engine which developed 96 hp at 7200 rpm. Its top speed was 175 km/h (108.7 mph).

The N 600 Touring is another small format car. It has a Honda two-cylinder transverse air-cooled engine of 598.7 cc, developing 38 hp at 6000 rpm, with a top speed of 125 km/h (77.7 mph).

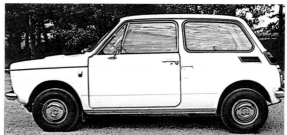

A classic in its design, the compact Civic has a 1.3- or 1.5-liter transverse engine and front-wheel drive. The body is available in a two-, three-, four- or five-door version. It first came out in July 1972, and since then several improvements have been made: its dimensions have been increased, its bodywork altered and independent rear suspension added.

The Accord is a front-wheel drive saloon launched in 1976. It has a four-cylinder transverse engine of 1.6 liters and independent suspension. Top speed is 163 km/h (101.3 mph).

The new station wagon known as the Shuttle is part of the Civic family. It has a five-door body and is almost 4 m (13.1 ft) long and 1.62 m (5.3 ft) wide; its height of 1.48 m (4.8 ft) makes for an extremely spacious interior.

1.2 m (4 ft) wide. Its top speed was 115 km/h (71.5 mph). The car was subsequently fitted with an engine of 500 and later 600 cc, while the 360-cc engine continued in regular production.

The first major innovation was launched at the 1968 Tokyo Motor Show in the form of the N 1300 – a five-seater four-door saloon with a four-cylinder transverse engine of 1298 cc, developing 96 hp, and front-wheel drive. Two

years later came the Z, a 2 + 2 with a rounded body and the same mechanics as the 360, the classic which formed the basis for the Life in 1971, an improved final version of the 360. This was followed a year later by the 1169-cc Civic front-wheel drive saloon.

These models have remained in production – with a few minor modifications – but have now also been joined by the Accord and the Prelude.

The agreement made with Austin-Rover for the production of the Acclaim (based on the Ballade) in Great Britain has proved an important landmark for the company, leading as it has to the development of the Rover 213, the latest product of the Honda-Austin-Rover agreement.

In 1982, 875,779 cars came off Honda's production lines, and their range is currently sold in ninety-two countries.

The Prelude coupé, brought out in 1978, is a 1.8-liter 2 + 2 with an output of 103 hp at 5500 rpm and a top speed of 180 km/h (112 mph). It has automatic transmission with four ratios and a five-speed gearbox.

The compact Ballade is sold in Great Britain under the Austin-Rover marque as the Acclaim. It has a 1.3- or 1.5-liter engine and front-wheel drive.

The Jazz is a small three-door car with a 1.2-liter engine. It first came out in 1981 and since 1983 has been available with a fuel-injected 100/110 hp turbo engine that gives a top speed of 180–190 km/h (112–118 mph).

The 1984 Civic, shown here in the CR-X coupé version (left) and the four-door saloon (right), also called the Ballade, has a 1.3- or 1.5-liter transverse engine.

Brought out in 1981, the Accord is also available with a coupé body. It has a 1.6- or 1.8-liter engine with a top speed of 172 km/h (107 mph). Above: the four-door saloon version of 1984.

JAGUAR
DAIMLER

One of the most famous British automobile manufacturers today, Jaguar owes its origin to two partners, William Lyons and William Walmsley, who in 1920 founded Swallow, a company which was set up to produce side-cars. Their low-price policy ensured the commercial success of their enterprise, and in 1927 they decided to branch out, changing their name to the Swallow Side-car and Coachbuilding Company. They started off building bodies for low-priced chassis, one of the most popular of which was the Austin Seven. The word "side-car" was then dropped from the company name and the first SS (Swallow Sports) car was launched at the 1931 London Motor Show. It had a six-cylinder two-liter Standard engine, developing 48 hp, coupled to a four-speed gearbox. The SS 90, the first "sports" version, was put on the market in 1935, with a 2700-cc 90-hp engine. The same year, a new four-door 2.7-liter saloon with an increased output of 104 hp provided a glimpse of the Jaguar lines of the future at a price of £395. However, the Jaguar marque was not born until 1937, when it appeared on a saloon with a 1.5-liter Standard engine. The next model had a 1776-cc 65-hp engine with a valve gear system using rods and rockers, and was very popular.

During the war, production was concentrated on aircraft components. The SS marque finally disappeared in 1945, when the company name was changed to Jaguar Cars Ltd. With the exception of 1946, at the end of which it was in the red, the newly formed company was extremely successful. In the early 1950s, Jaguar brought out their first truly innovative ideas of the post-war period, introducing the XK series, which included the XK 120, with a six-cylinder 3.4-liter long-stroke engine developing 160 hp at 5400 rpm. For the first time, the twin overhead camshaft engine was used on a standard tourer, which also had aerodynamic lines and independent front suspension. It was now that Jaguar began its competition successes, racing against Ferrari, Talbot and the best marques of the day for the World Manufacturers' Championship. Disc brakes appeared as an optional extra for the first time on the XK 150 of 1957, which had engines of up to 3800 cc and 265 hp.

Meanwhile, in 1951 had been launched the Mk VII six-seater saloon, with an XK 160-hp engine, aimed mainly at the American market. American orders reached a record $27 million with over 30,000 in six years. From 1953 onwards, automatic two-speed Borg-Warner gear change was available, and overdrive was introduced in the following year. The Mk series of saloons continued in production and the 1959 Mk IX had a separate chassis, standard disc brakes and power-assisted steering.

A new, smaller series began in 1960, with new engines and bodies, and on the Mk II, which was in production until 1969, 2.4-, 3.4- and 3.8-liter engines were available. The E-Type coupé with its extremely long bonnet appeared at the 1961 Geneva Motor Show, followed by a roadster version. In the early 1960s, after taking over Daimler, Jaguar entered into the production of buses and armoured cars, then went on to take over the Guy lorry factory, and the Coventry-Climax and Meadows engine factories. In 1966, however, the company gave up its independent status and joined the British Motor Group, which became the state-owned British Leyland in 1968. The XJ 6 and the new twelve-cylinder engine came out during this period. The E-Type went out of production in the 1970s.

While still maintaining their own range of saloons, Jaguar brought out new convertible models (inspired by the saloons) in 1984, and the company regained its independence at the end of the same year.

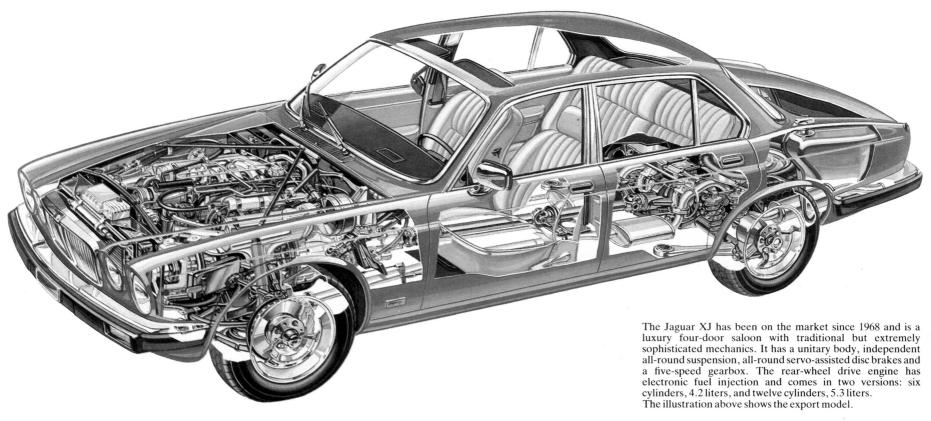

The Jaguar XJ has been on the market since 1968 and is a luxury four-door saloon with traditional but extremely sophisticated mechanics. It has a unitary body, independent all-round suspension, all-round servo-assisted disc brakes and a five-speed gearbox. The rear-wheel drive engine has electronic fuel injection and comes in two versions: six cylinders, 4.2 liters, and twelve cylinders, 5.3 liters. The illustration above shows the export model.

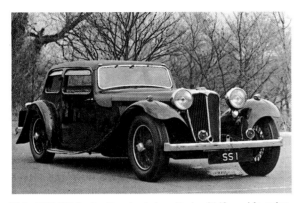

This 1934 SS1 had a Standard six-cylinder 2143-cc side-valve engine with an output of 48 hp, a four-speed gearbox, a single plate clutch and cable-operated mechanical brakes.

The 1936 SS 100 had a six-cylinder 104-hp engine with seven main bearings. With its short, two-seater chassis, it won many competitions. A certain number of SS 100s had a 3.5-liter 125-hp engine, 160 km/h (100 mph).

The XK series began with various versions of the 120, which had a new and very high performance twin overhead camshaft engine of six cylinders and 3442 cc, developing 160 hp, which won many races.

The 140 was an intermediate stage in the XK family: its six-cylinder engine remained unchanged at 3442 cc, but its output went up to 190 hp, to 210 hp on the 140 MC. The body had the rounded side profile popular at the time.

The third and most famous of the XKs was the 150, which had the normal six-cylinder 3442-cc engine developing 190 or 210 hp, increased to 250 hp on the S-Type. Launched in 1957, the 150 had optional front disc brakes.

The 1966 420 was the link between the Mk series saloons and the new generation of Jaguars. It was an imposing saloon, nearly 5 m (16.5 ft) long.

This imposing Mk X (Mark Ten) came out in 1961 as the last in the line of Mk saloons. It had a 3800-cc engine and a top speed of 190 km/h (118 mph). It handled excellently despite its size.

In 1961, the E-Type sports model was brought out in a coupé and roadster version. The 3.8-liter engine was increased in 1964 to 4.2 liters and 269 hp. The four-speed gearbox was fully synchromesh and it had a limited slip differential.

The new Jaguar cabriolets appeared in late 1983. The XJ-SC had both a new body design and a new engine – six cylinders, 3.6 liters, 228 hp, with fuel injection.

The Daimler 4.2 of 1984 has a six-cylinder fuel-injected engine which develops 205 hp at 5000 rpm, independent rear suspension and disc brakes.

The latest version of the Daimler Double Six saloon has a 5.3-liter V12 engine with an automatic gearbox, all-round disc brakes and a top speed of 240 km/h (150 mph).

The 1968 XJ6 had a twin overhead camshaft engine of six cylinders and 2800 cc. Servo-assisted disc brakes were later fitted. Above: a 1984-registered model.

LAMBORGHINI

Ferruccio Lamborghini founded his automobile factory in 1961 in Sant'Agata, a few kilometers outside Modena in Italy. Built for the production of exclusive cars with a very sporty line, the factory made its début with the 350 GTV coupé, which had a Scaglione-designed body, rear-wheel drive and a front-mounted twelve-cylinder alloy engine. Its top speed was 280 km/h (174 mph).

The first 350 was followed in 1964 by the GT version, and the 3.5-liter engine was then increased to nearly 4000 cc on the 400 2 + 2. The bodies were highly streamlined, but of questionable aesthetic appeal. It was not until 1966, with the launch of the P 400 Miura, that Lamborghini reached a peak in terms of quality as well as technical perfection. Its lines were well ahead of its time, yet elegant and streamlined, and it had a four-liter 350-hp engine with five-speed gearbox also built by Lamborghini. It was the first car to

have a transverse mid engine, after which the front-mounted engine was abandoned. Various versions of the Miura were produced, and it is still the pearl of many car collections today.

At the end of 1970, after an order from Bolivia for 5,000 tractors had been cancelled as a result of political changes there (Lamborghini had begun making his fortune with tractors immediately after the war), the company found itself in serious difficulties; Ferruccio Lamborghini decided to retire and handed over his factory to a group of Swiss. Since then, Lamborghini Automobiles has produced the ultra-aerodynamic Countach, the Urraco, the Jalpa and more recently (1982) the LMA – an off-road vehicle with the performance of a GT (twelve cylinders, 4754 cc, 332 hp) designed to operate in the desert and created specifically for the armies of the United Arab Emirates.

The first Lamborghini was the 350 GTV of 1963. This was followed a year later by the GT, which had a Touring body and modified engine with six horizontal instead of Weber vertical carburettors. The twelve-cylinder engine developed 270 hp at 6500 rpm, as opposed to the 360 at 8000 of the GTV.

The bodywork of the 1968 Islero GT was by Marazze in Varese and the mechanics were taken from the 400 GT – a 320-hp V12 engine with six twin-body carburettors. Only 125 were built.

The Espada is another Bertone body on the classic mechanics: V12, four liters, 326 hp, with a top speed of 245 km/h (152.3 mph).

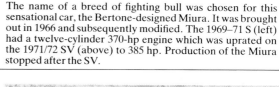

The name of a breed of fighting bull was chosen for this sensational car, the Bertone-designed Miura. It was brought out in 1966 and subsequently modified. The 1969–71 S (left) had a twelve-cylinder 370-hp engine which was uprated on the 1971/72 SV (above) to 385 hp. Production of the Miura stopped after the SV.

The Urraco came out in 1975 at the time of the oil crisis and was available with a two- or a three-liter engine. It remained in production until 1977.

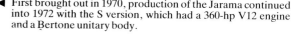

◄ First brought out in 1970, production of the Jarama continued into 1972 with the S version, which had a 360-hp V12 engine and a Bertone unitary body.

The 1981 Jalpa 350 had a 3.5-liter V8 engine, an output of 255 hp and a top speed of 248 km/h (154.2 mph).

The Countach LP 500 was brought out as a prototype in 1971 to replace the Miura, which was about to be phased out of production. In the LP 400 S series of 1972–8 (above), the engine was increased to four liters and the car was fitted with a rear spoiler on request. The LP 500 S series of 1982 (left) had a front spoiler and a 4754-cc 375-hp V12 engine.

LANCIA
AUTOBIANCHI

Very few motor manufacturing companies can boast of the total faithfulness of their production philosophies to the aims and guidelines of their founder in the same way as Lancia. Lancia has traditionally built cars which are technologically highly advanced and rich in innovatory features – features which increase their performance, reliability, safety and comfort – placing them in a class apart, exactly as Vincenzo Lancia (1881–1937) intended. By a trick of fate, even the company name has contributed to making this blend of history and technology unique.

The word "Lancia," which in Italian means a lance, conjures up an image of a slender object silently and smoothly speeding through the air, and these are – and always have been – the main characteristics of Lancia cars, from the very first chassis built in September 1907. Already faster and more powerful than other cars of the time, the first Lancia had a four-cylinder side-valve engine (although the brilliant Vincenzo Lancia had already prepared designs for a revolutionary overhead valve layout) which could develop 14 hp at 1250 rpm. This was a very high engine speed at that time, since other engines did not go above 1000–1200 rpm.

Officially registered on 29 November 1906, with the notary Ernesto Torretta, in the joint names of Messrs. Lancia Vincenzo and Fogolin Claudio, this Turin company was soon to see its technical supremacy and leadership become a recurring theme for over three-quarters of a century. The first true Lancia, that is the first complete car to bear the company name, came out in 1908 and was named after the first letter of the Greek alphabet: Alpha. The car was, in fact, almost too advanced for its day, for it was considered too fast and too light, having a four-cylinder 2543-cc engine with a high speed of rotation, a four-speed gearbox and an advanced cardan shaft transmission capable of reaching 90 km/h (56 mph).

The first Lancia was 3.8 m (12.5 ft) long and 108 were built between 1908 and 1909, some of them being sold abroad, particularly in England. The Alpha was followed by the Dialfa in 1908, the Beta in 1909 – the first car to have a monobloc engine – and the Gamma in 1910. It is interesting to note that the names Beta and Gamma were later used again by Lancia on more recent models, in 1972 and 1976 respectively. The Delta was the next to appear (another name which was used again in 1979), followed by the Didelta, the Epsilon and the Eta, which was driven by a 5-liter engine coupled to the transmission through a single plate dry clutch, one of Lancia's many technical innovations. Another technical novelty was the adoption of metal artillery wheels in 1912 to replace the wooden spokes, reminiscent of the old gun carriages. The Theta, of which almost 1,700 were built, came out in 1913 and was the first car in the world to have a built-in electrical system – all the other manufacturers were fitting them as accessories.

The B 20 coupé version of the Aurelia had a Pininfarina body and was without doubt one of the biggest successes in the history of Lancia. It was brought out at the 1951 Turin Motor Show and was in production until 1957, by which time 3,111 had been built. The six series had engines varying from the original 1991 cc to 2451 cc – all of them 60-degree V6. The car won the Monte Carlo Rally in 1954.

LANCIA

This was the first car built by Vincenzo Lancia: the Alpha, with four cylinders, a capacity of 2543 cc and a top speed of 90 km/h (56 mph). Above: the double phaeton.

One of the first six-cylinder engines ever built, a 3.8-liter, drove the Dialfa in the summer of 1908. The car's top speed of 110 km/h (68.4 mph) was considered "too fast," so only twenty-three were built.

The 1909 Beta had a 3120-cc 34-hp monobloc engine capable of 90 km/h (56 mph). It cost L15,000 and 150 were built.

The Gamma saloon came out in 1910 as a development of the Beta, built on a different size chassis. The four-cylinder 3460-cc engine developed 40-hp at 1500 rpm.

The first European car to have an electric starter was the Theta, a luxury car with an engine of nearly five liters. It came out in 1913 and was in production until 1919, by which time 1,696 had been built.

With a top speed of 115 km/h (71.5 mph), the Delta was brought out in 1911. It had a four-cylinder 4080-cc engine and was also built in a limited sports series, the Didelta.

The Eta came out in 1911 and, with a speed of 120 km/h (75 mph), was the fastest Italian car of its time, thanks to a four-cylinder five-liter engine which developed 80 hp at 1800 rpm. It also had the first-ever single plate dry clutch.

Lancia brought out its first post-war model in 1919: the Kappa (right) had a 4940-cc engine and top speeds of over 120 km/h (75 mph). It was followed in 1921 by the sports version, the Dikappa (shown below, in the roadster version, which could reach 130 km/h – 80.8 mph); and finally, in 1922, by the Trikappa (bottom right), which was the first to have a V engine. With its 98 hp and 130 km/h (80.8 mph), this was the flagship of the time and cost L69,000.

When Italy became involved in the war, Lancia was made an auxiliary war plant by government decree on 24 May 1915, and production was concentrated mainly on supplying vehicles for the armed forces.

After the war, the 1920s saw the launch of the Kappa (70 hp [120 km/h, 75 mph]). This was another car which was ahead of its day, having a variable angle steering column, electric pedal starter and a central gear lever, as opposed to one placed outside the body. The more sporty Dikappa, which had an 87-hp 130-km/h (80.8-mph) engine and metal spoked wheels, appeared at the same time, followed by the big Trikappa with its eight-cylinder, 4.5-liter engine, and

finally, in 1922, the Lambda, the most famous and most revolutionary model in the history of Lancia. The Lambda was the first car in the world to have a unitary body as opposed to the traditional "chassis" which, like the horse-drawn carriages, took all the road shocks, but more importantly it also had independent front suspension. Even the body was revolutionary, consisting of a metal framework covered in sheet steel. The Lambda was an enormous success and 13,000 were built, in eight different series, between 1923 and 1930.

Since then, almost every Lancia has been a success, each new model introducing more advanced and more sophisticated technological

features, which, combined with the superior quality of the materials, have become the hallmark of the company.

The year 1929 saw the launch of the Dilambda, a luxury vehicle with a V8 engine displacing nearly four liters. The Artena and the Astura were brought out in 1930, followed in 1932 by the Augusta, the first "popular" Lancia, and a car which has gone down in history not only for its numerous technical "firsts," but also for the "freewheel" device which used the vehicle's own inertia to cut down on fuel consumption. In 1937, Vincenzo Lancia, who was to die at the age of fifty-six the following winter, produced another stroke of genius with the Aprilia, a revolutionary

Brought out in October 1922, the Lambda had independent front wheels and a unitary body. It was in production until 1931, by which time over 13,000 had been built.

The Dilambda was launched in Paris in 1929. It was a luxury model with a four-cylinder V8 engine. One of its main features was the overhead camshaft.

The 1931 Astura was the big sister of the Artena and in terms of quality represented the peak of Lancia production during the 1930s.

The 1931 Artena had a narrow, V4 engine with a displacement of 1924 cc, a top speed of 115 km/h (71.5 mph) and an output of 55 hp at 4000 rpm. It cost L31,000.

The Augusta was in production from 1932 to 1938 and was the first of the Lancia runabouts. It had a 1196-cc engine, hydraulic brakes and an all-steel body.

One of the first aerodynamic cars in history, the Aprilia, launched in 1937, is considered to be Vincenzo Lancia's last masterpiece. It had independent wheels both front and rear.

The Ardea, built from 1939 onwards, was the first Lancia to have an engine displacement of under a liter: 903 cc, with a top speed of 108 km/h (67.1 mph) and a fuel consumption of 7 liters/100 km (40.35 mpg).

In 1950, the Aprilia was replaced by the six-cylinder 1754-cc Aurelia, called the B 10 (left), followed in 1951 by the two-liter B 21 and the B 20 coupé, which was designed by Pininfarina. The B 24 spyder of 1955 (right) was also designed by Pininfarina.

Based on certain existing mechanical parts, beginning with the Delta floorpan, the Prisma was brought out in late 1982 and revived the fortunes of Lancia. It was a front-wheel drive saloon and the first of Lancia's diesels. It had a 1.3-, 1.5- or 1.6-liter engine, independent suspension, front disc brakes and rear drums. The 1600 had all-round disc brakes.

The second series of the Appia came out in 1956 (the first series was launched in 1953), with a three-box body and an uprated 43-hp engine capable of 128 km/h (80 mph).

The Flaminia (1957–64) was brought out to replace the Aurelia. It was powered by a 2458-cc V6 engine which was later increased to 2775 cc, with an output of 125 hp.

The revolutionary Flavia came out in 1960 and was the first Italian car to have front-wheel drive, with a four-cylinder, horizontally opposed engine (initially 1500 cc) and all-round disc brakes.

The Fulvia coupé of 1965 was a small sports car with a highly individual design, driven by a 1216-cc 80-hp engine with a top speed of 160 km/h (100 mph). It underwent many more spectacular developments.

In 1971, the Flavia underwent further developments. The horizontal grille was replaced by the traditional vertical Lancia shield, and the 2000 was born. It was also available with a two-liter 125-hp fuel-injected engine.

The first Lancia of the "post-Fiat" era was the 1972 Beta, which had an original two-box body and a choice of three engines: 1.4, 1.6 and 1.8 liters. It was the first Lancia to have a transverse engine and gearbox.

The 1976 Gamma was designed by Pininfarina and had a flat engine of only four cylinders (2 and 2.5 liters). This somewhat marred its image as a medium-top class international car.

The 1979 Delta body, designed by Giugiaro, originally came with two engines (1300 and 1500 cc); a twin camshaft 1600 cc and a 130 hp "turbo" were later added to the range. A four-wheel drive prototype was also launched.

To satisfy a more traditional clientele, Lancia in 1980 brought out a three-box Beta, known as the Trevi. It was available with 1.6- and 2-liter engines. A two-liter supercharged version was added to the range in 1982.

model which remained in production until 1949. This was followed by the Ardea, a "mini" car of just 903 cc, which weighed only 750 kg (0.74 ton) and had a five-speed gearbox giving 14 km/liter (39.5 mpg).

The next cars to be brought out were the Aurelia, launched in May 1950, and then, coming gradually up to the present day, the Appia, Flaminia, Flavia (the first Italian front-wheel drive car, which also had a flat engine), Fulvia, Stratos, Beta, Gamma, Trevi, Delta and Prisma (on which a diesel engine was used for the first time in Lancia history), the very recent Thema and the "small car" (code name Y10), due for

Presented at the 1984 Turin Motor Show, the Thema has a wide choice of petrol engines (four and six cylinders) as well as diesel.

immediate launch, which is destined to take over from the A 112. The A 112 was brought out as an Autobianchi but sold through the Lancia sales network in line with group policy, Lancia having been taken over by Fiat in Autumn 1969 in an attempt to save the company from the grave financial difficulties which had compromised its chances of survival.

Today, Lancia is more than ever on the crest of the wave, with increasing sales both at home and abroad. In 1984 the company was able to secure almost 9 per cent of the Italian market, taking second place among the Italian manufacturers, after Fiat and ahead of Alfa Romeo.

◀ The up-market version of the popular Fiat 500, the Bianchina, shown here in the four-seater version with a vertical rear window, was in production from 1957 onwards in the Desio plant in Lombardy. Autobianchi was taken over by Fiat in 1967 and its cars were sold through the Lancia sales network after the latter merged with Fiat.

This "adopted" daughter of the Lancia sales network, the ▶ Autobianchi A 112 (marketed outside Italy simply as the Lancia) has proved extremely successful.

LOTUS

The Seven S4 of the 1970s was a new edition of the Mark 7 Seven of 1957. It was available with various sizes of Ford engine and also came as a two-seater roadster in fiberglass.

The Elite, the first car to have a fiberglass body, went into production in 1958/59. Its construction proved so expensive that it brought the company to the verge of bankruptcy.

Anthony Colin Bruce Chapman had always cherished a desire to found a company able to build sports cars distinguished by both elegance and competition performance. Hence, in 1948, with the help of Colin Dare and Rodney Nuckey, a new car was built for trials, the Lotus 1 (named after the flower). By 1952, the new company, also calling itself "Lotus," had begun to build chassis and suspension for sports cars. The Mark VI Lotus introduced features which can still be seen today on the modern Sevens. Development continued particularly on the chassis and suspension, the company's strongpoints, with the Mark 8, 9 and 10. Lotus used Bristol, Ford, Coventry-Climax and MG engines on their cars. The Mark 11 was the last in the series to incorporate a "Mark" number. Subsequent models were either given a symbolic name or the word "Type" followed by the number.

The Elite, the first Lotus to have a fiberglass body, was launched at the London Motor Show in 1957. Three years later, Lotus made its début in Formula One racing with Stirling Moss, who won the Monte Carlo Grand Prix. From then on, Lancia won victory after victory with Chapman's cars, which became better known on the world circuits than on the roads, although his road cars have the same sporty lines and performance.

The first Elan was the Type 26, a small soft-top of which 12,224 were built, followed by the Type 36 and the Type 45, also known as the Elan Series 3 and S3. Left: the S4 of 1972, which had a four-cylinder 1558-cc engine with twin overhead camshafts. The 1967 Elan +2S (right) was a 2 + 2 coupé with a 1.6-liter 119-hp engine and all-round disc brakes.

The 1974 Elite was the product of three years' work. The interior was by the Giugiaro coachworks. The four-cylinder two-liter Lotus engine has four valves per cylinder.

Brought out in 1967, the Europa had a modified Renault 16 engine. The Europa Special of 1972 had a four-cylinder 1.6-liter mid engine, with twin overhead camshafts.

The 1975 Eclat is a variation of the Elite with the same mechanics (two liters) and a new body. The series continued from 1982 as the Excel, with a 2.2-liter engine developing 160 hp at 6500 rpm. Its top speed was 216 km/h (134.2 mph).

The 1975 Esprit body was by Giugiaro, although the engine was still the same – sixteen valves, two liters. In 1980 this was increased to 2.2 liters, and a turbocharged version was brought out in the same year.

213

MASERATI

As is the case for almost all the other older marques, Maserati was a family name. In fact there were seven Maserati brothers, six of whom were fascinated by the newly born automobile (the other turned to painting) and who found work with Isotta Fraschini, Fiat and Bianchi. Alfieri Maserati eventually opened a workshop in his own name to build Isotta Fraschini engines and was soon joined by two of his brothers. However, it was not until twelve years later that the first true Maserati car came out of the workshop, 1500 cc supercharged, and known as the Type 26.

Maserati's production was characterized by sports models until after the Second World War, when the A6 was unveiled (1947). This had a six-cylinder 1500-cc engine with three carburettors, developing 65 hp, and a berlinetta body designed by Pininfarina. In 1954, the trident marque produced the A6 G54 sports model, which was designed for series production rather than the race track. It was available in spyder or coupé versions, designed by Allemano, Frua and Zagato, with a six-cylinder 2000-cc engine.

The insignia was apparently designed by Mario, the painter brother, who drew a stylized version of Neptune's trident from the monument in Neptune Square in Bologna. Series production gave the company a positive boost at the beginning of a long period of financial restrictions. The company officially announced its withdrawal from competition racing in 1957 and, on 1 April 1958, Maserati entered a period of controlled administration. The first signs of recovery were seen immediately, and production was concentrated on increasing sales of the 3500 GT (220 hp). Maserati's name was once again connected with racing, and in 1959 the company brought out a 5000 at the request of the Shah of Iran which aroused the interest of many coachbuilders. In 1962, appeared the Sebring berlinetta, named after the American circuit and designed by Vignale. It was a 2 + 2 with a six-cylinder 3485-cc engine developing 235 hp, with a top speed of 235 km/h (146 mph).

The four-door Quattroporte brought out in the following year was the first and only saloon ever produced by Maserati. It had a 4136-cc 260 hp V8 engine capable of reaching 230 km/h (143 mph).

In 1964, production settled down with a range that included the Sebring, the 3700 GTI, the Convertible (3692 cc) and the Quattroporte. In 1966, the 4.2 Mexico was brought out, a 2 + 2 berlinetta by Vignale which had the Quattroporte engine. That year also saw the appearance of the 4.7 Mexico, with a 4719-cc 290-hp V8 engine giving a top speed of 255 km/h (158.5 mph), and a Ghia-designed coupé, the Ghibli,

The Pininfarina-designed A6 of 1947 was the first Maserati not built for racing. It had a six-cylinder 1500-cc 65-hp engine and a top speed of 170 km/h (105.6 mph).

An updated version of the basic A6, the A6G had the same six-cylinder 1500-cc 65-hp engine, but the body was more rounded and had more passenger room.

The 5000 GT, shown above with a Ghia body, came out at the 1959 Turin Motor Show and was enormously successful, largely thanks to its 4935-cc V8 engine, which developed 350 hp at 6000 rpm.

The 3500 GT, in the version with fuel injection, developed 220 hp at 5500 rpm, with a displacement of 3485 cc. The body was built by Touring.

The 1962 Sebring was a Vignale berlinetta (with a coupé type 2 + 2 body), also available as a roadster. It had a six-cylinder 3.5-liter engine.

Another Vignale berlinetta, this Mexico 4.2, had the Quattroporte 90-degree V8 engine of 4136 cc, giving 260 hp at 5200 rpm, with four overhead camshafts.

The 1967 Mistral was produced in coupé and roadster versions, with two engines, 3692 and 4014 cc, the same as were used on the Sebring. It was the most expensive car of the range at the time, costing nearly eight million lire.

In 1971, the Bora coupé was brought out as the first mid-engined Maserati. It had a 4700-cc 310-hp V8 engine, supplied by four carburettors, and the body was a Giugiaro-designed two-seater.

The Biturbo – so called because of the two turbochargers supplying its V6 engine, one for each bank of cylinders – was brought out in 1982 when its list price of around twenty million lire raised many cries. However, the formula of its two-liter engine (now also available with 2.5 liters outside Italy) and 180 hp worked so well that the car became a commercial success and has made a significant contribution to Maserati's financial recovery.

with the 4.7 Mexico engine increased to 330 hp and a top speed of 280 km/h (174 mph).

In 1969, Frua designed the Mistral, in coupé and spyder versions, using the same 3692- and 4014-cc engines as the new Sebring. Its market success ever rising, Maserati was sold to Citroën by the Orsi brothers, who had taken over the company in 1937. A year later, the Indy was brought out, followed by the spyder version of the Ghibli and a new version of the Quattroporte with the Mexico 4700-cc engine. In the spring of 1970, the SM was launched, the product of an association between Maserati, who contributed the 2670-cc 170-hp V6 engine, and Citroën, who supplied a four-seater coupé body almost 5 m

(16.4 ft) long. Meanwhile, in 1971, the Indy's 4700-cc Mexico engine was replaced by an uprated 5-liter version. A few months later, the new Bora was unveiled, with a Giugiaro-designed body and the customary 4700-cc engine. After modifications to its tail design, the car was brought out again in the following year as the Merak. The style was the same, but it had a three-liter mid engine developed from that used on the SM. To continue the series, the name of another wind, the Khamsin, was given to the 2 + 2 Bertone berlinetta.

In April 1975, two months after the SS version of the Merak had gone into production, uprated from 190 hp to 220 hp and with its top speed

increased to 250 km/h (155.3 mph), Citroën announced its decision to put Maserati into liquidation. At this point, GEPI and the Italo-Argentinian Alejandro De Tomaso arrived on the scene and took over the company. On 8 August, an agreement was signed allowing Maserati to continue in operation, and by the Geneva Motor Show of 1976, the Kyalami had been brought out, with a 4135-cc 265-hp V8 engine.

It was not then until 1979 that the Quattroporte Mk III came out, with a 4.2-liter engine and a redesigned body by Giugiaro. In 1982, the Biturbo was launched – a two-liter six-cylinder, with a supercharger per bank, developing 180 hp.

Designed as both a coupé and a spyder, the Ghibli was available with a 4.7- or 5-liter engine. Brought out in 1966 by Ghia, it had pop-up headlights and a particularly smooth line. The spyder version was not brought out until 1969.

The 1972 Geneva Motor Show included this Boomerang coupé – a Giorgetto Giugiaro design on Bora mechanics. Note how the styling of the front end is connected to the windscreen in one single line.

In 1972, Giugiaro also designed the Merak, a development of the Bora of the previous year. The mid engine was a V6, derived from the SM three-liter, with three twin carburettors and electronic ignition.

The Khamsin – designed by Bertone as a 2 + 2 – was launched in 1973. The front-mounted five-liter 320-hp V8 engine gave top speeds of over 280 km/h (174 mph). The steering had progressive power assistance.

Eyecatching restyling of the De Tomaso (Longchamp) berlinetta led to the 1976 Kyalami with a V8 engine of 4135 cc capacity, giving 270 hp and 240 km/h (149.8 mph), and a 2 + 2 body redesigned for Maserati by Frua.

The first Quattroporte came out in 1963. An elegant, classic saloon, it had a 4136-cc V8 engine, developing 260 hp and giving a top speed of 230 km/h (143 mph). The last series in 1979 had more rounded lines designed by Giugiaro.

MAZDA

Mazda have a strong claim to being the record-breakers among Japanese manufacturers, not necessarily for their production levels, since the Hiroshima factory ranks only third on the national list after Toyota and Nissan, but for the high level of technology which has always been their hallmark, and for the company policy of concentrating on the production of small or very small-engined cars.

Mazda is the marque under which cars produced by the Japanese Toyo Kogyo Company Ltd. are known. The company grew up in Hiroshima in 1920 (as the Toyo Cork Kogyo Company) and concentrated solely on the production of cork until 1927. In 1928, it began making machine tools, and in 1931 built its first trucks, innovative three-wheeled, front-wheel drive vehicles which handled very well and could carry up to 2000 kg (39.4 cwt) economically.

Hiroshima is a tragically famous name in the history of the twentieth century: the Toyo Kogyo factory was completely destroyed by the atomic bomb in 1945. Yet, within ten years, the company was back in a position to begin production again, and, taking advantage of their pre-war experience with trucks and using a few automobile designs from the 1940s, Mazda brought out their first car in 1960. The R 360 was a two-seater mini coupé driven by a rear-mounted V2 engine, which had a displacement of only 356 cc and an output of 16 hp, yet gave a top speed of 105 km/h (65.25 mph) with a fuel consumption of approximately 3 liters/100 km (94.2 mpg). Two years later, the P 360 four-seater version came out, with a four-cylinder 358-cc 20-hp engine; a four-door version of the same model was also

The 323 is a two-box hatchback which had a front-mounted, four-cylinder 1000- or 1300-cc engine when it was first brought out in 1977. In 1980, the Familia (the name used on the Japanese market) was given front-wheel drive and a front-mounted transverse engine. It comes in a three-, four- or five-door saloon, and a cabriolet version.

The Savanna (or RX-7) was launched in 1978 and immediately became one of the most popular sports cars. Highly compact, it has very good road-holding, thanks to its low center of gravity and excellent weight distribution. Since 1983, it has also been available with a fuel-injected turbocharged rotary engine. The Savanna has taken part in various competitions and rallies, but has shown its greatest potential in endurance races.

produced, known as the Carol. By 1964 Mazda ranked third on the list of Japanese car manufacturers, with a range of four models, three of them completely new. Apart from a bigger Carol, with a 600-cc 28-hp engine, there was also the Familia, the Luce, and the exciting and highly advanced rotary-engined Cosmo. The Familia, a small two-box, three-door model with rear-wheel drive, had a front-mounted four-

cylinder engine of 782 cc, developing 42 hp, with a top speed of 105 km/h (65.25 mph). The Luce, designed by the Italian Bertone, had a choice of 9930- or 1484-cc engines, but the car that drew most attention was naturally the streamlined Cosmo coupé. This had a two-cylinder rotary piston engine with a total displacement of 800 cc and an output of 70 hp, making for a particularly sparkling performance. However, although the

Cosmo was developed and tested constantly, it did not get far beyond the prototype that had been unveiled at the Tokyo Motor Show in 1964.

Although the Luce had gone into production in 1966, in the case of the Cosmo it took another year before a practical outlet was found, with a 982-cc 110-hp engine (still using the rotary piston system) giving a top speed of 175 km/h (108.8 mph). This development marked the future

The first Mazda vehicle, a three-wheeler, came out in 1931, in which year 66 were built.

The 800 Sedan, known as the Familia, came out in 1964, followed immediately by a coupé version with an increased displacement of 985 cc.

Mazda's first passenger car appeared in 1960. The R 360 was a two-door coupé with a two-cylinder engine.

The new 360 and 600, which as the Carol came out in 1963, were fitted with a four-cylinder air-cooled engine.

The new 1966 Luce had a four-cylinder, water-cooled engine and a four-speed gearbox. The bodywork was by Bertone.

The Capella came out in 1970. The 616 version had a 1.6-liter, the RX-2 a Wankel twin-rotor engine.

A twin-rotor engine was still used for the Savanna (RX-3) in 1971, although a four-cylinder model was also current.

The 1972 Chantez was a small, two-door car, with a two-stroke engine of two cylinders, 359 cc, water-cooled.

The Luce (or RX-4), launched in 1972, was the first Mazda to incorporate pollution control devices. It had a Wankel rotary engine.

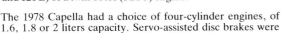

The 1967 Cosmo 110 S was the first car to have a twin-rotor Wankel engine. The 1975 version had a four-cylinder (121 and 121 L) or a twin-rotor (RX-5) engine.

The 1978 Capella had a choice of four-cylinder engines, of 1.6, 1.8 or 2 liters capacity. Servo-assisted disc brakes were fitted on the front and drums on the rear.

A new Familia was brought out in 1977. The 323 was sold with a 1- or 1.3-liter engine, increased to 1400 cc (above) in 1979 and to 1500 cc in 1980. A turbocharged version was added to the range in 1983. Below: the three-door hatchback of 1982.

The four-cylinder engine used on the 929 (or Luce) of 1977 had been increased to 1800–2000 cc. It was also available with a Wankel rotary engine.

The MX 02 of 1983 has a light aerodynamic carbon-fiber body. It has a sixteen-valve 1300-cc engine, four-wheel drive, electronically controlled suspension and an on-board computer.

The 1982 Luce or 929 (left) was the first car to have a turbocharged rotary engine. It has all-round disc brakes and independent suspension automatically controlled by a computer. Right: the 13 RE hardtop of 1984.

Front-wheel drive is just one of the innovations added to the new Capella (or 626) range of 1982. It also has independent suspension, and since 1983 has been available as a diesel. Above: the 2000 Saloon of 1984.

policy of Mazda, and the company is now the only one in the world – since Citroën and NSU ceased to do so – regularly producing cars powered by Wankel rotary engines.

From the Cosmo 110 S, R 100, Luce Rotary coupé, RX-2, Capella XR, Rotary and Familia Rotary TSS up to the present-day RX-7 twin-rotors, with their displacement of 2 × 573 cc (equivalent to 2292 cc in a traditional rotary engine), an output of 115 hp at 6000 rpm and a top speed of 200 km/h (124.3 mph), these cars represent the different stages of the company's success and its technical perseverence with a

The 1983 Cosmo is sold with the same engines as its twin series, the Luce. It has all-round disc brakes, ventilated at the front.

system that has been abandoned by other very famous manufacturers, discouraged by problems of excessive fuel consumption and pollution.

Today, Mazda production hinges on three families of models: Series 3 (323, with 1296-cc to 1490-cc engines), Series 6 (626, all with 1998-cc engines) and Series 9 (929, with 1970-cc engines), plus the RX-7 coupé, with twin rotary pistons.

In 1983, 944,716 cars were sold (679,173 of them outside Japan) as well as 397,177 commercial vehicles (255,742 abroad), and the company had a turnover of $5,055.42 million, an increase of 15.6 per cent over their 1982 figures.

MERCEDES-BENZ

The hundredth anniversary of the automobile is an occasion of particular historical importance for Daimler-Benz, as its celebration is so closely tied to the great technical discoveries of our company's founders, Karl Benz and Gottlieb Daimler.

Their inventions inaugurated the age of the motor car, giving Man a real answer to his natural desire for freedom and mobility, leading over the years to an unparalleled degree of social, economic and technical progress.

From the very outset, the history of the automobile has been one of constant technical innovation, with which, we are proud to say, the Daimler and Benz names have continued to be very closely linked through our company. Today, as in the past, our aim is to produce an organic whole which strikes a perfect balance between all the elements that go to make up the automobile.

Faithful to Gottlieb Daimler's motto: "The best or nothing," we do our utmost to ensure that our products respond to the greatest demands of safety, economy and ecology, while respecting the company's traditional standards of comfort, quality and value. In this way, we hope to be worthy of the legacy of Karl Benz and Gottlieb Daimler, both now and in the future.

Professor Dr WERNER BREITSCHWERDT   President of the Board of Directors, Daimler-Benz AG

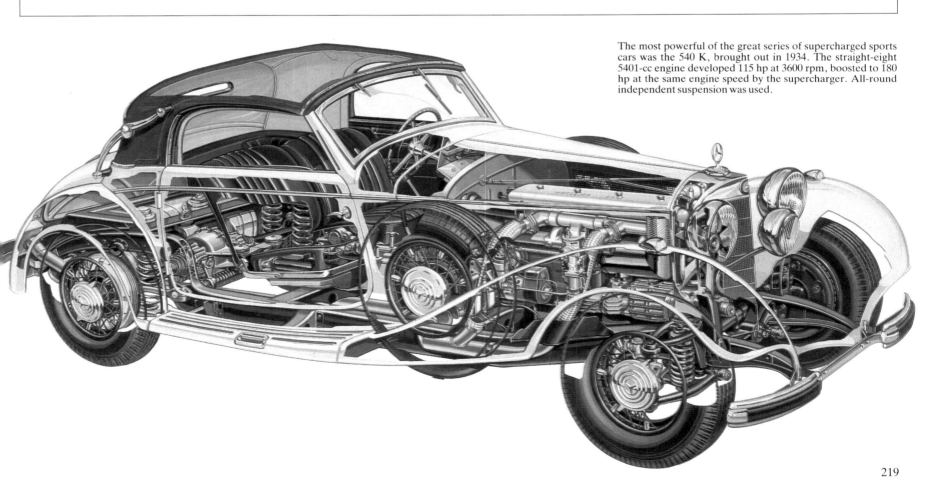

The most powerful of the great series of supercharged sports cars was the 540 K, brought out in 1934. The straight-eight 5401-cc engine developed 115 hp at 3600 rpm, boosted to 180 hp at the same engine speed by the supercharger. All-round independent suspension was used.

The engine designed by Daimler and Maybach, a single cylinder of 469 cc, developing 1.5 hp at 700 rpm, was installed in this small carriage in 1886 and gave a top speed of 16 km/h (10 mph).

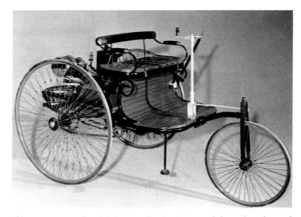

A new type of vehicle, perfectly harmonizing chassis and engine, was the car patented by Benz in 1886. This was a single cylinder of 984 cc, developing 0.9 hp at 400 rpm, with a top speed of 15 km/h (9.3 mph).

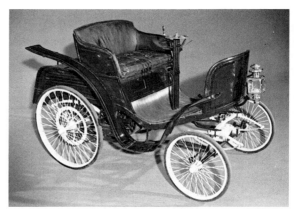

The 1894 Benz Velo was the first car in the world to be produced in series. It had a single-cylinder 1050-cc engine developing 1.5 hp, which was available in standard form or a version known as "the Comfortable" (above).

The "dos-à-dos" and the closed version of the Mylord of 1897 were fitted with a two-cylinder opposed 2.7-liter engine. The output was 9 hp at 900 rpm, giving a top speed of 40 km/h (24.8 mph).

The 35, brought out in 1900/01, was the first car to use the Mercedes name. The new four-cylinder T-head engine had side valves operated by an outer camshaft, and with its 5.9-liter displacement developed 35 hp at 1000 rpm, giving a top speed of 72 km/h (45 mph).

◀ Increasing power outputs on the developing engine demanded improved cooling systems. The Ideal 5 HP of 1899 was fitted with an additional water tank, tucked under the small front bonnet. The 1050-cc engine developed 4.5 hp at 750 rpm and gave a top speed of 40 km/h (25 mph).

Gottlieb Daimler and Karl Benz never met. Their respective efforts to conceive and develop what was later to become known as the automobile ran parallel over a period of forty years, during which their creativity and ingenuity enabled them to obtain truly extraordinary results for their time.

Daimler was ten years older than Benz and from 1872 to 1882 was chief engineer at the Gasmotorenfabrik Deutz, where the four-stroke Nikolaus Otto engine was produced and where Wilhelm Maybach was chief designer.

When he set up on his own with Maybach, Daimler in 1883 took out a patent for an original engine, the forerunner of one he fitted into a car body in 1886. In the same year, Benz, who was the owner of Benz & Company in Mannheim, where he produced stationary engines, presented his tricycle, the first vehicle to be designed as a rational engine-chassis unit. While Daimler Motoren Gesellschaft, founded in 1890, was adapting its own engines for all types of vehicles including boats and dirigibles, Benz continued perfecting his own vehicle and, in 1894, produced the Velo, the first car to be built in a small series. This vehicle was entered in the first car race in history, the Paris–Rouen, which was held that

same year. Both Benz and Daimler obtained excellent results and immediately realized the importance of competitions for the promotion of their vehicles. In fact it was from these races that the Mercedes marque was born, originating as the pseudonym of the Austrian Consul Emil Jellinek, who raced under the name of his eldest daughter. From 1898 onwards, Jellinek, who lived in Nice, was what we would now call one of Daimler's main agents, since he commissioned racing cars from him, starting with the Phönix 25 HP followed by the 35 HP. He undertook to buy thirty-six of the latter wholly on trust, and went on to sell Daimler cars under the name "Mercedes" which – thanks to its rapidly growing fame – was borne by all vehicles produced in Stuttgart from 1902 onwards. In 1900, Daimler died and Maybach took over the company.

Benz had his racing successes too, the most notable being the speed record of 205 km/h (127.4 mph) with the 200-hp Blitzen Benz on the Daytona track in 1909. This was followed by another record of 228 km/h (141.7 mph) in the following year.

The early years of the century were characterized by the steady development of automobile technology, two of the best examples being the

Mercedes Simplex and the Benz Phaeton. Thanks to Daimler's first six-cylinder engine, saloon cars were very soon able to develop 40–60 hp. These were highly satisfactory years for Mercedes, who won the first three places in the 1914 French Grand Prix and victory at Indianapolis in 1915. However, with war imminent, the large industrial companies were turned over to the production of war materials. Daimler built a factory in Sindelfingen for the manufacture of aeroplane engines, which Benz also began to produce.

The difficult years after the war forced the two companies to rescale their programmes; nevertheless, both Daimler and Benz began racing again in 1921, taking turns to win important successes.

Building on experiments made as early as 1885 and using to the full the experience he had gained in the field of aeronautics, Daimler in 1921 brought out two cars, one with a 1500-cc, the other with a 2600-cc engine, both with superchargers, which were also fitted on to their competition cars. Of the 269 successes confirmed in 1924 with Daimler or Benz cars, 92 were won with supercharged engines.

This was just the beginning of an era which was

to last until 1939. The Mercedes 15/70/100 and the 24/100/140 of 1924 were two examples of powerful and extremely comfortable saloons, the first in a long series of automobiles which appealed to a rich and demanding clientele.

In the early 1920s, eighty-six car factories were in operation in Germany, producing over a hundred different models. This rate of competition could not be sustained in such a critical period, and so, in 1924, an agreement of technical co-operation was made between Daimler and Benz which brought together three of the best designers of the day: Ferdinand Porsche, Fritz Nallinger and Hans Nibel. Although Porsche stayed at Daimler-Benz for only two years, leaving the design section under the direction of Hans Nibel, his contribution was an important one, especially with regard to the development of supercharged cars.

On 28 July 1926, the co-operation agreement became a full merger, resulting in the formation of Daimler-Benz AG, whose production was thenceforth distinguished by the Mercedes-Benz marque. Until 1930, the new company's range was divided between the Stuttgart, Mannheim and Nürburg models, the last of which were classics of their time, with their U-chassis, great rigidity and semi-elliptic leaf-springs. In the following decade, even more important technical innovations were made. The S and K models, developed from the supercharged 140, won countless competition successes, but the new SS and SSK versions were truly formidable vehicles with power-ratings which touched 225 hp. Of the series-produced vehicles, the 1930 170, of which 14,000 were built, represented an important stage in the evolution of the Mercedes. It had a six-cylinder engine, independent suspension with swinging half-axles, hydraulic brakes, thermostats and a gear change with overdrive. In 1933, a small series of eight-cylinder 380s, with a power-rating of 120 hp, was produced, which for the first time used independent front suspension with parallelograms and helical springs.

In the second half of the 1930s, Mercedes's production covered a range of different series of cars, from the small four-cylinder, rear-engine 130 limousine, 150 sport and 170 H to two extremely popular cars, the 170 V and the 230 six-cylinder with the V chassis, which were produced in a large number of versions. At the top of the range there were the 370 S and the very famous 500 K and 540 K with supercharged engines, and finally the Grosser Mercedes of 1938. This car came in a normally aspirated 150-hp version and a supercharged 200-hp version, and offered all the features that automobile technology had achieved by then, including a synchromesh five-speed gearbox.

In February 1936, the first diesel-engined vehicle available to the public was unveiled at the Berlin Motor Show. The 260 D was an extremely sturdy car produced from Benz's precombustion chamber engine of 1922, which had been fitted into an automobile as early as 1923. The owner of a transport company in Württemberg is reported to have covered 1,300,000 km (805,800 miles)

Considerably lighter than its predecessor, the 35 CV, the 1902–6 Simplex developed 40 hp. It was introduced at the Paris Motor Show in 1902.

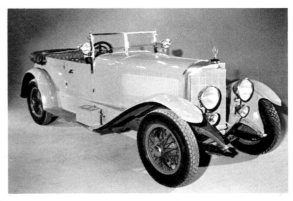

The 28/95 of 1914 had a six-cylinder 7.28-liter engine which developed 95 hp at 1800 rpm, giving a top speed of 120 km/h (74.5 mph). It won the Florio Cup in 1921.

The supercharged 1500-cc engine of this sporty 6/25/40 of 1921 developed 40 hp at 2800 rpm. Despite weighing 1800 kg (1.7 tons), it could reach a top speed of 110 km/h (68.3 mph).

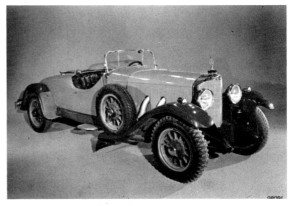

The Mercedes 24/100/140 of 1924 was the last car produced by Daimler before the merger. The six-cylinder 6.2-liter engine developed 140 hp at 2800 rpm with the assistance of a supercharger. The car's top speed was 125 km/h (77.7 mph).

The great supercharged sports cars built by Mercedes from 1926 onwards can be considered the pinnacle of motor technology in their day. The K of 1926 (shown here with a special Saoutchik body) was a shortened version of the 140. The S of 1927 had a displacement of 6.8 liters and developed 180 hp at 3000 rpm. Its top speed was 180 km/h (118.85 mph) and it weighed 1270 kg (1.25 tons). Although not a true racing car, it won fifty-three victories in 1928 and broke seventeen records. The evolution of the six-cylinder continued with the SS of 1928, with its capacity increased to 7.1 liters and an output of 225 hp. The lightened SSKL version of 1930 was partly designed for racing and was the last of this series, winning great victories between 1931 and 1932.

K – 1926

SS – 1928

◀ S – 1927

SSKL – 1930

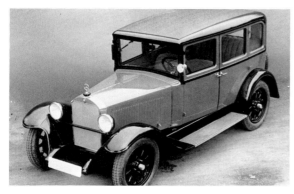

The Stuttgart was the first car to use the new Mercedes-Benz name and had a six-cylinder two-liter engine which gave 38 hp at 3500 rpm.

The Mannheim series was a range of six-cylinder vehicles in different versions, with engine displacements of 3–3.7 liters, developing 55–75 hp. They were built from 1926 onwards. The photograph shows the 1930 370 S, the last to be brought out, capable of 75 hp at 3100 rpm, with a top speed of 100 km/h (62.14 mph).

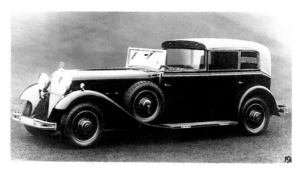

The Nürburg series consisted of large cars with eight-cylinder engines (4.6–4.9 liters), including this 110-hp F cabriolet brought out in 1931.

The Grosser Mercedes was the company's flagship throughout the 1930s. The series had an eight-cylinder 7.7-liter 150-hp engine, which could be boosted to 200 hp with the addition of a supercharger. Right: the 1930 cabriolet version of the Grosser Mercedes. Below right: the Keiserwagen of the same series. A new 230-hp supercharged version was built in 1938, illustrated here (below) in the limousine version.

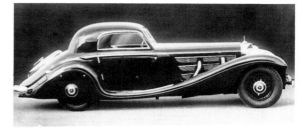

In 1934 appeared the 540, with a 5.4-liter engine which could develop 115 or 180 hp (with or without a supercharger). Two 1936 versions are illustrated, the coupé (above) and the two-seater 540 K roadster (below).

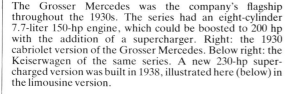

The small, rear-engined 130 of 1933 gave rise to a sports version (above) known as the 150 H, which had a four-cylinder 1500-cc engine developing 55 hp.

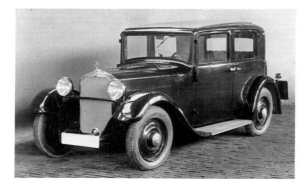

Between 1931 and 1935, over 14,000 six-cylinder 170s were built, with independently sprung wheels front and rear. This was one of the most popular Mercedes models of the 1930s.

The three-liter class was represented by the Mercedes 290, six cylinders and 68 hp, brought out in 1933. Above: the 290 Cabriolet C of 1933. Below: the two-seater 320 coupé convertible of 1937.

The four-cylinder 170 V (above) was brought out in 1935. It had an engine displacement of 1.7 liters and developed 38 hp. The six-cylinder 230, illustrated below in the cabriolet version, came out in 1938 and developed 55 hp at 3600 rpm.

Derived directly from the 300 SL competition model of 1952, the 1954 road version marked a return to big sports cars. The six-cylinder 2996-cc engine developed 215 hp at 5800 rpm and had a top speed of 260 km/h (161.56 mph). It had a tubular chassis with independent all-round suspension and distinctive "gullwing" doors, but gave way to a more conventional roadster in 1957.

with this car, changing the engine every 250,000 km (155,342 miles). Many of these cars are still on the road today.

The 1930s were epic years for Mercedes-Benz competition cars. The 354-hp W 25 dominated the 1934 and 1935 seasons, but in 1936 Alfa Romeo and Auto Union shared eight of the nine Grand Prix between them. The new W 125 managed to redeem itself fully in the following year, winning six Grand Prix out of eleven, thanks to its tubular chassis and a 646-hp engine which enabled it to reach 300 km/h (186.4 mph). In 1938, new regulations set the limit at 3000 cc, and so was born the W 154, which went on to win in Tripoli, Reims, the Nürburgring and Berne that same year.

The 1939 racing season was the last before the outbreak of the Second World War. Six years later, with 80 per cent of their factories destroyed, and their work-force gone, Daimler-Benz were faced with the daunting task of

reconstruction at all levels. Furthermore, they had lost the international outlets that Daimler himself had built up and which had been so courageously re-established after the First World War.

Nevertheless, by 1946, 214 type 170 V cars had come off the assembly lines, quickly followed by the new 170 D: Mercedes had made a comeback on the world market.

The 1950s marked the beginning of the modern age of the Mercedes-Benz and since then they have maintained a certain continuity in terms of technology and style, without abandoning their innovatory and at times avant-garde approach. The vehicle on which limousine development was based at that time was the 180 of 1953, which had a new tubular chassis forming a unit with the base to give great rigidity and guaranteeing a very comfortable ride. The body had a large area of glass and its overall lines were to form the basis for later Mercedes-Benz models, particularly

with regard to the design of the front. Various other versions of this model were produced with larger engines.

In 1954, production began on another historic vehicle, the 300 SL, which was developed from the competition version of the same name. For the first time, a direct fuel injection system was used and, in spite of its 215 hp and top speed of 267 km/h (166 mph), it could accelerate smoothly in fourth from 25 km/h (15.5 mph). One of its distinctive features was its gullwing doors, but these disappeared in 1957 with the introduction of the roadster version. The 1955 competition model 300 SLR won first and second places in the Mille Miglia, at the Nürburgring, in the Targa Florio, in Sweden and in the Tourist Trophy. The same year saw launched on to the market the 190 SL, with four cylinders giving 105 hp and 180 km/h (112 mph). Stylistically, it was very similar to the 300 SL, but its chassis was based on that of the 180.

The Mercedes 260 D was the first series car to have a diesel engine. The four-cylinder 2.6-liter engine developed 45 hp at 3000 rpm. Top speed: 97 km/h (60.27 mph); average fuel consumption: 9.5 liters of diesel per 100 km (29.74 mpg).

The performance achieved with the 170 S was later improved with the six-cylinder 220 of 1951. This car developed 80 hp at 4600 rpm and had a power-to-weight ratio of only 16.5 kg/CV (39.916 lb/hp).

Fitted for the first time with a "safety cell" passenger compartment in the body, the 180, developing 52 hp at 4000 rpm in the original version, was the model for the most popular Mercedes saloons of the 1950s. A 40-hp diesel version was brought out in 1955 (the output was increased to 43 hp two years later). The larger capacity 190 was produced in 1955, and in 1958 appeared the 190 D.

With the six-cylinder 300 series, Mercedes in the 1950s regained its reputation for highly sophisticated large-capacity cars. Left: the 300a of 1951, with a 2996-cc displacement and an output of 115 hp (increased to 125 with the 300b in 1954). It had an overhead camshaft valve gear with vibration dampers. Its top speed was 160 km/h (100 mph) and the rear suspension was electrically adjustable. Right: the 300 Sc coupé of 1955 had a top speed of 180 km/h (111.85 mph). Its six-cylinder engine had direct fuel injection and developed 175 hp at 5400 rpm.

The 220 of 1954 (2195 cc, 85 hp) had the same structure as the 180 and was the first of the six-cylinder series that became the top of the Mercedes range in the 1950s. The output was increased to 100 hp in 1956 with the 220 S, and to 115 hp in 1958 with the 220 SE injection model. Above: the 220 S saloon of 1956. Below: the 220 S cabriolet A of the same year.

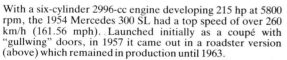

With a six-cylinder 2996-cc engine developing 215 hp at 5800 rpm, the 1954 Mercedes 300 SL had a top speed of over 260 km/h (161.56 mph). Launched initially as a coupé with "gullwing" doors, in 1957 it came out in a roadster version (above) which remained in production until 1963.

In 1959 the 220 was launched. The range comprised three versions: the 220, with six cylinders, 2.2 liters and 95 hp; the 220 S, with 110 hp; and the 220 SE, with 120 hp. Between 1959 and 1965, 313,798 were built, many of which were exported.

The years 1954 and 1955 were memorable for Mercedes-Benz Grand Prix vehicles. The 250-hp W 196 was twice driven by Fangio to win the world championship, and important victories were also won by Moss and Taruffi. At the end of the 1955 season, Mercedes retired unbeaten from competition racing, never to return at the same level again.

In 1959, the problem of safety was methodically tackled for the first time in studies for the new 220. This aspect had already been considered in the past, giving rise to the adoption of safety measures such as the 180 chassis and safety cone locks, which since 1951 have prevented the doors of the Mercedes-Benz from remaining locked in the event of an accident.

At least eighty pre-production vehicles were used in crash tests, which allowed for a large number of measures to be adopted, including extensive padding of the passenger compartment in order to reduce risk and injury in the event of accident. In 1961, the 220 SE coupé used disc brakes for the first time, and since then these have been standard on all Mercedes-Benz vehicles. Subsequently, the 190 petrol and diesel versions, and the 300 DE, were launched, followed in 1963 by the 190 SL. This was replaced by the 230 SL, with its distinctive pagoda roof. This was followed by the 6300-cc V8 600, which became the new flagship of the range. In the following years, even more importance was attached to research into safety, which led to the development of the concepts of "active safety" (accident prevention by means of improved technical features and safer driving), and of "passive safety" (the reduction of the conse-

quences of an accident). For the new 200 D-280 SEL series of 1969, the first version of an experimental sports vehicle, the C 111, took shape. For a decade, this was a travelling laboratory for experiments into new technical developments, among them the Wankel rotary engine and synthetic body materials, and for further research into the diesel engine and aerodynamic design. Among the records set by this vehicle on the Nardo circuit in 1978, one in particular stands out – the speed average of 314.463 km/h (195.398 mph) over twelve hours.

Brought out in collaboration with Bosch, the ABS system prevented the wheels locking when braking on any road surface, including ice, making it possible to control the direction of the vehicle at all times.

As far as passive safety is concerned, as well as

In 1982, Mercedes returned to the "compact" car sector with the W 201 series. It was launched in December with the 190 (1997 cc, 90 hp) and the 190 E (1997 cc, 122 hp), the latter fitted with an electronically controlled mechanical injection system. A year later, the 190 D came out, a 1997-cc 72-hp diesel. The rear suspension system on all versions is particularly sophisticated, as each wheel has five three-dimensional variable geometry arms.

The two-seater 190 SL was built from 1955 to 1963, on a chassis very similar to that of the 180 and 220 saloons. The four-cylinder 1.9-liter engine developed 105 hp at 5700 rpm and had a top speed of 170 km/h (105.6 mph).

In 1961, the 190 and 190 D (four-cylinders, 1897 cc, 75 and 50 hp respectively) were given new bodies, following the lead set by the design of the 220. In 1965, the 200, 230 and 230 S (right) petrol versions were introduced, the last with six-cylinder engines, as well as (left) the 200 D diesel.

Detailed research into safety led to the development of a new body in 1965. Impact absorption zones at the front and rear became important new features of "passive safety." The 250 S, 250 SE, 300 SE and 350 SEL were the models launched.

The successor to the Grosser Mercedes of the 1930s, the 600 came out in 1963 with a 6.3-liter 250-hp V8 engine and air suspension. It was available in a normal version or a pullman with a larger wheelbase.

In 1963, the 230 SL made its début, with a six-cylinder 2.3-liter 150-hp engine. The capacity was changed in 1966 to 2.5 liters (250 SL) and again in 1968 to 2.8 liters (280 SL). The car remained in production until 1971.

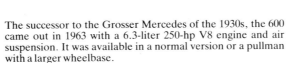

In 1968, the "new generation" Mercedes were introduced, with petrol engines of four (200, 220) or six cylinders (230, 250). The 200 D and 220 D were offered as the diesel versions.

Two coupés were brought out in 1968 – the 250 C and the 250 CE.

The new sports 350 SL roadster (two-seater) and the SLC coupé (longer wheelbase and four seats) were introduced in 1971. The six-cylinder 280 SL and 280 SLC came out in 1974, while the 450 SLC 5.0 appeared in 1978. The 380 SL and the 500 SL were fitted with a new generation of V8 engines, brought out in 1980.

The new W 123 series (known by its internal production number) was brought out in 1976 and originally consisted only of saloons. However, an estate version (the T series) was added in 1977 (below).

In 1972, the new Series S was launched, with the 280 S, 280 SE, 350 SE and 450 SE. The 450 SE 6.9 was added to the range in 1975 with, among other things, hydropneumatic suspension. The 300 SD turbodiesel was brought out in 1977 for the American market.

A change in both design and technology came about in 1979 with the Series S (W 126), which had new 3.8- and 5.0-liter V8 engines (380 SE and 500 SE), and also one of six cylinders, 2791 cc (280 S and SE). Longer wheelbase versions are indicated by the letters SEL. The 300 SD Turbodiesel is reserved for the United States. The 380 SEC and 500 SEC coupés were brought out in 1981.

Mercedes-Benz joined the off-road vehicle manufacturers in 1979 in association with the Austrian company Steyr-Daimler-Puch. They used the engines from the W 123 series for the 240 GD, 300 GD, 230 GE and 280 GE, built in open or estate versions, the latter in two wheelbase lengths. Above: the 240 GD SW short wheelbase.

◄ In 1983, the 190 E 2.3-16 sports version was launched at the Frankfurt Motor Show with four valves per cylinder on its four-cylinder 2299-cc engine. It has an output of 185 hp, a top speed of 230 km/h (143 mph) and accelerates from 0–100 km/h (0–62.14 mph) in eight seconds. The Mercedes range for the 1980s is completed by the new W 124 series, brought out in 1984 to replace the W 123.

tests carried out in 1971 with the experimental vehicle (ESV), important results have also been obtained with the air-cushion system (Airbag): this inflates in a fraction of a second in the event of a violent frontal impact, preventing the body of the driver from hitting the windscreen and the dashboard when he is thrown forwards; an electronically operated seatbelt keeps the front passenger firmly held in his seat. In 1978, an excellent off-road vehicle was brought out in collaboration with the Austrian company Steyr-Puch.

Current Mercedes-Benz production falls into three ranges: the compact W 201 series launched in 1982, which is a return to the smaller vehicle; the large limousines, estate cars and coupés, which in both petrol and diesel versions are very roomy and comfortable; and the S series, superior limousines of which the SEC and SL are sports versions.

Mercedes-Benz is one of today's most active companies in the field of research into both reducing pollution and finding alternative sources of energy. In the case of the latter, plans for a gas turbine, experimentally adopted on the 1981 Auto 200 prototype, are already at an advanced stage, although its development depends on the use of ceramic materials which are not as yet economically viable. Hydrogen and electric power are also being investigated, although here the size and weight of the necessary tanks and accumulators offer problems.

Although it has officially abandoned all competition activities, the Mercedes-Benz company has been involved in important road trials over the last few years, winning the London–Sydney rally of 1977 in a 280 E , and the Paris–Dacca rally of 1983 with a 280 GE off-road vehicle driven by the Ickx–Brasseur team.

MITSUBISHI

The origins of the modern Japanese industry date back to 1870, when Yataro Iwasaki founded a small navigation company called Tsukumo Shokai. In 1911 his successor, Mitsubishi Goshi Gaisha, divided the industrial empire that had developed from the navigation company into different sectors, including shipyards, banks, mines and insurance companies; as a result each became independent.

A few years later, in 1917, Mitsubishi automobiles came into existence with the arrival of the model A, the first car on the Japanese market to sell in sufficient numbers to justify production on an industrial scale. Three years later, the Mitsubishi aircraft division was also formed and carried out final testing of the first military fighter for aircraft carriers. In 1923, the factory began to build trucks, which were needed for emergency reconstruction operations after Tokyo had suffered a terrible earthquake. The Mitsubishi Heavy Industries group was created by a merger between the shipyards and the

aircraft industry in 1934, and the following year saw the first Japanese diesel truck come off the production lines – the predecessor of the present-day series of trucks and buses grouped under the name Fuso.

During the war, Mitsubishi excelled itself with a wide range of products, the most important of which were twin-engine bombers. In 1946, construction began on a scooter, which was given the auspicious name "Silver Dove" and was put on the market with the Mizushima, a small, three-wheel truck. The first economy car, the Mitsubishi 500, came out in 1960, but it was not until five years later, in 1965, that real expansion began, when Mitsubishi built a factory in Thailand, the fruit of a joint venture with a local company. In 1971, following an agreement with the American company Chrysler, the various Mitsubishi ranges were introduced on to the American market, a move that boosted the gradual expansion of certain Chrysler subsidiaries throughout the world. The following

year, for example, saw the opening of Chrysler in the Philippines; the company was immediately renamed the Canlubang Automotives Resources Corporation. Production then began in Indonesia, where vehicles were brought out with the marque of the three diamonds of the Iwasaki family combined with the three oak leaves of the Yamanouchi family.

In 1975, Mitsubishi cars were exported to Great Britain, Holland, Belgium and Luxembourg. In the following year, the market was expanded to include Finland and Norway, and eventually took in Denmark, West Germany, Switzerland and Austria. In 1977, an agency was opened in Europe. In 1979, Mitsubishi gained control of a third of Chrysler Australia, taking 99 per cent the following year. The new Gallant and Sapporo series came out in 1980, with a 2.3-liter turbodiesel engine, followed by the Tredia, Cordia, Lancer and the turbocharged off-road version, the Pajero. Today Mitsubishi specializes in supercharged petrol and diesel engines.

The Starion is a successful 2 + 2 coupé which was brought out at the Geneva Motor Show in 1982. The two-liter turbo engine has electronic fuel injection. The car has all-round servo-assisted disc brakes, a five-speed gearbox and a very carefully researched aerodynamic body. The top speed is 220 km/h (136.7 mph).

The first Mitsubishi automobile, the Model A, was brought out in 1917 and was the first Japanese car to be built in series.

The 500 of 1960 was the first economical Japanese model, following a request from the government for a popular car.

The 1962 Minica was a small, four-seater saloon with a two-cylinder two-stroke 359-cc air-cooled engine.

The Colt 600 (above left) was followed in 1965 by the Colt 800 (left), a two-door, five-seater saloon driven by a three-cylinder in-line, water-cooled engine. The 1000 had four cylinders, as did the 1100 (above) which also had a fully synchromesh four-speed gearbox.

The 1976 Sapporo coupé (below) was developed from the 1973 Galant (above). In Japan, they are known respectively as the Galant Sigma and the Galant Lambda, and in the USA the Dodge Challenger and the Plymouth Sapporo. Available with 1.6- or 2-liter engines; since 1980, with a 2.3-liter turbodiesel.

The 1982 Lancer (above) had a 1.2-, 1.3- or 1.6-liter engine, disc brakes on the front and drums at the rear. Only the GT model had all-round disc brakes. In 1983, the Lancer was updated in design and engines. It is now available with a 1.8- or 2-liter engine. The Lancer Turbo (below) has two Bosch electronic fuel injectors. It is sold in the United States as the Plymouth Arrow.

Launched at the Tokyo Motor Show of 1981, the Cordia coupé (left) and Tredia saloon (right) have front-wheel drive with 1.4- to 1.8-liter engines. A 1.8-liter turbo has also been available since 1983.

The Colt of the 1980s is a two-box, front-wheel drive having a "Super Shift" four-speed gearbox with an overdrive with two ratios, offering four gears for fast cruising and four for economical driving. A 1.6-liter turbo and a 1.8-liter diesel have been available since 1983 (above).

The four-wheel drive Pajero is a new off-road vehicle with 2.6-liter or 2.3-liter turbodiesel engines and independent front suspension.

MORGAN

Henry Frederick Stanley Morgan founded his factory for the production of three-wheeled cars in 1910. He met with considerable success, both in competitions and on the market, until 1935, when a change in government meant that financial assistance for cars with "one wheel less" was stopped. Morgan found himself in a difficult position and was forced to make hasty modifications to his products in order to fall into line with his competitors, who had been producing four-wheel versions for some time. The first four-wheeler built by Morgan was the 4/4 of 1936 which used a four-cylinder horizontally opposed engine of 1122 cc. The company continued producing three-wheelers until 1952.

The first important change came after the Second World War, when in 1950 the Plus 4, with a Standard-Vanguard 2100-cc 68-hp engine, was produced at the Malvern Link plant. The Plus 4 replaced the 4/4: it had the same body as the former, although the bonnet was slightly longer, and boasted another important new development in the shape of hydraulic brakes. Morgan won many competitions with this car, including wins in the RAC and Portuguese rallies. In 1954, the car was available with an optional Triumph TR 2 engine having a displacement of 2000 cc, twin carburettors and a top speed of 160 km/h (100 mph).

The 4/4 reappeared later, at the 1955 London

Motor Show, with a Ford 100 E engine (1172 cc, side valves, three-speed gearbox with the gear lever mounted on the dash). Other Ford engines, developed from those used on the Anglia and the Cortina, were also later used on this model. When Triumph stopped making its large, four-cylinder engines in 1968, Morgan began using the Buick-derived Rover V8 (3528 cc) on its Plus 8, which could reach up to 210 km/h (130.5 mph). Morgan's reputation rests on the quality of its hand-crafted cars: the plant did not have an assembly line, and this tradition remained unchanged when Peter Morgan took over from his father in 1959. In 1974, the Plus 8 cost about £2,163 and was produced at a rate of nine a week.

The first Morgan two-seater was built in 1911, the year after the company was formed. It was the first in a long line of three-wheel cars and had an open-topped body with a canvas hood.

This record-breaking car was built in 1930. Still using three wheels, it reached a speed of 115.66 mph (almost 190 km/h) on the Brooklands circuit. Note the fairing on the third wheel.

In 1936, the three-wheel models were produced in four-seater versions such as this F4, which used the Ford four-cylinder 1172-cc engine. In the same year, Morgan began production of four-wheel cars.

The 4/4 coupé series began in the immediate post-war period with this 1949 model, which still had an open body and a waterproof canvas hood.

In 1950, the Plus 4 came on to the market, with a Standard-Vanguard 2100-cc 68-hp engine. Morgan introduced hydraulic brakes on its cars with this model.

The Plus 4 Plus was a 1965 coupé which, with its closed body, represented a departure from the classic line of the Morgans. The most popular engine available was the Ford.

The Plus 8 is still in production today. It uses the Buick 3528-cc 155-hp V8 engine (assembled at the Rover plant), with which the car can reach up to 210 km/h (130.5 mph).

The 4/4 is now available with a choice of four-cylinder 1660-cc engines, one a Ford and the other a Fiat, both with a five-speed gearbox and disc brakes on the front. The bodies are two- or four-seaters, both similar in design and both open-topped.

NISSAN-DATSUN

It is now a hundred years since the automobile was invented and the enormous impact of this mode of transport on many aspects of life is felt throughout the world. The transport revolution it engendered has brought us tremendous economic growth and led to the establishment of a widely motorized "automobile society."

The twenty-first century, the new era of the "information society," will soon be upon us, with all the advantages microelectronic technology can offer. We have yet to see how the information age will develop, but we believe the automobile, one of the most significant inventions in the history of civilization, will never lose its utility, whatever changes are made to our society in the future. Nevertheless, the auto industry must continue striving to develop the safest, most efficient vehicles possible, perfectly matched to the needs and convenience of mankind. To this end, we aim to maximize the automobile's great contribution to society, to enable it to perform the even greater role it must play in this new era.

The aim in founding the Nissan Motor Company in December 1933 was to establish a fully fledged automobile industry in Japan. In spite of the many difficulties this effort entailed, Nissan succeeded in establishing Japan's first mass-production system for the manufacture of automobiles. Continuous efforts to develop and apply new technology, and achieve new heights in quality, have made Nissan one of the leading car manufacturers in the world. One of the most fundamental aims of our company has always been to contribute to the development of society through the manufacture of the best possible automobiles of the times. It is this same spirit that will underlie our efforts to develop an automobile of the future in perfect harmony with the needs of the age.

Katsuji Kawamata

KATSUJI KAWAMATA   Chairman, Nissan Motor Company Ltd

The Leopard and the Leopard TR-X differ practically in name only. Following the trend of Japanese cars over the last few years, this car is a further example of the research carried out into aerodynamics and has a body with large areas of glass. It is available with a 2-liter or a 2-liter turbocharged engine, both with fuel injection, and with a five-speed or (on the turbo) a three- or four-speed automatic gearbox.

In 1919, the company's cars were known as Dats. The Type 41 was a four-seater runabout with a four-cylinder engine.

The first car to appear after the merger between Dat Motor Company and Jitsuyo Jidosha Seizo was the 1924 Lila Type JC (above), followed by the two-seater roadster (right).

Another Dat, the Type 51, came out in 1923.

The first Datsuns came out in 1932, available in various versions, but all with a limited engine capacity and at a low price. Left: the Type 10. Right: the Type A.

The Type 12 of 1933 was a continuation of the small-engine Datsun car line, with a displacement of 747 cc.

This 1934 phaeton had a new type of front grille and a four-cylinder 10-hp engine.

The Type 14 came out in 1935 and still formed part of the company's range of small cars.

The second largest Japanese car manufacturer with regard to the number of cars produced, and the third largest automobile empire in the world after General Motors and Toyota, Nissan operates mainly in the automobile and commercial vehicle sectors, with limited activity in the aerospace industry and in the manufacture of textile machinery, machine tools, industrial machinery and marine engines.

With an average annual turnover of $16 billion, and with about 59,000 employees who, in common with other large Japanese companies, have a very high per capita productivity level, Nissan operates through a dozen main factories

in Japan and through twenty-five assembly plants in twenty other nations throughout the world. In Europe, Nissan is present in Spain (Motor Iberica), Ireland (Datsun Ltd) and Italy, where it produces the Arna in association with Alfa Romeo. In the United States, Nissan has subsidiaries in California, Tennessee and Hawaii.

As for most other Japanese companies, the foreign markets provide a privileged hunting ground for Nissan, who send about 55 per cent of their turnover abroad; the remaining 45 per cent is retained for the home market.

Nissan is one of the oldest automobile

manufacturers in the East. An engineering company, the Kwaishinsha Motor Car Works of Tokyo, had built a rather traditional motor car, which had gone into regular production by 1912; a completely new car, the DAT, was brought out two years later, named after the three partners in the company, Den, Aoyama and Takeuchi. The Dats were produced and sold alongside commercial vehicles and were built from 1925 onwards by the Dat Motor Car Company, which became the Dat Automobile Manufacturing Company in 1926, with its headquarters in Osaka.

In 1930, after a period devoted mainly to the manufacture of industrial vehicles, Dat went

231

In 1937, a decision was taken to extend production with the help of the American Graham-Paige company. This gave rise to this six-cylinder Nissan 70 Special Sedan.

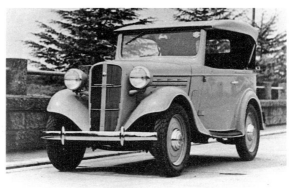

From 1937, the Datsun range shared the market with Nissan. This is a 1938 Datsun Type 17.

The cars brought out between 1948 and 1950 were the same as the pre-war models. Above: a Datsun DX Type DB. Below: the Standard Type DA.

This 1952 Datsun was a small, neat, sports model.

The 1953 Datsun DS 5 still echoed pre-war lines.

The 1955 Datsun 110 had a four-cylinder 860-cc side-valve engine. The four-speed gearbox was fully synchromesh.

The Datsun 210 (above) was entered in the Australian rally together with the Sakura (right). The 210 came first and the Sakura fourth in Class A.

The Skyline of 1957 belonged to Prince Motors, who joined the Nissan group in 1965. It had a four-cylinder engine.

The 1961 310 was also called the Bluebird. Its original 1189-cc capacity was later increased to 1300 cc. It had drum brakes and a three-speed plus reverse gearbox.

The 1960 Nissan Cedric had a four-cylinder 1883-cc engine, but this capacity was later increased to 2000 cc. In 1964, the Cedric was available with a diesel engine, the first to be brought out by Nissan.

In 1965, the Nissan range was extended with a prestige model, the President, available with either a six- or an eight-cylinder 3-liter engine.

The Datsun 1500 sports model was called the Fairlady, and the coupé the Silvia (right). It had Dunlop disc brakes on the front. Above: the 1967 Fairlady 2000.

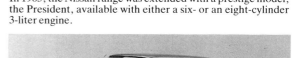

From the Bluebird, a model was developed in 1967 with an increased engine displacement of 1.6 liters.

The 1968 Skyline 2000 had a six-cylinder engine, a four-speed gearbox and servo-assisted brakes.

From its first appearance in 1966, the Datsun 1000 (also known as the Sunny) was an immediate market success. It had a four-cylinder 988-cc engine and drum brakes.

The 1971 Datsun Cedric was sold in various versions (220 C, 240 C, 260 C) with an engine displacement of 2 to 2.6 liters. ▶

The Nissan President was given a new body in 1973. It had a 3- or 4.4-liter V8 engine.

The coupé Fairlady Z appeared in 1969 with a six-cylinder 2-liter engine. The Z 432 appeared at the same time, with a more powerful engine (160 hp instead of 130).

In 1973, the new Datsun Violet (or 140J/160J) was brought out. It had a 1.4- or a 1.6-liter engine. It won the African Safari Rally in 1979 and 1980.

The Nissan Cherry came out in 1970 and was the first of the company's front-wheel drive cars. It had a transverse engine, a twin-body carburettor and independent suspension.

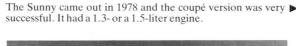

The restyled Bluebird of 1979 was also available with fuel injection, either in a turbocharged or a diesel version.

The 1979 Datsun Cedric 2000 came out with a new turbo model. It had a computer and ECCS to control the fuel injection.

The 1976 Bluebird was available with engines ranging from 1.6 to 2 liters. Above: the 1800 SSS.

The Sunny came out in 1978 and the coupé version was very ▶ successful. It had a 1.3- or a 1.5-liter engine.

The Laurel 2000 was restyled in 1980. It had a 1.8- or a 2-liter engine and belonged to the mid range of the market.

A new model, the Langley, came out in 1980 with the same structure as the Pulsar series. It had a 1.3- or a 1.5-liter engine and front-wheel drive.

The front-wheel drive Auster came out in 1981 with a 1.6- or a 1.8-liter engine.

The 1981 Skyline was available with a four- or six-cylinder engine, and had rear-wheel drive.

The Liberta (above) and the Pulsar of 1982 had a 1.3- or 1.5-liter, or a 1.5-liter turbocharged, engine with fuel injection.

The 1982 Micra (known in Japan as the March) is a front-wheel drive compact with an all-alloy 988-cc engine.

The 1982 Laurel Spirit was put on the market with a 1.3- or 1.7-liter engine and front-wheel drive.

The 1982 Prairie (above) is developed from the Nissan Sunny. It is a very roomy car (1.60 m/5.24 ft high) and has sliding rear doors. The engine is either 1.5 or 1.8 liters and it has a five-speed gearbox. The Sunny (below) comes with a wider range of engines (1.3, 1.5 and 1.7 liters diesel) and is known in the United States as the Sentra.

The 1984 Gloria has the new 2000- or 3000-cc V6 engines; a diesel 2.8-liter version is optional.

The 1984 Skyline also has a new engine, a 2000-cc DOHC. It has a five-speed gearbox and all-round disc brakes.

The 1984 Stanza (or Auster) is a front-wheel drive model with a 1600- or an 1800-cc engine, the latter with fuel injection. It has servo-assisted front disc brakes.

The 1984 Bluebird has front-wheel drive and a choice of 1600- to 2000-cc engines or a turbocharged 1800-cc version with electronic fuel injection. A 2-liter diesel is also available.

The brand-new 1984 Fairlady Z is available with the new 2- or 3-liter turbocharged engine with electronic fuel injection. It has servo-assisted disc brakes.

back to producing motor cars, bringing out the Dat 91, followed by the Datson in 1931. In that same year, the Japanese company was taken over by the Tabota Imono Company group and the name changed from "Datson" to "Datsun" in 1932, combining the original "Dat" with the word "sun," symbol of the Japanese empire. In 1933, with a capital of ten million yen, the Jidosha Seizo Company was formed in Yokohama for the manufacture of Datsun cars. The company name was finally established in 1934 as the Nissan Motor Company Ltd. In the period leading up to the Second World War, the small Datsuns were

inspired by the British Austin Seven, and the Nissan cars followed the style and themes of the large American cars such as the Graham-Paige. After involvement in the manufacture of military equipment during the war, Nissan went back to civilian production in 1946, manufacturing industrial vehicles, while the Datsun cars produced were simply rehashed pre-war models. The Nissan marque reappeared after 1960.

Meanwhile, as the result of an agreement made with British Austin, Nissan began building the A 40 under license from 1952 onwards; this was followed by the A 50. The engines were

British-inspired. In 1959, the Datsun 310 sparked off the successful Bluebird series (in 1965, over 200,000 had been exported, mainly to the USA) and in 1960 the Cedric marked the relaunch of the Nissan marque. The first diesel produced by the company came out on a 1964 model.

Since then, Nissan has earned a reputation for itself both in terms of technical reliability and style, and has suffered no setbacks in its expansion and development. Production figures illustrate the company's success: in 1982 the group produced 2,958,000 units, after a record 2,117,800 in 1980.

The Silvia range was launched in 1979 because the company wanted to create a series of sporty cars with an on-board computer. The Silvia has the same frame as the Gazelle. The four-cylinder 1800- or 2000-cc engines are standard, but a 1.8-liter turbocharged version with fuel injection is also available. Above: the 1984 model.

This 1985 Pulsar is a two-door coupé with front-wheel drive which, with its 1.5-liter engine, belongs to the mid-lower end of the market. Mounted transversely at the front, the engine develops 85 hp, increasing to 115 hp on the turbo version. It is also available with a 1.5-liter fuel-injected 95-hp engine or a 1.7-liter diesel. The top speed is between 160 and 185 km/h (100-115 mph).

PEUGEOT-TALBOT

SIMCA – SUNBEAM

At a time when our country is celebrating "a hundred years of the automobile," I cannot help but feel great pride at the thought that the history of our company is so closely linked to that of the motor industry.

This great celebration of the French motor car is an invitation for manufacturers and public alike to look back on an industry which, from the beginning of the century to the present day, has continued to develop and expand, to the extent that it now represents one of the most important industries in our country, playing an essential role in our dealings with other countries.

The history of the automobile is open-ended, and the centenary of the motor car, although an important stage, is but a milestone in this history. Looking back over the history of the car enables us to appreciate the wealth of experience gained by each manufacturer, in the most varied sectors, from conception to production, in terms of design, the reduction of fuel consumption, in competitions and so on.

Automobiles Peugeot has made a notable contribution to the evolution of the automobile: the Peugeot cars that have appeared on the market for over a century have often introduced important new technological developments, which have also won the company a solid reputation in the field of sport. With regard to fuel economy, valuable research has been carried out by Peugeot in association with L'Agence pour la Maîtrise de l'Energie.

I am confident that Peugeot's continuous striving to update, adapt and improve the automobile will enable the company to participate ever more actively in the future development of the industry.

ROLAND PEUGEOT   President of the Supervisory Board of Directors, Peugeot S.A.

The 402 of 1935 was an innovative car with fully automatic transmission, a dash-mounted gear lever, headlights placed behind the radiator grille and a four-cylinder 2-liter 60-hp engine with rods and rockers.

This 1892 vis-à-vis was one of the first Peugeot models to use the Daimler V2 engine.

The Type 19 was in production from 1897 to 1902 with a Peugeot two-cylinder horizontal engine.

The Type 20 of 1902 had an eight-seater omnibus body on a two-cylinder engine mounted under the front seat.

The front mudflaps on this 1905 double phaeton were designed to protect passengers from the dust.

Many changes were made to the Type 69 (known as the Bébé) from the 1905 model to that of 1913 (right). With its original single-cylinder engine changed to four cylinders, 856 cc and 10 hp, the Bébé could reach 55 km/h (34.2 mph).

The first examples of Peugeot vehicles to have their own power source were the steam-powered tricycles designed by Serpollet in 1888. The Peugeot machine-tool factory had faith in the horseless carriage from the very start and by 1889 had already tested two quadricycles with petrol engines. The construction of automobiles, however, began in 1891, when the factory dedicated practically all its resources to the construction of the automobile as we understand it today. All the first Peugeots were known as a "Type" followed by an identification number; among the models of the day – a time when it was not uncommon to find up to a hundred models in the range of just one manufacturer – one of the most famous was the Type 39. This was the first of the company's cars to have a four-cylinder 1042-cc engine coupled to a four-speed gearbox (just under a hundred were built). There was also the popular Type 69, nicknamed the "Bébé," of which over four hundred were built after 1905, using a single-cylinder 652-cc 6-hp engine.

The Peugeot factories were first established in Valentigney and Audincourt, and then in Lille; the Sochaux factory was opened in 1913, and in 1902 production was concentrated in Lille and Audincourt. For a few years after the Sochaux plant was opened, production was given over to the manufacture of trucks: the first of these to bear any resemblance to our modern versions was the Type 109 which, with a maximum load of three tons, could still reach 20 km/h (12.5 mph). Industrial vehicle production was given a great boost by the war, but then slowed down. In the period leading up to the war, Peugeot cars won many races, including the 1913 Indianapolis 500. Peugeot were producing a complete range of vehicles for all uses in a style which is still their distinguishing feature today; their cars were sturdy, high-class vehicles with an excellent finish, and were therefore not particularly cheap to buy. However, Peugeot specialized mainly in the production of utilitarian models like the Bébé. The Quadrilette, based on the same lines as the Bébé and launched at the Brussels Motor Show in 1920, subsequently led to the development of the 5 CV, which hit a record production figure of 82,904 chassis.

The history of the modern Peugeot, however, did not begin until the 1929 Paris Motor Show, with the launch of the 201. This completely new car, which was originally fitted with an 1122-cc engine, earned Peugeot their reputation as a manufacturer of tough, reliable vehicles. Three years later came the 301, a more refined model than the 201, making the beginning of Peugeot's new aim to supply their customers with "useful" cars. The 301 was also available in a family version or as an estate. During this period, the lines of the 201 and 301 bodies had become more and more elegant and attractive, creating a distinctive "style" very much in keeping with current trends of the time.

In 1934, the first aerodynamic tests were carried out on the 301; at the beginning of the same year, Peugeot launched the six-cylinder 601, which proved to be unsuccessful. The 401 came out in the same period, but no other model could match the 201, of which 142,000 were built before it finally went out of production in September 1937. The aerodynamic series began in 1935 with the 402 prototype, which had the headlights set behind the grille. It was with this model that the numbering system began which is still in use today to identify the cars. After the 402, which cost about 24,000 f. for the basic saloon, Peugeot launched the 302 at the 1936 Paris Motor Show; this was a new and scaled-down version of the 402. The most significant innovation on it was the use of a synchromesh gearbox, and it was the first tourer to be fitted with a diesel engine (1938).

Production slowed down during the war and almost ground to a halt as a result of the damage caused by the Allied bombers. It picked up again immediately after the war, although at a slower rate, with the 202, which had been brought out in 1938. This was replaced towards the end of 1947 by the 203, of which over 685,000 were built. With a unitary body and a 1300-cc 45-hp engine,

Like other companies, Peugeot during the war concentrated on the production of military vehicles such as this machine-gun carrier of 1915.

An elegant 174 landaulet of the post-war period, of which 810 were built between 1922 and 1928. It had a four-cylinder sleeve-valve engine.

The first 201 was brought out at the 1929 Paris Motor Show. It was the first small-engined car to be produced in a large series in France. The M model came out in 1936.

A new model was added to Peugeot's range in 1932. It was the 301, which came in various versions with the same 1465-cc 35-hp engine as the 201.

Another successful car, the 302, remained in production from 1936 to 1938, during which period 25,000 were built.

The 401 model (shown above in the taxi version) came out in 1934, and 13,545 were built. The four-cylinder 1720-cc engine had an output of 44 hp.

Brought out in 1948, the 203 had angled valves and a hemispherical head, a feature that was only used on luxury car engines at that time.

The 403 was launched in 1955. In 1959, it was fitted with a very modern, Peugeot-designed diesel engine.

The 404 of 1960, designed by Pininfarina, was an enormous success. The diesel-engined coupé version did very well racing at Monthléry and in the African rallies.

The 204 of 1965 had a light-alloy engine with front-wheel drive and an overhead camshaft. Four-cylinder in-line engine of 1130 cc, top speed 138 km/h (86 mph).

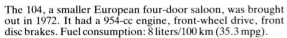

The 104, a smaller European four-door saloon, was brought out in 1972. It had a 954-cc engine, front-wheel drive, front disc brakes. Fuel consumption: 8 liters/100 km (35.3 mpg).

Another new model, the 504, was launched in 1968 in saloon, coupé and cabriolet versions, the last two designed by Pininfarina.

The 304 of 1969 had a transverse 1.3-liter 70-hp engine, front-wheel drive and an overhead camshaft.

The 604 of 1975 had a 2664-cc V6 engine which was the result of collaboration between Peugeot, Renault and Volvo. This engine was also used on the 504 coupé and cabriolet.

The 954-cc Peugette roadster was designed by Pininfarina and came out in 1976. Only one was built.

When the 205 came out in 1983, it was immediately hailed as a major breakthrough, representing a completely new concept of the car. The transverse engine was available with a displacement of 954, 1124 or 1360 cc. It had front-wheel drive and a four- or five-speed gearbox. The diesel version, the GTI and the Turbo 16 were brought out later, the last a mid-engine Rally model with four-wheel drive.

this remained in production for almost twelve years without any major modifications.

In April 1955, Peugeot began their association with the coachbuilder Pininfarina. Since then, their cars have been produced with the marque of the lion rampant, first used on the modern 403, which was brought out in both a saloon and an estate version. The 403 was given an 1800-cc 48-hp diesel engine in 1959.

A more modern version of the 403 was launched in May 1960 – the 404. This was available with a 1485- or 1618-cc carburetted petrol engine (the fuel-injection model was brought out later) or a diesel engine of almost two liters. An important feature of the 404 was its versatility, for it was available as a saloon, coupé, cabriolet, family car or all-purpose van. A total of 2,450,000 were built, and by August 1963 Peugeot were already celebrating the production of their millionth 403.

Meanwhile, in the commercial vehicle sector, the front-wheel drive J7 van was brought out. With its large carrying capacity, it was in fact one of the few vans in its category in which, in spite of its limited outer dimensions, a man could stand upright. It was available with the same petrol or diesel engines as the 403. In April 1965, front-wheel drive was introduced on the small,

new 204, which had a 1130-cc 58-hp petrol engine. The 4 series expanded over the years to include the 304 (a more powerful 204 with a different body) and the 504, which was the flagship of the range until the arrival of the 604. This followed the small, new 104, the fruit of an agreement with Citroën.

In 1978, the Peugeot-Citroën group gained control of Chrysler operations in Europe, by then including Simca. As a result of the new agreement, the old and no longer used Talbot name, which belonged to the British Sunbeam and the French Talbot and Matra, was brought back into use.

The history of Peugeot continues with the 5 series, on the market today in the form of the 205, 305 and 505, all with carburetted and fuel-injected petrol engines, as well as turbocharged diesel.

Simca

Simca was the brainchild of a man named Pigozzi, who wanted to build Fiats under license for the French market. He began with the assembly of the 508 Balilla and the Simca-Fiat 5, which was based on the design of the 500 Topolino. From

The 505 came out in 1979, since when over twenty different versions have appeared on the market, including the 160-hp fuel-injected 505 turbo.

The Vera 02 diesel prototype, shown at the 1982 Geneva Motor Show, marked an important step in Peugeot's research into energy saving systems. It had a fuel consumption of 3 liters/100 km (94.2 mpg) at 90 km/h (56 mph) from a 1360-cc engine.

The first Simca was, in fact, the Fiat 508 Balilla, assembled at the Nanterre plant in 1935 and marketed under the name Fiat-France.

Built entirely in France to the design of the Fiat 500 Topolino, the Simca-Fiat 5 (left) came out in March 1936, a few months before the Topolino was launched on the Italian market. It had a four-cylinder 569-cc 13-hp engine. It was followed by the 6, a new version of the 500 C (above right) in 1949.

Another Fiat (the new Balilla 1100) was the model for the Simca 8 of 1945, which proved enormously successful in France. Four-cylinder: 1098 cc, 32 hp.

The Simca 9 Aronde (left) of 1951 signalled a final departure from the Fiat-inspired lines. It was a four-door saloon with a unitary body and a four-cylinder in-line engine of 1221 cc and 45 hp. It was followed by a two-door model, the Grand Large (above right). A Monthléry model came out in 1959 with a 1290-cc 56-hp Rush engine.

The 1308 came out in 1975 with a 1442-cc engine developing 85 hp at 5600 rpm. It was based on the same mechanics as the 1100, with a five-door saloon body.

The most successful Simca was the 1000. The four-cylinder in-line 944-cc engine developed 35 hp, later increased to 44 hp. It was rear-mounted and water-cooled.

This three-door saloon came out in 1977 under the Talbot-Simca-Sunbeam marque. It was available with three different engines – 0.9, 1.3 or 1.6 liters – and had a unitary body and four-speed gearbox.

1936, the Fiat-Simca 5 was built entirely in France to Fiat designs; proving highly successful, it was followed by the 8 and the 6. The company's reputation also grew as a result of the cars modified by Amédée Gordini, whose association with Simca in the construction of competition cars lasted until 1951. In 1954, the company took over Ford-France and in 1958 passed 15 per cent of its shares to Chrysler, who assumed complete control between 1963 and 1970, giving rise to the formation of Chrysler France. Company production increased steadily during this period, thanks also to the success of the 1000.

Not even the Talbot sports marque managed to survive the post-war crisis. After Anthony Lago gave the company over to Simca in 1959, it brought out this Talbot-Lago America coupé. It was fitted with a BMW V8 engine, something completely new for the company, which had previously used the Ford V8. Only twelve were built.

From 1970 onwards, cars were coming off the production lines with either the Chrysler marque (160, 180 and 2 liters) or the Simca marque (1307, 1308). The Simca marque is still used with the Matra (also taken over by Chrysler) as well as with Talbot and Sunbeam.

Talbot

Founded in London in 1903, Clément-Talbot concentrated mainly on the production of competition cars, although road versions were also built, and a four-cylinder 3800-cc, known simply as the Talbot, was on the market from 1906 onwards. From that date, various versions of the 12 HP were entered in many races and won many victories, as did the 25 HP, and also a special single-seater with which Percy Lambert was the first ever to cover 160 km (100 miles) in an hour.

After the war, Clément-Talbot was taken over with Sunbeam by the French company Darracq (forming STD – the Sunbeam-Talbot-Darracq group) and a confusing period began in which sports cars were produced on both sides of the Channel and entered in competitions under any one of the three marques. In 1920, the cars went under the name "Talbot-Darracq."

Despite the financial problems which led the company to ruin, Anthony Lago, who had been responsible for marketing vehicles as Talbot Lago or Lago Talbot, resumed production again immediately after the war, although without much success. The company was saved from complete closure, however, when it was taken over by Simca in 1959; it was they who made the connection which was to result in Talbot and Peugeot's rising together from the ashes of Simca.

The Talbot Matra Bagheera three-seater coupé came out in 1973. It had a unitary body made of polyester resin reinforced with fiberglass and a 1294-cc 84-hp engine (increased after 1979 to 1442 cc and 85 hp).

The Talbot Matra Murena, shown above in the 1980 S version, was directly developed from the Bagheera and was available with a 1.6- or a 2.2-liter engine, with top speeds of 182 and 200 km/h (113 and 124.3 mph) respectively.

The Solara three-box saloon comes in various versions (LS, GL, GLS, SX) with 1.4- to 1.6-liter engines. It has a transverse front engine, a four-speed gearbox (only the SX has five speeds) and servo-assisted brakes.

The Tagora has a 2-, 2.3- or 2.6-liter engine on the GLS, DT and SX versions. The last of these has an engine developing 165 hp at 6000 rpm, all-round disc brakes, an on-board computer, an electronic rev-counter and transistorized electronic ignition.

The Pininfarina-designed Samba cabriolet has a 1360-cc engine with an output of 72 hp at 6000 rpm. It has a five-speed gearbox and a top speed of 160 km/h (100 mph).

The successful Horizon range of 1983 has been completed with diesel versions (LD and EXD: 1.9 liters, 65 hp with injection pump) and the Premium (1592 cc, 90 hp).

PORSCHE

Ferdinand Porsche was seventy-three years old when the first car was brought out bearing his name. It was built at the small Gmünd workshop where the Porsche Büro had moved to after the war, to resume operations repairing military vehicles. The company was active from as early as 1929, and with the benefit of the experience gained by Porsche at Lohner, Mercedes and Austro-Daimler, the Kronenstrasse workshop in Stuttgart became a true design center, where some of the best brains of the time were using the most advanced techniques to build all types of vehicles from automobiles to armoured cars and motor cycles.

Commercially speaking, the pre-war master-piece was undoubtedly the Porsche 60, the definitive prototype for the Volkswagen. There were, however, other exceptional projects, such as the Grand Prix Auto Union mid-engined models that came out in 1934. After this date, the rear-mounted engine became an established tradition with Porsche and was used on the first 356, which came out in 1948 with a four-cylinder Volkswagen 1131-cc engine. The engine was originally to have been mounted centrally, but this idea was abandoned because of problems of cost and reduced passenger space. The car was officially launched at the Geneva Motor Show in 1949, together with a coupé version. The output from the three hundred and fifty-sixth car designed by the Porsche Büro was 40 hp at 4000 rpm with a top speed of 150 km/h (93.2 mph). The flat chassis had a central tunnel with transverse torsion bar suspension. Forty-six 356s, all with hand-beaten aluminium bodies, were built at Gmünd.

In 1950, Porsche returned to Stuttgart, where the production capacity was increased following an agreement with the Reutter coachbuilders for the supply of bodies, this time made of steel. In 1952 the new plant was opened at Zuffenhausen. Ferdinand Porsche had died the previous year, leaving the management of the company in the capable hands of his son Ferry.

The 356 was fitted with engines, the displacements of which were being continually increased, but all had a basic specification of horizontal cylinders, with an air-cooling system in which the fan was vertical. In 1951, a 1300-cc engine was adopted, followed by a 1500-cc engine the year after. The 356 A of 1956 came with a 1300-cc (in production until 1957) or a 1600-cc engine. The 356 B of 1959 was the result of moderate restyling and used three different versions of the 1600-cc engine, the most powerful of which was the Super 90, named after the amount of horsepower developed. The last in the series was the SC in 1963 (95 hp).

From 1955 onwards, the Carrera was also in production, with a twin-camshaft engine which had first been used on the 1953 RS Spider, the first Porsche to be designed for competitions. With an output which reached 130 hp with the 2000 of 1961, the 356 GS Carrera models were very successful in GT races.

A worthy successor to these outstanding cars was the 1964 904 GTS, which preserved some of the tourer-racer ambivalence, a characteristic which disappeared altogether on the following six-cylinder 906, launched in 1966. This heralded a long series of successful cars in the sport-prototype category, which followed on from each other with exceptional continuity in terms of technical and stylistic development (907, 908 and 917) throughout the late 1960s.

Attempts to break into Formula 1 in 1961 and 1962, however, were not so successful, for during those two years Porsche crossed the finishing line first on only one occasion, at the French Grand Prix in 1962, with Dan Gurney at the wheel.

The year 1964 saw the launch of the six-cylinder 911, one of the most important sports cars of the post-war period. The engine used was another flat version arranged longitudinally over a central gearbox. The air-cooling system also remained unchanged, although it was given a horizontal fan. The original displacement of 2000 cc was increased to 2200 cc in 1969, 2400 cc in 1971 and 2700 cc in 1973. The 3000-cc engine, brought out in 1975, was fitted originally on the Carrera and then from 1979 on the unified model, the 911 SC, the displacement of which was

The definitive version of the 356 was brought out with a displacement reduced from the 1131 cc of the prototype to 1086 cc, and this remained unaltered until 1953. The aluminium roadster weighed only 596 kg (1314 lb) and the coupé version, its output reduced to 48 hp, won in its class at the 1951 Le Mans 24 Hours at an average speed of 122 km/h (75.8 mph).

The 356 B was brought out in 1959. The engine had a displacement of 1582 cc and an output of 60, 75 or 90 hp, with top speeds of 160, 175 and 180 km/h (99.4, 109 and 112 mph) respectively. From 1952 onwards, the 356 was fitted with a new gearbox with the patented bush synchromesh system later used by many other companies.

The 928 came out in March 1977 with another 4474-cc front-mounted V8 engine and transaxle transmission. The independent rear suspension was highly sophisticated, with fully converging compensating arms. The original 240-hp model was joined in 1979 by the 928 S, which had an increased displacement of 4664 cc and an output of 300 hp. Its top speed is 250 km/h (155.4 mph).

The first front-engined Porsche, the 924, came out in November 1975. It had a four-cylinder 1984-cc engine developing 125 hp at 5800 rpm, transaxle transmission. In 1978, the Turbo was presented, with an increased output of 170 hp at 5500 rpm, giving a top speed of 230 km/h (143 mph).

Brought into production in 1964, the 911 originally had a 2000-cc engine with an output of 130 hp at 6100 rpm and a top speed of 210 km/h (130.5 mph). In 1965, a new version, the 912, was introduced, using the four-cylinder Super 90 engine. The Targa version followed, with a big rear roll-bar and removable middle roof section.

increased to 3200 cc with the 1983 SC Carrera. In twenty very successful years, the output increased from the original 130 to 231 hp. A model was also brought out in 1975 with a KKK turbocharger which, with a displacement of 3000 cc, could develop 260 hp at 5500 rpm. September 1977 saw further developments with the 3300-cc 300-hp engine. However, the success of the 911 was not affected by the launch in 1975 of the 924, followed in 1977 by the 928, both of them fitted with the revolutionary (for Porsche at least) front-mounted engine with transaxle transmission. The 924 has a four-cylinder 1984-cc engine developing 125 hp and since 1978 has also been available in a 170-hp turbo version. The 928, on the other hand, has a powerful 4474-cc V8 engine. The 928 S model of 1979 has a

displacement of 4664 cc and develops 300 hp; the 1981 944 is a variant of the 924 with a four-cylinder 2479-cc engine.

An agreement with Volkswagen in 1969 culminated in the birth of the VW-Porsche marque, which produced only one car, the relatively unsuccessful mid-engine 914. However, despite the demands of very high-level production, Porsche has continued to undertake design for third parties, a fine example being the 542 saloon designed for Studebaker in 1953, which had a rear-mounted, air-cooled V6 engine.

The car did not go into production. In a similar tradition, Porsche has always been keenly involved in sports racing, and the 911 alone has collected many great wins both on the track and in rallies, as well as in great road trials, notably the 1983 Paris–Dakar. At the same time, the ranks of the prototypes have been enriched by the successful new 936, 956 and 962 models.

In 1983, the company's achievements extended to Formula 1, with the turbo engine, designed for the Techniques d'Avant Garde, with which the McLaren went on to dominate the 1984 season.

The most powerful 911 is the 1977 Turbo, which has a 3299-cc engine with a KKK turbocharger and can develop 300 hp at 5500 rpm. Capable of 0–100 km/h (62.1 mph) in only 5.4 seconds from a standing start, its top speed is 260 km/h (161.5 mph). It has a four-speed gearbox.

In production since 1981, the 944 has a four-cylinder 2479-cc engine developing up to 163 hp at 5800 rpm. It has electronic fuel injection and a top speed of 220 km/h (137 mph). The 220-hp turbo version introduced in 1974 has a top speed of about 250 km/h (155.3 mph).

The 1982 cabriolet version of the 911 has the 2994-cc SC mechanics, in production since 1979. The output was 204 hp at 5900 rpm and top speed 235 km/h (146 mph). In 1983, the whole range was given the 3164-cc engine, developing 231 hp at 5900 rpm, giving a top speed of 245 km/h (152.2 mph).

Sold under the Volkswagen-Porsche marque, the mid-engine 914 was in production until 1975. Available in two versions, of four cylinders, 1679 cc, 80 hp and of six cylinders, 1991 cc, 110 hp, with top speeds of 175 and 200 km/h (109 and 124.3 mph) respectively, it had a five-speed gearbox.

RENAULT

In 1898, Louis Renault brought out his first automobile. The following year he invented shaft drive, one of the great milestones in the history of the motor car, which represented the start of a great adventure for the extraordinary personality behind this manufacturer. Very soon it was to turn into an extraordinary technological and commercial adventure too.

With about thirty-three million cars built since the post-war period, the Renault marque now figures on the major world markets, constantly consolidating its image, which is based on a philosophy giving priority to the reliability and sturdiness of the engines, low fuel-consumption and a high degree of comfort. These aims have been applied to a whole gamut of cars designed to satisfy every possible consumer need: from as early as the 1930s, the choice of models ranged from the 6 CV NN to the prestigious 40 CV, the saloon used by heads of state.

After the war, Renault became a state-run concern and gradually developed into a large multinational company, accumulating both technical and commercial successes. These ranged from the 4 CV (750 cc), the first example of a popular, rear-engine, four-seater with independent wheels all round, to the Renault 4, brought out in the 1960s and very quickly becoming the symbol of the young, an economical car par excellence, and the Renault 16, which introduced the concept of the modern dual-purpose car. The 1970s saw the success of the Renault 5, a car which satisfied public taste because of its great versatility and of which over five million have been built to date.

Always at the forefront in terms of technology, Renault was the first company successfully to test turbocharged petrol engines in motor racing; it then took advantage of its findings by using the system on a large scale in standard production.

BERNARD HANON   President-Managing Director of the Régie Nationale des Usines Renault

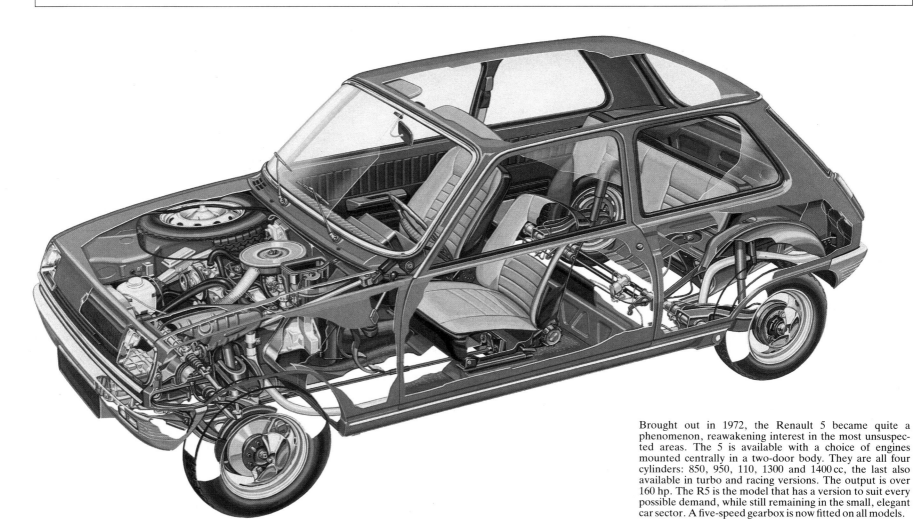

Brought out in 1972, the Renault 5 became quite a phenomenon, reawakening interest in the most unsuspected areas. The 5 is available with a choice of engines mounted centrally in a two-door body. They are all four cylinders: 850, 950, 110, 1300 and 1400 cc, the last also available in turbo and racing versions. The output is over 160 hp. The R5 is the model that has a version to suit every possible demand, while still remaining in the small, elegant car sector. A five-speed gearbox is now fitted on all models.

The most famous French automobile factory owes its existence to the passion for mechanics demonstrated by Louis Renault from an early age. The son of a cloth merchant, by 1888, when he was eleven years old, Louis had already converted his room into a laboratory. The following year, he travelled unobserved on the tender of the Paris–Rouen steam locomotive in order to see for himself how it really worked. A year later, he had his first taste of speed on the road, when his father took him for a drive in his steam-powered car. After that memorable experience, Louis persuaded his father to buy him an old Panhard engine for which he devised various uses, although his efforts were increasingly directed towards the real passion of his life, the motor car. When he was twenty-one years old, after he had finished his military service, he bought a 3/4 HP De Dion-Bouton and hired some men with whom he worked day and night to convert and improve it. With a completely newly designed gearbox, the totally updated and transformed "quadricycle" made its first trip under the plane trees of Billancourt one evening in November 1898, reaching a speed of 50 km/h (31.1 mph). This may be considered the first Renault, signalling the birth of an industry which was to change the course of the French economy in the field of automobile production.

In the early twentieth century, the Renault workshops expanded in Billancourt around the house in which Louis had been born. Immediately after the First World War, in 1920, Renault built a bridge across the Seine to the Ile Séguin, where the headquarters of the Régie now stand. Formerly the site of a stadium and gardens, the island has now been totally taken over by the Renault car works. In the period between the two wars, French cars earned a reputation for their rationalized construction and design, so much so that both Renault and Citroën cars were taken as examples to Germany and other countries where the automobile industry was still in its infancy.

In 1938/39, just before the Second World War which was to upset Renault's production, 45,388 cars and 15,613 industrial vehicles came off the assembly lines of the Ile Séguin (in the same period, Citroën produced 61,460 and Peugeot 52,796 cars). The outbreak of the war seriously affected the factory's activities: production continued, but was limited to the manufacture of industrial vehicles. Louis Renault died in October 1944, the year of the liberation of Paris. His position as head of the company was taken over by Pierre Lefaucheux, until 11 February 1955 when he died in a tragic car accident while on his way to Strasburg to give a lecture to a group of Catholic students.

Lefaucheux and his successor Dreyfus both sat at the very same desk from which Louis Renault had given his orders. Similarly, those who had worked with him at all levels in the factory also kept their places during the reconstruction operations and afterwards. They were the same team who in 1939 had designed the Juvequatre, the car which should have more securely established Renault on the European market.

The Renault 3/4 came out in 1898, based on a De Dion-Bouton tricycle. It was driven by a single-cylinder air-cooled engine of 198 cc (3/4 hp), capable of 35 km/h (21.7 mph). In 1899, Louis Renault introduced his first real voiturette, the single-cylinder 237-cc 1.3/4-hp Type A. The car was capable of 45 km/h (28 mph) and was featured on Renault's first ever advertisement, which appeared in the magazine *Nature*.

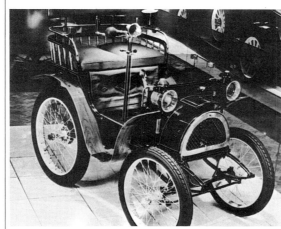

On 25 April 1901, Renault exhibited the single-cylinder 450-cc 4.5-hp cabriolet on their stand at the Paris Motor Show. The car weighed 500 kg (1102 lb), had a top speed of 40 km/h (25 mph) and was water-cooled with side radiators.

The first versions of the type G closely resembled the Type D of 1901. The single-cylinder 860-cc 6-hp engine was water-cooled with side radiators of twelve elements. Its top speed was 40 km/h (25 mph).

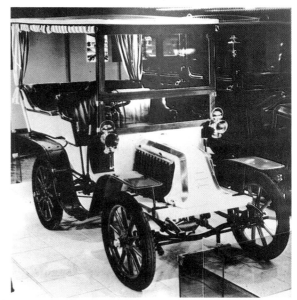

The two-cylinder 1720-cc 14-hp engine was the first to be produced entirely by Renault. This Type H of 1902 had a top speed of 65 km/h (40.4 mph) and weighed 800 kg (1765 lb). It was directly developed from the G.

◄ In the 1902 racing season, the Renault brothers dominated the scene: Marcel won the Paris–Vienna at a record average speed of 71 km/h (44.12 mph) with the first four-cylinder Type K, which had a Billancourt-built engine.

In 1903, the Type L had a single-cylinder 10-hp 940-cc water-cooled engine capable of 40 km/h (25 mph). A few special bodies were built for it, such as that pictured above.

Similar to the previous year's model, the two-cylinder 8-hp Type AG coupé of 1906 was mainly designed for taxi companies. Its chassis alone cost 5,700 f. at the 1905 Paris Motor Show.

The Type V-1 of 1907 was a four-cylinder 20-hp saloon which had an excellent reputation for sturdiness. Its many admirers included the son of the King of Siam.

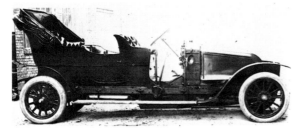

The 1908 Type X-1 had a four-cylinder 3050-cc 14-hp engine (bore × stroke = 90 × 120 mm/3.5 × 4.7 in). The chassis cost 13,000 f. and was normally fitted with an open four- or five-seater body.

The Type AX two-seater cabriolet built in 1910 had a two-cylinder 1060-cc 8-hp engine. The car was to cause a strike among the workers, who said they would not accept their work being timed with a stopwatch.

This closed coupé was built on the Type AG-1 mechanics in 1909. It had a two-cylinder 1205-cc engine with an output of 8 hp (80 × 120 mm/3.1 × 4.7 in) and a top speed of 55 km/h (34 mph). It cost 5,000 f.

The Type BX replaced the X-1 in 1910. It had a larger body and incorporated numerous improvements. Its engine was of four cylinders, 3050 cc and 14 hp; its length was 4.35 m (14.27 ft) and its weight 1550 kg (1.5 tons).

Also from 1910, the above saloon had the mechanics of the Type BY, a four-cylinder 4390-cc 20-hp engine, and came in two wheelbase lengths: 435 or 455 cm (14.27 or 15 ft). It weighed 1450 or 1650 kg (1.4 or 1.6 tons).

This 1912 shooting-brake had the mechanics of the Type CC with a four-cylinder 3560-cc 14-hp engine. The chassis alone cost 12,000 f. The car had a special body.

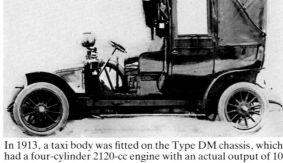

In 1913, a taxi body was fitted on the Type DM chassis, which had a four-cylinder 2120-cc engine with an actual output of 10 hp although rated at 11 hp. It was developed from the CQ series of 1912.

A cheap new car, the Type GS, was introduced in 1920, with an elegant body and the new spokeless wheels. The engine developed 10 hp. The photograph shows the closed version.

This coupé was developed from the 1914 Type EE and had a six-cylinder 5100-cc 22-hp engine (bore × stroke = 85 × 158 mm/3.3 × 6.2 in). The engine included a dynamo to recharge the batteries. ▶

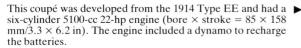

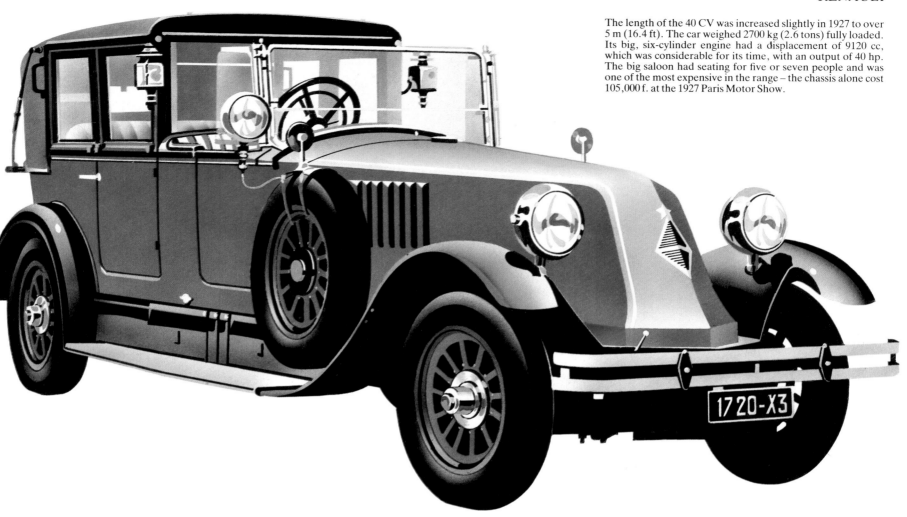

The length of the 40 CV was increased slightly in 1927 to over 5 m (16.4 ft). The car weighed 2700 kg (2.6 tons) fully loaded. Its big, six-cylinder engine had a displacement of 9120 cc, which was considerable for its time, with an output of 40 hp. The big saloon had seating for five or seven people and was one of the most expensive in the range – the chassis alone cost 105,000 f. at the 1927 Paris Motor Show.

This roadster had a Type GR body, that is, it was 20 cm (7.8 in) shorter than the FS of similar engine size. The 18 CV of 1920 had a four-cylinder 4535-cc engine and a top speed of 75 km/h (46.6 mph). It cost 33,000 f. on 1 September 1919.

This three-seater cabriolet was built on the Type IG chassis in 1921. It had a four-cylinder 2120-cc 10-hp engine and was available in both a left-hand and a right-hand drive version.

They were also the team who between 1942 and 1944 had secretly designed the strange prototype that in its final form was to become the 4 CV, the first car to be produced in vast numbers and raise the fortunes of the French state industry. When he was appointed acting director on 4 October 1944, Lefaucheux found himself with a factory that had been bombed twice by the British and once by the Americans, with 4,000 destroyed cars, 10,000 broken windows, and machinery which had been ruined by the raids and was in any case about twenty years old. Out of 38,000 employees in 1938/39, 14,000 still remained at Billancourt, and of these 8,000 were set straight on to the work of reconstruction. Meanwhile, efforts were made to finalize Renault's situation as a state company, and on 16 January 1945 the nationalization of the Usines Renault was officially published. The signatories were the President of the provisional government, Charles De Gaulle, Robert Lacoste, Pierre Mendès-France, Alexandre Parodi and René Pleven. The decree marked the birth of the Régie Nationale des Usines as a state company, which it remains

This three-seater closed coupé, developed from the 10 CV Type IG, had a four-cylinder 10-hp engine. Renault intended it to be as popular in France as Ford's Model T in America.

This 1923 roadster used the mechanics of the Type KZ. It had the normal four-cylinder 2120-cc 10-hp engine, but its all-round brakes were an innovation.

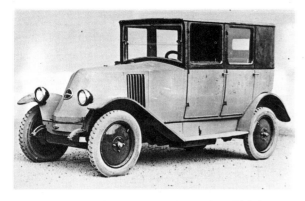

The Type NN, a four-cylinder 6-hp model which became extremely popular in the four-door, four-seater version shown above, came out in 1924. Its displacement was 950 cc and it cost 19,550 f. in December 1925.

The Type NN of 1927, shown here in the drop-head coupé version, was a 2 + 2 with the traditional mechanics of the Renault range: four cylinders, 950 cc, 6 hp, and 75 km/h (46.6 mph). It cost 27,000 f.

The Vivastella Type ACR 1 saloon was introduced in 1935 with a five- or seven-seater body and two wheelbase lengths. With its six-cylinder 4-liter 23-hp engine, it could reach 130 km/h (80.8 mph).

Closed bodies were becoming increasingly popular, as in the case of the 1925 Type MG (above), which had a six-cylinder 4767-cc 18/22-hp engine. The chassis alone cost 53,900 f. in the normal version and 56,900 f. for the longer one.

The Reinastella was a Type RM with an eight-cylinder 7125-cc 41-hp engine giving a top speed of 125 km/h (77.7 mph). It cost 14,000–17,000 f. The saloon version of 1932 (above) was capable of 145 km/h (90 mph) and was available as a five- or seven-seater.

The 1937 Juvequatre (Type AEB 2) was a completely new model and the first Renault to have independent front-wheel suspension. It had a four-cylinder 1003-cc engine, a top speed of 95 km/h (59 mph) and weighed 725 kg (0.71 ton).

In 1928, this Vivasix, a Type RA with a six-cylinder 3180-cc 15-hp engine, became widely popular. Notable for its new rear suspension, it is shown here in the four-seater saloon version.

The 1935 Celtaquatre Type ZR 2 had a four-cylinder 1463-cc engine capable of 100 km/h (62.14 mph). It was a two-door, four-seater saloon weighing 1300 kg (1.3 tons) fully loaded and 880 kg (0.9 ton) empty. It cost 16,500 f.

The 1937 Viva Grand Sport (Type ACX 3) had a six-cylinder 4085-cc engine, giving 130 km/h (80.8 mph). It weighed 2100 kg (2.1 tons) fully loaded. The four-door, six-seater saloon (above) cost 32,900 f.

to this day. Pierre Lefaucheux was appointed director-general of the company on 31 March.

The first vehicle of the post-war period (1,045 industrial vehicles had come off the assembly lines in August, before the liberation of Paris) was assembled on 10 October, scarcely six days after the arrival of Lefaucheux. A few days later, the rate of production increased to five units a day, and rose to thirty before Christmas. It was the early months of 1945, however, which marked the beginning of Renault's true recovery: Billancourt produced sixty vehicles a day on its assembly lines, a remarkable effort considering the problems posed to industries by the shortages of raw materials. The 4 CV was launched in the midst of disagreements between the management, the majority of whom were in favour of producing a higher class vehicle. Lefaucheux had drawn up a proposal for the production of 300 new 4s a day; until then the plant had shown a daily potential of only 250 units.

The idea of the 4 CV dated back to before the war, when Louis Renault was received by Hitler in Germany and saw the plans for the KDF (Kraft Durch Freude), the small car which a short time later was to become the Volkswagen (the "people's car"). The first prototype of the 4 CV had only two doors and the bonnet was so rounded that it bore a very close resemblance to the German VW. Its all-steel monocoque body was revolutionary for its time, and still ultra-modern when it went into regular production on 12 August 1947 with a four-cylinder 760-cc rear engine and rear-wheel drive.

Lefaucheux's secret weapon, which proved the wisdom of his decision, was the introduction of the first complex of automatic machines into the factory to speed up the assembly and so increase the rate of production. His reasoning was backed by the knowledge that the success of the flourishing American industry lay in the economical management of series production.

The outcome proved him right, despite the fact that, in April of the same year, the Régie had had to overcome its first strike. This did not prevent 35,000 lorries and 32,000 cars being produced in 1948; meanwhile the 4 CV was enjoying great market success and was winning many speed trials, often coming first in its class. As a parallel development, the company was extending to markets abroad and by 1949 these were accounting for 20 per cent of production.

In 1950, Renault had to face their first crisis as a result of overselling abroad. This in fact came about as a result of unprecedented interest from the USA, where the Régie was aiming to penetrate the market by supplying 1,000 cars a month. The United States ordered no fewer than 3,000 4s in only one month. With a total of approximately 50,000 employees, Renault increased their daily production rate from about 300 to 500 units, and their production capacity was fully booked up for months in advance. This situation led to the rapid formulation of a policy of decentralization, so that 4s were thereafter assembled in the most remote corners of the world, from Great Britain to Belgium, South Africa and even Australia. Meanwhile, in April 1950, Renault launched the Prairie and the Colorale (a name composed from *COLOniale* and *ruRALE*), which were designed primarily for commercial use, with front-mounted engines and rear-wheel drive. However, the fact that the Billancourt factory could not be extended (it was now in the very heart of Paris) presented a serious obstacle to the internal expansion of Renault. Lefaucheux ordered the construction of another plant, using the best materials available, at Flins, some 40 km (25 miles) from Paris. Safety had become a matter of prime concern to Renault ever since 1917, when a wall had collapsed in Billancourt killing 250 workers.

Meanwhile, Renault were becoming well established on a market which was clearly moving in an uphill direction, and in November 1950 the prototype of the Fregate was launched. Construction of this model was begun in Billancourt, but was then transferred to the new plant at Flins, where production progressed at a rate of fifty a day from March 1952. Throughout this period, the 4 was still winning races as a result of the daring and enthusiasm of the private drivers who entered them in competitions. A

racing division was therefore set up in Renault and a sports series of the 4 CV with a 1062-cc engine brought out.

After the death of Pierre Lefaucheux, who had no natural successor, the Régie found itself without a director. Pierre Dreyfus, a ministry official, was appointed to the position; he was already involved in the automobile industry in his capacity as technical advisor to the Ministry of Industry and as inspector-general of industrial production. It was during this period under Dreyfus that "project 109" was initiated. This led to the development of the Dauphine, successor to the 4, from which a great deal of experience had been gained. Launched in December 1956, the Dauphine (which owed its name to the fact that the 4 CV was considered the "queen," and therefore its successor was naturally a "dauphine" or princess) was immediately exported to the United States, where the manufacturers hoped it would win a place on the market as successful as that held by the 4. On 8 March, the Dauphine was presented to the press and the public at the Geneva Motor Show, while in the USA it was offered at a market price of $1,600, $400 dollars less than the cheapest car available at the time.

Another project was launched on 5 September 1956, which resulted in a new speed record for a turbine vehicle: 309 km/h (192 mph) set in the

USA on the bed of the salt lake at Bonneville by the 270-hp Renault "Shooting Star." By 1957, over 4,000 Americans had bought 4 CVs and over 28,000 Dauphines, which were being produced at a second line in Flins and also at a plant in England. The French balance of payments deficit led to the government's making an agreement with the Régie, allowing them to export at least two-thirds of the increase in production, with the result that Renault exported nine out of every ten of the 50,000 surplus. With a daily production rate of a thousand units, the one hundred thousandth Dauphine was made less than a year from its first appearance on the assembly line.

One of Dreyfus's trips to the USA to evaluate Renault's market potential resulted in the development of a new car, the Floride, directly derived from the mechanics of the Dauphine and also available in a cabriolet version. The name of the Floride was later changed in the USA to the Caravelle. At the end of 1958, Renault celebrated production of their millionth 4 CV and their five hundred thousandth Dauphine, a large percentage of which had been sold in the USA. Meanwhile, in France, a special limited new series of the Dauphine was being designed with a more sporty line by Amédée Gordini, who was to leave his mark on small sporty Renaults for a long while after. In Dieppe, production began on the RDL, later known as the Alpine, which became

This was the most famous Renault of the early post-war years. Designed in secret during the war, the prototype came out in 1946. The series was launched on 12 August 1947, all the cars painted desert-sand yellow, using a bulk supply of paint from Rommel's Afrika Korps, because there was still no other paint available at the time. In the following year, some black 4 CVs were also built. The 4 CV had a four-cylinder 760-cc 4-hp engine and remained in production until the arrival of the R3/R4.

The Colorale series made its début in May 1950 with a 2383-cc 46-hp engine. The Colorale Savane was also available as a shooting-brake (above).

The Caravelle replaced the Floride from the spring of 1963. It had a 956-cc 48-hp engine and the four-speed gearbox was up to date, although it had no synchromesh on first gear.

The R4L had the same engine as the R3 and 4, which also came out in 1962, but differed from them in having a third side window and a chrome finish. It had a four-door body and a rear hatchback for ease of loading.

The rear-engine R8 saloon of 1964 had a four-cylinder 956-cc 48-hp engine. It was given a new dashboard in the same year it appeared. An R8 Major was also available, with an 1100-cc engine.

The 1970 R10 Major saw the introduction of a more powerful engine, increased from 1108 to 1289 cc, with an output of 52 hp. It was no different in style from the previous model, with the exception of the nameplate on the back.

With a four-cylinder 1565-cc engine, the new R16 of 1971 was slightly more powerful than previous versions and had an optional automatic gearbox. It remained in production for sixteen years.

The 15 TL was brought out in 1972, using the R12's 1289-cc 68-hp engine (8 hp more because of its twin-body carburettor). It cost 15,500 f.

The R17 TS of 1972 was a more powerful version of the R15, with a 1565-cc engine (the same as on the R16) uprated to 120 hp. Because seventeen is an unlucky number in Italy, the R17 was launched on the Italian market as the 177.

The popular 1108-cc 47-hp engine was used again on the R6 TL, a five-door model that was very roomy for its category. The front end and roof-line of this 1974 model were modified.

The 1974 R12 TR combined the design of the TL with the mechanics of the TS. It had a 1289-cc 60-hp engine and a three-speed automatic gearbox.

The R20 TL, brought out in 1976, had a 1647-cc 90-hp front-mounted engine, a two-box body and excellent road-holding.

one of the company's competition cars.

In October 1958, Renault made an agreement with Alfa Romeo to assemble the Dauphine in Italy and to sell the car on the Italian market under the name Dauphine-Alfa Romeo.

Expansion of the world markets, however, remained one of Dreyfus's main concerns, and agreements were therefore made for the construction of plants abroad. Sales agreements using existing local networks were made in Latin America (Brazil and Argentina), Algeria and in India, where Renault was chosen to build the "people's car." However, with the outbreak of the Indo-Pakistani conflict, the project was abandoned.

By the end of 1959, Renault was estimated to be the sixth largest automobile manufacturer in the world, but at the beginning of 1960 the first signs of alarm were felt on the American market, where sales of the Dauphine dropped by 33 per cent in comparison with the previous year. It was a period of stagnation on the US home market, and the French product also suffered, faced with the problem of adjustment to the specific

The R30 TX, introduced at the 1978 Paris Motor Show, had a 2663-cc 142-hp V6 engine with K-Jetronic Bosch fuel-injection. As well as differing from the R20 in its engine, it also had a better finish.

The R14 GTL of 1979 was distinguished by its ultramodern body design. It had a 1218-cc 57-hp engine, a four-speed gearbox and front-wheel drive. The R14 was also available in a more powerful version, the TS, which developed 69 hp.

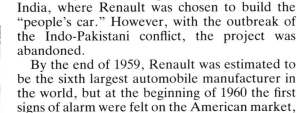
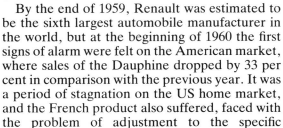

The new 25, brought out in 1984, has taken over from the previous "flagship", the 30 TX, As well as a 2664-cc 144-hp electronically injected engine, the 25, like the 30, is also available with four cylinders of 2000 cc, developing 103 hp, or with a capacity of 2200 cc. A 2068-cc diesel engine, which comes in a naturally aspirated 64-hp and a turbocharged 85-hp version is also available. The body design of the 25 is unquestionably one of Renault's most successful in the last decade. The interior design, in particular, is perhaps unique in the amount of room allowed for the rear seats.

requirements of the American motorist.

In France, meantime, preparations were under way on projects 112 and 113, the future R4 and R8. An error was then made on project 114, which was to have been a large, six-cylinder vehicle, designed to replace the Fregate. Once the accounts had been done, however, it emerged that the price of the car ought to have been 25 per cent higher than that of the Fregate. The swift and decisive personal intervention of Dreyfus established the parameters of the new car, which was to have four cylinders and an innovative line, and be practical and functional, as well as competitive in price. The result was the R16,

product of project 115; it remained in production for sixteen years and had features that are still retained today. While the R8 and the 410 derived from it still had the "all-rear" format, the R4 and the R16 were of the "all-forward" type, heralding a new generation of Renault cars. As a parallel development to car production, Renault had also begun to manufacture the Estafette: this was a commercial vehicle for door-to-door deliveries which was replaced by the Trafic only at the beginning of the 1980s. In early 1966, a partnership agreement was made between Renault and Peugeot in which the two companies had tried for many years to involve Citroën. In

1969, the R12 appeared and was immediately brought out in a TS version. This was followed shortly afterwards by the 15 and 17 coupés. In 1972, the R5 was launched, a front-ranking car which raised the fortunes of the Régie on the European markets.

The rest are all current: the R14, R20/30, R18, R9, R11, R25 and the Fuego coupé. These cars have raised Renault's status in the markets of many countries; diesel versions have been introduced; and Formula One experience has led to the fitting of turbochargers on both diesel and petrol engines. In 1980, the company acquired 46.4 per cent shares in American Motors.

The TX version of the R5 came out in 1982 with a 1300-cc twin-carburettor engine. The TX is distinguished by its excellent finish, which includes electric windows.

The "American" version of the 18, designed to appeal to the US market, was brought out through Renault's associate company, AMC. It has a 1647-cc 96-hp engine.

The Fuego's 1565-cc engine develops up to 132 hp with the aid of a turbocharger. This 1983 version is also available with 1647-cc petrol and 2068-cc (88-hp) turbodiesel engines.

The R9 has a new 1595-cc 55-hp diesel engine, a four-speed gearbox and a three-box body. The R9 represents Renault's entry into the small diesel car market.

The application of the 1596-cc engine to the R11 (1984) has opened up the possibilities of a small-engine diesel with a two-box body. It is available in three- and five-door versions.

The Espace is the estate car of the 1990s, built with spaciousness in mind. An extremely versatile car, it has a 2-liter petrol engine, seven seats and generous loading space.

ROLLS-ROYCE

BENTLEY

It is certainly unique in the history of the motor car that a meeting between two gentlemen in Manchester in May 1904 created a marque which became the symbol for excellence all around the world: the name of these two gentlemen – Charles Rolls and Henry Royce.

For eighty years now, Rolls-Royce have managed to maintain a reputation which was based on the simple policy of Henry Royce: "take an existing part and make it better." This perfectionism, which applies from the selection of first class materials right through to final quality control, resulted in the production of 95,000 motor cars to date, and about 60 per cent of these vehicles are still on the road.

Rolls-Royce have never been avant-garde. The solid company philosophy, however, to strive for the highest levels of mechanical reliability, safety, longevity and unrivalled comfort, have proved right. The Rolls-Royce and Bentley motor cars (Bentley Motors was acquired by Rolls-Royce in 1931), today produced at a rate of around 2,200 units per annum, have become legends – legends of traditional, classical elegance much appreciated in the contemporary world of hectic developments and rapid changes.

ROLLS-ROYCE

The new Phantom II, in production between 1929 and 1935, had an engine of six-cylinders arranged in two blocks of three, with an aluminium head. The four-speed gearbox was coupled to the engine. After 1933, there was synchromesh on third and fourth and after 1935 also on second.

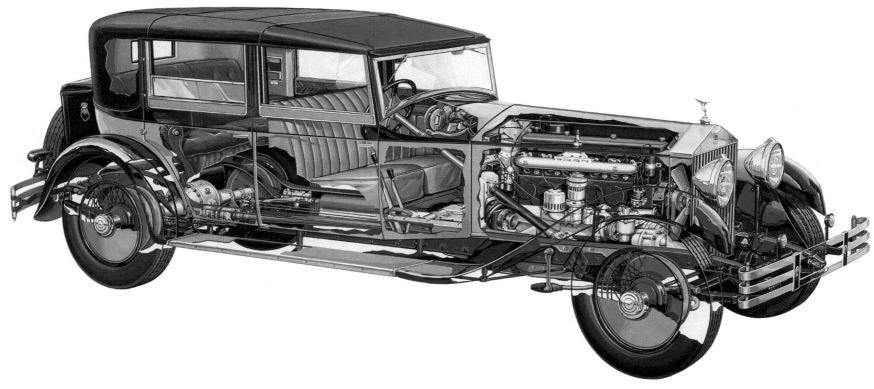

In 1904, only three 12 HPs were built. They had engines of 1800 cc.

The 10 HP of 1904 to 1906 had a two- or four-door body, but still used the same 1800-cc engine.

This 15 HP came out in 1905 with a three-cylinder 3-liter engine, a three-speed gearbox with reverse and direct third.

A limousine body was fitted on the 30 HP of 1905/1906. It had a 6-liter engine of six cylinders arranged in three groups of two, and a four-speed gearbox with reverse and direct third.

With C. S. Rolls driving, the 1905/1906 20 HP won the 1906 Tourist Trophy at an average speed of 63.25 km/h (39.30 mph). The four-cylinder engine had a displacement of 4000 cc.

The Silver Ghost of 1907 was the car which earned the company its reputation as a manufacturer of high-class cars. It was in production until 1925, by which time 6,173 had been built.

The slogan used since 1907 for the launch of the Silver Ghost – "the best car in the world" – still fits the image of the Rolls-Royce company today.

From the very start, the prime objective of Frederick Henry Royce and Charles Stewart Rolls was to combine their ambition and dedication with the knowledge and technology of the early twentieth century to create the best possible car. Henry Royce was producing electric cranes and dynamos in Manchester through his company, Royce Ltd., and was already forty years old when he bought a foreign, two-cylinder Décauville in 1904.

Although it was not one of the worst cars of its day, the French vehicle did not fully satisfy him, so Royce, who also wanted to diversify production in his electrical goods factory, built three two-cylinder, 10-hp cars. There was nothing revolutionary about these cars, but they were built with a high degree of precision and were extremely sturdy, in line with the high standards of quality which Royce had learnt to appreciate during his apprenticeship with the Great Northern Railway.

The first Royce cars were ready on 1 April 1904 and were solid, silent, vibration-free – in so far as a two-cylinder of that time could be – and also flexible. One of their most important features was that the engine could be kept idling and then taken up to 1000 rpm in a simple manner, at a time when most other cars required considerable

adjustment to the carburettor, the air intake and the ignition to obtain the slightest variation in engine speed.

Royce had effectively succeeded in building a car that was far superior to his Décauville. Word of his success soon spread and reached Charles Rolls, the British importer of Panhards, who was greatly impressed by his ideas and determination, and was keen to meet the new builder. Over lunch one day, they discussed plans to build a new car, the Rolls-Royce, which would lay down new standards of excellence.

Obviously, therefore, the Rolls-Royce cars were never to have "only" two cylinders, and the first cars were built with three (only six of these were made) and four-cylinder engines.

The new luxury cars were an immediate success, and their reputation was heightened by their race wins, the first of which was the triumph of the light four-cylinder 20-hp in the 1906 Tourist Trophy. This victory was followed by a new record on the Monte Carlo–London run and by wins in the USA, including the Silver Trophy in Empire City and the new record for cars up to 60 hp at Ormond Beach, Florida. These successes were all achieved with the cars developed from the original Royce prototype, of which fewer than a hundred were built between 1904 and 1907.

The first true Rolls-Royce, the 40/50 HP, which only later became known as the Silver

Ghost, was brought out at the Paris Motor Show of 1906, already featuring the distinctive doric arch top on the radiator – that Greek "temple" which is still retained in a stylized form today. Its six-cylinder engine had a displacement of almost 7 liters and had side valves and double ignition. It developed 48 hp and gave a top speed of 105 km/h (65.2 mph).

The most outstanding and unusual feature of the car was the full-pressure lubrication system, while the chassis – the bodies were individually produced by a number of coachbuilders – cost £985. Even in those early days, the engines could do over 30,000 km (18,750 miles) before needing a service.

In 1907, the company moved from Manchester to Derby, and shortly afterwards a service was set up to provide technical inspection at the customer's own home; a Rolls-Royce driving school was also opened.

From 1908 onwards, the company followed a single-model policy and Rolls had meanwhile branched out into the aeronautics industry. In fact, it was in a flying accident in 1910 that Rolls was killed, in a Wright biplane which fell from a height of only 7 m (23 ft).

In 1911, the "Spirit of Ecstasy" appeared for the first time on the radiator of the Silver Ghost. The famous winged figure was modelled by Charles Sykes at the suggestion of the young Lord Montagu of Beaulieu.

In 1925, the Phantom I took over from the Silver Ghost. It had a six-cylinder 7668-cc overhead-camshaft engine, and 2,212 were built. In 1929, it was replaced by the Phantom II (right), which had a new chassis, a six-cylinder engine to which was coupled a four-speed gearbox, a dry single-plate clutch and semi-elliptic leaf-spring suspension both front and rear. In all, 1,767 were built.

The 20/25 HP of 1929 had a six-cylinder monobloc overhead-valve engine. In 1932, it was fitted with a four-speed, fully synchromesh gearbox. By 1936, when it ceased production, 3,827 had been built.

In 1936, the 25/30 HP came out, with its six-cylinder engine increased to 4257 cc. The four-speed gearbox had synchromesh on third and fourth.

Brought out in 1938, the Silver Wraith was still in production after the war with the same six-cylinder 4257-cc engine (increased in 1955 to 4887 cc). The front brakes were hydraulic, and an automatic gearbox was available after 1952. Left: the 1938 saloon. Right: the 1955 Touring Limousine.

The 1935 London Motor Show saw the introduction of the Phantom III, a new twelve-cylinder 7340-cc model. The transmission consisted of a four-speed synchromesh gearbox (except for first and reverse) and it had independent coil-spring front suspension.

In production between 1950 and 1956, this Phantom IV limousine had a Park Ward body. Only sixteen were built, for the Royal Family and heads of state. It had a straight-eight 5675-cc engine.

Various versions of the Silver Cloud I were in production between 1955 and 1959. It had a four-speed automatic gearbox coupled to a six-cylinder 4887-cc engine. In 1959, it was replaced by the Silver Cloud II (below), which had an eight-cylinder 6230-cc engine. The brakes were servo-assisted.

Between 1949 and 1955, 760 Silver Dawns in nine different series were built. They were equipped with six-cylinder 4257-cc engines whose capacity was later increased to 4566 cc.

The Phantom VI of 1968 was the most prestigious of the Rolls-Royce range. It had a 6750-cc V8 engine and all-round drum brakes.

Despite the fact that other companies had been using the electric starter motor since 1914, because of the company's cautious attitude towards accepting innovations they were not fitted on Rolls-Royce cars until 1919.

More than 6,000 Silver Ghosts were built, with many different types of body, up to 1925 and it was even used as an armoured car in the First World War. During the war, Rolls-Royce increased production of aircraft engines, giving rise to the creation of an aeronautical division.

The legendary Silver Ghost was followed by the various Phantoms (I, II, III), the Twenty (which was the cheapest in the range), the 20/25, 25/30 and the Wraith – the last Rolls brought out before the outbreak of the Second World War.

After the death of Henry Royce in 1933, the two Rs enamelled on the radiator were changed from red to black. By this time, Rolls-Royce had already become a legend – a legend which still lives today, fuelled by the detachment of a company which reveals no details of its own

engines but simply describes them as "sufficient," and which wants its cars to be so silent that you can hear the clock tick at 100 km/h (62.14 mph).

Legend apart, however, Rolls-Royce and Bentley (another glorious marque which was taken over in 1931 by Rolls-Royce) still produce cars which may have been equalled or even bettered, technologically speaking, by the products of other companies, but which, with regard to class, style, quality of materials and price, are most certainly unrivalled.

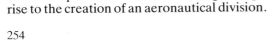

Brought out in 1965, the Silver Shadow had a new all-round disc brake system. The 6.2-liter V8 engine was increased to 6.7 liters in 1970 on the Silver Shadow II, (right).

The Camargue coupé was designed by Pininfarina. It has a 6750-cc V8 engine, an automatic General Motors Turbo-Hydramatic gearbox, and independent suspension.

The four-door Silver Wraith II saloon was launched at the 1977 Geneva Motor Show. It has a 6.75-liter V8 engine with a unitary body.

The 1980 Silver Spirit was given a new aerodynamic line and a roomier interior, and the glass area was increased by 30 per cent. The engine is the usual 6.75-liter V8, with an automatic gearbox and air-conditioning as standard.

Distinguished by certain modifications to the interior, the Silver Spur has the same technical features as the Silver Spirit, but is 10 cm (3.9 in) longer.

This Bentley was called the Mulsanne after a famous bend on the Le Mans La Sarthe circuit. It has the same mechanics as the Silver Spirit series and is recognizable by its classic Bentley radiator, with the famous winged B. The 1982 Turbo (below) is a 6.75-liter turbocharged V8 with a top speed of 220 km/h (136.7 mph).

The Corniche is the coupé and cabriolet version of the Silver Shadow. The body is produced by Park Ward-Mulliner. This élite two-door, four-seater cabriolet was brought out in 1971 with a unitary body, a Turbo-Hydramatic automatic gearbox, independent suspension front and rear, all-round dual circuit disc brakes and a top speed of 190 km/h (118.1 mph).

▼

SAAB

The first Saab was made in Sweden in 1949 by two aeronautical engineers who wanted to build a particularly aerodynamic car. The drag coefficient of this first Saab has not been matched since: the new 9000 has a coefficient of almost 0.35, whereas its predecessor had 0.32.

In a world economy which sees companies formed into holdings as safe, Saab is in an ideal position. It produces just 120,000 cars a year and owes its financial security to Scania (a major manufacturer producing industrial vehicles) and to the Aerospace Division which designs and builds aircraft for the defence of Swedish territory. An important agreement was recently made with the American Fairchild company for the production of a twin-engined turboprop.

Saab also has a strong sporting tradition, especially in rallies, in which it has enjoyed periods of great success, particularly in races through snow and ice such as the Monte Carlo Rally and the Thousand Lakes.

The first series-produced Saab, the 92, was brought out in 1949. It had a 764-cc two-stroke engine.

The Saab sports car range went under the name "Sonett." The first model (two cylinders, 750 cc) appeared in 1956, followed in 1966 by the Sonett II (above), with a three-cylinder 846-cc 60-hp engine and a synthetic body.

The company's designs changed in 1968 with the new 99 – a two-door saloon with a four-cylinder 1700-cc Triumph engine. The 1975 99 EMS (below) had a 2000-cc Saab engine with fuel injection, developing 110 hp DIN.

The 93 (three cylinders, 748 cc) came out in 1955, following the style of the 92. Over the years, various other versions were produced.

The 95 was simply a family version of the 93. Brought out in 1955, it was a five- or seven-seater with a slightly increased engine power: three cylinders, 843 cc.

Outwardly very similar to the previous models, the 96 of 1960 had a three-cylinder 843-cc engine with an output of 14 hp and a top speed of 120 km/h (74.5 mph). It was also built in a GT and a sports version.

In 1984, Saab updated its range again with the 9000 Turbo 16, ▶ which has a four-cylinder 1985-cc 175-hp engine. The body was designed by Giugiaro.

Available as a three- or five-door model, the 900 came out in 1978 and was an immediate success. It was built in GL, GLE and turbo versions, with 2-liter engines. Above: the 1980 Turbo.

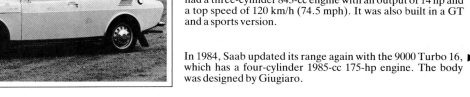

TOYOTA

TOYOTA

The history of this Japanese giant only began in 1935, but by 1971 Toyota was already the third largest world producer of cars and industrial vehicles after American Ford and General Motors. Breaking away from typical trends in the Japanese market, Toyota has concentrated on producing classic cars, and has shown less interest in avant-garde design. Toyota cars have very few electronically operated gadgets, and the production and planning philosophy behind them is more in line with that of the West, which has resulted in their greater popularity than other Japanese cars on world markets. The company had its inception in the textile industry, the Toyota Automatic Loom Works becoming the Toyota Motor Company in 1935 to take advantage of the economic situation, the most favourable since the birth of the automobile industry, to extend its field of operation to the motor car. Having no planning programme of its own, Toyota looked to the American industry for inspiration, a choice which was determined not only by the quality of American products, but also by the growing demand for Japanese cars on the American market. The Toyota Al was inspired by the Chrysler Airflow saloon, considered to be one of the most modern and most successful models of its day. The AA was developed from it in the following year, 1936, with a straight-six 3.4-liter engine, overhead valves and an output of 62 hp. The rounded lines of the car were classic and overall it was quite a successful model. A few months later, the AB roadster was also brought out, followed three years later by the AE, which was launched on to the market with a smaller body and a reduced engine displacement of 2258 cc. Unlike the Western industry, Toyota did not stop producing civilian vehicles during the war, but continued with a vehicle project alongside massive production of war material. The BA was not American-inspired and was not put on the market until 1943, although it had first been produced in 1940, based on the PV 60, one of Volvo's most successful models.

The Japanese have followed a tradition of

This Tercel was brought out as an estate car of advanced design, its carrying capacity increased as a result of its height. It has front-wheel drive, but can also engage the drive on the rear wheels. It has a 1452-cc 83-hp engine.

Toyota's first model, the A1, came out in 1935. A 3400-cc 62-hp saloon capable of carrying five passengers at 100 km/h (62.14 mph), it was in fact a prototype, of which only three were built.

From its introduction in 1936, 1,404 AAs were built, derived directly from the A1 prototype. The same six-cylinder 3.4-liter 62-hp overhead-valve engine was used. It remained in production until 1943.

The second Toyota model was this AB Phaeton (also brought out in 1936 and developed from the AA), of which 353 were built before it was taken out of production in 1942.

In 1939, production began on the Toyota AE. It was smaller than the AA and had a four-cylinder 2258-cc 48-hp engine with a top speed of 100 km/h (62.14 mph). Between 1941 and 1943, 76 were built.

The 1940 BA had the familiar 2.3-liter 48-hp engine with a top speed of 100 km/h (62.14 mph). One of its characteristic features was an extensive use of wood, because all steel was needed for war materials.

A new and more powerful version of the 3.4-liter engine (75 hp) was fitted on the 1943 AC, which could reach over 100 km/h (62.14 mph), and of which 115 were built.

The Toyota luxury prototype came out in 1944. The B limousine could carry seven people and was capable of 120 km/h (74.6 mph) with the "normal" 3.4-liter engine, which had been uprated to 85 hp.

The SA was the first Toyota of the post-war period, and 215 were built before it ceased production in 1952. It had a four-cylinder 1-liter 27-hp engine with a top speed of 87 km/h (54 mph).

The SD, designed as a taxi, had a 995-cc 27-hp engine and a top speed of 77 km/h (47.8 mph). It was in production from 1949 to 1951, during which time other versions were built.

The SF was in production for two years (from 1951) and 3,653 were built. It was a five-seater fitted with a four-cylinder 1-liter engine with a top speed of 79 km/h (49 mph).

A new four-cylinder 1453-cc 48-hp engine was used on the ▶ five-seater RH Super introduced in 1953. It was replaced in 1955 by the Crown RS, after 5,845 had been built.

The first real all-Japanese car was this 1955 RS Crown, available with four doors and a 1.5-liter 58-hp engine, with a top speed of 100 km/h (62.14 mph). Many versions were produced.

almost invariably basing any industrially produced object on an existing model, but with the universally acknowledged skill of being able to make the copy better than the original. The BA copied the lines of the Volvo, but its engine had updated mechanics, with a four-cylinder 48-hp version.

Post-war production began in 1947 with the introduction of the SA, the first of the S series. Various S models were brought out from 1947 to

1951, finishing with the SF, which had a reduced engine capacity and a smaller, squarer body, inspired this time by the Fiat 1400. Expansion of the market, however, and the relative production peaks which followed, were most noticeably felt in 1955, with the introduction of the R series, in particular the RS Crown, a saloon measuring almost 3 m (13.1 ft) in length, with a four-cylinder, 1.5-liter engine. Two years later appeared the Corona, a small, 1000-cc saloon

aimed at the more popular end of the market.

Universal acceptance of the range was confirmed in the early 1960s, when Toyota began to penetrate foreign markets, exporting large numbers of cars, especially to the USA. The range consisted of ten versions of four basic models: the Publica 700-cc four-cylinder, designed to cover 20 km on one liter of petrol (56.5 mph); the 986-cc Corona four-door, four- or five-seater; the 1500-cc Tiara RT 20 (also

This car was built for family use or as a taxi. The Corona ST 10 four-door saloon of 1957 had a four-cylinder 1-liter 33-hp engine, weighed 960 kg (2116.4 lb), and was 3.91 m (12.8 ft) long and 1.47 m (4.8 ft) wide.

In 1960 appeared the second generation of the Corona, with a four-cylinder engine of 986 cc, increased to 1500 cc in 1961. The photograph shows the 1961 four-door saloon.

The 1000 of 1961 (known on the home market as the Publica) had a two-cylinder air-cooled engine of 700 cc, increased to 1000 cc on the export model. It had a top speed of 155 km/h (96.3 mph).

The second series of the Crown was brought out in October 1962. Completely redesigned, it was available as a saloon or an estate with a 1900-cc 90-hp engine.

The Sport 800 of 1964 was based on the mechanics of the Publica. It had a two-cylinder 790-cc 46-hp engine and a top speed of 155 km/h (96.3 mph), with a fuel consumption of 31 km/1 liter (87.6 mpg).

The 2000 GT first appeared as a prototype in 1965 and was brought into production two years later, after which 351 were built. It had a six-cylinder 1988-cc 150-hp engine and a top speed of 220 km/h (136.7 mph).

The Corolla two-door saloon was brought out in November 1966 with a four-cylinder 1.1-liter 60-hp engine and top speed of 160 km/h (100 mph). A four-door version and an estate car were also available.

The third generation of the Crown appeared in 1967. It had a six-cylinder 1988-cc 105-hp engine with overhead camshaft (a four-cylinder model was also available in Japan) and came both as a saloon and an estate car.

The 1968 Sprinter was the sports model of the Corolla. The 1077-cc engine developed 73 hp with a top speed of 160 km/h (100 mph). It had a two-door body and from September 1969 was fitted with a 1200-cc engine.

The 1968 Cressida was a four-door saloon which weighed 990 kg (2182.6 lb) and had a 1591-cc 100-hp engine. It was also available as a two-door hardtop and an estate car.

The third generation of the 1000 (April 1969), this two-door saloon had a four-cylinder 933-cc air-cooled engine developing 58 hp at 6000 rpm. Its capacity was increased in September to 1200 cc.

The Carina saloon was introduced into the range between the Corona and the Corolla in December 1970. Above: the two-door 1600 De Luxe saloon with a four-cylinder 1588-cc 100-hp engine.

available as an estate); and the Crown six-seater saloon with a 1900-cc engine and an output of 80–95 hp, depending on the compression ratio. All these models were built to a classic design, with a front-mounted engine and rear-wheel drive, a unitary body, independent front wheels with a rigid back axle and drum brakes. The Publica, which had an air-cooling system instead of the water cooling used on the rest of the range, was the only exception.

In about the mid-1960s, Toyota brought out a new engine for the Crown with six cylinders, an overhead camshaft, an output of 105 hp and a displacement of two liters. As well as this, it also brought out a 2600-cc V8 show car called the Century.

The Tiara then went out of production and was replaced by the new Crown, driven by a 1500- or 1600-cc engine. Two new sports models arrived in the early 1970s, based on the saloon mechanics: a

790-cc roadster and a 2-liter coupé with a straight-six engine. In fact, important technical innovations were made on this engine, which had a twin overhead camshaft instead of a single version; the output also increased, from 105 to 150 hp, giving the car a top speed of 200 km/h (124.2 mph). In 1970, Toyota's annual production exceeded a million and a half units – over half of which were for export – in seventeen different versions. The company's commercial success

In April 1973, the Starlet made its début as part of the 1000 range. It was a 1166-cc coupé of 74 hp. A four-door saloon version was brought out in October of the same year.

The 1977 Chaser was a coupé version of the Cressida. The Hardtop SGS (above) had a six-cylinder 1988-cc 125-hp engine, but was also available with four cylinders of 1800 or 2000 cc.

The Corsa came out at the same time as the Tercel and also had front-wheel drive. The 1500 GSL (above) had a 1452-cc 83-hp engine. A 1300-cc version of both the Corsa and the Tercel was introduced on the home market.

The second generation of the Starlet (February 1978) was a two-box, three- or five-door model with a 1290-cc 72-hp engine. In 1980, the car was restyled and rectangular headlights were fitted.

The 1978 Tercel was the first of the Toyota front-wheel drive cars. It had a completely new four-cylinder 1452-cc 83-hp engine. Available in two-, three- and four-door versions.

The Celica was brought out in late 1970. The 2000 GT Liftback of 1973 (above) had a four-cylinder 1968-cc engine with twin overhead camshafts and an output of 145 hp.

The Celica Supra 2800G (also available with a six-cylinder two-liter engine) was restyled in April 1978. It had a 2759-cc 145-hp engine coupled to a gearbox equipped with overdrive.

The Camry version of the Celica was available only as a sedan. It came out in 1980 with a four-cylinder 1600- or 1800-cc engine. A new two-liter engine was added in August 1980. The 1800 XT (above) had a 1770-cc 95-hp engine.

The fourth generation of the Cressida had engines of four cylinders and 1800 or 2000 cc, and six cylinders of 2759 cc (above) or two liters, and developed 145 hp. It was available in a saloon or a four-door hardtop version.

The third generation of the Carina was available with five engines from 1500 to 2000 cc. Above: the 1832-cc 1800 EFI, developing 100 hp at 5400 rpm. This version came out in 1981.

The third generation of the Cressida came out in 1976. It was lighter and more compact, with a six-cylinder 2600-cc or a four-cylinder 2000-cc engine. Above: the larger version, with a 2563-cc 135-hp engine.

The Land Cruiser was already in production in 1951. It was an off-road vehicle with a 3168-cc 93-hp diesel engine. Also available with a 4200-cc petrol engine and three wheelbase lengths: 2.3, 2.4 and 3 m (7.5, 7.8 and 9.8 ft).

The estate version of the Land Cruiser came out in 1980. It had a 3431-cc 98-hp diesel engine, but was later given six cylinders of 4000 cc. It was also available outside Japan with a petrol engine (4200 cc).

The 1981 2800 GT Soarer is a high-performance model with a six-cylinder 2759-cc engine developing 170 hp at 5600 rpm. A further three engines, one a turbo, were also available.

Brought out in 1983, the seventh generation of the Corona was a four-door saloon available with four different engines – one of 1500 cc, two of 1800 cc and a 2000-cc diesel. Above: the 1800 EX Saloon AD, with a 1832-cc 115-hp engine.

rocketed in 1971 when the number of versions available increased to forty-five, for such a wide range meant that Toyota was able to suit all the car-importing markets, who were able to import the vehicles best suited to the specific demands of their countries. This remarkable increase in the number of car versions available was the result of the introduction of the Sprinter, the Carina and the Celica.

The off-road version, the Land Cruiser, deserves a particular mention. It has been in production since 1951, but came out in a diesel version in 1974. The success of this particular vehicle on all the world markets is proof of the quality of the Toyota product. The Land Cruiser has been successfully used for both civilian purposes and military.

Toyota's world range included three versions of the Publica with 800-, 1000- and 1200-cc engines; nine Corollas with 1200- and 1400-cc

engines, and saloon or coupé bodies; four Sprinters, also with the 1200- and 1400-cc engines; three Carinas and four Corollas with the same 1400- and 1600-cc engines; seventeen Coronas ranging from 1500 to 1900 cc; four Crowns, all with 2-liter engines but in a choice of four or six cylinders; and one Century with a 4-liter V8 engine. Naturally, this range was further extended by the off-road versions and industrial vehicles. Since taking over the Hino factory in 1966, Toyota has also been producing numerous other models, which are less well known on European markets. The Hino factory's financial difficulties were resolved when it was taken over by Toyota, to which it passed on all its technology. Hino had specialized in the production of all types of industrial vehicles, including tractors for exceptional loads and four-wheel drive vehicles suitable for off-road uses and work in quarries and on building sites. The company

had also produced a small number of cars, which remained in production for a short while after Toyota's takeover.

Over the years, Toyota has greatly altered the design of its own cars, with the result that they are now perfectly suited to the particular requirements of each market throughout the world. Sales suffer only in those countries where quota restrictions are in force to protect the market by limiting the number of imported cars. Conversely, sales are high on the markets of other non-manufacturing countries, such as Switzerland.

Recently, Toyota has introduced the Tercel, a 1450-cc front-wheel drive estate which can engage four-wheel drive by bringing in the drive to the rear axle. This was brought out to satisfy the demand for a car which can engage four-wheel drive both on normal roads and in snow or mud.

The five-door Vista had an 1800-cc engine developing 100 hp at 5400 rpm. Available in thirteen different body versions and finishes, in up to three boxes. Above: the 2000 cc.

The Sprinter Carib (as the Tercel was known on the home market) came out in 1982. It is a 4 × 4 with a four-cylinder in-line 1.5-liter engine and top speed of 160 km/h (100 mph).

The 1982 new Century had a 3994-cc V8 engine developing 190 hp. This high output was needed because the saloon was over 5 m (16.4 ft) long and weighed 1780 kg (1.75 tons).

VOLKSWAGEN

The automobile will be a hundred years old in 1986, and in the same year Volkswagen will celebrate its fiftieth anniversary. This car was the brainchild of Professor Porsche and his associates in the 1930s, but it was not until the end of the Second World War that he managed to overcome all the obstacles.

For many Germans, as for over a hundred and fifty other nations throughout the world, the Volkswagen was to become the symbol of mobility, independence and safety.

Its legendary economy, toughness and technical reliability were the reasons for its success, and over twenty-one million cars have been produced at the factory. The Volkswagen became synonymous with the post-war German economic boom, not only because of its technical features, but also because it represented the first economical "people's car."

Its economy, reliability and technical refinement are now mirrored in the new generation of Volkswagens which replaced the legendary Beetle in the early 1970s. Future technical progress on a world-wide scale now hinges on the Golf, Passat, Polo and Scirocco models.

CARL H. HAHN   Chairman of the Board, Volkswagen Werke AG

In the course of nearly forty years in production, the Beetle has been continuously modified and improved without significant changes to the character on which was founded its formidable success. The most important innovations were the hydraulic braking system and the fully synchromesh gears, adopted in 1950 and 1960 respectively. In 1972, a more modern version was brought out, the 1303, with a curved windscreen and larger front luggage space. The Karmann cabriolet was derived from this and continued in production until 1976.

The Porsche-Zündapp Type 12. Built in 1932, this prototype had a stellar five-cylinder 1200-cc engine developing 26 hp at 3000 rpm. It was water-cooled, had a four-speed gearbox, and was 3.33 m (10.9 ft) long.

One of the thirty pre-series cars built in 1936 and called the Volkswagen 30. Displacement 985 cc; output 23.5 hp at 3000 rpm; top speed 100 km/h (62.14 mph); length 3.99 m (13.09 ft); wheelbase 2.40 m (7.87 ft); weight 600 kg (1322.77 lb).

Porsche-NSU Type 32. Various examples of this model were built between 1933 and 1934 following the same basic conception as its predecessor (rear engine, central gearbox). It had a flat-four air-cooled engine with a capacity of 1.45 liters, developing 20 hp at 2600 rpm.

The Porsche Type 60 of 1938. With this, the final lines of the future Beetle were decided, but mass-production could not begin until 1945. The 1131-cc engine developed 25 hp at 3300 rpm with a top speed of 100 km/h (62.14 mph). The four-speed gearbox had synchromesh on the top two. Dimensions: 4050 × 1540 × 1500 mm (159.4 × 60.6 × 59 in). Weight: 720 kg (1587.33 lb).

The 1962 version, with a sun-roof and an 1192-cc 40-hp engine. The Beetle went out of production in Germany in 1975, but is still built in Mexico (VW Sedan), Brazil (VW Fusca), Nigeria (VW Beetle) and Peru (VW 1300).

The idea of a "people's car" was conceived in the 1930s when the German government recognized that the time was ripe for a larger section of the public to be mobilized. The programme that was worked out included extending the road networks and producing a new runabout. Ferdinand Porsche, formerly employed at Mercedes, had run his own workshop in Stuttgart from 1928 and had designed two projects for a "car for all," first of all for Zündapp and then for NSU. He was subsequently commissioned by the Ministry of Transport to take charge of the Volkswagen project.

The basic features of the new car were made known at the Berlin Motor Show of 1934: it was to be not too small, economical, sturdy, fully equipped but low-priced, and capable of smooth running at 100 km/h (62.14 mph) on the German motorways under construction. The project was supervised by the Association of German Automobile Industries under the direction of Porsche.

In 1936, the first prototype was ready. It had all the latest features, including independent torsion bar suspension, power brakes with cams and rubber engine mountings. The engine was an air-cooled flat-four 23.5-hp designed in two versions, two- or four-stroke, the latter of which was eventually chosen for use. The practically definitive version built in 1938 was the result of co-operation between the design offices of Porsche, NSU and Daimler-Benz, and the

The first Volkswagen soft-top was built as a one-off. A small series was then produced by the Herbmüller coachworks until the definitive version was presented in 1949. This marked the beginning of the association with the Karmann coachworks.

The off-road model (Porsche Type 82) produced during the war had four-wheel drive and a five-speed gearbox. Some models had a front roller for driving over difficult terrain. Over 14,000 small amphibious vehicles were also built on the same base mechanics.

collaboration of Reutter & Co. coachbuilders. The development of the car was based on the results of research carried out in the previous year over almost two and a half million kilometers (over a million and a half miles) with thirty experimental vehicles. The four-stroke engine was uprated to 24 hp and proved extremely reliable in road tests.

The reaction of the critics and the public towards the car was one of great enthusiasm. However, the Association withdrew from the operation and was replaced by a state-funded organization. Volkswagen GmbH was placed in charge of Porsche, Dr Lafferenz and Mr Werlin, and a plant was built near Wolfsburg Castle, around which developed the city where the employees were to live. While construction was under way, the government introduced the VW savings scheme which allowed anyone to reserve one of the new cars, by paying RM 5 a month (a considerable sum at the time); in just a few months, almost 170,000 had been ordered.

The production programme included plans for a saloon and a cabriolet, and Porsche also developed an aerodynamic competition version. The war, however, brought the entire operation to a halt. The new plant was requisitioned and turned over to the production of war materials. During the war, Volkswagen used the design of

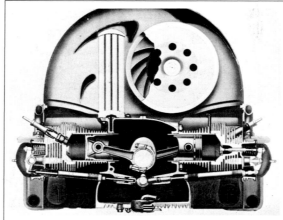

The engine of the first series Volkswagen (1945) was directly developed from the 958 cc of 1936/37. Except for a slight increase in displacement in 1954 (1192 cc, 30 hp at 3300 rpm), it remained practically unchanged until a completely updated version was brought out in 1960, which developed 34 hp at 3600 rpm with the same displacement.

the future Beetle as a basis for the production of a small, off-road vehicle and an amphibious version, building 14,276 of the latter, of which around a hundred are still in use. At the same time, the Wolfsburg plant also produced 630 "civilian" saloons, for which the war proved a hard testing period.

In 1945, with 60 per cent of their factories destroyed, Volkswagen began a programme of reconstruction and reorganization from which a stronger company was to emerge. Of the 1945 Beetle only one original feature has remained unchanged: the front bonnet-catch. The rest has been continuously modified and perfected to make this particular Volkswagen one of the most reliable cars ever produced.

An assembly plant was built in Brazil in 1953 which became an independent production center in 1959. VW Mexico SA was formed in 1964, and plants were later opened in South Africa and in various developing countries.

Even in the past, however, the VW marque has not only been limited to the Beetle. In 1955, an interesting Ghia-designed 1200-cc coupé was brought out with the collaboration of Karmann, which was also available in a cabriolet version. In 1961, the 1500 was launched in sedan, family and cabriolet versions. Although it used the same base scheme as the Beetle, with the same engine and suspension, the new car was the product of a completely original project, a special feature being the reduced height of its engine – only 40 cm (15.75 in) – providing luggage space above it.

Another model, the Brasilia, was developed from the 1500 and was produced in Brazil until 1982. Towards the end of the 1960s, NSU had

The 1200 Karmann Ghia coupé of 1955 was based on the Beetle chassis and was later fitted with a 1600 cc engine.

The Volkswagen 1500 of 1961 had a flat-four 1493-cc engine developing 45 hp at 3800 rpm, air-cooled, with a four-speed gearbox and torsion-bar suspension. It was 4.22 m (13.84 ft) long and weighed 860 kg (1896 lb). The 1600 of 1965 and the 411 of 1968 were subsequent developments.

The K70 was the first modern front-wheel drive Volkswagen. The four-cylinder in-line 1605-cc engine developed 75 hp at 5200 rpm. A 90-hp version was also produced. Overhead camshaft valve gear and power-assisted front disc brakes. Length: 4.42 m (14.5 ft).

The Passat was brought out in 1973 to a Giugiaro design and was completely updated in 1981. It has a 1300- or 2000-cc petrol engine, and there is also a 1600-cc diesel in both naturally aspirated and turbo versions. An estate car has also been produced, together with a two-door model for the US market (VW Quantum).

Produced by Karmann on a Golf base and mechanics, the ▶ Scirocco coupé, brought out in 1974 to a Giugiaro design, was totally updated in 1981.

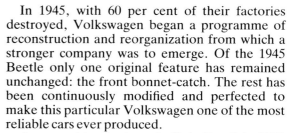

Current Volkswagen production covers three basic models. The smallest is the Polo, brought out in 1975 with an 850-cc engine to which the 1100 cc and the 1300 cc derived from the Golf were later added. In 1981, a new estate version of the body was brought out (below), as well as a coupé. A three-box version, the Derby (above), combines features of the two models.

The Golf, a worthy successor to the Beetle, was designed by Giorgio Giugiaro. Six million were built of the first version, brought out in 1975, both in Wolfsburg and in Mexico (VW Caribe), in the USA (VW Rabbit), in Yugoslavia and South Africa. Over the years, it has had various petrol engines, ranging from 1100 to 1800 cc in capacity, and a revolutionary small 1500-cc diesel (brought out in 1976, increased to 1600 cc in 1980 and subsequently fitted with a turbocharger). In the autumn of 1983 it was replaced by a new version with a completely different body.

gone ahead with development of the K 70, a new medium-sized saloon which boasted some very advanced features. Its launch, which had been planned for the Geneva Motor Show of 1969, was put back because of the sudden merger of Audi and NSU, and the incorporation of the new company (Audi-NSU-Auto Union AG) into the Volkswagen group.

Production of the new car, this time under the name of the Volkswagen, began in October 1970 at a new factory in Salzgitter. The K 70 later provided the conceptual basis for the development of all the current cars of the group. Another new marque, Volkswagen-Porsche, had also appeared in 1969, for the production of the 914, a mid-engined sports car.

A period of total modernization and extension of the range had begun, requiring an exceptional investment in terms of technology and finance in order to build cars that were in keeping with the changing times and would prove worthy successors to the Beetle. The Golf, Polo and Passat, in particular, have achieved this objective with, perhaps, even better results than expected.

To complete the picture of production on a world-wide scale, Volkswagen's more recent models include the GOL, designed and produced in Brazil, with an engine based on that of the Beetle but with a more modern body in two and three sizes (VW Voyage), and the ex-Chrysler models (Dodge Polara 1500 cc and the Dodge Dart 5200 cc), built in plants taken over by VW from the American company in Argentina, Brazil and Australia in about 1980.

Developed from the Golf first series and produced at the Karmann works, the cabriolet (above) has the same engines as the saloon, except for the diesel version. The export version for the USA is known as the VW Rabbit Convertible.

The 1984 version of the Golf is more aerodynamic, roomy and comfortable. The body has been lengthened (17 cm/6.7 in) and widened (4 cm/1.6 in), and the luggage space has been increased by 30 per cent. The engines are of 1300–1800 cc (petrol) or 1600 cc (diesel), the latter either aspirated or turbo.

Launched in 1981, the Santana is the three-box version of the Passat. The petrol engines range from 1600 to 2000 cc and the diesel is 1600 cc, either aspirated or turbo. The Santana is also built in China and, following an agreement with Nissan, in Japan.

The 1979 Jetta was also produced in Mexico as the VW Atlantic. The new 1984 model is particularly aerodynamic in line and is available in a two- or a four-door version, with a 1300-, 1600- or 1800-cc petrol engine, or a 1600-cc diesel.

VOLVO

Cars and the industry which produces them play a decisive role in the economic development and employment situation in most industrialized countries.

When Volvo started building cars in 1927, the work-force was small and the cars were handbuilt. Today, Volvo is the largest industrial enterprise in Scandinavia, with 76,000 employees world-wide and a scope of operations which, in addition to transport equipment, also includes energy, food processing and engineering. The very foundations of Volvo's product philosophy today – which is characterized by high standards of quality, safety, comfort and performance – were established as long ago as 1927, when the very first Volvo car was built. Over the years, Volvo has also introduced innovations in many fields, including safety, that have become a standard to live up to for the rest of the automotive industry. Examples include the laminated windscreen, the three-point seat-belt, a body construction which incorporates a safety cage and has energy absorbing crumple zones at the front and rear, dual triangular-split braking systems, and much more.

Volvo took a further step forward in its pioneering work in 1970/71 when it was the first European car manufacturer to establish a crash-investigation team. By detailed and thorough study of accidents, the Volvo safety researchers and engineers have accumulated invaluable information, to the benefit of the product and the safety of the customer.

The Volvo Car Corporation has been a public limited company within the Volvo Group since 1979. Thanks to aggressive product development and marketing endeavours, the Corporation has succeeded in strengthening its position among the car manufacturers of the world. Since 1980, it has increased its sales by about 35 per cent, close to 100,000 cars. The most important markets for Volvo cars are Scandinavia, Western Europe and North America. In 1983, Volvo sold 365,000 cars. Approximately 85 per cent were sold outside Sweden, which makes Volvo one of the world's most export-orientated car manufacturers.

ROGER HOLTBACK   President, Volvo Car Corporation

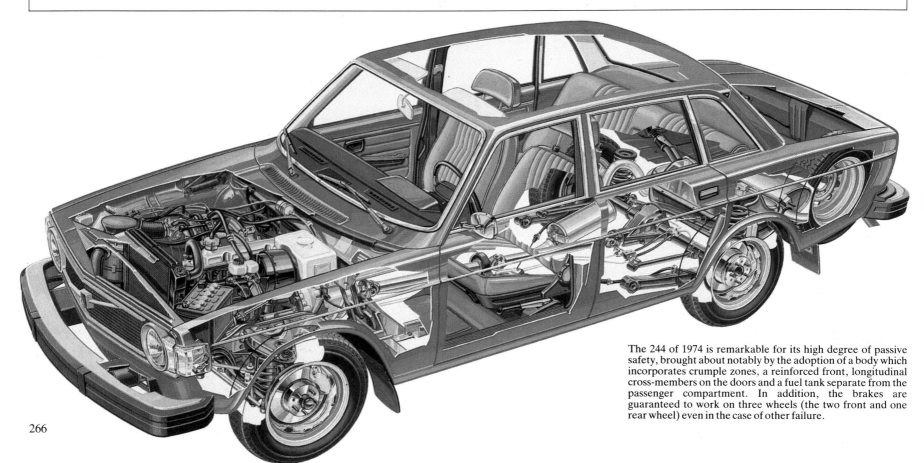

The 244 of 1974 is remarkable for its high degree of passive safety, brought about notably by the adoption of a body which incorporates crumple zones, a reinforced front, longitudinal cross-members on the doors and a fuel tank separate from the passenger compartment. In addition, the brakes are guaranteed to work on three wheels (the two front and one rear wheel) even in the case of other failure.

Assar Gabrielsson and Gustav Larson founded Volvo in 1926, using the name which already belonged to the Swedish ball bearing company SKF. Volvo, derived from the Latin *volvere*, means to rotate. It was in fact with the financial assistance of SKF that the two partners managed to get construction of the first thousand vehicles under way. The emblem they used was the symbol for iron. The first car, the ÖV 4, later renamed the Jacob, had an engine of nearly two liters and a top speed of 60 km/h (37.3 mph).

Production in series began at the end of April 1927. This was followed by the PV 4 with its all-round breaking system, of which 770 were built between 1927 and 1929. Alongside this, Volvo produced the six-cylinder range, which lasted until 1950. The TR 671 taxi, a seven-seater with a 65-hp engine, appeared in 1930, and in 1933 the industrial vehicle line was modified to fit Hesselman engines, which were produced under license. These used diesel but had spark ignition.

The PV 36 (known as the Carioca) had synchromesh gear change, six seats and independent wheels, used the aerodynamic concepts of the Venus Bilo (produced in 1933) and had an all-metal body for the first time. In 1935, there was an important change in the stock-market quotations for Volvo shares, with the increase from 4 to 13 million kr. capital and the incorporation of Pentaverken, who manufactured engines. By the end of 1938, 35,000 vehicles had been built, but production slowed down with the outbreak of war.

In 1944, the four-cylinder PV 444 went into production, continuing until 1958. In 1956, the P121/22, known as the Amazon, came out and secured even greater success on the market. In 1975, Volvo took over the Dutch company DAF, and as a result of the union the 66 was launched, followed by the 340 series. Meanwhile, the 144 (1966) and the 164 (1968) were brought out, which developed into the 240 series in 1974.

In the meantime, Volvo had also become famous for its estate cars, which made up 30 per cent of the 240 series. A further boost was given to the company with the introduction of the 740/760 series, which came out in February 1982.

The TPV was designed for the Swedish army and had the long-wheelbase taxi body and four-wheel drive. The engine was the usual six-cylinder 3670-cc one, produced in 1946.

The first Volvo, the ÖV 4, was in production from April 1927 onwards. The four-cylinder engine had a displacement of almost two liters, with a top speed of 60 km/h (37.3 mph). Above: the sporting version.

The PV 652 was brought out in 1930 and was a variation of the 651. It had the same 3000-cc engine, but the hydraulic brakes were new, as was the synchromesh gearbox.

The PV 51-52, introduced in 1936/37, followed the lines of the Carioca, but the more powerful, six-cylinder 3670-cc engine developed 86 hp at 3400 rpm, and the body was lighter.

The PV 444 was the first Volvo to break away from previously adopted lines. It had a unitary body, a four-cylinder 1410-cc engine developing 40 hp, a three-speed gearbox and a top speed of 110 km/h (68.3 mph). Various versions of the PV 444 were produced up to 1958 (the one illustrated from 1955 to 1957). Modifications were made each time it was updated.

The PV 650 of 1930 had a closed body such as today would be called a coupé, with a six-cylinder 3010-cc 55-hp engine. It had mechanical brakes on all four wheels.

The 673, in production from 1931 to 1934, had a six-cylinder 3266-cc 65-hp engine. The bodywork was distinguished by its seven seats, and it was in fact used as a taxi.

The new PV 801-802 taxis were also fitted with the normal six-cylinder 3670-cc engine, but had a larger, eight-seater body. They were built from 1938 to 1947.

The first studies for the PV 60 date back to 1939, but it was not officially launched until 1944. The biggest innovation was its independent front suspension. It had a six-cylinder 3670-cc engine.

In February 1982 was launched the 760 GLE, with a 2800-cc V6 engine. This was followed immediately by a six-cylinder 2400-cc VW-produced turbodiesel, then a four-cylinder 2300-cc petrol engine with a turbocharger and an intercooler.

The P 1900 of 1956/57 had a glass-resin body and a 1410-cc engine developing not much more than 40 hp. Only sixty-seven were sold on the export markets for which it was designed.

The Series 120 estate had a 1780-cc 85-hp engine and led the way for the modern Swedish family models. Various versions were in production from 1962 to 1969.

The P 130, in production from 1961 to 1970, was in 1984 fitted with a special seat designed to support the spine in the correct position, introducing a completely new concept of comfort.

The 144 saloon, brought out in 1966, was the first Volvo to combine their successful design with a high degree of active and passive safety. It had a 1780-cc 85-hp B18 engine.

The 144 was followed almost immediately by the 142 (1967), which had the same body but two doors instead of four. It was a great success on the Swedish market.

Launched in 1975, the 264 had a new front end and a 2.7-liter V6 engine produced jointly by Renault and Peugeot. It was the flagship of the Swedish company's range until the arrival of the 760.

The 66 was produced after the takeover of DAF. The 1108-cc 47-hp or 1289-cc 57-hp Renault engines were coupled to the automatic variable transmission by different diameter pulleys and chains. The 66 was in production from 1976 to 1980.

The 345 is the five-door version of the 343 brought out in collaboration with DAF. From 1982 to the present day, it has been fitted with a 1397-cc engine, followed by the B19 carburetted and 1900-cc fuel injection versions. The three-box 340 and 360 were introduced in 1983.

OTHER COMPANIES

AC

Formed in England for the construction of automobiles in 1900, Autocarriers became AC in 1922 and made a name for itself with the production of a three-wheeled van with a single-cylinder engine. AC was also known for its 1991-cc six-cylinder engine, in production from 1919 to 1963, with an original output of 40 hp increasing gradually to 105 hp. The company experienced a difficult period in between the two wars, but was chosen in the 1960s by Caroll Shelby, a former driver, to produce his 4.7- to 7-liter Ford-engined cars. AC-Shelby-Ford continued to flourish until 1969. When Shelby left, AC continued to use Ford engines for the high-performance coupés it built in conjunction with the Italian coachbuilders Frua. The 3-liter AC 3000 ME coupé came out in 1980.

AC 3000 Sport – 1980 (GB)

Alpine

The Société des Automobiles Alpine, known simply as Alpine, was founded in 1955 by Jean Rédélé. Its first model, the A 106, was a small fiberglass saloon brought out in conjunction with the Michelotti coachbuilders, based on the contemporary Renault 4 mechanics. Rédélé raced this car in its class in the 1952 and 1954 Mille Miglia, and also achieved good results in the Coupe des Alpes and the Monte Carlo Rally. His first workshop soon expanded into a factory with a surface area of 13,000 sq. m (15,548 sq. yd), producing other models which became consistently more competitive. The 1963 A110 had a central backbone chassis and its engines were derived directly from the Gordini-produced R8 and Caravelle. As the company became more and more successful, it developed closer ties with Renault, who supplied increasingly powerful engines, a typical example of which was the modified R 16 TS engine used on the 1600 coupé, with five-speed gearbox and Gordini R8 suspension. Throughout the 1960s, the company won countless competition successes hand in hand with Renault. The A 310 was a road version of the A 110 fitted with the V6 engine used on the R 30. More recently, Alpine has introduced its own sports version of the small Renault 5, first in an aspirated version, then with a turbocharged 1400-cc engine developing 110 hp. Alpine cars are sold exclusively through the Renault network.

Avanti

The Avanti Motor Corporation factory rose from the ashes of Studebaker in 1965, and was created by two former Studebaker-Packard agents, N. Altman and L. Newman. They decided to take over the plant and build an updated version of the Avanti – the last Studebaker model – with a 5763-cc 290-hp Chevrolet V8 engine in a fiberglass body. The 1984 Avanti II still has a 5-liter V8 engine with an output of 180 hp.

AZLK (alias Moskvich or MZMA)

Founded in the Soviet Union for the assembly of units to be sent to the Gorki Automobilova Zavod (better known as GAZ), the company continued in this line of operation from its foundation in 1929 until 1940, when three complete cars were built. Based on a British Ford, these were known as the Kim 10. After the war, in 1946, the company changed its name to the Moskovskij Zavod Malolitrajnnich Avtomobilej (MZMA) and by 1947 cars were coming on to the market under the name "Moskvich." The first model, the 400, was in fact a product of the war, since the 1936 Opel Kadett assembly lines were then in Russian-occupied territory and the Moskvich 400 was effectively a Russian version of the Kadett. In 1956, the situation changed radically with the launch of the 1220-cc 402, which was no longer inspired by the Opel. A year later, the first Russian estate car, the 423, came out, followed in 1958 by the 407, which had a 1358-cc 45-hp overhead-valve engine. It was not until six years later, however, with the launch of the 408, that a completely new line appeared. The company reached its first million vehicles in 1967 (the second came in 1974), and in the same year the 412 was brought out, the first Russian car to have an overhead camshaft. During this period, the factory moved its head office to Ishevsk, near the river Ish, where the company name was changed again to AZLK (Avtomobilnji Zavod Imeni Leninskogo Komsola) and production began on commercial vehicles. The Moskvich 1500 was launched in 1975, with an 83-hp engine and bodywork similar to the 412. Production continues today with the saloon and the estate lines, powered by 1.5-liter engines.

Daihatsu

The history of the motor car in Japan only dates back as far as 1923, when it took off on an unprecedented scale. At that time, alongside the engines which had been their main product since 1907, Daihatsu brought out a new line in the shape of a motor tricycle which was to stay on the market for nearly twenty years. In 1958, Daihatsu launched their first three-wheeled car, the Bee – a four-door version with a two-cylinder 540-cc rear-mounted air-cooled engine. This was followed five years later by the Compagno, a four-door model which came as a saloon, coupé or estate, with a four-cylinder 797-cc engine. It was later given a fuel-injected 958-cc engine and front disc brakes. In 1968, Daihatsu was

Alpine A310 – 1982 (GB)

Avanti – 1967 (GB)

Daihatsu Charade – 1978 (J)

De Tomaso Pantera – 1972 (I)

taken over by Toyota and the company is best known today for its compact off-road model, available with a petrol or diesel engine, and the compact front-wheel drive Charade.

De Tomaso

Founded in 1959 by the Argentinian Alejandro De Tomaso, the company took over the Ghia and Vignale coachbuilders and was then itself taken over by the Ford Motor Company. It was extremely active in competition racing with Formula 2, minor formulae, prototypes and even a Formula 1 when De Tomaso brought out a roadster, the Vallelunga, in November 1963. This was followed by a small saloon with the 1.5-liter Ford Corsair engine uprated to 105 hp. Four years later, De Tomaso presented two more new models at the Turin Motor Show, the Pampero roadster, developed from the Vallelunga, and the Mangusta, a big sports model with a Ford V8 engine and a displacement of nearly five liters. They also introduced the Rowan electric car at Turin, built in conjunction with the Rowan Company and the Ghia coachbuilders, but the model never progressed beyond the prototype stage. De Tomaso opened a new factory on the outskirts of Modena in 1968 and brought out the definitive version of the Mangusta: 305 hp and 4700 cc, with a top speed of 250 km/h (155.3 mph). It was followed two years later by the Pantera, a natural development of the Mangusta, which also had a Ford engine, but this time in a 5730-cc 330-hp version. The 1970 Turin Motor Show saw the launch of a four-door, high-performance saloon, the Deauville, which had the same engine as the Pantera but coupled to an automatic transmission. It was just under 5 m (16.4 ft) long with a top speed of 240 km/h (150 mph). Two years later, the Longchamp coupé came out as a direct development of the Deauville, with a Ghia body and the same mechanics as the saloon. Immediately afterwards, the Pantera 290 was launched at the Geneva Motor Show as a "quieter" version of the Modena sports car. It was similar in design, but had the V6 Ford Capri engine, uprated to 210 hp. Production of the Pantera continued at the end of 1972 in the former Vignale plant under the direct control of Ford. A hundred cars were built in 1982.

Hindustan

Although founded in 1942, this Indian company did not begin building cars until the 1950s, limiting itself simply to the assembly or manufacture of European and American cars under license. One of the most popular Hindustan models, of which 22,000 were built in 1970 alone, was the Ambassador Mk II. This was an Indian remake of the Morris Oxford II. The uprated Mk 4 is the company's latest product.

Holden

The merger between Holden's Motor Body Builders Ltd and the General Motors Australian division led to the formation of Holden in 1931. With capital supplied by American GM, Holden built British and American models in Australia between the two wars. The first car built after the war was the FX, which was in effect a 1938 Buick, for production plans were halted as a result of America's involvement in the war. It was a 2.2-liter saloon which proved to be quite popular on the market. It was followed by an updated model, the FJ, in 1954 with a more modern design. The automatic Powerglide gearbox was introduced in 1965 on the HD model, which bore an even closer resemblance to the European and US cars. Two years later, it was followed by the Torana, fitted with engines of gradually increasing power up to a six-cylinder 3300-cc 193-hp version with a top speed of 195 km/h (121.2 mph). The 1980s range includes the Gemini, an export version of the Isuzu of the same name, the Camira and Commodore, based on Opel models, and the Statesman series.

Holden Premier – 1967 (GB)

Hyundai

Founded in Korea in 1967, the Hyundai Motor Company had begun producing automobiles by November 1968 with a version that had the same name as a European model: the Cortina. In January of the following year, Hyundai began to manufacture trucks and dumpers, supported by the Japanese company Mitsubishi, which provided them with the benefit of its experience and technology. The first South Korean bus was brought out by the newly formed company in the same year. It was not until October 1974 that the first original car, the Pony saloon and coupé, was launched at the Turin Motor Show, with a 1200-cc engine (later increased to 1400 and then 1600 cc) and two-box body. These were followed two years later by an estate car and pick-up version. This line has kept its name, but the bodywork has been improved by Giugiaro and the mechanics have been steadily perfected. The 1983 Stellar was also designed by Giugiaro.

Innocenti

In 1960, the first of the unusually shaped A 40 saloons, which had bodies reminiscent of an estate car, came off the Innocenti production lines in Lambrate, Italy, as the result of an agreement with the British BMC group. The A 40 was followed by the Innocenti 950 roadster, which had a Ghia (Turin) body and the same engine as its predecessor, but in a twin carburettor version to increase the output. The second

Innocenti 1000 – 1975 (I)

series A 40 of 1963 had an increased displacement of 1098 cc and a top speed of 135 km/h (84 mph), and the same engine was used on the S roadster version. In May of the same year, the IM3 five-door two-box saloon came out, with disc brakes, Hydrolastic suspension, front-wheel drive and a transverse engine. This car proved to be rather unreliable, however. It was followed by the J4, which had a 1098-cc engine with a reduced output of 58–50 hp. All the engines were imported from Britain while the bodies were built in the Lambrate plant near Milan, which had already made a name for itself by having promoted Innocenti tubes all over the world before the war and Lambretta scooters immediately afterwards. The Italian version of the Mini was produced from the Austin-Morris model and was launched at the 1965 Turin Motor Show. The company entered a period of crisis when its founder, Ferdinando Innocenti, died in 1966. Six years later, it was taken over by British Leyland and immediately began production of the 1300 Mini Cooper and the Regent, based on the British Allegro. When the industrialist De Tomaso took over, the Mini was redesigned by the coachbuilder Nuccio Bertone and assumed its present form, although the same engine was used. Today, the Mini has a three-cylinder 1000-cc Japanese Daihatsu engine in naturally aspirated turbo and diesel versions. The plant also produces parts for the Maserati.

Isuzu

When the company was formed in 1937 after a merger between Ishikawajima and the Tokyo Gas and Electric Company (which also gave birth to Hino, later taken over by Toyota), its major production line was trucks and vehicles for building sites. It first extended its operation to include cars in 1935, assembling the British Hillman Minx under license and adding a Japanese-built engine in 1961. In 1962, the Bellet saloon was brought out, with a four-cylinder 1471-cc engine (later increased to two liters) and was replaced by the 1600-cc Florian. Both cars were also available as coupés designed in Italy by Giugiaro and Ghia. Another speciality of Isuzu was the construction of off-road vehicles, the most recent being the Trooper diesel, which follows the new generation of Japanese four-wheel drives.

Isuzu Florian 2000 – 1983 (J)

Otosan

Otosan was formed in 1967 in Istanbul and builds Anadol cars in conjunction with the British Reliant Motors. The first Anadols were fitted with the 1200-cc Ford Anglia engine on a fiberglass body. In 1973, a four-door model and an estate

were brought out, the latter fitted with a Ford 1.6-liter engine. Anadol has also brought out the STC 16 coupé, using the same engine as the estate car.

Puma

Founded in 1962 by Gennaro Malzoni, an Italian emigrant to Brazil, Puma is one of the youngest car manufacturing companies in the world. Its first car was a front-wheel drive coupé using the three-cylinder DKW engine produced by Vemag, fuelled by a two-stroke mixture. However, the Puma marque did not appear until the next model, brought out in 1966. The company took the name Puma Industria de Veiculos SA in 1975. In 1967, the Vemag factory was taken over by Volkswagen Brazil and ceased production of the DKW engine used until then. Puma subsequently made an agreement with VW to supply its 1584-cc engine. The company also changed the design of its coupés, which became more aerodynamic and sporty. In 1973, a new four-seater (2 + 2) coupé was put on the market with a four-cylinder 2512-cc or a six-cylinder 4093-cc Chevrolet engine. The GTI coupé was modified in 1980, and has the engine and chassis of the VW 1600.

Reliant Kitten 850 – 1975 (GB)

Reliant Scimitar GTE – 1970 (GB)

Reliant

The history of this company began in 1935, when T.L. Williams decided to found a factory to continue building the Raleigh motor tricycle. The motor-cycle engines used until 1938 were replaced with the 747-cc Austin Seven engine at the end of that year, but this caused the factory production problems. Reliant therefore obtained rights to produce the engine themselves, and did so in almost unaltered form until 1962. The first Reliant tourer, shown at the 1951 London Motor Cycle Exhibition, was a small, four-seater roadster with a four-speed synchromesh gearbox and, of course, three wheels. Modifications to the bodywork produced the 1956 saloon, the first to have a fiberglass body, starting a tradition which the company continued to follow from then on with all its models. In 1962, they stopped producing the Austin Seven engine and went on to a light alloy, 598-cc 24-hp version, developed and built entirely by Reliant. Reliant's assembly system, which kept separate the mechanical and body parts, meant that the cars could be built in other factories and in countries less technologically advanced at the time, and so Reliant was built in Greece, Turkey and Israel. In 1961, Reliant finally launched a traditional four-wheel model, the Sabra, on to the home market, first with 1.7-liter Ford Consul and later with six-cylinder 2.5-liter Ford Zephyr engines. The more successful Scimitar coupé was launched in 1965, with a 2500-cc 120-hp Ford Zephyr engine and later a 3-liter 146-hp Ford V6. Production of Scimitars reached a peak with the introduction of the estate model in 1968, which was available from 1972 with the six-cylinder Ford Granada engine. Reliant had bought its only competitor in the three-wheel market, Bond Cars, in 1969, and with them in 1974 brought out the two-seater Robin saloon, with a 748-cc engine. The 1975 Kitten had an 848-cc engine, and in 1980 the Scimitar soft-top was brought out, with a 2.8-liter V6 engine.

Seat

This Spanish company was formed in 1950, but its first car, a 1400 equivalent of the same Fiat, only left the assembly line in 1953. In fact, Seat (Sociedad Española de Automobiles de Turismo – Spanish Touring Automobile Company) built cars under license from Fiat, but in a range no longer particularly up to date on other European markets. Spanish import regulations were so severe that the only way to overcome this problem was to build a factory directly on Spanish soil, or at least to come to an agreement with a local manufacturer, so Seat was formed with the help of the INI (the Spanish equivalent of the IRI). The 1400 was followed in 1957 by the 600, which was also available in a new four-door version. Seat has also produced its own personalized 1500 and 850, followed by the 124 and the 1430, a variation which is only available in Spain. The Pamplona version of the 124 was exported to other markets after Fiat took it out of production. It was then relaunched, following the agreement with Seat, and became a firm favourite with taxi drivers on account of its toughness and reliability. The 124 1600 coupé came out in 1970, followed by the 1800 diesel, and then in 1972 the two- and three-door 127 (now available in a five-door version known as the Fura), and in 1974 the 133. The launch of the Ronda (the Spanish version of the Italian Ritmo) on to other European markets immediately caused a controversy which the Paris court of arbitration resolved by deciding in favour of Seat and allowing them to continue exporting. Since then, the company has also assembled 1200- and 1500-cc Porsche-designed engines and gearboxes. The Ibiza came out in 1984, following an agreement with VW, and the Spanish company is now producing other models from Volkswagen's range.

Seat Ronda – 1983 (E)

Seat Ibiza – 1984 (E)

Skoda 105 GL – 1984 (CS)

Skoda

This Czechoslovak company began producing automobiles in 1925, although the Skoda name was already known for the manufacture of industrial vehicles and arms, especially machine guns. The first Skoda cars closely resembled Laurin & Klement models. By late 1925, however, the 110 and 120 had replaced the old cars, which Skoda had continued to produce along the lines of Laurin & Klement. These were the forerunners of the new Skoda, and the company established itself as one of the major Czechoslovak car manufacturers. Both the 110 and the 120 had four-cylinder engines with displacements of 1794 and 1944 cc, developing 25 and 30 hp respectively. The 120 became the 4R in 1928 and formed the basis for the six-cylinder 2918-cc 6R. In the following year, an eight-cylinder, nearly 4-liter model appeared, of which only a few were built. Skoda really made its name in 1933 with the 420, a tough, reliable runabout with an engine of almost a liter. The Popular and the Rapid were both developed from the 420 and were slightly more powerful versions with a superior finish. On the large car market, Skoda continued producing the six-cylinder 2.5-liter Superb of 1935, which was also developed from the 1928 6R. The size of the engines used on the Superb was gradually increased to 3 liters, but the car was never a great success. At the outbreak of the Second World War, the Skoda range included the Superb, the Favorit four-cylinder 2091-cc saloon, the 1588-cc Rapid and two versions of the Popular, one with a four-cylinder 995-cc and the other with a newer, 1089-cc overhead-valve engine. This engine remained in production until 1964. After the war, the company's operations returned to the production of civilian cars, starting with a remake of the Popular, the 1101. This remained in production until 1954 and was the only Skoda product for five years. In 1959, the Octavia was brought out as a development of the 440 and was also produced in a sports version (Skoda had won many international rallies even before the war). Known as the Felicia, it was originally fitted with a 1100-cc engine, but a more powerful 1200-cc 53-hp was used later. Radical changes in 1964 led to the entire range being taken out of production with the exception of the estate car, which was based on the Octavia and replaced by the new 1000 MB. The most important innovation on the new car was that the engine was mounted at the rear, replacing the traditional front-engine, rear-wheel drive arrangement. The 1000 MB had a 42-hp engine and a top speed of 125 km/h (77.7 mph). In 1970, a more powerful version was prepared, with an 1100-cc engine uprated to 47 hp; in the following year, the two cars became known as the 100 and 110. Even today, Skoda still uses the same arrangement as the basic model developed from the 1954 1000 MB in the 105, 120 and coupé versions.

Subaru

The Fuji Heavy Industries Group, formed in 1953, included several companies involved in a wide variety of activities. Subaru was the motor-manufacturing arm, beginning in the late 1950s with the introduction of the 360, a small, two-cylinder, two-stroke model with a monocoque frame. Various modifications to the body shell and the engine led to the development in 1970 of the R2, which had independent suspension and redesigned bodywork. In 1974, this was joined by the Rex, with its cut-off rear. On the threshold of the 1980s, Subaru brought out a new modification on its 1800-cc top model – the possibility of engaging the drive on the rear wheels to give a second drive axle. Subarus are now available in a standard range of saloon, coupé and family versions. Nearly all the models come in the three versions; on some, additional drive can be engaged on the rear wheels. The modern Subaru factory has the financial backing of the Fuji group, to which it belongs, and its expansion is still in its early stages.

Subaru 1800 Hardtop – 1979 (J)

Subaru 1300 DL Hatchback – 1979 (J)

Subaru 700 – 1981 (J)

Subaru 5WD 1800 Hatchback – 1983 (J)

Suzuki GX Coupé – 1980 (J)

Suzuki

Suzuki first began producing machines in 1909 for the textile industry and it was not until ten years later that cycles and motor cycles went into production. In 1954, the company name was changed from the Suzuki Loom Manufacturing Company to the Suzuki Motor Company. The first car in regular production was the Suzulight of 1961, which had a four-seater body and a two-cylinder 360-cc air-cooled engine (obviously developed from their motor cycles) which could reach a top speed of 85 km/h (53 mph). The 800 Fronte came out three years later, with a three-cylinder engine, a roomier body and front-wheel drive. Suzuki's development in the automobile market has since extended to include small industrial vehicles, often with four-wheel drive. The very compact, elegant 410 off-road model was recently brought out, originally with an 800-cc engine, but this has now been replaced with a 970-cc version. In 1982, the Cervo Turbo was launched, and in 1983 the Cultus SA 310.

Tatra

The origins of this Czechoslovak marque date back to 1850, when I. Schustala set up a coachbuilding factory in Nesselsdorf in the Austro-Hungarian Empire. The workshop expanded until, forty-one years later, work began on the production of railway wagons. The company changed its name in that period and Hugo Fischer Von Rösselstamm became director, from 1897 giving a new boost to the construction of automobiles. In 1898, the Präsident came out, driven by a two-cylinder horizontally opposed rear-mounted Benz engine. In 1899, it was the basis for the Météore and the Type A, and a racing model was also brought out which took part in the Paris–Vienna. In 1906, the Ledwinka-designed four-cylinder S 20/30 was brought out, with a top speed of 85 km/h (53 mph). This was followed in 1910 by the S 40/50, which had a six-cylinder engine fitted as standard, with the electrical system incorporated. At the end of the First World War, the political situation changed radically with the fall of the Austro-Hungarian Empire and Nesselsdorf found itself in Czechoslovakia. The company changed both its nationality and its name, and was from then on known as Tatra, after the nearby mountain chain that forms the border with Poland. Tatra's most important product at that time was the Type II, which was another Ledwinka design. Before the Second World War, Tatra was building medium-sized air-cooled models and a small series of "flagship" cars differing from the rest mainly in that they were water-cooled. With the outbreak of war, production was turned over to the supply of war materials. As a result, the company began to specialize in industrial vehicles, which they continue to manufacture to this day. At the end of the war, Tatra went back to producing the same models as five years before: the Tatraplan was brought out in 1949 and was replaced in 1957 by the V8 2.5-liter 100-hp 603. Various updated versions of the T 603 remained in production until 1975 (T 613), in a period when Tatra changed form and production concentrated mainly on industrial vehicles. Today only the "presidential" models remain of the range, with the 3500-cc V8 613 in pride of place.

Trabant

Trabant belongs to the group of companies which was created as a result of the reorganization of German companies after the Second World War. VEB took over the Audi and DKW plants, and began manufacturing automobiles in 1949 under the IFA marque, which remained in operation until 1955. It then changed to AWZ (until 1958) and in 1959 became known definitively as Trabant, which is its name today. The first Trabant, the P 50, came off the production line in 1958 with a two-cylinder 500-cc 18-hp engine and front-wheel drive. It had a top speed of 90 km/h (56 mph), which was also made possible by its light, fiberglass body. Two years later, the P 50 was replaced by the 500, which had some minor design modifications and slightly increased horsepower. In 1963, the 600 came out, its displacement increased to 594 cc, followed a year later by the 601, which had a completely different fiberglass body. The 601 today is still one of the most popular runabouts on the Eastern European market, where it has made a major contribution to the motorization programme.

TVR

Originally formed under the name "Layton," changed to "Grantura" in 1962/63, the company became known definitively as TVR in 1966. The first TVR had a honeycomb fiberglass body and a 1100-cc Austin A40 engine. Thirty of these were built, most of them open-topped, and they were sold in the USA under the name "Jomar." A coupé with the same frame, but with modified suspension, was brought out in 1960. Ford or Coventry-Climax twin overhead camshaft engines were originally used, although the MGA (1600 cc) and MGB (1800 cc) engines were later fitted. TVRs were also famous for being available in kit-form. The 1962 TVR Mk III was also sold in America with a 4.7-liter 285-hp Ford V8 engine which gave the car a top speed of 260 km/h (161.5 mph). In 1965, TVR went into liquidation and the new management decided to base its production on cheaper models. The Trident came out in 1965 and was reintroduced in 1968 with the 1.6-liter Ford Cortina engine. In 1970, the range included the Vixen and the Tuscan, both with Ford engines. In 1980, the Tasmin (Ford four-cylinder) was brought out, followed in 1983 by the Tasmin 350, which had a Rover 3.5-liter V8 engine.

UAZ

Founded in the Soviet Union in 1941, UAZ started out producing trucks. From 1954 onwards, its range also included the GAZ 69 AM off-road vehicle, of which 250,000 had been built by 1965. Since then, this model has been built under license in Romania and in North Korea. The UAZ 469 B, not launched until 1972, is the most up-to-date Soviet off-road vehicle. It is available with a petrol or diesel engine and has earned a certain degree of popularity on all European markets for its toughness, although its performance does not match up to other off-road models available.

Wartburg

In 1898, the Fahrzeugfabrik Eisenach chose the name "Wartburg" under which to market the Décauville it was building under license. In 1903, the Wartburg marque disappeared altogether, until it was revived by BMW in 1930 for a 748-cc two-seater. When the Eisenach factory took the name VEB in 1953 (the same company also produced the Trabants), it began producing the IFA F9 front-wheel drive model with a three-cylinder 900-cc two-stroke engine, and this led to the very similar 1955 Wartburg 311. Five years later, the model was fitted with an automatic gearbox. The 353 went into production in 1966 and is still in the range today (three cylinders, 992 cc).

YLN

There is a car factory even on the island of Formosa: the Yue Loong Motor Company Ltd, which produces cars under license from Japanese Nissan. The cars are in fact directly derived from Nissan products such as the Datsun Cherry (since the agreement between Nissan and Alfa Romeo, also known on European markets as the Arna). YLN has also been producing scooters for some years under license from the Italian company Innocenti. The YLN range also includes a few Japanese-based off-road vehicles.

Zastava

Formerly an arms and machine-tool factory, the Yugoslav company ZCZ (Zavodi Crvena Zastava) first began building automobiles in the 1950s, when it produced Fiat models under license. One of its first models was a local version of the 600, followed by the 1300, which enjoyed a certain degree of popularity. In the mid-1970s, Zastava production concentrated on the 101, a Yugoslav version of the Fiat 128. It had the same engine, but the rear bodywork was substantially altered. In fact, the Zastava 101 had become a two-box car with a rear hatchback, unlike the Fiat 128 which was a compact four-door with a boot and three-box body. The Yugo 45 version of the Fiat 127 is a three-door front-wheel drive saloon.

ZAZ

Founded in 1958 in a former tractor factory, this is one of the most recent Russian factories. ZAZ made its début on the market in 1960 with the ZAZ 965, which had a body that was highly reminiscent of the Fiat 600 and a 746-cc 23-hp rear-mounted V4 engine. It was used as the basis for the next model, the 965 versions A and B, on which the engine displacement was increased to 867 cc and the power output to 27 hp. The B version also had an electromagnetic clutch controlled by the gear lever. The introduction of the 966 B in 1966, with a body that was vaguely reminiscent of the American Fords or even the NSU Prinz, although it was slightly larger, signified a radical change. It was, however, a notable improvement on the previous models, with an increased output of 30 hp and much more passenger space, even including a reasonably sized boot. At the end of the 1960s, ZAZ brought out a small off-road vehicle noted for its excellent handling in snow, with four-wheel drive (which could be engaged by bringing in drive to the front axle) and a special gearbox. The 969 came out in 1970, followed in 1972 by the 968, which is still in production today, with a 1196-cc V4 engine. One of the main features of the ZAZ models is the extremely low retail price in comparison with other cars on the Russian market.

ZIL

The Russian company ZIL began operation in 1916 as AMO, building its first basic automobiles on concepts that were still very close to those of the old carriages. The factory was given a complete facelift and renamed the Zavod Imjeni Stalina (ZIS) in 1931. Subsequently this was changed to ZIL – Zavod Imjeni Likhacheva – after the name of the director of the plant, Likhachev. The first small series of cars was produced in 1933, using the Buick 5650 straight-eight engine. The ZIS 101 came out in 1936 with a steamlined, aerodynamic body, following the current trend in the USA. The 101 represented a turnabout in Russian automobile technology, with the introduction of windscreen demisters, a synchromesh gearbox and even a thermostat, dual-effect dampers and the twin-body carburettor. The ZIS 101 remained in production until 1940, when the 101/A was brought out, with a modified front end. In 1946, ZIS/ZIL went into operation again, introducing a new "flagship" on to the market which was a virtual copy of the Packard 180. It had a 6-liter 140-hp engine, weighed 2.5 tonnes (49.2 cwt) and was 6 m (19.7 ft) long. It was used as an official saloon, a taxi and even an ambulance, and remained in production until 1958, when a 6-liter 200-hp V8 ZIL III came out, introducing the two-speed automatic gearbox. The 114 of 1967 had a longer wheelbase and body, and was also fitted with a bigger, 7-liter light-alloy engine instead of cast iron. Disc brakes and electronic ignition were introduced on the 114, as well as the first central door-locking system. The 117 short wheelbase saloon (3.30 m/10.8 ft) came out in 1972 and was also available as a soft-top (117 V). In 1978 came the 4104 Limousine with a 7.7-liter V8 engine.

INDEX

Numbers in italic refer to an illustration

273

274